Educational Leadership

Knowing the Way, Showing the Way, Going the Way

Edited by
Carolyn S. Carr
Connie L. Fulmer

ScarecrowEducation
Lanham, Maryland • Toronto • Oxford
2004

Published in the United States of America
by ScarecrowEducation
An imprint of The Rowman & Littlefield Publishing Group, Inc.
4501 Forbes Boulevard, Suite 200, Lanham, Maryland 20706
www.scarecroweducation.com

PO Box 317
Oxford
OX2 9RU, UK

British Library Cataloguing in Publication Information Available

Library of Congress Cataloging-in-Publication Data

Educational leadership : knowing the way, showing the way, going the way
/ edited by Carolyn S. Carr, Connie L. Fulmer.
    p. cm.
  "2004 NCPEA yearbook"—Pref.
  Includes bibliographical references and index.
  ISBN 1-57886-172-1 (hardcover : alk. paper)
  1. School management and organization—United States. 2. School
administrators—Training of—United States. 3. Educational
leadership—United States. I. Carr, Carolyn S. II. Fulmer, Connie L., 1949–
LB2805.E3472 2004
371.2—dc22

                                                        2004011468

∞™ The paper used in this publication meets the minimum requirements of
American National Standard for Information Sciences—Permanence of
Paper for Printed Library Materials, ANSI/NISO Z39.48-1992.
Manufactured in the United States of America.

NCPEA OFFICERS FOR 2004–2006

President
Michael "Mick" Arnold, *Southwest Baptist University*

President-Elect
Duane Moore, *Oakland University*

Past President
Elaine L. Wilmore, *University of Texas, Arlington*

Executive Director
Theodore Creighton, *Sam Houston State University*

Executive Board
2003
James E. Berry, *Eastern Michigan University*
Dwain Estes, *McNeese State University*

2004
Angus MacNeil, *University of Houston*
Jesse J. McNeil, *University of Texas, Arlington*

2005
Judith Aikan, *University of Vermont*
Fred Dembowski, *Lynn University*

2006
Minnie Andrews, *Northern Arizona University*
Carolyn S. Carr, *Portland State University*
Gary Martin, *Northern Arizona University*

NCPEA HONOR ROLL OF PRESIDENTS, 1947–2004

1947	Julian E. Butterworth, *Cornell University*
1948	William E. Arnold, *University of Pennsylvania*
1949	Russell T. Gregg, *University of Wisconsin*
1950	Clyde M. Campbell, *Michigan State University*
1951	Dan H. Cooper, *Purdue University*
1952	Walter K. Beggs, *University of Nebraska*
1953	Robert S. Fisk, *University of Buffalo*
1954	Van Miller, *University of Illinois*
1955	Harold E. Moore, *University of Denver*
1956	Walter A. Anderson, *New York University*
1957	A. D. Albright, *University of Kentucky*
1958	Jack Childress, *Northwestern University*

1959	Richard C. Lonsdale, *Syracuse University*
1960	William H. Roe, *Michigan State University*
1961	Howard Eckel, *University of Kentucky*
1962	Daniel E. Griffiths, *New York University*
1963	Kenneth McIntyre, *University of Texas*
1964	Luvern Cunningham, *University of Chicago*
1965	William H. Roe, *Michigan State University*
1966	Willard Lane, *University of Iowa*
1967	Harold Hall, *California State University, Los Angeles*
1968	Kenneth Frasure, *SUNY, Albany*
1969	Samuel Goldman, *Syracuse University*
1970	Malcolm Rogers, *University of Connecticut*
1971	Paul C. Fawley, *University of Utah*
1972	Gale W. Rose, *New York University*
1973	Anthony N. Baratta, *Fordham University*
1974	John T. Greer, *Georgia State University*
1975	C. Cale Hudson, *University of Nebraska*
1976	John R. Hoyle, *Texas A&M University*
1977	J. Donald Herring, *SUNY, Oswego*
1978	Charles Manley, *California State University, Northridge*
1979	Jasper Valenti, *Loyola University of Chicago*
1980	Max E. Evans, *Ohio University*
1981	Lesley H. Browder Jr., *Hofstra University*
1982	John W. Kohl, *Montana State University*
1983	Bob Thompson, *SUNY, Oswego*
1984	Donald L. Piper, *University of North Dakota*
1985	Robert Stalcup, *Texas A&M University*
1986	Robert O'Reilly, *University of Nebraska, Omaha*
1987	Donald Coleman, *San Diego State University*
1988	Charles E. Kline, *Purdue University*
1989	Larry L. Smiley, *Central Michigan University*
1990	Frank Barham, *University of Virginia*
1991	Paul V. Bredeson, *Pennsylvania State University*
1992	Rosemary Papalewis, *California State University, Sacramento*
1993	Donald Orlosky, *University of South Florida*
1994	Paula M. Short, *University of Missouri, Columbia*
1995	Maria Shelton, *NOVA Southeastern University*
1996	Clarence Fitch, *Chicago State University*
1997	C. M. Achilles, *Eastern Michigan University*
1998	Robert S. Estabrook, *Stephen F. Austin State University*
1999	Cheryl Fischer, *California State University, San Bernardino*
2000	Michael Martin, *University of Colorado, Denver*
2001	Judith Adkison, *University of North Texas*
2002	Paul M. Terry, *University of Memphis*
2003	Elaine L. Wilmore, *University of Texas, Arlington*
2004	Michael "Mick" Arnold, *Southwest Baptist University*

Contents

Part II: Knowing the Way

Part III: Showing the Way

Contributing Authors

C. M. Achilles, *Eastern Michigan University*
Michael "Mick" Arnold, *Southwest Baptist University*
Roger L. Barnes, *Bowling Green State University*
G. Thomas Bellamy, *University of Colorado at Denver*
James E. Berry, *Eastern Michigan University*
Jo Blase, *University of Georgia*
Joseph Blase, *University of Georgia*
Jeffry S. Bowman, *Bowling Green State University*
Charlotte Boyle, *Creighton Elementary School District, Phoenix, Arizona*
Fred Brown, *National Association of Elementary School Principals*
Tricia Browne-Ferrigno, *University of Kentucky*
Peter J. Burke, *Edgewood College*
Herminia Cadenas, *California State University, Los Angeles*
Carolyn S. Carr, *Portland State University*
Theodore Creighton, *Sam Houston State University*
Arnold Danzig, *Arizona State University*
Jeanne R. Fiene, *Western Kentucky University*
Richard Flanary, *National Association of Secondary School Principals*
Richard Fossey, *University of Houston*
Connie L. Fulmer, *University of Colorado at Denver*
Carole Funk, *Sam Houston State University*
Josué González, *Arizona State University*
Sandra Harris, *Stephen F. Austin State University*
John R. Hoyle, *Texas A&M University*
Kay Hunnicutt, *Arizona State University*
Karen E. Jenlink, *Stephen F. Austin State University*
Patrick M. Jenlink, *Stephen F. Austin State University*

Albert Jones, *California State University, Los Angeles*
Gary Kiltz, *Arizona State University*
Donna Macey, *Arizona State University*
Angus MacNeil, *University of Houston*
Stephen K. Miller, *University of Louisville*
Julie Milligan, *Arkansas State University*
Michael J. Murphy, *University of Colorado at Denver*
Rodney Muth, *University of Colorado at Denver*
Joe Nichols, *Arkansas State University*
Azadeh Osanloo, *Arizona State University*
Anita Pankake, *University of Texas-Pan American*
Rosemary Papalewis, *California State University, Sacramento*
Barbara Polnick, *Sam Houston State University*
Kenneth F. Reiter, *University of Colorado at Denver*
Connie Ruhl-Smith, *Bowling Green State University*
Marcia Salazar-Valentine, *Bowling Green State University*
Gwen Schroth, *Texas A&M University–Commerce*
Steven P. Shidemantle, *Katy Junior High School, Katy, Texas*
John Shindler, *California State University, Los Angeles*
Alan Shoho, *University of Texas at San Antonio*
James Smith, *Bowling Green State University-Firelands*
Elsie Szescy, *Arizona State University*
Clint Taylor, *California State University, Los Angeles*
Youlanda C. Washington, *Oldham County Schools, Buckner, KY*
Louis Wildman, *California State University Bakersfield*
Terrence Wiley, *Arizona State University*
Sarah E. Worsham, *Southwest Baptist University*
Michelle D. Young, *University Council for Educational Administration*
Judith A. Zimmerman, *Bowling Green State University*

Review Board

Preface

Education in the United States is in a time of reexamination and redefinition as professors, practitioners, and politicians reflect upon the past and look toward a future characterized by massive change around the world. The National Council of Professors of Educational Administration is deeply involved in this process of shaping our national educational reform agenda. The theme of the 2004 NCPEA Yearbook, *Educational Leadership: Knowing the Way, Showing the Way, Going the Way*, reflects the organizational initiatives begun during the past year to shape this important professional and political effort.

A new NCPEA initiative is being forged to bring practitioners and professors into a collaborative relationship around the practice of educational leadership for this new era. A collegial conversation has begun with the National Association of Secondary School Principals (NASSP), the National Association of Elementary School Principals (NAESP), and the University Council of Educational Administration (UCEA) joining NCPEA as partners in looking toward the futures of each of our organizations in the service of our schools and our professions. As a unique expression of this new relationship, leaders of each of these organizations, addressing this new leadership trend toward collaboration, were invited to contribute to Part I of this yearbook.

Taking the lead in addressing the yearbook educational leadership themes, Part II, *Knowing the Way*, addresses the knowledge base of our field with an eye toward both past foundations and future educational reform. Best practices in preparing future educational leaders are a continuing concern and focus of research, and are the subject of the manuscripts selected for Part III, *Showing the Way*. Finally, ethics, diversity, and social justice remain central concerns of ongoing professional development of both practitioners and professors, and are the focus of Part IV, *Going the Way*, as writers describe current and future directions for educational leadership preparation programs.

The organizational framework of the 2004 yearbook reflects all three of the themes described here. The audience is practicing school leaders in PK–12 schools and university faculty who direct preparation programs for leaders in those same PK–12 schools. According to the tradition of NCPEA, the Cocking Lecture is included here and reflects the educational reform movement which concerns all of us today. This year the Living Legend Address is also included and reflects our organization's historical evolution. Other contributors to the volume consist of active members of NCPEA and others who responded to the call for manuscripts issued at the 2003 conference in Sedona, Arizona. Similarly, reflecting the active membership of NCPEA, volunteer reviewers came forward to serve as the Review Board and select the quality manuscripts to be included in the volume. Each manuscript underwent blind reviews by a minimum of three reviewers. In addition, both editors read and critiqued all of the manuscripts. Members of the Executive Board were consulted when questions arose.

This yearbook is the product of contributions from many persons, without whom it could not have become a reality. A debt of gratitude goes to "Mick" Arnold, the current NCPEA President, who suggested the theme of this year's conference, which in turn serves as the focus and title of the yearbook. Ted Creighton, the NCPEA Executive Director, provided direction, assistance, and support throughout the year, and the Executive Board members were generous in their advice, historical insight, and encouragement throughout the project. Special thanks go to my graduate assistant, Rachel Richards, who contributed many hours helping to bring the project to fruition. Particular thanks go to the editorial staff at Scarecrow Press, especially Cindy Tursman, who was always encouraging and unfailingly responsive to my requests for assistance. Finally, I am especially grateful for the assistance of Connie Fulmer, the associate editor, for her major involvement in every step of the project.

CAROLYN S. CARR
APRIL 2004

I

INVITED CHAPTERS

President's Message

Educational Leadership: Knowing the Way, Showing the Way, Going the Way

Michael "Mick" Arnold

The theme of the 58th Annual Summer Conference is adapted from a quote, used with permission, by John Maxwell. The theme is appropriate, as the National Council of Professors of Educational Administration (NCPEA) has undertaken the task of researching our knowledge base (knowing the way). To further our commitment the profession and to continue our effort to learn from each other, the idea of best practices also seemed to fit well to the ideas and philosophy of the organization (showing the way). Finally, the issues concerning who we serve and the ethics of our profession in context of social justice and servant leadership ('going the way) tie the theme together.

The *American Heritage Dictionary* defines knowledge as "the state of knowing or the sum or range of what has been perceived, discovered, or inferred." The challenge of compiling a knowledge base for educational administration was met by the board following discussion in Sedona at the summer conference and during the fall retreat. As a result of this, Jim Berry was asked to take on the tasks of leading the effort. Following months of work by Jim Berry, the board invited several leaders in our field from NCPEA as well as leaders from other organizations to have a conversation related to the knowledge base during the regular board meeting in February. The conversation was open and frank. From the discussion, comments, and minutes of the meeting, sixteen critical themes emerged. The board took this information and generalized the themes into workable categories. From the work of Jim Berry and others we have begun the initial task of compiling a knowledge base. NCPEA must be proactive in its effort to compile an educational administration knowledge base. We must continue to engage other professional organizations to support our effort. The knowledge base must support practical and scholarly aspects of leadership and educational administration. Author Hays Sulzberger stated, "A man's judgment cannot

Michael "Mick" Arnold, Southwest Baptist University

be better than the information on which he has based it." The continued effort of NCPEA as it relates to the knowledge base of our field will ensure that we and those that follow will know the way.

Several years ago, I sat down and wrote a brief story entitled *Whose Hero Are You?* In that story I addressed people in my life that had impacted who I am and who I would become. I noted that my friends, father, and other family members had impacted me in ways that I didn't realize at the time. In each case, they took the time to show me. In much the same way NCPEA continues to take the time to show others and share what we do to make our profession better. Showing the way by sharing best practices so that others may work to develop the leaders in schools that will impact young people is a task that NCPEA has and continues to embrace. The members of this organization have not only openly shared what they are doing, but NCPEA members have also taken up the mantle of showing others outside our organization through leadership and collaboration.

Leadership must be grounded in the concept of service. George Washington said that a leader must be careful not to get too far ahead of his troops or he may be perceived as the enemy. Leadership cannot be successful unless you are willing to meet the needs of others. We are in the business of developing leaders for today's schools. How can we develop these leaders without giving them an understanding that to lead you must first learn to serve? Leadership must be more than telling. Leaders must be humble, under the authority of others, accountable for their actions, have high moral character and see the value of those around them. As part of the capstone class at Southwest Baptist University, I share with students a quote from William Authur Ward. I would like to leave you with his words.

> From Listening to Serving
> We must be silent before we can listen.
> We must listen before we can learn.
> We must learn before we can prepare.
> We must prepare before we can serve.
> We must serve before we can lead.

Cocking Lecture

Change the Damn Box

C. M. Achilles[1]

PROLOGUE

To initiate discussion about issues at the heart of the Cocking Lecture, I've used some current events as a starting place. In the Call for Proposals (AERA, 2003), the theme for the 2004 American Educational Research Association conference is "Enhancing the Visibility and Credibility of Educational Research." This noble theme is long overdue. A portion of the 2003 Cocking Lecture is about research in education and education administration (EdAd).

In its call for proposals, AERA (2003) seems almost to dismiss EdAd as important ("the very core") in schooling. Consider one conference "sub theme" and substitute EdAd for "teacher" if you want to feel proud.

Teacher Learning and Development. Teachers and their work are at the very core of the educational enterprise. It is through the teacher that all other aspects of the educational system come into contact with the learner, making teachers central to any meaningful change in educational practice. Educational researchers have studied various aspects of teaching and teacher learning for several decades, accumulating an increasingly robust body of knowledge relevant to teacher practice. . . . At the same time, the role of institutions of higher education in the preparation and continuing education of teachers is being questioned. Thus, it is important to understand the process of teacher change and to identify effective ways of fostering teacher learning. As researchers, we have a particular responsibility to bring the tools and findings of our research to bear on these issues. (p. 34)

Why didn't AERA make the above comment about research on teachers and teaching and *also* about EdAd? The "Call" omits administration and organization of schools. A portion of the Lecture is about *administration and organization of education*, student outcomes, and research B and EdAd preparation (the next topic).

C. M. Achilles, Eastern Michigan University

The *UCEA Review* (2003, Spring) continued the discussion of preparation for EdAd, and especially the role of universities. Because of my lengthy tenure in EdAd and long concern about EdAd preparation, I read two articles in detail. Rather than relying on research, Young (2003) discussed what we know "intuitively" about poor or effective EdAd programs. For 30 years, I've seen most of the points presented (e.g., internships, recruitment, evaluation). Hull (2003) listed a series of recommendations that, with minor editing, parallel *Leaders for America's Schools* (Griffiths, Stout, & Forsyth, 1988).

Ironically both Young and Hull discuss research and research use and EdAd preparation, but both also recommend following paths in EdAd preparation that lack credible, valid, and visible research support (e.g., ISLLC, Professional Development or PD). Note Bok's (1987) comment that a lack of a knowledge base (KB) and firm anchor keep EdAd drifting from fad to fad. Points expressed by Hull and by Young are important. They have been expressed before in much the same way. EdAd fails to act decisively, change, and to take charge of its field and preparation. EdAd must take charge of the field. Now, or (as Griffiths said in 1988), R.I.P. . . .

INTRODUCTION

In this presentation I emphasize three ideas (all gall is divided into three parts!) that need action if we are serious about improving Education and Education Administration (EdAd). As the National Council of Professors of Education Administration (NCPEA) has occasionally asked my advice as an "Elder," I unabashedly draw upon some 36 years of professing in EdAd., more than 44 years in education.

I touch upon the three fairly broad topics in much too limited a fashion, and probably without the requisite scholarship of citing numerous others. I recall Carl Glickman once saying that it is the height of impoverishment to cite one's own work. The three areas covered, all normative claims, are:

1. EdAd should focus on schools and schooling, with attention to and research on schooling outputs. (Make schools better places for kids.)
2. Major knowledge base (KB) conundrums in EdAd need resolution for if any field is to grow, so must its KB.
3. Points 1 and 2 need to shape preparation programs for EdAd: If EdAd persons don't take charge of EdAd, others are more than willing to.

Consider the Box

Each of us has probably both heard and used the adjuration about how to be creative: "Think out of the box." Patterson (2003) called it "breaking out of our boxes" (p. 568). If "the box" is so confining that we must always think out of it to improve, we should examine the Box: We should *change the Box*.

The Box is both a metaphor and a reality on three dimensions: a) the structure of the Box, or the setting, b) the neatly wrapped processes and ways of doing things, and c) the mindset of being Boxed in. The Box in this presentation is some of all three of the preceding, but I emphasize structure—the organization and processes—for a) delivering schooling, and b) for EdAd preparation. My often contrarian ideas about EdAd have usually been met with polite one-handed applause. Since January, 2002, I've added a strange ally to my refrain for EdAd to focus on schools and make schools better places for kids. The ally is scientifically based research (SBR). The "strange" is that SBR, is, in my mind, the only useful part of the No Child Left Behind (NCLB) Act, an abomination more aptly called the No Child Left Testers' Full Employment Act.

Since 1967, I've collected bits and pieces about EdAd specifically and education improvement efforts in general as part of trying to determine why, over the years, education reform has been cyclical and mostly stagnant. Explaining these views about school improvement, EdAd, and SBR to educators seems as daunting as explaining three dimensions to a native of Flatland (Abbott, 1952).

At Bozeman (29th NCPEA, 1975) Hoyle called learning environments places "where two or more people gather in the name of education" (p. 1). Hoyle continued:

> Most recent writings on the subject of learning environments have been grounded in the theoretical models . . . (that) hold that institutional and individual characteristics interact in schools and determine student learning. In spite of the tremendous amount of energy expended by researchers of learning environments, *no clear-cut relationship exists between the environment and student achievement.* . . . The complexity of the environment may be such that even valid measures are extremely difficult to relate to student outcomes: However, researchers committed to improving school environment realize that the benefit of analyzing those environments comes when we can successfully predict student cognitive and affective outcomes. (p. 1. Emphasis added)

By the 55th NCPEA at Houston, Lunenburg (2002) addressed the topic of "Improving Student Achievement: Some Structural Incompatibilities." (Although Fred and I disagree on some conclusions, his focus on structure is important. Consider the on-going work of Hoy and Sweetland on learning *structures*.) Some premises that appear in Lunenburg are used here, although some conclusions are different. (I've omitted the references that appear in the original). Quotes are from Lunenburg (2002, pp. 5–27). CMA notes are in [ ].

- The mantra that school is the unit of improvement was based on the misguided belief that individual teacher professionalism would produce excellent schools (p. 5) [Alas, more Professional Development or PD. See also Young, 2003.]
- The main reason for the failure of these reforms to endure and penetrate the classroom is that many of the principal *structures* . . . remain remarkably stable . . . (p. 6, emphasis added).
- If school improvement efforts are bent to fit comfortably into schools as they are currently structured . . . improvement efforts will be weakened and unrecognizable by the time they reach the classroom (p. 6). [Especially if EdAd people don't study and learn about them.]
- Put another way, school administrators have little to do with the technical core of education (teaching and learning) . . . and in many cases *there is no support*

from the organizational infrastructure that surrounds them. (p. 7, emphasis added) [Call this statement "A."]

And in the ensuing discussion of A structural incompatibilities, we find:

• School administrators, then, do not manage instruction. They *manage the infrastructure, surrounding the technical core of teaching and learning* (p. 8, emphasis added). [Call this statement "B."]

These last two quotations contain what I consider an important and structural incompatibility. Consider these two points (A and B) as premises in syllogistic form.

A. There is no support from the organizational infrastructure.
B. School administrators . . . manage the infrastructure.
C. Therefore . . . (?).

I. THE FOCUS ON SCHOOLS AND SCHOOLING

In the 1960s, when I began my study of EdAd, the field was called the administration and organization of education. Organization included the idea of structure (Lunenburg, 2002) and the early idea of Hoyle (1975) on learning environments. Much of school *organization* and the organization variables are "administratively mutable,"[2] or variables that an administrator has some possibility to control, as distinct from "status" variables such as a student's gender or ethnicity, or even socioeconomic status (SES). One would expect that administrators who wish to be successful would know much about administratively mutable variables that influence outcomes of schooling, and how to engage these variables. Unfortunately, my own research suggests that the prior picture is not true.

My major premise is that EdAd should focus on schools, schooling, and outputs of schooling, with attention to, use of SBR, theory, and exemplary practice to improve education. First, EdAd persons must have a clear idea of preferred outputs of schooling contexts, such as that the "learning environment" should be pleasant, safe, healthful, and support desired outcomes. I have argued elsewhere that schooling variables and outputs should be administratively mutable, and improve student achievement in at least four or five categories. The ABCD's or Abecederian Compact (Achilles, 1999) are similar to Comer's desiderata for school as described by Haynes and Emmons (1997). Student achievement is positive in:

Academics, as shown by test scores and other indicators
Behavior and discipline in and out of school
Citizenship and participation in and outside of school
Development into productive, contributing, humane adults with constructive self-concepts (Achilles, 2003, p. 9).
Category E could be Economic Sufficiency.

The emerging list in Table 1 offers SBR-supported education-improvement, administratively mutable, ideas that are organization-based. According to Deming's theory

that is addressed a bit later, administrators are responsible for changes in the organization. To address these types of changes, EdAd persons must know about them and
their usual outcomes. Do EdAd persons know?

One Example of What Gets Attention

A common component for school improvement is the ubiquitous call for Professional Development (PD) or Staff Development (SD).[2] PD as used here excludes advanced degree work. However, even advanced degree work is suspect. An unpopu-
lar study by Haller, Brent, and McNamara (1997) called into question the value of
advanced preparation in EdAd if preparation is continued in traditional ways. (Mainline EdAd outlets shunned publishing this study!)

Table 1.   Emerging List of SBR Results Influencing Schooling Outcomes Positively on ABCD Dimensions: Change the Box

Instructions: 'Brainstorm' ideas onto the list. Provide a source (i.e., author, study) or research for
an idea (e.g., class size, K–3 Project STAR). Estimate cost as high, moderate, medium, or low.
(References available).

A. Organization (Related to Deming's 85%–94%)

 1. Appropriate-size learning groups for the task. Class size, if the class is the unit of
    organization for instruction. STAR, K–3; SAGE; Many studies. (Achilles, 1999). Low cost if
    done in accordance with the research.
 2. Attention to school size (K. Cotton, Fowler & Walberg, V. Lee), such as Learning
    Communities, Academies, School Within a School, etc. (Low Cost).
 3. Tutoring (Bloom's 1984 2-Sigma problem) (Reading Recovery) (High Cost).
 4. Transitions (Elementary-Mid/Mid-HS). (Low/Moderate Costs). See also #2, 17) (J. King-Rice,
    S.H. Achilles, M. Wilson).
 5. Eliminate or greatly reduce retention in grade (Harvey; STAR; Holmes & Matthews, Shepard
    & Smith; etc.) (Low costs or a cost savings).
 6. Non-graded or multi-graded schools (especially work in Australia; Pavan; Goodlad &
    Anderson); (Low cost). See #7.
 7. Multi-age (Australian studies: Pavan, Goodlad & Anderson) (Low cost) See #6.
 8. Quality Pre-K (Perry Pre-School and its longitudinal findings.)(Moderate/High cost but
    positive, cost-effective returns if well done). (Barnett, Head Start, Schweinhart & Weikart).
    See #29.
 9. Cohorts, The Cohort Effect: Most research is on adults. STAR . Morrill (2003). (Low to no
    cost).
10. Looping. Little solid data, some small studies. (Low cost). See #6, 7, 11.
11. The Class Teacher (Denmark). See Morrill, *Kappan*, Feb. 03. (Low cost, high outcome). (A
    type of looping).
12. "Hands-on" learning opportunities (Use of time and space). (Low cost).
13. Use of Time in Schools (National Commission on Time and Learning, 1994; Goodlad, 1984;
    Time on Task Studies). (Low cost). Recapture wasted time in schools: "Prisoners of Time."
    See #31.
14. Participation (Cooperation, Involvement, Engagement, etc.) (Finn; Voelkl; Rumberger;
    Lindsay). STAR. (Moderate/Low cost).
15. Relationships (J. Comer, et al.) (Moderate/High costs, depending on methods).
16. Herzberg's "Motivators;" "Motivation" research (Maslow, Herzberg). (Costs?).
17. Effective Schools (Edmonds, Lezotte, etc.). (Low/Moderate costs).

18. "Community/Family" (Bateman, Small-class research, etc.). (Low costs). This generates psychological sense of community (PSOC).
19. Coherence (Newmann, Bryk, et al.), Seamless In-class Transitions (SSS). Reduce "pull-outs." (Low costs).
20. Use of Teacher Assistants (Para-pro): (Gerber, et al., Finn, et al., Achilles, STAR papers; Haberman; Title I Evaluations). (Aides should have minimum time and use in classes). (Low cost or cost savings).
21. "Structures" studies: (Hoy, Sweetland). (Low/Moderate costs).
22. Capacity Building. Spillane, others. (Low cost).
23. Theories of Practice: (Keedy & Achilles). (Low or no cost). See also NAS evaluations (RAND: Bodilly, et al., 2003).
24. Cooperative Learning (Slavin, Johnson & Johnson, etc.). (Low/Moderate costs).
25. Facilities, Air Quality, "Sick Buildings." (J. Prout). (Cost could be high).
26. Ways to address Student Mobility (e.g., migrants, etc.). (Costs?)
27. Full-Day Kindergarten (in a small class). (STAR, "Test Score Value of K;" Barnett's work with Head Start). Moderate/Medium Cost, but cost effective). See Slavin, Wasik, etc. *Early Prevention of School Failure.* Head Start, Krueger.
28. Delivery Model (Planned, Coherent vs. Fragmented, A Pull-Out@) (STAR, SSS, Newmann et al., B. Taylor in CMA Monograph, and notes to AASA (2003) pages 4-5) (See Title I Critique) (Low/Moderate costs).
29. Parent/Community Involvement. (Epstein, Hoover-Dempsey, Ho & Willms, Chicago Child-Parent Centers). (Low cost). See also Quality Pre-K.
30. Teacher use. Teaching, Redeployment of Personnel. The National Commission on Teaching (D. Hammond, 1968, p. 6), Sharp (2002).
31. High quality, qualified teacher in every classroom;
32. What teachers *know and can do* is one of the most important influences on what students learn. . . . (Emphasis added).
33. School reform cannot succeed unless it focuses on creating the conditions in which teachers *can teach and teach well.* (Emphasis Added). (Cost?).
34. Reconfigurations of time use in school: Block, Copernican, Year-round, Extended day and/or year. Canady & Rettig; Carroll. (Moderate cost). See #13.
35. Homework, Appropriate uses of: (Cooper, H.) (Low cost).
36. Alternative schools, home schooling.
37. Add more.

B. Curricular and Instructional Issues Supported by Organization Changes

- Developmentally appropriate schooling (Piaget; Feuerstein; Vygotsky; Dewey; Perry Pre-School)
- Teaching/Learning styles (Dunn & Dunn; Campbell; Gardner).
- Problem-Based Learning; Projects, Service and Community Learning.

C. Personnel Focus (New PD Forms)

- Job-Embedded PD (Tienken, 2003; Caufield-Sloan, 2001).
- Teacher "Conversation" [See reviews (note 4) e.g., Showers & Joyce; Keedy; Achilles & Gaines] (Low cost).

D. Summary

Tables 1 and 2 together build a case that the Deming (2000) estimate that 85%–94% of the problem resides in the organization and not in the workers may be reasonable. Organization change should be a primary task of administration. *Change the Damn Box!* Now.

The snare is set early and easily. Calls for professional development (PD) or staff de-velopment (SD), or in-service programs, are usually high on the list of education-improvement strategies. In a field whose core business includes instruction and in which many practitioners hold titles such as staff developer or human resource consultant, calls for more PD or SD as a primary capacity-building tool for education improvement are seldom questioned. Many professors have an in-service moonlighting business that may expand dramatically with the reauthorization of the Elementary and Secondary Educa-tion Act of 1965 (PL 89–10), mislabeled as the No Child Left Behind (NCLB) Act which recommends lots of SD and funds it through Title II. Over many years, PD has received huge expenditures of time, funds, and effort: PD is touted in the same NCLB that argues for scientifically based research or SBR. One would expect demonstrable, cost-effective replicable SBR evidence of successes as a base for the NCLB support of PD, but none is presented in NCLB, or in studies I could find (See Table 2). The depth and ubiquity of the problem are evident in the question, "Can you provide two or more high quality, replicable, independent empirical studies (SBR) of the positive effects of PD on teacher behavior and especially of its subsequent effects on student short and long-term success as usually measured?" See Appendix A for definitions (Glossary).

Teachers seldom clamor for more PD. Regardless of self-reports and surveys, scant, if any, replicable, empirical evidence (SBR) has related PD to a) changes in teacher behavior and b) improved student outcomes. Many articles and ideas for im-provement perpetuate PD with unsupported assertions that PD is required. However, many studies that have demonstrated improved education outcomes and have also included and assessed a PD component [such as Student Teacher Achievement Ra-tio or STAR (Achilles, 1999; Word et al., 1990), class-size reduction or CSR in Cal-ifornia, and other class-size studies] do *not* find observable PD-driven teacher changes even if teachers self-report them. The absence of such findings is particu-larly notable in relation to organization changes, such as class size, that consistently *do* provide replicable student gains.

The constant focus upon PD, nearly to the exclusion of other improvement strate-gies has derailed education improvement. This focus wrongly blames teachers and (indirectly) teacher preparation for presumed education deficiencies and shields other possible causes such as EdAd failures. *DISCLAIMER*: This paper is not an *attack* on PD, but it does *raise questions* about lack of leadership approaches to capacity building that meet the SBR test.

A Research, Theory, and Logical Alternative
Dennis Sparks, the executive director of the National Staff Development Council (NSDC) noted that "A . . . quality improvement expert W. Edwards Deming esti-mates that 85% of barriers to improvement reside in the organization's structure and processes, not in the performance of individuals" (1995, p. 3). Intriguing. If this is correct, then PD for workers could only get at 15% of the barriers to improvement even if PD were 100% successful (improbable)! So, thinking outside of the box by tinkering with PD is not likely to get much done except continuously blame teach-ers, misdirect improvement work, punish students, etc.

Table 2. Sample of Articles and Studies That Encourage PD but Fail to Find or Provide SBR Evidence of Teacher Change or Student Gains

Source/Focus/Design	*Design/Outcome/Quota*
Bodilly, et al., (2003). RAND evaluation of NAS implementations.	". . . reforms such as NAS—including teacher-reported collaboration, professional development, and revised instructional practices—were *not* related to student achievement."
Carpenter (2000). Reviewed school reform efforts (1990–2000). Findings: . . .	". . . PD (and other reforms) have had little impact on student achievement or on school improvement."
Covert, S. (2003). Review of research for a dissertation on PD. (E. Michigan U.)	"Given the lack of studies which demonstrate PD effects on teachers or student outcomes. . . " Argues for attention to theory to guide PD.
Garet, et al., *AERJ* (2002). Focus on teacher learning	National probability sample (n=1027). Teacher self-reported info. on a survey. No evidence of student gains.
Guskey, T. R. (2003). Review of 13 lists of "effective PD." Dearth of SBR work and evidence of outcomes. Mostly "surveys of opinions." (p. 749)	". . . lists could be described as 'research level.' But that research rarely includes rigorous investigations of the relationship between the noted characteristics and improvements in instructional practice or learning outcomes."
Guskey, T. R. (1997)	"Research needs to link PD and student learning."
Haller, Brent, & McNamara (1997). Advanced training in EdAd.	No measurable difference on Effective Schools@ indicators of advanced training in EdAd.
Newmann, King, & Youngs, *AERJ* (2000), and *American J. of Education*. Broadly theoretic and conceptual paper. School capacity focus.	"The case for substantial investment in [PD] is vulnerable because of an absence of research that links specific forms of [PD] to changes in teacher learning and practice and to student achievement gains . . ."
Tienken (2003). Review of research for a dissertation on PD (Seton Hall U.)	Minimal evidence of PD changing teacher behavior or student achievement. Job-embedded PD seems promising. (Expensive)

In his last years, Deming revised his 85%–15% estimate of the problem. The front page of the Business Section of the *Los Angeles Times* (December 5, 1993) quoted Deming at a California seminar, "All that happens comes from the system, not the workers. It's absolutely frightening, just frightening." See also Deming's (1993) book, *The New Economics* (2nd edition, 2000):

> In my experience, most troubles and most possibilities for improvement add up to proportions something like this:
>   94% belong to the system (the responsibility of management)
>   6% are attributable to special causes

No amount of care or skill in workmanship can overcome fundamental faults of the system. (pp. 33–34)

Consider the idea that *administrators are responsible for the organization, especially those variables that are administratively mutable.*

Given (a) Deming's claim that organization problems are directly connected to an organization's structure and management (85%–94%) and that only a few are related to personnel (workers), (b) the continuing pervasive finding of little demonstrable student gain or teacher change from PD, and (c) an espoused goal of EdAd for improving education, we must stop exhorting people to "think out of the Box" to improve education. If it is the Box, *change* the damn Box. Start by making administratively mutable organization adjustments aligned with findings of "good" research (SBR). Changes should be in concert with useful, time-tested theories and consensually validated exemplary practices or informed professional judgment (IPJ).

The list in Table 1 contains SBR (demonstrated) "things" that advance education efficiency and effectiveness and improve schooling. Evaluate, expand, and advance EdAd's KB. Add to the list, but exclude for-sale "Programs" unless they meet SBR, theory, and Informed Professional Judgment (IPJ) tests.

II. THE KNOWLEDGE BASE (KB) CONUNDRUM

NCPEA and UCEA and other groups have struggled constantly with EdAd's "knowledge base" (KB). Achilles has written considerably about the KB, as have Hoyle, the Interstate School Leader Licensure Consortium (ISLLC) people, and many others. "Ed Ad still seems to be searching for its KB, much like a playful puppy pursuing its own tail in ever hilarious circles" (Achilles, 2000, p. 4). The following five paragraphs from Achilles (2000, pp. 4–5) summarize the KB conundrum.

When he was president of Harvard, Bok (1987) questioned that education even had a KB. He presaged a condition that exists today as educators jump from one fad to another, and acquiescence to "mandates" to reform education in ways shown by substantial research, theory, and IPJ *not* to work (e.g., retention in grade). Bok said:

Because they have neither a strong profession nor distinctive body of knowledge to impart, education faculties have no firm anchor for their programs or curricula. Instead, external forces *push them first in one direction, and then in another.* (p. 46, emphasis added)

Culbertson (1990) pointed to the squishy KB in EDAD as set forth in texts that professors teach from. He argued that much of what was supposed to be research-based wasn't. [English (2002), has commented about the text problem.]

First, borrowed concepts tend to enter textbooks before they are adequately tested in school systems. The result is that such concepts may be used indefinitely in training programs even though their actual relations to school management and leadership practices remain unknown. (pp. 102–103)

There is not a minimum KB generated by practice, either. If there were, where is *The Handbook of Exemplary Practice in EDAD*?

Clearly, without consensus on its KB, EdAd can't even be as well off as medicine, a field that at least "tells it like it is." The *New York Times Magazine* (Jaubar, 2003) featured a series on medicine and medical education. One MD (Sanders, 2003) reflected on the Dean at her medical school saying ". . . half of what we teach you here is wrong—unfortunately, we don't know which half" (p. 29). Another MD noted: "1999 Institute of Medicine report estimated that 98,000 deaths occur in the United States every year because of medical errors. Most of these deaths, the report said, do not occur because of individual mistakes but because of *flaws in the way hospitals and clinics operate.*" Citing a tragic transplant issue, the doctor reported that "the fault was *not in any one individual* but rather *in the structure* of care . . ." (Jaubar, 2003, p. 35, emphasis added). Burton (2003) noted that "Five percent of doctors are said to be responsible for more than half of malpractice post-trial payments" (p. 48). The medicine scenario sounds eerily like the Deming 85%–94% contention and the prior arguments against PD as the *primary* way to "improve" education outcomes.

Others confirm my observations both about the EdAd KB and the potential for research to support a professional KB of practice (e.g., Achilles, 1990, 2000). My research includes surveys (see Appendix B), reviews of EdAd preparation programs, discussions with EdAd persons, and considerable reading of EdAd student work. My conclusions are that (a) EdAd practitioners do not know the administratively mutable variables that influence schools, schooling improvement, and student outcomes, (b) EdAd preparation-program curricula do not include them, and (c) many professors don't know them either. This last point should not be surprising given the constant findings of studies of the EdAd professoriate (Campbell & Newell, 1973; McCarthy, et al., 1988; McCarthy & Kuh, 1997, as cited in McCarthy 1998). McCarthy (1998, p. 5) reported that for EdAd professors, the "most preferred periodical was the *Kappan.*" This replicated earlier studies where the *Kappan, Educational Leadership, NASSP Bulletin*, etc., were the primary reading for EdAd professors. Haller and Knapp (1985), and Achilles (1990, 1997, 2001) have argued that many EdAd articles that are called "research" should be called dissemination or service; they rehash points of view and do not report research that emphasizes students and outcomes.

At the very least, EdAd journals should emphasize research related to school improvement and professional practice, because to be successful, an administrator must know three domains that I've simplistically called WHAT, HOW, and WHY. The EdAd person must know, relative to schooling and student outcomes:

1. WHAT to do: (The foundational KB of schools, schooling outcomes, etc., based on valid, reliable, replicable SBR research);
2. HOW to get the WHAT done: (Leadership skills, etc.); and
3. WHY something should (or should not) be done: (Legal, moral, ethical, statute, policy, court decisions, etc., reasons).

The third section addresses context of issues raised in the first two parts of the paper and suggests how these several considerations could lead in to solid preparation

programs that will help persons become effective, respected, and efficient administrators who are stewards of other peoples' children and money. Appendix C contains
a real-life scenario to demonstrate the conundrum presented here.

III. TAKE COMMAND OF EDAD PREPARATION

The "structural incompatibilities" of Lunenburg (2002), "learning environments" of
Hoyle (1975), the considerable work on structures (Hoy & Sweetland, 2001), and
numerous works on class sizes that are structures for teaching (Project STAR,
SAGE, CSR in California, etc.) can help EdAd persons think about changing the
Box. In writing about creativity in schooling, Hennessey (2003) recalled that the
idea of creativity and the Box (structure, here) have been around awhile. The research here is about both structures and processes.

> The work of Seymour Sarason speaks eloquently to this problem of *effecting change
> within the schools*; and in fact, his seminal book on this subject is titled *The Culture of
> School and the Problem of Change* (1971, revised 1996). . . . Sarason demonstrates how
> long-standing *educational structures and practices*, both at the institutional level and
> within individual classrooms, *stifle reform efforts*. . . . Moreover, Sarason points out that
> reasoned arguments for the abandonment of these control systems have been met in the
> past and will continue to be met with strong protests from various groups (classroom
> teachers, administrators, unions) who believe they must defend their power . . .
>   Sarason (1990) . . . Fortunately for our nation's children, Sarason and a handful of
> others like him will continue to work to make his message heard: *Schools should and
> must exist to serve students.* (p. 28, emphasis added)

That telling quotation about Sarason's work helps explain why high-quality EdAd
preparation is required. How many EdAd professors or practitioners would recognize the problem(s) expressed in the quotation? How many would know some SBR-
supported steps to address the problems? Should the problems be addressed? By
whom? The questions get complex and answers will be murky. Don Willower told
me once that a reasonable answer to most EdAd problems is "It depends." I agree,
but I believe that EdAd as a field should answer "it depends" clearly in terms of
WHAT, HOW, WHY. That is, depending on the problem, EdAd people should know
What to do, How to do it, and Why!

To provide a framework for considering both EdAd preparation and the concept
of profession, conceptualize a professional as knowing WHAT to do (the basic KB),
HOW to use or get the WHAT done, and WHY (or why not) do something. (Details
are in Appendix D.) Without a solid, field-specific KB, there is no professional expertise, so there is no reason why anyone who knows about change, fund management, public relations, etc., can't run a school, right? Without all three "legs"—the
WHAT, HOW, WHY, the field and its preparation are wobbly.

- Consider a lawyer with fine speaking skills but ignorant of law.
- Consider a preacher with good oratory but absent of any theology.
- Consider an MD with great bedside manner but no medical knowledge.

- Consider a CPA with mastery of math but no knowledge of tax laws.
- Consider a general with leadership skills but weak military science.
- Consider an EdAd person or program . . . (See Appendix B.) Alas!

The quotation of the medical school Dean . . . "half of what we teach you here is wrong—Unfortunately, we don't know which half" (Sanders, 2003, p. 29) should be a wake-up call to EdAd to return seriously to the KB issue. With the preceding ideas as a foundation, I offer several recommendations to help the EdAd field take charge of and reclaim the important task of preparing "Leaders for America's Schools." Recommendations relate to a framework and WHAT to do. The HOW effort needs to be serious, scholarly, practical, collaborative, and focused.

Recommendation 1. Focus EdAd upon schools, schooling outcomes, making schools better places, etc. Set clear goals and mission (e.g., The Abecederian concept works for me. The field needs consensus on some goal.)

Recommendation 2. Conceptualize the EdAd KB in the WHAT, HOW, WHY framework and (a) deliver it that way (courses, experiences, assessments, and (b) evaluate all three dimensions relative to the goals set in Recommendation 1. That is, if behavior, citizenship, and development are valid goals, then outcome evaluation by test scores only is inadequate and lacks content validity.

Recommendation 3. Work collaboratively with "stakeholders," but define and insist on establishing and using a professional KB based upon research (SBR), theory, and IPJ, tempered with the WHY elements.

To provide some direction for decisions, I suggest that criteria be clearly delineated and agreed upon in advance. Several examples of such criteria are in Appendix E where I have used my research on class size as the focus. Class size is an organization for instruction that is administratively mutable but widely misunderstood and poorly implemented in EdAd. The class-size issue provides one interesting example of the points I have touched on in this presentation.

CONCLUSION

I have tried to summarize my years of concern about EdAd as a field and about EdAd preparation. I have provided some ideas for improvement based on experience, reading and synthesis of scholarly works, critique (considering points of view and then making a judgment), and some logic.

The final section provides a simple, but functional, structure to conceptualize, develop, deliver, and assess both the EdAd KB and preparation programs for EdAd. Admittedly the final section is extremely brief, but change must start somewhere. At this point, I am concerned with trying to establish a foundation and framework.

Thanks for listening. Think well. Act wisely. Start soon. R.I.P.?

NOTES

1. Some material in this presentation has appeared in the same or slightly modified form in other authored or co-authored works by Achilles. Specific sources include Achilles (in press), Achilles (2003), and Achilles and Finn or Finn and Achilles articles and papers on class size.

I thank NCPEA President (2003) Elaine Wilmore and the NCPEA Executive Board for extending me the honor of presenting the 2003 Walter Dewey Cocking Lecture to NCPEA. The ideas here certainly will not be new to many NCPEA faithful, but I was asked to think about and build upon my full range of experiences in EdAd, including reading, research, practice, critique, and also to consider the future. I've tried to synthesize several papers (1984–2003) on preparation, EdAd, changes, and combine those ideas with some current events.

Although I surely have left some off the following list, my debt to folks like John Hoyle, Dave Erlandson, Don Coleman, Phil West, Dwain Estes, Jim McNamara, Rosemary Papalewis, Jim Berry, Bob Beach, Ted Creighton, Ley Browder, Emett Burnett, Lloyd DuVall, Don Willower, Jack Culbertson, and many other NCPEA stalwarts is probably obvious. Less obvious may be the impact that early NCPEA influentials had: Orin Gruff, Edgor Morphet, R.L. Johns, Ted Reller, Dan Griffiths, Max Abbott, Clyde Campbell, Dick Lonsdale, Dan Davies, Bob Blackman, Norman Boyan, Ben Sachs, and others, all of whom I had opportunity to work with or to learn from at NCPEA.

I thank David Berliner for his dialogue regarding Professional Development (PD) that I've used as an example in this presentation.

Nevertheless, any obvious stupidity in this is entirely my pleasure to add: A sense of play is important.

2. Definitions are important in research and in discourse. Key terms that I use in this paper are defined in Appendix A, Glossary.

REFERENCES

Abbott, A. (1952). *Flatland: A review of many dimensions.* New York: Dover Publications, Inc.

Achilles, C. M. (2003, Winter). Thoughts about education administration and improvement. *Journal of Thought, 38*(4), 103–121.

Achilles, C. M. (2000, August). *Drama in education administration (EdAd): A morality play or a farce?* Paper presented at NCPEA, Ypsilanti, MI.

Achilles, C. M. (1999). *Let's put kids first finally: Getting class size right.* Thousand Oaks, CA: Corwin Press.

Achilles, C. M., Dickerson, C., Dockery-Runkel, L., Egelson, P., & Epstein, M. (1992). *Practical school improvement: The Mary Reynolds Babcock project at Moore School.* Paper presented at the annual meeting of the American Educational Research Association, San Francisco, CA.

Achilles, C. M., Reynolds, J., & Achilles. S. H. (1997). *Problem analysis: Responding to school complexity.* Larchmont, NY: Eye on Education.

American Educational Research Association. (2003, May). Call for proposals. *Educational Researcher, 32*(4), 33–45.

Biddle, B. J., & Berliner, D. C. (2002). Research synthesis: Small class size and its effects. *Educational Leadership, 59*(5), 12–23.

Bodily, S. J., Gill, B. P., Berends, M., Kirby, S. N., Dembowsky, J. W., & Caulkins, J. P. (2003). Hard lessons learned from educational interventions. *Rand Review, 27*(1), 1–10, retrieved 5/11/03 from < http://www.rand.org/publications/randreview/issues/spring2003/crashcourses.html >

Bok, D. (1987, May–June). The challenge to schools of education. *Harvard Magazine, 89*(5), 47–57, 79, 80.

Boyd-Zaharias, J., & Pate-Bain, H. (2000). Early and new findings from Tennessee's Project STAR. In M. C. Wang & J. D. Finn (Eds.), *How small classes help teachers do their best* (pp. 65–98), Philadelphia, PA: Temple University Center for Research in Human Development.

Burton, S. (2003, March 16). The biggest mistake of their lives. Four interviews conducted by S. Burton. *New York Times Magazine*, 48–51.

Campbell, R. F., & Newell, L. J. (1973). *A study of professors of educational administration.* Columbus, OH: UCEA.

Carpenter, W. A. (2000, January). Ten years of silver bullets: Dissenting thoughts on education reform. *Phi Delta Kappan, 81*(5), 383–389.

Caulfield-Sloane, M. R. (2001). *The effects of staff development of teachers in the use of higher order questioning strategies on third grade students' rubric science assessment.* Unpublished Ed.D. dissertation. Seton Hall University, Orange, New Jersey.

Covert, S. L. (2003). *Transferring professional development to the classroom.* Unpublished EdD Dissertation, Eastern Michigan University, Ypsilanti, MI.

Crane, J. (Ed.). (1998). *Social programs that work.* New York: Russell Sage Foundation.

Culbertson, J. A. (1990, Fall/Winter). Tomorrow's challenges to today's professors of educational administration. 1988 W. D. Cocking Lecture to NCPEA, Kalamazoo, MI. *The Record in Educational Administration and Supervision, II*(1), 100–107.

Darling-Hammond, L. (1998, January–February). Teachers and teaching: Testing policy hypotheses from a national commissions report. *Educational Researche, 27*(1), 5–15.

Deming, W. E. (1993, 2000). *The new economics for industry, government, education (2nd ed.).* Cambridge, MA: The MIT Press.

Dunkin, M. J. (1996, Summer). Types of errors in synthesizing research in education. *Review of Educational Research, 66*(2), 87–97.

English, F. W. (2002, January). The penetration of educational leadership texts by revelation and prophecy: The case of Stephen R. Covey. *Journal of School Leadership, 12*, 3–22.

Feuer, M., Towne, L., & Shavelson R. J. (2002). Scientific culture and educational research. *Educational Researcher, 31*(8), 4–14.

Finn, J. D., & Achilles, C. M. (1999, Summer). Tennessee's class size study: Findings, implications, misconceptions. *Educational Evaluation and Policy Analysis, 21*(2), 97–107.

Finn, J. D., Gerber, S. B., Achilles, C. M., & Boyd-Zaharias, J. (2001, April). The enduring effects of small classes. *Teachers College Record, 103*(2), 145–183.

Garet, M. S., Porter, A. C., Desimone, I., Birman, B. F., & Yoon, K. S. (2001). What makes professional development effective? Results from a national sample of teachers. *American Educational Research Journal 38*(4), 915–945.

Griffiths, D. E., Stout, R. T., & Forsyth, P. B. (Eds.). (1988). *Leaders for America's schools.* Berkeley, CA: McCutcheon.

Guskey, T. R. (2003). What makes professional development effective? *Phi Delta Kappan, 84*(10), 748–750.

Guskey, T. R. (1997). Research needs to link professional development and student learning. *The Journal of Staff Development, 18*(2), 28–34.

Haller, E. J., Brent, B. O., & McNamara, J. H. (1997, November). Does graduate training in educational administration improve America's schools? *Phi Delta Kappan, 79*(3), 222–227.

Haller, E. J., & Kleine, P. F. (2001). *Using educational research.* New York: Longman.

Haller, E. J., & Knapp, T. R. (1985, Summer). Problems and methodology in educational administration. *Educational Administration Quarterly, 21*(3), 157–168.

Haynes, N. M., & Emmons, C. I. (1997, February). *Comer school development program effects: A ten-year review, 1986–1996.* New Haven, CT: Yale Child Study Center School Development Program.

Hennessey, B. A. (2003, Fall). The social psychology of creativity in the schools. *Research in the Schools, 9*(2), 23–34.

Hoy, W., & Sweetland, S. (2001). Designing better schools: The meaning and measure of enabling school structures. *Educational Administration Quarterly, 37*(3), 296–321.

Hoyle, J. (1975). Analyzing learning environments. Paper presented at NCPEA (No date on the draft), Bozeman, MT.

Hoyle, J. (1991, Fall/Winter). Educational administration has a knowledge base. *The Record in Educational Administration and Supervision, 12*(1), 21–28.

Jaubar, S. (2003, March 16). When doctors slam the door. *New York Times Magazine,* 32–35.

Keedy, J. L., & Achilles, C. M. (2001). The intellectual firepower needed for educational administration's new era of enlightenment. In T. Kowalski & G. Perreault (Eds.), *21st century challenges for school administrators* (pp. 89–100). Lanham, MD: Scarecrow Press.

Krueger, A. B. (1999). Experimental estimates of education production functions. *Quarterly Journal of Economics, 114,* 497–532.

Krueger, A. B., & Whitmore, D. M. (2000, April). *The effect of attending a small class in the early grades on college-test taking and middle school test results: Evidence from Project STAR.* Cambridge, MA: National Bureau of Economic Research. Working paper 7656. Retrieved from www.nber.org.papers/w7656.

Lewit, E. M., & Baker, L. S. (1997, Winter). Class size. *The Future of Children: Financing schools, 7*(3), 112–121.

Lunenburg, F. C. (2002). Improving student achievement: Some structural incompatibilities. In G. Perreault & F. Lunenburg (Eds.), *The changing world of school administration* (pp. 5–27). Lanham, MD: Scarecrow Press.

McCarthy, M. M. (1998). The "new" educational leadership professor. In R. Muth & M. Martin (Eds.), *Toward the year 2000: Leadership for quality schools. 6th Yearbook of NCPEA.* (pp. 3–15). Lancaster, PA: Technomic.

McCarthy, M. M., & Kuh, G. D. (1997). *Continuity and change: The educational leadership professoriate.* Columbia, MO: UCEA.

McCarthy, M. M., Kuh, G. D., Newell, L. J., & Iacona, C. M. (1988). *Under scrutiny: The educational administration professoriate.* Tempe, AZ: UCEA.

McRobbie, J., Finn, J. D., & Harman, P. (1998, August). *Class-size reduction: Lessons learned from experience.* San Francisco, CA: West Ed.

Mosteller, F. (1995). The Tennessee study of class size in the early school grades. *The Future of Children, 5*(2), 113–127.

Newmann, F. M., King, M. B., & Youngs, P. (2001, January). *Professional development that addresses school capacity: Lessons from urban elementary schools.* Portions from a paper presented at AERA, April 28, 2000.

Patterson, W. (2003, April). Breaking out of our boxes. *Phi Delta Kappan, 84*(8), 568–574.

Sanders, L. (2003, March 16). Medicine's progress, one setback at a time. *New York Times Magazine,* 29–31.

Sharp, M. A. (2002). *An analysis of pupil–teacher ratio and class size.* Unpublished Ed.D. dissertation. Eastern Michigan University. Ypsilanti, MI.

Showers, B., & Joyce, B. (1996). The evolution of peer coaching. *Educational Leadership, 53* (6), 12–16.

Sparks, D. (1995, Winter). A paradigm shift in staff development. *Professional Staff Development: The ERIC Review, 3*(3), 2–4.

Sparks, D., & Loucks-Horsley, S. (1989, Fall). Five models of staff development for teachers. *Journal of Staff Development, 10*(4), 40–57.

Tienken, C. H. (2003). *The effect of staff development for teachers in the use of scoring rubrics and reflective questioning strategies on fourth-grade students' narrative writing performance*. Unpublished EdD Dissertation, Seton Hall University, South Orange, NJ.

Word, E., Johnston, J., Bain, H., Fulton, B., Zaharias, J., Lintz, N., Achilles, C. M., Folger, J., & Breda, C. (1990). *Student/teacher achievement ratio (STAR): Tennessee's K-3 class-size study. Final report and final report summary.* Nashville, TN: Tennessee State Department of Education.

Young, M. D. (2003, Spring). From the director. . . . Let's practice what we teach. *UCEA Review, XLV*(2), 6–8.

APPENDIX A: GLOSSARY/DEFINITIONS

Administration is the crafty blend of the science of managing and the art of leading. Managing deals with conserving and maintaining the good and useful (a smooth ship); Leading is initiating, changing, and improving. (See Achilles, Reynolds, & Achilles, 1997 for more detail).

Administratively Mutable refers to things over which the Administrator has sufficient control to adjust or change. For example, this would exclude status variables such as gender, or race, and include "the Box" as discussed here: context, resource allocation, etc. I thank Emil Haller for extending my thinking on this important concept. Obvious administratively mutable changes include staffing, time use, facilities changes, re-allocations of resources.

Average Class Size is the sum of all students regularly in each teacher's class divided by the actual number of regular teachers in those specific classes. If the four 2nd grade rooms have 14, 16, 18, 18 (n = 65), the average grade-2 class size is 16.25 (or 16) students.

Class Size(s) "The number of students for whom a teacher is primarily responsible during a school year" (Lewit & Baker, 1997, p. 113). This is an addition problem. Class size is an organization for instruction important to teachers, parents, students. It is administratively mutable.

Class-Size Reduction (CSR) includes processes involved in achieving class sizes smaller than presently in place. Often this means changing the class size from 25 to 16 or so. One needs accurate pre and post data to support the change process.

Inservice Training refers to short-term training, usually a specific workshop or large-group session to present information or a basic skill, easily lea·ned, usually delivered via one-way communication. There typically is no follow-up.*

Job-Embedded Staff or Professional Development is PD that in education specifically emphasizes teaching or instruction skills and knowledge related to student outcomes. Examples include action research and evaluation, structured study groups, peer coaching, mentoring. There is mounting evidence that this works

---

* These are adapted from operational definitions used in two recent EdD dissertations: Covert, 2003, pp. 16–17 and Tienken, 2003, pp. 14–15. In both studies the researchers explored the connection of PD to observed change in teacher behavior. Tienken connected job-embedded v ork to measure student improvement in writing (experimental design). Covert sought to determine if any changes in teacher behavior persisted at least a full year in teacher use of running records (descriptive and time-series design).

(teacher behavior, student achievement), but it is expensive, labor intensive, and produces gains in a single area, such as writing skills (e.g., Tienken, 2003; Caulfield-Sloane, 2001; Achilles et al., 1992).*

Professional Development (PD) is on-going, planned, continuing education through which certified, qualified education professionals improve skills, knowledge, and attitudes/dispositions related to assisting clients (e.g., students) achieve goals of the organization (i.e., improved student performance and outcomes). A primary interest is to improve the professional's long-term value in workplace performance. Interaction and two-way communication are part of the long-term effect. PD (as distinct from personal improvement) should have at least two levels of observable, measurable impact: 1) to improve the participant's observed professional practice when measured against stated criteria, and 2) to influence positively the achievement of students when measured against desired outcomes. The new professional practice will be sustained.*

Pupil-Teacher Ratio (RTR)—"The number of students in a school or district compared to the number of teaching professionals" (McRobbie, Finn, & Harman, 1998, p. 4). In some venues all educators are part of the computation, including counselors, administrators, etc. In this division problem, the divisor is very important. PTR is a way to assure equitable distribution of funds and is important to administrators, policy persons, etc. The difference between PTR and class size in USA elementary schools is about n = 10 (Sharp, 2002).

Staff Development (SD) involves workplace related workshops, training and knowledge offered to both professional and support personnel. The focus may not be on personal and job-related topics of interest and value to staff and to organization maintenance or health (e.g., retirement planning, first aid, diversity training, conflict resolution, policies/procedures related to law, etc.), rather than on classroom performance.

APPENDIX B: SURVEY OF RESEARCH-BASED STUDENT
IMPROVEMENT PRACTICES (K–12)

I'm collecting information for a paper. Results will be anonymous. Your participation is completely voluntary. Please return responses to the person who distributes this form.

1. Please list some key research-based concepts *that improve student schooling outcomes* that you have been *taught directly* in formal Education Administration (EdAd) courses at the Master's, Ed.S., or Ed.D. levels (not in-service efforts, or on-the-job training). Criteria for including the concept here:

---

* These are adapted from operational definitions used in two recent EdD dissertations: Covert, 2003, pp. 16–17 and Tienken, 2003, pp. 14–15. In both studies the researchers explored the connection of PD to observed change in teacher behavior. Tienken connected job-embedded work to measure student improvement in writing (experimental design). Covert sought to determine if any changes in teacher behavior persisted at least a full year in teacher use of running records (descriptive and time-series design).

a—Research based

b—Improved student outcomes
c—Taught in formal EdAd classes

1. *Elementary Level (K–8 or so)*
   Concept

   | WHAT to Do |

   _____ A
   _____ B
   _____ C
   _____ D
   _____ E
   _____ F

2. *Secondary Level (8–12 or so)*
   Concept

   | WHAT to Do |

   _____ A
   _____ B
   _____ C
   _____ D
   _____ E
   _____ F

2. If you were also taught *HOW* to do a concept you entered into question A above, mark that item (x) in the space at the left of your entry.

3. Identifier Information:
   1. *Your EdAd Program Level:*   Master's, Ed.S., Doctoral   (Please circle one.)
   2. State ——————————— 3. Years experience in EdAd ———————

                                   Thank You.

4. If you are interested in the results, please complete this last item.

Name: ——————————— Address: ———————————
Date: _____   ———————————

APPENDIX C: A REAL-LIFE SCENARIO OF PD VS. THE BOX

Scenario.   Pat's pre-service teacher preparation in running records (RR) to assess and assist beginning readers and appropriate use of portfolios as a way to monitor student-growth. Pat demonstrated solid knowledge of these skills and used them satisfactorily in student teaching, usually while the regular teacher helped students with whom Pat was not working. The classroom teacher praised Pat's work.

After employment, Pat's first-grade class, like others in the building had 29 students considered "about average" with a couple of "included" students. Pat's plan called for RR (each child observed weekly), portfolio assessment that would involve parents, and individualized work emphasizing "the basics" of language and numbers.

Pat soon found that there was not time for RR and portfolios. These and other skills learned in teacher preparation soon faded in favor of large-group instruction, rote, testing, worksheets, and classroom management. Pat learned crowd control. Colleagues told Pat to "forget college idealism." "Welcome to the real world."

An esteemed district supervisor returned from a conference enthusiastic about PR and sold the idea to the administrative council, which mandated RR training for all K–3 teachers. Pat dutifully attended 20 hours of training and demonstrated the use of RR, including diagnosing a student's needs and re-teaching. When the supervisor conducted a follow-up visit, she wrote an unfavorable observation indicating Pat's non-use of RR, a "scene" repeated in other K–3 classrooms. The supervisor reported to the administrative council: "We brought the K–3 teachers the most up-to-date tools, and even after extensive PD with follow-up, the teachers won't use what we required. No wonder we can't improve!"

Unfortunately, the above scenario is not uncommon. More unfortunately, there are great alternatives. Administrators seem not to know them or to try them.

APPENDIX D: CHARACTERISTICS THAT DEFINE "PROFESSION" AND SERVE AS A BASE FOR DECISIONS ABOUT COMPETENCE IN THE PRACTICE OF THE PROFESSION (ADAPTED FROM ACHILLES, 1999, P. 133).

A Profession Has Certain Definable Elements:

- A body of knowledge (knowledge base or KB) that members use to address client (people) problems. This KB constitutes a field's *basic skills* and information to guide the practice (WHAT to Do).
- A method or methods of inquiry to advance, assess, and access the KB and its applications. (Use of the KB is not predictable or immutable.)
- Validated skills and processes to apply the KB to achieve goals, solve problems, and benefit clients: consensually validated exemplary practice and IPJ (HOW to proceed).
- Intellectual decision making based on "informed professional judgment" (IPJ factor). Flexibility.
- Standards of conduct and application (code of ethics), e.g., Oath of Hippocrates. "Primum Non Nocere" (at least, do no harm). Ethics, Laws, Policy (WHY)
- Entry requirements (licensure, certification) and internship or some guided practice before full licensure.
- Provisions to maintain and advance the field and for members to keep current with changes and improvements.
- Public perception of quality and value of the field's KB.
- Self-regulation, sanctions.
- Common language, Effective communication.
- Others (?)

APPENDIX E: TABLE E–1: COMPARISON OF STAR DESIGN, PROCESSES, AND FACTS WITH ONE SET OF "PRINCIPLES OF INQUIRY"*

Although no universally accepted description of the principles of inquiry exists, we argue nonetheless that all scientific endeavors . . .

*Feuer, M. S., Towne, L., & Shavelson, R. J. (2002, November). Scientific culture and educational research. *Educational Researcher, 31*(8), 4–14.

Scientific Endeavors

1. Pose Significant Questions That Can Be Investigated Empirically. The initiating law required questions and processes. Researchers added others.

2. Link Research to Relevant Theory. STAR began in 1984, so some design and theory issues we now know (2003) were not yet refined. Table 8 is a summary of some theories supporting STAR.

3. Use Methods that Permit Direct Investigation of the Questions. The variable of focus was class size so

Star Design, Processes, and Facts

1. STAR was driven by two significant, major questions: What is the EFFECT of small classes in primary grades on the 1) Achievement and 2) Development of students? Researchers addressed secondary questions required or implied in the legislation: Effects of a) full-time teacher aide, b) training, c) duration, d) cohort, and e) random assignment. (See Table 5.) Researchers studied other questions: teacher quality (by credentials), comparisons of sample with state averages, checks on "randomness," time use, teaching processes, incentive value . . .

2. STAR was deeply rooted in prior research and theory. Theories are evident in the design, data forms, analysis steps. Additional theory and refinements were "teased out" during the study (1984–1990), as data were analyzed (some data still await analysis), as STAR played into Project Challenge, and while students progressed throughout their schooling for longitudinal results (they would graduate from high school in 1998, if on schedule).

3. "Effect" required an EXPERIMENT (Campbell & Stanley, 1963, Design #6), ofsufficient Duration (4-years),

(continued)

APPENDIX E: TABLE E–1: COMPARISON OF STAR DESIGN, PROCESSES, AND FACTS WITH ONE SET OF "PRINCIPLES OF INQUIRY"* (*Continued*)

Scientific Endeavors

only class size was manipulated: the Aide was a Pupil-Teacher Ratio

Star Design, Processes, and Facts

Magnitude (at least 80 classes of each type—eventually 11,600

(PTR) element. STAR represented school as it is normally operated.

students). The experimental plan was small class (S) at 13–17; regular (R) at 22–25; and full-time Aide (RA) at 22–25. Within-school design was parsimonious, reduced school-level effects, eliminated control group mortality, moderated the "Hawthorne Effect" if it might be a factor (Appendix A summarizes the experiment).

4. Provide a Coherent and Explicit Chain of Reasoning.
Longitudinal class-size studies were needed to test duration. Without an experiment, effects of SES, teacher, principal leadership, etc. clouded the class-size issue/effects.

4. Much of the reasoning appears in the STAR Report literature review, data research questions, sample, and instruments, observation data, design. Prior to STAR there was disagreement on the effects of group (class) size on student outcomes. Before establishing statewide class-size limits, Tennessee lawmakers and policy persons sought evidence about class size and paraprofessionals. They commissioned STAR.

5. Yield Findings that Replicate and Generalize across Studies and Work continues here as more states, and local districts move into class-size changes. Note international work in Australia, England, Netherlands, and Sweden.

5. STAR results have been replicated and generalized in state studies (e.g., SAGE in WI), by state law (e.g., HB 72 in TX); in observations (SSS); in case studies (e.g., Rockingham Co., NC); in large (n = 15,000) and small (n = 1,200) district (Burke Co., NC; Litchfield, MI); in Title I schools (n = 16) in a large district; in single schools (SC, NC, LA)> "Micro" comparisons contrast with "macro" or statewide events (e.g., NC, TN, TX, IA, UT) and even in NV that did some PTR and in CA, a "near text-book case of doing it wrong" (Biddle & Berliner, 2002). Results are always positive.

6. Disclose Research Data and Methods to Enable and Encourage Professional Scrutiny and Critique**
STAR data, methods, and outcomes are in the Final Report, papers and

6. The Spencer Foundation assisted PIs to organize, clean, and post STAR data on the Web. After the final report was accepted, data were provided to researchers in London

articles by the PIS, dissertations, and other print sources.

and later to persons in the USA. Critique is evident in some journal articles. "Scrutiny" is in the hands of the secondary analyzers, and has seldom been rigorous, absent pre-conceived ideology.

Table E-2: Crane*** Criteria for Social Science Research Demonstrated by Using the STAR Research

Crane Criteria and Questions	STAR's Facts
1. Do the benefits outweigh the costs? YES	1. In the short term (K–3), there were no definitive data, in the "follow-up studies": yes; in the STAR reanalysis yes; in alternative implementation yes. See Krueger (1999), Finn & Achilles, 1999; Finn et al. 2001).
2. Does the program have a statistically significant effect on the treatment group? YES	2. Yes. This statistically significant difference was found each year, all years, and in many combination of analyses done by STAR persons and by others (as far away as London).
3. What is the magnitude of the program's effect? *(Shown in Effect Size or ES).*	3. Effect-size (ES) results were .17–.40 in the early analyses. Effects were about twice as high for minority children as for Anglo children, grades K–3 (each year, all years). Grade-equivalent analyses show *(continued)*

Table E-2: Crane Criteria for Social Science Research Demonstrated by Using the STAR Research (*Continued*)

Crane Criteria and Questions	STAR's Facts
	continuing growth even after students leave small classes (see #4) (Finn & Achilles, 1999; Finn et al., 2001).

** The narrowness of most STAR critiques that the *STAR Report and Papers* (The Primary Sources) were read by few (e.g., Mosteller, 1995; Burke, Co. administrators; SAGE staffers; SERVE personnel; doctoral students). Few persons engaged the four Principal Investigators (PI's) in discussions or asked important questions so they could understand STAR outcomes. Professor Mosteller (1995) actually explained that in reality STAR was THREE studies (STAR, LBS, CHALLENGE).

***Crane, J. (Ed.). (1998). *Social Programs that Work.* New York: Russell Sage Foundation, 324 pages.

4. How long do the effects of the program last? *(At least into high school and beyond.)*

4. Positive academic and social effects of K-3 small classes are highly visible in H.S. and beyond including in college-entrance tests (Boyd-Zaharias & Pate-Bain, 2000; Krueger, 1999; Krueger & Whitmore, 2000).

5. What is the relationship of the evaluator to the program? *(Independent.)*

5. The STAR evaluator was a contracted independent expert. STAR personnel did secondary analyses. The external expert's work is (and was) the primary analysis accepted and published. Others have re-analyzed STAR data with similar results.

6. Can the programs and its results be replicated? *(Yes.)*
7. Can the program maintain its effectiveness on a larger scale? *(Still being assessed. Yes, if well implemented.)*

6 & 7. They have been consistently replicated in well-designed class-size analyses. Replication of STAR have been achieved in single districts, and in general policy implementation. Reported gains and ES for well-conducted studies are similar. Evaluations of state-wide small-class efforts in CA, and the results in TX (HB 72, 1984) suggest large-scale benefits, but these results are less definitive than STAR or SAGE in Wisconsin, probably because of less-controlled implementations.

Table E-3: A Six-Level Phase Model to Guide Practitioners in Decisions

Care is required in selecting options for education policy especially if the research for education is conducted by persons from other disciplines that may have criteria for acceptance and publication different from those in education. Various criteria have been combined into a six-level model to help policy persons and practitioners sort the issues into valid and invalid claims based upon reasonable criteria. The serious task of educating America's youth requires more than data being called "valid" by the sound-byte media.

Level I. The base for intelligible research is clarity of definition. Before considering "research" ideas, carefully evaluate the definition of terms to assure that the "research" base is accurate. Check its fidelity to the policy or program being considered. All reputable research should have a section on definitions, and the research and data should relate explicitly to the defined terms.

Level II. Assess research and results against established criteria, such as Crane (1998): (a) Benefits outweigh costs? (b) Statistically significant effect? (c) Magnitude and longevity of the effect? (d) Relationship of evaluator to the project? (e) Replicability? (f) Maintenance of effects on larger scale, etc.

Level III. Assure that the author(s) avoided errors that slant reviews of research. Dunkin's (1996) nine types of errors can be guidelines: (a) Unexplained selectivity; (b) Lack of discrimination; (c) Erroneous detailing; (d) Double counting; (e) Non-recognition of faulty author conclusions; (f) Unwarranted attributions; (g) Suppresssions of contrary findings; (h) Consequential errors; and (i) Failure to marshal evidence relevant to a generalization.

Level IV. Consider possible conflicts of interest. Does the author have significant monetary or reputational stake in a specific point of view? Does the research rest, at least, partially, on independent, unbiased work of reasonably disinterested persons?

Level V. Referee and ideology. Are sources used in the decision process refereed? Are the publications from a generally non-biased outlet, as distinct from ideologically driven sources (e.g., some think tanks)?

Level VI. Synthesize and evaluate the results of Levels I–V within the local context where the policy or program is proposed. Does this make sense for you?

This six-level phase model provides a process to guide a decision. If the policy or program fails Level I, the action is over. A policy or program that has high *value* (potential impact) must reach a high level in the model, say Level IV or V if it is to be considered seriously. At that point, the leader should visit the primary research before making a final decision, and conduct a thorough literature review. (See also Crane [1998] and Feuer, et al. [2002] Appendix E that relate STAR research to the elements of Scientifically Based Research or SBR).

2003 Living Legend Lecture

Practice of Theory to Theory of Practice: The Prime Directive

Rosemary Papalewis

> Few things are harder to put up with than the annoyance of a good example.
>
> Mark Twain, *Pudd'nhead Wilson* (1894)

Good morning, President Wilmore, NCPEA Executive Board Members, and esteemed colleagues. I cannot tell you of a greater honor for a professor of Education Administration than to receive the Living Legend award. I am deeply humbled among you. NCPEA has served me well—my beacon for moral, ethical, compassionate behavior for students I teach; collegiality among my peers; my colleagues and friends from Sacramento State, Drs. Carlos Nevarez, Ana Garcia-Nevarez, Rosemary Blanchard and Cirenio Rodriguez; and the members of our community of NCPEAers, especially the many of you that have served as mentors to me.

In order to shape the future, we should understand our "roots." Let me begin with some of the thoughts of those who preceded us. The first course designed to train principals was taught in 1881 by William T. Payne, a former superintendent and later an education professor at the University of Michigan. Almost 100 years ago, in 1904, Cubberley and Strayer became the first professors of Education Administration in this country (Willower & Culbertson, 1964).

Sixty years later Willower and Culbertson wrote that emphasis in our field must move in the direction of theory, research and content differentiation. Campbell (1964) wrote more specifically to the kind of professors sought in Education Administration.

> In seeking talent for the professorship . . . we should look for men [and I am sure he would add women now] who are bright, who are young, who have dealt with the major ideas of Western culture, who have exhibited some independence and creativity, and who have a commitment to education. (p. 19)

Rosemary Papalewis, California State University, Sacramento

In seeking these ideal professors of Education Administration, the American Association of School Administration (AASA) in their *1960 Yearbook* listed the ideal staffing for our departments. Possibly, this is an early precursor to their role in the standardization of our field.

    3 senior faculty members
    5 associate faculty members
    2 assistant faculty members
    10 graduate assistants
    7 secretaries (Griffiths, 1964, p. 30)

I am sure you will all agree with me that we only wish for these staff ratios.

In this seminal book edited by Willower and Culbertson (1964), three theories were offered as policy frameworks for our field to consider: the propinquity/free lunch theory; the great man, or more appropriately today the giants theory; and, the scientific journal theory. The propinquity theory was based on approximation to how those in our field were housed. Department faculties were advised to be near one another for cross fertilization to occur. The free lunch theory suggests the same. I agree with Hughes (1988) who likened administrative expertise as something to be caught like measles, by working closely with more experienced colleagues. But approximants could also increase individual rancor, hence this theory was seen as lacking.

The great man theory meant employ "giants" in our field for university and departmental fame. These giants were not to be expected to become team players. The scientific journal theory was meant to harness the intellectual activity of the department. Create a scientific refereed journal and the intellectual activity will increase among the faculty and bring esteem to a department. Since many journals in our field exist today, faculty like me are founding editors of student journals that utilize colleagues as referees.

The final piece of history I will share pertains to the 1960's theories relating to practice. The administrator as practitioner was viewed as an outcome of a complex marriage of practice and theory enlivened by the tension between practice and theory (Willower & Culbertson, 1964).

    It was believed that practice brought two gifts:
        The wit to bring theory to its matter . . . make sense of ideas, and
        The wit to bridge what theory must become coherent. (p. 64)
    Theory brought three gifts:
        Depth and breadth of coherent knowledge beyond experience,
        Breaching walls of personal and social class prejudice, and
        Expansion and refreshment to experience. (p. 64)

As a field of study, we claim more than a century of knowledge development (see Appendix). We anchored our discipline in the medical model of theory and practice. Joseph Schwab (1964) pointedly argued that the theory movement reflected a false model both for inquiry and training. He stated that medicine's "theory of practice" with the study of biological science and medicine—what diseases and pathologies there are, their symptoms, etiology, causes and treatment is equivalent in Education Administration. He suggested that the study of the school—the missions it undertakes, and patterns it has used, its strengths and weaknesses, needs and problems— is parallel with the medicine model.

Over 100 years later, we today wrestle with such questions as, "Can anyone run a school? A university? What are the education administrative theories? Has comparative analysis helped the field of study? Is the business model better for our field than the medical model? Do the requirements of the No Child Left Behind "nickelbe" (2001) make sense?

Eleven years ago I wrote a vignette with mentors of mine, Chuck Achilles and Lloyd DuVall, which featured Socrates discoursing with a student named Neuprof on the possible causes of the loss of prestige and power felt by colleges of education and departments of educational leadership (Papalewis & Achilles, 1992–1993). Eleven years later this dialog remains relevant.

I believe we need to focus our attention on what Shapiro & Stefkovich (2001) have termed our personal and collegial ethos, our customs, practices and institutional contexts. Wilcox and Ebbs (1992) wrote of universities as custodians of knowledge and power. They wrote of three contexts: students, in terms of their increasingly diverse needs; professors in terms of their scholarship; and leadership in terms of shared governance.

I will briefly identify the current state of affairs for both K–12 and higher education. I include higher education from the perspective that we train all levels of educational leaders as well as serve in leadership positions within our institutions.

The recent RAND report titled *Who Is Leading Our Schools? An Overview of School Administrators and Their Careers* (Gates, Ringel, Santibanez, Ross & Chung, 2003), preceded by McCarthy's research (1998; 1999), focused on career patterns and future policy directives. The RAND 2003 report studied characteristics of current school administrators, their movements in and out of the field and their incentives. The results in Table 1 show that age is increasing for first-time principals; there is no shortage of credentialed candidates; the number of administrators is stable; the 1990's saw a dramatic increase in female administrators, and a slightly smaller increase for minority administrators.

Table 1. Characteristics of School Principals

	Public School		Private School	
	1987	*2000*	*1987*	*2000*
Number of Principals	77,890	83,909	25,401	26,231
Average Age	47.8	49.3	46	49.9
Average Contract Length (months)	11.1	N/a	11.3	N/a
Average Years of Experience as Principal	10.1	9.0	8.0	10.2
Percent Women	24.6	43.7	52.0	54.6
Percent Minority	13.4	17.8	7.0	11.1

Rand, 2003

Table 2. Characteristics of University Presidents

Characteristics	2001 %	1986 %
Women	21.1	9.5
Minority	12.8	8.1
Currently Married	83.1	85.0
Hold Doctoral Degree	76.4	76.6
Age	57.5	52.3
Years in Present Job	6.6	6.3
Years as Full-Time Faculty	8.0	6.4

Center for Policy Analysis, 2003

The RAND findings show that over 99% of all public school principals have had some teaching experience; there is little evidence of principals leaving to enter a new field; and, there is no evidence that more experienced principals choose not to work in low socio-economic urban schools.

The recent ACE study titled *The American College President, 2nd Edition* from the Center for Policy Analysis (April 28, 2003) displays the characteristics of university presidents (see Table 2). Similar to principals, age is likewise increasing for first-time university presidents, there is a dramatic increase of female presidents, with a modest increase for minority presidents and a slight increase in the number of years spent in full-time faculty positions. Table 3 displays the top three fields of study for presidents.

Both studies were done for very different reasons. The ACE report is meant to inform the changing field of university presidents, by tracking their past. The RAND study is meant not only to inform but to direct future policy initiatives based on their study and has a feel of *a priori* perspective. The RAND study reaches conclusions that are indicative of research used by some to further a particular point of view while reflecting popular political policy development.

THE HATFIELDS AND THE McCOYS

Now that we have a sense of the current state of our students in their occupations, let us review the theory of practice and practice of theory debate. Culbertson wrote (1988) that NCPEA helped nurture the new movement by providing forums where scholars could challenge existing research and advocate theory-based norms to professors in attendance from across the nation.

Griffiths (1988) wrote of the administrative theory movement and outlined three primary events that impacted the development of administrative theory. First, in

Table 3. University President's Top Three Fields of Study

2001	%	1986	%
Education	43.8	Education	43.8
Humanities	14.3	Humanities	14.3
Social sciences	13.5	Social sciences	13.5

Center for Policy Analysis, 2003

1946 the W. K. Kellogg Foundation gave funds to support Education Administration projects. Second, in 1947 NCPEA was founded, and third, in 1947 AASA began standardization for preparation in Education Administration courses. These three events, along with W. Cocking serving as the Editor of *School Executive Magazine* (Achilles, personal communication, August 8, 2003), created the foundation for our profession.

Griffiths (1988) concluded that:

1. Better research into Education Administration was needed.
2. Research must be theory based.
3. Social scientists used some of the same theories, and social scientists were to guide professors of Education Administration.

Of special significance was a forum held in Denver in 1954, which Halpin (1970) has described as follows:

> At that meeting the first "real" confrontation between behavioral scientists and professors of Education Administration took place. Coladarci (of Stanford), Getzels (of Chicago), and Halpin (then of Ohio State University) pointed out to the group—and not gently—that what the CPEA (Cooperative Program in Education Administration, funded by the Kellogg Foundation, founded 1950–51) Centers and members of NCPEA were doing in the name of research was distinctly a-theoretical in character and sloppy in quality. The reception that these three behavioral scientists received at that meeting can scarcely be described as cordial. (p. 16)

At that 1954 meeting the NCPEA committee approved a plan for a book titled *Administrative Behavior in Education* (Campbell & Gregg, 1957). I brought my copy for anyone here who would like to see it. It is quite well done. Also, during 1960's the *Journal of Education Administration* and *The Educational Administration Quarterly* began.

In opposition to the theory-driven field of study, Greenfield in 1975 stated, "Academicians who assume that social-scientific secrets can explain how organizations work or how policy should be made, indulge at best in premature hope and at worst in a delusion" (cited in Culbertson, 1988, p. 20). Greenfield commented that researchers in Education Administration wrote of organizations as if they were real. Greenfield espoused that there should be no single paradigm, only theories of Education Administration that should be limited to specific types of organizations which exist in carefully defined contexts.

Culbertson wrote that both Greenfield and Harris stressed that organizations cannot be equated with objective phenomena, "that organizations do not think, choose, or act as theories claim; rather individuals do" (p. 20).

During this same time Hughes (1988) described how UCEA moved the field in the direction of comparative approaches. Reller (1962) argued that field studies in a foreign country were an effective way to provide better understanding of educational changes in the U.S. This became the purview of the research institutions, often leaving the local community and state education initiatives in the hands of regional comprehensive institutions. As Willower and Forsyth (1999) stated, "However much NCPEA and UCEA share and emphasize similar purposes, an underlying exclusivity issue remains" (p. 7). This was evidenced by the comparative world studies versus the local school district action-based research.

Today the social-political terrain is very rough for public education, at all levels. Achilles (1999, p.171) recently wrote that American education has been suffering a legacy of neglect from tax abatements, media attacks, and unrealistic comparisons to outcomes in other nations, to declining facilities, class-size-increase creep, inattention to research results, policies that result in unfunded liabilities, faddism, political and polemic pronouncements (ad nauseam).

Likewise, the internal debates within Education Administration continue. Donmoyer wrote

> At most research universities, Education Administration must engage in a continual process of self-justification. One way to succeed in this process is to appear to be as similar to the high status disciplines, especially the hard sciences, as possible. A theoretical knowledge base is key element in maintaining this appearance, however irrelevant the knowledge base may be to practitioners of the field. (1999, p. 122)

In describing his experiences in serving as the editor of an American Educational Research Association journal (*Educational Researcher*) Donmoyer lamented the lack of healthy debate, that is rich in depth. He stated,

> . . . [When we] engage in discussion and debate, it will be hard for them not to re-enact the sort of adversarial scripts employed in the past, despite the fact that such scripts did little to promote understanding of a rival's position and functioned primarily to reassure each debater and his (or, in a few instances, her) supporters of the correctness of their a priori point of view. . . . I am in the last year of a three-year term as the editor of the American Educational Research Association journal, *Educational Researcher*. I had hoped to use my tenure as editor to encourage the sort of cross-perspective interaction I am talking about here but found this difficult to do. Responses arrived long after articles appeared; policies required they be sent out for review; reviewers did not always respond in a timely fashion; rejoinders also required review. The whole process was elongated, exceedingly formal and more than a little artificial. (1999, pp. 39–40)

What was written about our field in the first Education Administration (see Table 4) collection of writings was the juxtaposition of scientific knowledge development

Table 4.   Seminal Edited Books in Education Administration

- 1957 *Administrative Behavior in Education: A Project of the National Council of Professors of Educational Administration.* Edited by R.F. Campbell and R.T. Gregg.
- 1988 *Handbook of Research on Educational Administration: A Project of the American Educational Research Association.* Edited by N. Boyan.
- 1999 *Handbook of Research on Educational Administration, Second Edition: A Project of the American Educational Research Association.* Edited by J. Murphy and K. Seashore Louis.

characterized best by Griffiths versus Greenfield. The second Education Administration collection of writings was characterized best by Donmoyer's utilitarian approach, the Big Tent. He wrote that, "When we recommend contradictory things, we almost guarantee that research will be used selectively as a political weapon insteau of as a tool to help resolve educational disputes intellectually rather than through the use of brute power" (1999, p. 35).

Following this line of thought, Murphy (1999) wrote, ". . . [The] current era [is] a dialectic one . . . [where reform initiatives] link the worlds of theory and practice both for purposes of knowledge generation and for purposes of administrative preparation" (p. 35). Yet, today's political climate challenges the notion that theory generation is appreciated or wanted.

For practitioners the growing trend is to work outside the organization with top executives more as politicians resolving conflicting demands on the organization—schools or universities. The debate today is found in the No Child Left Behind drive to measurable standards. English wrote to NCPEA last fall (September 30, 2002) alerting us, as he termed it, to the ruthless drive for reduction of variance in preparation programs.

English stated that ELCC/NCATE standards with ISLLC are meant to drive out competition. He cited leaders in our field who believe that too many university/college programs are inadequate in their preparation programs. I would argue that NCATE could be described as the "logo" to what he terms the profoundly anti-theoretical and very homogeneous view of Education Administration. He wisely reminds us that the top five Education Administration programs in the country are not NCATE affiliated: Harvard, Wisconsin-Madison, Vanderbilt, Stanford, and T.C. Columbia (*U.S. News and World Report*, April 10, 2000). English believes that standards lead to standardized courses and programs, followed by a standardized faculty, all of which culminates in mediocrity.

Outspoken critics argue differently. Also, found on the NCPEA website is the article by Hess (January, 2003), where he contended that Education Administration is a sub-specialization of the sprawling field of leadership and management. He wrote, with conviction laced with chicanery, I feel, that too often civic leaders and public officials privately express contempt for most public school administrators. He finds contemptible the notion that only former teachers can lead and that advanced degrees are required. He supports this with the notion that "Today's America executive workforce is admired across the globe and business schools are among the nation's most prestigious educational units. This all transpired without formal licensing, i.c., Bill Gates or Michael Dell never did [an] MBA" (p. 19).

Equally interesting is an article dated May, 2003, found on the NCPEA website in which Finn (2003) made five major points (see Table 5). Finn stated that alternative approaches minimizes hoops and hurdles and regulatory hassles looking for talent rather than paper credentials. Is minimizing the hurdles—practice for practice sake—the only road left? He then cited that eleven states offer alternative routes for the superintendent and principal certification, with two states, Michigan and South

Table 5.   Finn's Five Reasons for Pursuing Alternatives

1. Conventional certification requirements . . . must be radically reduced . . . with criteria that stress leadership qualities.
2. Recruit from both inside and outside schools.
3. School district must play major role in training.
4. Schools' leaders (Superintendent and Principals) must have sweeping authority over their responsibilities.
5. Pay [administrators] well and expect results. (Finn, 2003, p. 2)

Dakota, requiring no licensure. He also stated that most alternate routes are controlled and operated by colleges and universities.

Feistritzer's (2003) findings show that certification practices across the U. S. coincided with Finn's statement—nearly all states require that public school administrators have prior teaching experience, and most alternate route programs are controlled and operated by colleges and universities.

In contrast to the notions that licensure should not include university study or regulated practice is the recent work of Laczko-Kerr & Berliner (September, 2002). In accessing the effectiveness of under-certified teachers on student academic achievement, they found that teacher preparation programs result in positive effects on academic achievement of low-income, primary-school children. The Teach for American program was noted as a harmful policy initiative that systematically provides an inferior education to the children of the poor. Such policies increase differences in achievement between the performance of poor children, often immigrant and minority children, and those children who are more advantaged. Rhetorically asked, doesn't this have implications for the training of principals and presidents?

In response to Finn's manifesto, Lasley (2003) appears on the NCPEA website stating that Finn's manifesto is the all too familiar conservative policy palliative: simplify entry requirements, introduce competition among training programs and relax the terms of employment for school leaders. The recent RAND report supports these same conclusions that formal barriers such as certification requirements and informal district hiring practices all but exclude those without teaching experience from considering administrative positions and policy makers believe must address these barriers.

And, what about the training of our universities leaders? Lazerson, Wagener & Moneta (July 28, 2000) liken universities to cities requiring the training of competent managers. Managerial roles have become larger, more complex, and more intrusive because the higher-education industry has become larger, more complicated, and more important. Again, where does the role of theory to practice belong? Basinger (April 25, 2003) cited Donna E. Schalala saying the role of the president has dramatically change to be what the provost now has been hired to do and that is to be the academic leader. Presidents today are fundraisers (see Figure 1). They are increasingly coming from outside higher education positions (see Figure 2).

Today, schools and universities are often subject to the "business model" which focuses mainly on accountability. With such a forced focus are we also subjected to

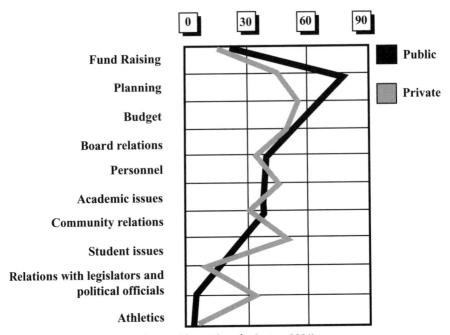

Figure 1. Top Issues Occupying Presidents' Time (by Sector: 2001)

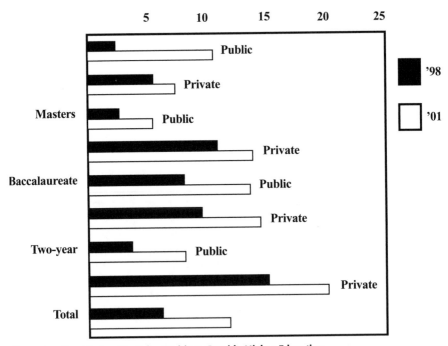

Figure 2. Presidents with Prior Positions Outside Higher Education

the possible abuses? A recent article in the *Sacramento Bee* (Schemo, July 11, 2003) regarding No Child Left Behind accountability proclaimed "Texas: It was Enron accounting." Just as with Enron accountability, in a successful business one of the outcomes is actually making a profit versus reporting a profit, Enron style. The same could be said for schools. If one of the real outcomes is actually lowering the dropout rate, we cannot permit this sort of behavior exemplified by the Houston school district; 54% of the 5500 who left school in 2000–2001 were not reported as dropouts when they should have been. This could be called Arthur Andersen accounting!

Indeed, sound research such as class size was completely omitted from NCLB (Achilles, Krieger, Finn & Sharp [February, 2003]. Is this the direction we want to go? As Chester Finn stated, pay well and expect results. Martha McCarthy (2001) told us the bad news that we have no studies tracking leadership preparation to student performance. In ten to fifteen years, will we have research that speaks to the harm done by unprepared administrators, as we now have for teachers?

So whose leadership qualities do we stress? Whose theories tell us practice is the best preparation model? Whose standards? Whose values?

FINDING THE PRIME DIRECTIVE

Maldonado, Skaruppa & Wolman (1999) stated that "universities not only have ethical and moral obligations to their students . . . [they] should design curriculum content that reflects social issues such as environmental problems, poverty, racism, world hunger, and issues of justice and world peace" (p. 206). Curricular content is what professors are responsible for, which includes seeking truth and stating truth. Honest academic content is found on most codes of professional ethics relating to universities.

I began this discussion on theory to practice to theory of practice using our common history in Education Administration to highlight the development of where we have come from and where we are today. The issue of standards leading to prescribed homogenized "like" programs is genuine, as is the lack of theory that benefits practice, such as class size reduction (Achilles, 1999). Practices that support successful schooling for all students (Achilles, 1999; Papalewis & Fortune, 2002) should be the primary goal of our licensure and degree programs.

Paula Silver began her 1983 textbook describing the theory experience:

> Discovering what theory is can be an exhilarating experience—like finding a special and exalted plan of existence, a rarefied, crystal-clear atmosphere where everything sparkles with the logic of pure abstraction. To grasp what theory is, beyond any mere definition, is to have a flash of insight about the nature of abstraction, a gasp of recognition that the words represent not mundane tangibles but inventions of the creative mind. (p. xiii)

Where has this sense of exhilaration gone? As Donmoyer (1999, p.38) told us, the question is never merely what works. The values implicit in criteria must be assessed. That question must always be followed by a series of other questions: For whom does it work? What and whose values are implicit in the criteria we use to assess utility? Are these values defensible? Are they more defensible than the competing values implicit in alternative ways of doing the business of administrative research, theory construction and practice?

The ethics of our profession speak to the best interests of the students. UCEA speaks to a new theory, the ethics of community. Ted Creighton, our executive director, personifies the building of community though his activities to build partners with most professional organizations relating to the field, including a few who may not see us as relevant.

The practice of theory and the theory of practice require us as the representatives of truth to assess not only what is just, but who has the power, who is silenced, who benefits and who is hurt by our decisions. Our collective decisions in Education Administration must bear this scrutiny. Our prime directive (yes, as in Star Trek) is to do no harm.

In closing, I propose (see Table 6) an NCPEA Ethical Guideline that links theory of practice to research-based practices that ask us these questions: Who benefits from decisions we make in our knowledge base and preparation programs? From our research and teaching? From our consulting and grants received? Who is hurt or left out by our decisions? What are the long term implications of our decisions? As a former school administrator I always ask myself am I *walking the talk*? Do my students and colleagues see me inspiring them to be honest, caring and collegial with one another?

The NCPEA 2002 Corwin speaker, Dr. Jeffrey Glanz (2002) spoke of the key components needed of all leaders: courage, enthusiasm, humility, imagination, and good judgment. Alas, he omitted knowledge as a Knowledge Base.

Imagine:
An MD with great bedside manners & no medical training
A lawyer with persuasive ability & no law training
A cleric with fine oratory but no theology
A general with leadership but no military science, etc.

And you have what Glanz and Finn, etc., all proclaim (Achilles, personal communication, August 8, 2003)!

I hope that consideration of the relationship of theory to practice today and in the future will help all of us better enact these qualities of successful, *knowledge-based* leaders, and maybe I have met even one of these criteria today.

Table 6.   Ethical Guidelines for Theory, Research and Practice

NCPEA—Ethical Guidelines Theory Research and Practice

We must ask ourselves,
Who benefits from our research?
Who is hurt by our research?
What long-term implications is my research suggesting?
Am I "walking the talk" with my research?
How are my interests advantaged? Disadvantaged?
Am I inspiring to students, colleagues, and site-based leaders?

REFERENCES

Achilles, C. M. (1999). *Let's put kids first, finally: Getting class size right.* Thousand Oaks, CA: Corwin Press.

Achilles, C. M., Krieger, J. D., Finn, J. D., & Sharp, M. (February, 2003). *School improvement should rely on reliable, scientific evidence. Why did "No Child Left Behind" leave class size behind?* A symposium presented at the Conference-Within-A-Convention American Association of School Administrators, New Orleans, LA.

Achilles, C. M. (Personal communication, August 8, 2003).

Basinger, J. (2003, April 25). More power for provosts: The second in command has more duties and influence than ever before. *Money & Management, The Chronicle of Higher Education.* Retrieved June 25, 2003 from http://chronicle.com/cgi2-bin/printable_verity.cgi

Boyan, N. (Ed.). (1988). *Handbook of research on educational administration: A project of the American educational research association.* New York: Longman.

Campbell, R. F. (1964). The professorship in educational administration: Preparation. In D. J. Willower and J. A. Culbertson (Eds.), *The professorship in educational administration* (pp. 15–28). Columbus, Ohio: University Council for Educational Administration.

Campbell, R. F. & Gregg, R. T. (Eds.). (1957). *Administrative Behavior in Education.* Sponsored by NCPEA. New York: Harper & Brothers Publishers.

Center for Policy Analysis. (2003, April 28). The American college president; 2002 edition. *Center for Policy Analysis, ACE Net.* Retrieved June 25, 2003 from http://acenet.edu/bookstore/index.cfm?pubID=280

Culbertson, J. A. (1988). A century's quest for a knowledge base. Chapter 1. In N. J. Boyan (Ed.), *Handbook of research on educational administration* (pp. 3–26). New York: Longman, Inc.

Donmoyer, R. (1999). The continuing quest for a knowledge base: 1976–1998. In J. Murphy & K. S. Louis (Eds.), *Handbook of research on educational administration, 2nd edition* (pp. 25–43). New York: Longman.

English, F. (2002, September 30). *Memorandum about the policing functions of ELCC/NCATE and the standardization of university preparation programs in educational administration.* Retrieved July 2, 2003 from http://www.ncpea.org

Feistritzer, E. (2003). Certification of public-school administrators: A summary of state practices. *The National Center for Education Information.* Retrieved July 2, 2003 from http://www.ncei.com

Finn, C. (2003, May). *The Fordham Foundation better leaders for America's schools: A manifesto.* Retrieved July 2, 2003 from http://www.ncpea.net/

Glanz, J. (2002) *Leading with soul and conviction: Essential qualities and virtues for effective leadership.* Address given at the annual National Council of Professors of Education Administration Conference, Burlington, Vermont.

Greenfield, T. B. (1975). Theory about organization: A new perspective and its implications for schools. In M. G. Hughes (Ed.), *Administering education: International challenge* (pp. 71–99). London: Athlone.

Griffiths, D. E. (1964). The professorship in educational administration: Environment. In D. J. Willower and J. A. Culbertson (Eds.), *The professorship in educational administration* (pp. 29–46). Columbus, Ohio: University Council for Educational Administration.

Griffiths, D. E. (1988). Administrative theory. In N. J. Boyan (Ed.), *Handbook of research on educational administration.* New York: Longman, Inc.

Halpin, A. W. (1970). The fumbled torch. In A. Kroll (Ed.), *Issues in American Education* (pp. 156–183). New York: Oxford.

Hess, F. M. (2003, January). A license to lead? A new leadership agenda for America's schools. *Progressive Policy Institute 21st Century Schools Project.* Retrieved July 2, 2003 from http://www.ncpea.net/

Hughes, M. G. (1988). Comparative educational administration,. In N. J. Boyan (Ed.), *Handbook of research on educational administration.* New York: Longman, Inc.

Laczko-Kerr, I. & Berliner, D. C. (2002, September 6). The effectiveness of 'teach for America' and other under-certified teachers on student academic achievement: A case of harmful public policy. *Education Policy Analysis Archives, 10,* 37. Retrieved July 2, 2003 from http://epaa.asu.edu/epaa/v10n37/

Lasley, T. (2003). *Crossing the ideological divide: A response to better leaders for America's schools: A manifesto.* Retrieved July 10, 2003 from www.ncpea.org

Lazerson, M., Wagener, U., & Moneta, L. (2000, July 28). Like the cities they increasingly resemble, colleges must train and retain competent managers. *The Chronicle Review, 46,* 47. Retrieved June 25, 2003 from http://chronicle.com/cgi2-bin/printable_verity.cgi

Maldonado, N., Skaruppa, C. & Wolman, C. (1999). Cultivating moral commitment: Perceptions of twelve leaders regarding the role of the university degree programs. In L. T. Fenwick (Ed.), *School leadership: Expanding horizons of the mind and spirit* (pp. 206–221). Lancaster, PA: Technomic Publishing Company, Inc.

McCarthy, M. (1998). The "new" educational leadership professor. In R. Muth & M. Martin (Eds.), *1998 NCPEA yearbook: Toward the year 2000, leadership for quality schools* (pp. 3–16). Lancaster, PA: Technomic Publishing Company, Inc.

McCarthy, M. (1999). Evolution of educational leadership preparation programs. In J. Murphy & K. S. Louis (Eds.), *Handbook on research in educational administration* (pp.119–140). New York: Longman.

McCarthy, M. (2001). Challenges facing educational leadership programs: Our future is now. *Newsletter of the Teaching in Educational Administration Special Interest Group of the American Educational Research Association, 8,* (1), 1.

Murphy, J., & Seashore-Louis, K. (Eds.). (1999). *Handbook of research on educational administration, second edition: A project of the American Educational Research Association.* San Francisco, CA: Jossey-Bass, Inc., Publishers.

Murphy, J. (1999). Changes in preparation programs: Perceptions of department chairs. In J. Murphy & P. Forsyth (Eds.), *Educational Administration: A decade of reform* (pp. 170–191). Thousand Oaks, CA: Corwin Press.

No Child Left Behind (NCLB). (2001). *Conference report to accompany H. R. Rep. No. 107–334,* 107th Congress, 1st session.

Papalewis, R. & Achilles, C. M. (1992–1993). Vignette: The newproph. *National Forum of Educational Administration and Supervision Journal, 9,* (2), 84–89.

Papalewis, R. & Fortune, R. (2002). *Leadership on purpose: Promising practices for African American and Hispanic students.* Thousand Oaks, CA: Corwin Press.

RAND, Gates, S. M., Ringel, J. E., Santibanez, L., Ross, K. E. & Chung, C. H. (2003). *Who is leading our schools? An overview of school administrators and their careers.* Santa Monica, CA: RAND Education.

Reller, T. (1962). A comprehensive program for the preparation of administrators. In J. Culbertson & S. Heneley (Eds.), *Preparing administrators: New perspectives.* Columbus, OH: UCEA.

Schemo, D. J. (2003, July 11). Dropout miracle was a myth? *Sacramento Bee* citing the *New York Times* (A5, A 24).

Schwab, J. J. (1964). The professorship in educational administration: Theory—art—practice. In D. J. Willower and J. A. Culbertson (Eds.), *The professorship in educational administration* (pp. 48–70). Columbus, Ohio: UCEA.

Shapiro, J. P., & Stefkovich, J. A. (2001). *Ethical leadership and decision making in education: Applying theoretical perspectives to complex dilemmas.* Mahwah, NJ: Lawrence Erlbaum Associates, Publishers.

Silver, P. F. (1983). *Educational administration: Theoretical perspectives on practice and research.* Cambridge, MA: Harper & Row, Publishers.

Twain, M. (1894). *Pudd'nhead Wilson.* Retrieved July 9, 2003 from, http://etext.lib .virginia.edu/modeng/modengT.browse.html

U. S. News and World Report. (2000, April 10). Specialties: Programs in 10 areas ranked best by education school deans (p. 94).

Wilcox, J. R., & Ebbs, S. L. (1992). The leadership compass: Values and ethics in higher education. *Ashe-ERIC Higher Education Report No. 1.* Washington, DC: The George Washington University School of Education and Human Development.

Willower, D. J., & Culbertson, J. (1964). Preface. In D. J. Willower and J. A. Culbertson (Eds.), *The professorship in educational administration* (pp. v–viii). Columbus, Ohio: UCEA.

Willower, D. J., & Forsyth, P. B. (1999). A brief history of scholarship on educational administration. In J. Murphy and K. S. Louis (Eds.), *Educational Administration, 2nd edition* (pp. 1–23) San Francisco, CA: Jossey-Bass Publishers.

APPENDIX: TIMELINE OF EDUCATION ADMINISTRATION

469 B.C.	Socrates
427 B.C.	Plato
384 B.C.	Aristotle
1881–1882	The first course designed to train principals and superintendents is created and taught by William T. Payne, a former superintendent and professor of education, University of Michigan
1875–1900	A Science of Education and Management curriculum designed by practitioners (Professors Payne and Harris)
1900s	Elements of business management and education included in preparation
1901–1925	Science of School Management (Professors Cubberley and Strayer)
1920s	Elwood Cubberley began first training program (Stanford) in Education Administration, Instructional Leadership.
1926–1950	Education and Management Science widens and deepens (Professors Dewey, Sears, Mort, Moehlman and Sargeant)
1947	NCPEA founded with the mission to improve educational leadership
1951–1966	Leap toward Administrative Science (Professors Getzel, Griffiths, Halpin, Coleman, and Schwab)
1954	NCATE (National Council for Accreditation of Teacher Education) founded
	Today, 33 national educational associations form the council.

1957	UCEA founded with the mission to improve professional preparation of educational administrators
1970–1980s	Effective schools + instructional leadership
1997	ISLLC (Interstate School Leaders Licensure Consortium) founded by the Council of Chief State School Officers to develop model standards and assessments for school leaders. Today, its policies are adopted in 35 states
2002	SLLA (School Leaders License Assessment) developed by Educational Testing Service and ISLLC. *The ETS School Leadership Series* is a set of performance-based assessments for the licensure and professional development of school superintendents, principals and other school leaders.

Some Thoughts from Practice to Preparation

Fred Brown and Richard Flanary

In his best selling book, *The Da Vinci Code* (2003), author Dan Brown leads the reader on a search down blind alleys, dead-ends, and a maze of confusing and conflicting evidence for the elusive Holy Grail. The story line is not unlike the search for the knowledge base for educational administration: a journey fraught with more than its share of mystery, confusion, and conflict.

Two national practitioner organizations, the National Association of Elementary School Principals and the National Association of Secondary School Principals, have long understood the fluidity, yet consistency needed to effectively lead institutions as complex as elementary, middle, and high schools. Schools are dynamic organizations with constantly changing needs and expectations, reflecting the communities and cultures they serve. These same communities experience cultural, social, and political change requiring the community to adjust. Principals and other school leaders for these schools need both the knowledge and skills to enable them to address change as they work to improve their learning communities, ultimately resulting in improved student learning.

Similarly, individuals charged with the responsibility of preparing future school leaders at the university level understand the extremely wide disparity between what can be taught in a typical thirty-six hour preparation program and the vast array of challenges that face these students as they begin their school leadership careers. Compounding this dilemma is the paradigm shift that has occurred in the expectations for schools and their leaders. The shift from universal access to ensuring performance has changed the face of the profession and is requiring a transformation of practice and a redesign of leadership preparation. Practitioners in school leadership have traditionally been guided by the accumulation of craft knowledge and practice

Fred Brown, National Association of Elementary School Principals
Richard Flanary, National Association of Secondary School Principals

that serves as a model for the field; however, the craft knowledge and artifacts of practice have changed as new expectations emerge. Unlike other professions, many new school leaders do not go directly from preparation to practice, permitting newly learned knowledge and skills to languish in the absence of a laboratory of opportunity. The effect of this gap between preparation and practice is exacerbated by the culture of expectations that holds the inexperienced principal to the same accountability standard as the very experienced principal. Other professions provide an incubation period for newly practicing professionals that create realistic expectations commensurate with their knowledge and skill.

The focused conversation involving NAESP and NASSP held on February 21, 2004, during the NCPEA Executive Board Meeting in San Francisco was a step in the right direction. The conversation framed around the knowledge base for educational administration and its role in adequately preparing new principals to effectively lead schools was timely and productive. This meeting offered an opportunity for the educational administration faculty and the practitioner organizations to share their perspectives regarding the preparation of school leaders in an open and frank manner.

The discussion dealt with the role of standards and their impact on the preparation of school leaders. Since most states have either adopted or adapted the ISLLC Standards, the combination of the ISLLC and ELCC Standards served as a catalyst for much of the discussion.

Neil Shipman and Joe Murphy wrote in the introduction to *Interstate School Leaders Licensure Consortium: Standards for School Leaders,*

> One intent of the document is to stimulate vigorous thought and dialogue about quality educational leadership among stakeholders in the area of school administration. A second intent is to provide raw material that will help stakeholders across the education landscape (e.g., state agencies, professional associations, institutions of higher education) enhance the quality of educational leadership throughout the nation's schools. (1996, p. iii)

There is no question that these standards have stimulated vigorous thought and dialogue as evidenced by the debate during the NCPEA meeting and at most other meetings with gatherings of more than two professors.

The second stated purpose, however, is more problematic. To what extent have the standards enhanced the quality of educational leadership in the nation's schools? Determining the answer to this question is as elusive as the search for the Holy Grail. The answer may lie in the eyes of the beholder. To some, the standards have finally caused the educational administration profession to coalesce around a common set of knowledge, performances, and dispositions. To others, the standards are antitheoretical and have created more mediocrity than excellence. Whatever the answer, the reality facing universities, professors, and practitioner organizations is that practitioners continue to be critical of their preparation programs, preparation programs continue to enroll students with no motivation to become a principal, and alternate preparation programs have taken on a mystical quality with no research to back up their effectiveness. These realities collide with the continuing shortage of qualified leaders, the increasing accountability standards, the impending sanctions dealt out by NCLB and the resulting reactions of communities.

An additional complicating factor is that some of the states and universities, in accepting the ISLLC Standards, view them as summative, rather than as the threshold for which they were intended. The ISLLC Standards and the revised ELCC standards were developed to serve as a baseline of what effective school leaders should know, encouraging universities the freedom to personalize their preparation programs from this starting point to meet the needs of their respective constituents. Consequently, the State Leaders Licensure Assessment (SLLA) was developed to assess the baseline and not to serve as the final arbiter in program effectiveness.

NAESP and NASSP are encouraged by the conversation begun in San Francisco. The time for "circling the wagons" has passed. It is our hope to continue to be an integral partner in the discussion as all parties strive to overcome philosophical and political differences and focus as a single profession on the requisite skills and knowledge that will enable our common partner, the school principal, to be effectively prepared and supported as they work daily to improve student achievement in our nation's schools. We believe the goal is both admirable and attainable.

Your partners in the profession,

Fred Brown, NAESP
Associate Executive Director for Professional Services
Richard Flanary, NASSP
Director, Center for Principal Development

REFERENCES

Brown, D. (2003). *The Da Vinci code*. New York: Doubleday.
Shipman, N., & Murphy, J. (November 2, 1996). *Introduction. Interstate School Leaders Licensure Consortium: Standards for School Leaders (p. iii)*. Council of Chief State School Officers, State Education Assessment Center.

Preparing School and School System Leaders: A Call for Collaboration

Michelle D. Young

Over the past two decades individuals, associations, consortiums, and commissions have distributed countless reports urging change in educational leadership preparation programs (Young, Petersen, & Short, 2002). These reports challenged programs and professors to move quickly to implement reform, and many responded to the call for rethinking and redesign. Yet it is now 2004, and the calls for change and reform in educational leadership preparation programs persist. A number of different conclusions can be drawn about this. Critics of higher education prefer to dismiss efforts that have been made, and instead paint pictures of educational leadership preparation as sloppy, outmoded, out-of-touch, and unaccountable. Through my work with the University Council for Educational Administration (UCEA) and the National Commission for the Advancement of Educational Leadership Preparation (NCAELP), I have come to a very different conclusion. Substantive and sustainable change in the preparation of school and school system leaders requires the commitment and involvement of stakeholders both within and outside of higher education. Quality preparation must be a collaborative endeavor.

COLLABORATION IS CENTRAL TO SUBSTANTIVE AND SUSTAINABLE CHANGE

Key to the success of any effort to meaningfully change the preparation of school and school system leaders is a commitment among educational leadership stakeholders to finding common ground and working interdependently toward the realization of jointly developed goals (Young, Peterson, & Short, 2001). Higher education cannot do this important work alone, nor can any other stakeholder group.

In 1987, the National Commission for Excellence in Educational Administration (NCEEA), recognizing the necessity of collaboration, established the National Policy

Michelle D. Young, University Council for Educational Administration

Board for Educational Administration (NPBEA) to facilitate collaborative efforts focused on improving the preparation and practice of educational leaders. The NPBEA is made up of ten national organizations—four representing higher education (University Council for Educational Administration, American Association of Colleges for Teacher Education, National Council for Professors of Educational Administration, and the National Council for the Accreditation of Teacher Education), three from elementary and secondary education (National Association of Elementary School Principals, National Association of Secondary School Administrators, Association for Supervision and Curriculum Development), and two governance associations (National School Boards Association and the Council for Chief State School Officers). The American Association for School Administrators (AASA), one of the policy board's founding members, recently withdrew from membership. As conceived by the NCEEA, it was hoped that the NPBEA would conduct periodic national reviews of programs, encourage the development of quality preparation, hold forums to discuss issues in educational administration, create a national certification board for advanced professional standing, and publish papers on critical national policy issues (Thompson, 1999).

In the beginning, the NPBEA was very active. It sponsored study groups, forwarded recommendations, held convocations, published newsletters and monographs, and developed national standards for preparation and practice. Later efforts have been more focused, including the development of the ISSLC standards in partnership with CCSSO, the development of educational leadership accreditation standards for NCATE, a proposal to develop the American Board for Educational Leadership (ABLE) to provide national certification to educational leaders, and co-sponsorship of NCAELP with UCEA. Clearly, collaboration at a national level has made a difference in the field of educational leadership. However, as a field, we have found it difficult to capitalize on the synergy offered through collaboration at a more local level.

For years, we have heard calls for collaboration in the preparation of school and school system leaders. In fact, calls for collaboration have been voiced throughout the field of education. For example the Association of Teacher Educators (ATE) argued that

> Political networks are needed to provide the base for improved research and better professional development. Because partnerships are vital to the future strength of teacher education, the education professions must join with outside groups such as the business community, industry, parents, government agencies, mass media, and various social agencies in a coalition directed to improving schools by improving the competence of teachers. Also, because partnerships involve both organizations and individuals, professional education associations, individual teacher educators, and other stakeholders in the effort must join together to advocate state and federal action and to work with governors and state legislators as well as national political leaders in government, the private sector, and agencies and foundations. (Association of Teacher Educators, 1991, p. 3)

Like the ATE's charge, the NCEEA's recommendations included a call for collaboration in the improvement and delivery of preparation of educational leaders. The NPBEA reiterated this call, pointing out a need for school/university partnerships to provide sites for clinical programs and applied research, the importance of "vigorous and systematic recruitment programs" to attract promising candidates, and the significance of maintaining full-time faculty who are clinically oriented as well as research oriented. (Thompson, 1999, p. 99)

More recently, the NCAELP emphasized the importance of collaboration and stressed the idea that the stakeholders that make up our field are interdependent—rather than independent, as one would assume by examining the way we currently operate. Currently, it seems that individuals decide to seek leadership preparation, programs admit and provide training, districts seek and hire leaders, and professional associations provide professional development and networking opportunities. In some places this process is more or less collaborative, but collaboration is not the norm.

THE NEED FOR COLLABORATION AMONG KEY STAKEHOLDERS

It is my contention that the lack of collaboration in our field for decades has undermined efforts to identify, prepare, place, induct and develop leaders for our nation's schools. Let's take, as an example, the selection of candidates for graduate programs in departments of educational leadership. Many believe the process typically used (e.g., Creighton & Jones, 2001) to select and admit candidates has greatly contributed to the lack of quality leaders in America's schools and, as a result, blame universities. However, this issue is not as clear-cut as some would have us believe. A number of factors impact the population that eventually applies and is admitted into the typical educational leadership program. These include:

- individual decisions and goals;
- encouragement from a mentor or colleague;
- program location;
- number of hours required to complete the program;
- financial cost of completing the program;
- recommendations from professional associations, colleagues, mentors, and family members;
- graduate school entry standards;
- program entrance standards;
- program recruitment strategies;
- size and quality of the applicant pool;
- administrative internship requirements;
- program difficulty; and
- program quality. (Young & McLeod, 2001)

Although the admissions standards of some educational leadership programs are woefully inadequate, increasing the rigor of entrance criteria alone will not ensure that the individuals admitted to preparation programs could become high-quality instructional leaders. Comprehensively addressing the issues of who applies and who is admitted to leadership programs will require collaboration between universities, practitioners, professional organizations, and state licensing agencies, among others. A collegial approach to recruitment and selection is needed. As a field, we must consider it our collective responsibility to ensure that tapping, recommending, recruiting, selecting, and retaining along with preparing, inducting, and mentoring are done well.

Preparation programs are already influenced by multiple stakeholders. As the NASSP pointed out over ten years ago, there are five categories of stakeholders with an interest in high quality preparation:

1. The higher education institutions that provide preparation and services to school administrators
2. State agencies and governmental units that license administrators and establish policies and regulations relative to administrative performance
3. Local and intermediate districts that employ school administrators
4. Professional organizations at state and national levels that represent the interests and offer professional development opportunities to school administrators
5. Other agencies such as centers, academies, unions, etc. that provide advice, training, and other services to school leaders. (NASSP, 1992, p.16)

Although each of these stakeholder groups has an interest in quality preparation and a responsibility to support quality preparation, rarely have the activities deriving from these groups been coordinated. "Rather than functioning symbiotically, the agencies have tended to pursue their own policies and programs" (NASSP, 1992, p. 177). So it was ten years ago; so it is today. This simply cannot go on. Quality preparation depends on coordinated and collaborative efforts. Moreover, because universities are the central site or provider of preparation, they should take responsibility for ensuring and encouraging both the coordination and the collaboration.

Collaboration is critical to the improvement of preparation programs. Candidate selection constitutes only one of the interdependent issues affecting school leadership preparation that will require a planned, collective response[1]. As a field we need to develop a plan for future collaboration in the preparation of school and school system leaders. My suggestions for key stakeholders are listed here, without embellishment, and developed in the course of the chapter. I believe we must do the following:

1. As a field we must understand how stakeholders might work collaboratively in a coordinated effort to improve preparation;
2. As a field we must decide how best to identify, attract, recruit, and screen candidates for leadership preparation;
3. As a field we need to come to consensus about the elements of quality preparation;
4. Based on these elements, universities must radically restructure their programs in collaboration with the field;
5. We must develop a process for evaluating our programs that provides valid and reliable measures of the success of our preparation efforts and that can be used to improve our programs; and

6. As a field we must take a more active role in supporting the improvement or
closure of programs that fail to provide quality preparation to future school and
school system leaders.

Collaborative efforts to change and deliver educational leadership preparation are
not likely to dominate the field unless explicit efforts are made to make this happen.

STAKEHOLDERS WORKING TOGETHER

Hart and Pounder (1999), among others, have made a strong case for the importance
of a strong and vibrant collaborative relationship with field practitioners as an essential element in any pre-service administrator's learning experiences. Although there
seems to be universal agreement regarding the importance and benefits of connecting
preparation programs to practice (Cambron-McCabe, 1999; Leithwood & Steinbach,
1995; Milstein, Bobroff, & Restine, 1991), few institutions actually implement programs that are truly collaborative and demonstrate organizational commitment from
all parties (Fusarelli & Smith, 1999). However, I firmly believe that if programs are
to be effective, stakeholders must be intimately involved in preparation, from conceptualization through recruitment and selection of students, course delivery, mentoring, field internship supervision, and evaluation (Young et al., 2001).

During its last meeting, the NCAELP recommended that we identify regions
where collaboration was working and learn from those efforts how stakeholders in
other areas might work collaboratively in a coordinated effort to improve preparation. As a result NCAELP is watching the efforts of the Southern Regional Education Board (SREB) very closely. SREB has learned a great deal from the universities and school districts involved in their University Leadership Development
Network. The following excerpt from *Universities in the Lead* is revealing.

> Universities and school districts are "uneasy collaborators," says Patrick Forsyth. The
> are institutions "that are quite different in how they operate and how they think." The
> history of school university relationships is marked by fits and starts, failed initiatives,
> and the residue of districts. As universities work to redesign their school leadership pro-
> grams, they must also work to overcome this history and find common ground on which
> to collaborate. (Norton, 2002, p. 5)

In addition to building relationships of trust, it is important that we understand how
best each stakeholder can contribute to program improvement. For example, it
would be useful to (a) develop a list of stakeholders that have a role in leadership
preparation, (b) identify potential roles each could play in program redesign, course
planning and delivery among other essential tasks, and (c) construct planning and
preparation models based on an analysis of the above.

IDENTIFYING FUTURE LEADERS

Part of the conversation about how stakeholders can work together to improve
preparation should include a focused conversation on how future leaders should be

identified. For too long we have depended primarily upon self-selection into educational leadership preparation. This must change. As a field we must decide how best to identify, attract, recruit, and screen candidates for leadership preparation. According to Cambron-McCabe (1999), the success of such endeavors depends upon first identifying our core educational purposes, which she notes "is central to transforming what we do" (p. 219).

Members of the NCAELP agreed that the individuals whom we admit into our program should be strong instructional leaders. Together this group acknowledged that the primary purpose of having school principals and district leaders is children; that the primary purpose of having schools, teachers, classrooms, buildings, etc., is children; and that the primary purpose of having schools of education *in* our universities is children. Therefore, it was agreed that the *ultimate purpose* of our leadership preparation programs *must be* supporting the education of our nation's children (Young, 2004). This requires that we not only provide high-quality preparation experiences, but that we also admit individuals into our programs who understand how to support student learning.

Currently, leadership programs do very little recruiting, relying instead on methods (e.g., word of mouth) that do little more than attract the same kinds of students that most programs already serve (Creighton & Jones, 2001). However, there are some current efforts from which we can learn. For example, the University of Texas at Austin has an excellent collaborative process in place that targets the identification of instructional leaders. The process involves "informed tapping" which differs from what most people think of when they hear tapping. Informed tapping is founded upon substantive conversations between university faculty and the field of practice focused on the characteristics of individuals who are likely to become effective instructional leaders. Together university faculty and practitioners look for excellent teachers, those with demonstrated leadership and a proven record of raising achievement among diverse groups of students. The process is followed by an assessment center type program admissions screening and several class room-based observations of the candidate's teaching abilities.

However, universities and school districts are not the only groups that should be playing a role in the selection of leadership preparation program candidates and, thus, future school leaders. States and professional associations also have important roles to play. At a minimum one would expect these stakeholders to consider how state policy and association outreach and mentoring might contribute.

QUALITY PREPARATION

As a field we need to come to consensus about the elements of quality preparation. As a starting point, we may want to agree to a set of irreducible minimums in professional preparation. The ISSLC standards, for example, could serve as an irreducible minimum for the content and competencies of school leaders. Viewing ISSLC as a minimum provides program stakeholders with a foundation from which to build programs that are appropriate for their particular contexts. This was the spirit of the NCAELP's anchoring statement.

The National Commission for the Advancement of Educational Leadership Preparation declares that the profession of educational leadership should be grounded on our best understandings of and latest research on student learning and school and school system improvement. We declare that preparation programs need to be built from that foundation; that is, their primary purpose must be to prepare leaders to create schools in which all children are successful. In order to meet the goal, we declare that preparation programs should be constructed collaboratively, should be congruent with the recently adopted NPBEA and NCATE standards (i.e., The ISLLC Standards for School Leaders), and should be evaluated in terms of their effectiveness in equipping graduates to create schools in which all youngsters are successful. (NCAELP, 2002)

NCAELP has also identified a set of program characteristics that seem to indicate program quality. These include:

- Planned recruitment, screening, and selection of students;
- Planned recruitment and retention of a core of full-time leadership faculty with contemporary professional experience;
- Professional development of faculty;
- Involvement of stakeholders in planning, teaching, and field internships;
- Reasonable teaching and advising loads for faculty;
- Advisory board of educational leadership stakeholders;
- Collaboration with state agencies;
- Development of program around a set of standards;
- Alignment of program to best practices in adult learning and leadership preparation;
- Coherent program design and delivery; and
- On-going programmatic evaluation and renewal. (Young, 2002)

This list, of course, represents just one perspective about what works in leadership preparation. The Association of Colleges and Schools of Education in State Universities and Land Grant Colleges and affiliated Private Universities have published a brochure that presents t heir perspective, titled "Increasing Instructional Capacity in Schools." Another example is a set of input standards recently commended by the NPBEA. What we need to do at this point is come to some consensus about what quality preparation consists of—what the irreducible minimum is—and we must do this as a field.

Part of this conversation should also involve differentiating between preparation and readiness as well as readiness planning. In other professional fields (e.g., engineering, business, medicine), preparation program graduates are considered prepared but not necessarily ready to practice independently in their chosen profession. Indeed, other professions invest heavily in the readiness of program graduates. The typical scenario looks something like this: (a) a candidate graduates from a preparation program, (b) the candidate is hired by a firm, (c) the firm trains the candidate for the work s/he will do, and (d) the candidate receives on-going professional development over the course of his or her career to ensure that her or his skills and knowledge are up to date and useful to the firm. Although most of our school districts do not have the resources to ensure that their job candidates receive proper readiness training and ongoing professional development, we as a field do. Moreover, it is our responsibility to ensure that preparation is not the end of the line with regard to leadership development. Stakeholders should determine how to make leadership development a seamless and lifelong process.

RESTRUCTURING PROGRAMS

Based on the program elements we as a field determine to be irreducible minimums, preparation programs must be radically restructured to support quality preparation that is based on substantive and sustained collaboration with the field. The history of educational leadership is full of attempts to redesign preparation programs[2] (Björk & Ginsberg, 1995; Murphy & Forsyth, 1999; Jacobson, Emihovich, Helfrich, Petrie, & Stevenson, 1998; Griffiths, Stout, & Forsyth, 1988; McCarthy, Kuh, Newell, & Iacona, 1988; Murphy, 1992, 1993, 1999b; Pitner, 1988; Short, 1997). Although some have been more successful than others (Björk & Ginsberg, 1995), few if any have reflected the interdependence and comprehensiveness that substantive and sustainable change will require (Young et al., 2002).

Part of this conversation must involve a mapping of how preparation will be planned and delivered, what resources will be needed, who will be involved, and what each stakeholders roles and responsibilities will be. With regard to the university, key challenges must be identified (policies on curriculum development and delivery, faculty evaluation, and load) and plans must be developed to meet those challenges.

One great challenge is inertia. In many programs, the structures predate most if not all of the faculty, creating a normative understanding of "the way things work around here" (Young et al., 2001, p. 9). Additionally, program content and specialty areas were, by and large, borrowed from technical areas already existing within universities (Murphy & Forsyth, 1999). Because these structures (e.g., evening courses held during the work week, courses offered during the university fall and spring semesters, courses held on the university campus, courses focused on traditional disciplines) and content areas, which maintain the status quo, tend to serve the faculty and staff more so than the students, few faculty feel compelled to question them.

Moreover, because universities generally do not support team teaching in calculating faculty load or recognize the added time and resources that structural improvements, content changes, and additional contributions to student learning would require, these changes involve commitments from faculty members that go well beyond the responsibilities of their jobs (Young et al., 2001). Although, those involved in such changes are likely to feel more satisfied with their work and believe they are better serving their students, they will also be overworked and their work may go unrecognized and unrewarded within their own institutions. Regardless, some faculty members have questioned traditional structures, and they have responded to the need for program improvement with extraordinary commitment. It has happened at Hofstra, the University of Miami-Ohio, Harvard, Fordham University, the University of Utah, Wichita State University, the University of Virginia, the University of California-Berkeley, the University of Missouri-Columbia, and the University of San Diego, among others.

Key to the success (and in some cases a lack of sustained success) of many of these efforts was institutional support. Thus, it is essential that as stakeholders map out restructured programs that they consider issues of institutional support. For example, stakeholders must determine whether departures from traditionally university-sanctioned practices are needed (e.g., from changes in promotion and tenure) (Owens & Steinhoff, 1992). Moreover, McCarthy (1999) suggested that changes in university norms would require more than faculty advocacy. "Such changes are unlikely without additional leverage from outside the field as well as support from national groups, such as the NPBEA and professional associations" (p. 205). Young and colleagues (2001) agree that outside leverage is essential.

> If, as a profession, we believe that programs should include more faculty with practical orientations and dedicate more time to collaborating with colleagues and practitioners, devising growth plans for individual students, conducting applied or action research, monitoring student progress, team-teaching courses, providing meaningful internship experiences, and observing students in their schools, then as a profession we must take collective responsibility for influencing universities to support these initiatives. (p. 18)

PROGRAM EVALUATION

We must develop a process for evaluating our programs that provides valid and reliable measures of the success of our preparation efforts and that can be used to improve our programs. Stakeholders frequently cite the disconnect between what is taught in many university preparation programs and what practitioners need to be able to do in their schools and school districts (Cambron-McCabe, 1999). This criticism may be related to the fact that we currently do not have reliable data upon which to base our programmatic efforts. A disconnect is likely, regardless of how well a program's content is aligned to national standards, if faculty have no reliable way of determining how well they are preparing leaders for the field. Although many program faculty now collect data, most forms of evaluation do not reveal how well students will perform once they are in the field. "Until we have a process for determining whether or not educational leadership preparation has any of the impacts that we hope for them, it is not likely that we will have adequate information to engage in effective program development" (Young et al., 2001, p. 10). Without evidence of success, few faculty may be willing to sustain the extra work program reform requires.

Fortunately, a number of researchers in collaboration with UCEA and the NCAELP are focusing their efforts. This group is working on a research project that has two sub-streams.

1. A longitudinal study of leadership preparation programs and the impact of their graduates on (a) the leadership they exercise, (b) the changes their leadership yields in their organizations, and (c) the impact of these changes in improving student achievement and other school outcomes.

2. A backward mapping study of (a) effective schools, (b) the nature of leadership, and (c) the source of the principals' leadership skill development.

Recognizing that there is no direct causal link between leadership preparation and student learning, these scholars have broken down the linkage by examining the following factors: (a) pre-conditions of program participants, (b) program components and related "through-puts," (c) direct student learning outcomes, (d) first order changes or leadership outcomes, (e) mediating factors, (f) second order changes where the focus is organizational outcomes, and (g) third order changes which focus on the link between leadership and learning. Now, there is no question that there are methodological challenges to linking leadership preparation to student learning. But the current dearth of information substantiating how preparation programs contribute to the practice of leadership and the performance of students, makes this kind of research critical, Moreover, our need to better understand the relationship between leadership preparation and leadership practices makes this kind of research compelling.

SUPPORTING QUALITY

My call for collaboration reflects my assumption that collaboration is the most likely path to quality and sustainable educational leadership preparation program improvement.

> The commitment of stakeholders to a system of collaboration and consensus will promote confidence and trust, discernible growth, and the attainment of mutual goals. Jointly agreed upon structures and relationships that support mutual trust among stakeholders must replace the existing uncontrolled free market structures. . . . Shared responsibility for collaborative goals also supports communication, experimentation, and innovation. (NASSP, 1992, p. 30)

However, the success of these efforts depends on true commitment to a set of common goals and a common vision of the leaders we need in our schools.

Once stakeholders have determined how to work collaboratively and in a coordinated way, once they have settled on a strategy for identifying, attracting, recruiting, and screening candidates for preparation programs, once they have come to a consensus about the elements of quality preparation, once they have determined how best to restructure programs, once they have agreed upon and developed a process for evaluating programs that provides valid and reliable information that can be used to improve our programs, then they must focus their efforts on the question of how to support and sustain quality leadership preparation. Although, sustainability and support are issues that will be addressed within the other five activity areas, at some point, it must become the sole focus of our efforts.

Although key issues to be considered here will be resources for specific program improvement efforts (e.g., faculty professional development), questions must be raised about program accreditation by state and national entities, licensure, certification, and recertification. In each of these areas we should seek a strengthening of requirements rather than a weakening. In teacher education, research has demonstrated a positive relationship between certification and teacher effectiveness. Studies employing national, state, and other data sets have reported significant relationships between teacher education and certification measures and student performance at the levels of the individual teacher (Neville & Robinson, 2003). Similarly, at the 2000 NCPEA conference, Cecil Miskel argued that a strong link exists between weakening state licensure requirements and the ability of educational leadership programs to prepare effective leaders. He argued that strong and quality state licensure requirements are necessary to ensure that all programs adequately prepare school and school system leaders. State licensure can play an important function in ensuring that only well-prepared and qualified individuals are provided licenses to lead.

With regard to program accreditation, we as a field we must take a more active role in supporting the improvement or closure of programs that fail to provide quality preparation to future school and school system leaders. Program accreditation should be considered a key tool for both courses of action. We simply cannot let programs that are failing to prepare effective educational leaders continue to license or certify individuals to work as vice principals, principals, superintendents and other school and district level leaders. If we do, we are responsible for the inevitable and terrible negative outcomes for the children, schools, and communities that those unqualified individuals fail.

This suggestion undoubtedly has an advocacy orientation to it, and according to Shipman, "many educational leadership professors are still operating as they were taught 30 years ago that school leaders should not be politically active or involved. Thus, they are hesitant to be proactive on any issue that has political overtones" (2001, p. 18). However, we must get used to being proactive. This is not the time to withdraw and hope that this issue will pass. It won't. Moreover, this is an area in which we can make a difference. Both accreditation and licensure and certification agencies provide opportunities for those effected to impact policy making and to make implementation decisions within their own environments.

Like in the other five areas discussed above, stakeholder collaboratives must address the issue of supporting quality in leadership preparation. Action plans should be developed that involve promoting quality programs and essentially "disowning" programs that do not meet the agreed upon standards of quality. Stakeholder collaboratives should focus on building coalitions with governmental organizations whose continuing support is essential for the long-term sustainability of programs, they should focus on building essential resources for effective preparation efforts, and they should focus on impacting key points of leverage, like certification and licensure policy.

CONCLUSION

Education is the single common ground and hope left in an increasingly splintered society and the success of children is at the very center of the leadership profession. To prepare educational leaders for the numerous settings and changing requirements is not an easy business. Given that that there are a variety of programs, most would agree that the underlying goal and orientation of leader preparation is the development of competent and pedagogically oriented leaders committed to the successful education of *all* children. What has become increasingly evident in the last thirty years of the twentieth century is that school leaders cannot ensure the success of every child single-handedly; likewise, the preparation of educational leaders must be conducted in a collaborative manner. Universities that prepare educational leaders, professional organizations, and field-based practitioners need each other in order to achieve this goal. Yet, to date few, if any, universities, professional organizations, policy makers, school administrators, and the private sector employ their collective potential to improve the profession of school leadership (Young et al., 2001).

Educational leadership preparation must meet the needs of our current and future school children. Teachers, principals, central office personnel, educational administration professors, researchers, regional service center personnel, Department of Education personnel, and other stakeholders have this goal in common—we are all working for the benefit of the children in our schools, school districts, regions, and states. However, if we are to realize the goal of ensuring educational excellence and equity for all children, we must first recognize that our work, at its core, is interdependent. Based on this understanding, we must rethink leadership preparation, how it is planned and how it is delivered. This will require that stakeholders come together and commit themselves to seeking common ground, to building shared goals, and to working collaboratively toward their realization. No single organization, group, or individual can create the kind of changes for leadership preparation that are needed. Substantive change requires collaboration.

NOTES

1. Others issues include but are not limited to: the development of program content, program delivery, mobilizing program resources, and providing post-programmatic induction, mentoring and networking opportunities.

2. Recommendations for significant changes in such areas as the clinical experiences/internships (Forsyth, 1992; Griffiths, Stout, & Forsyth, 1988; Murphy, 1993; Owens & Steinhoff, 1992; Pitner, 1988); administrative skills (Murphy, 1999a); differential instructional methods (McCarthy et al., 1988); and changing the entire structure of preparation programs (McCarthy, 1999; Short, 1997) have become commonplace in the literature of our profession.

REFERENCES

Association of Teacher Educators. (1991). *Restructuring the education of teachers.* Reston, VA: Author.

Björk, L. G., & Ginsberg, R. (1995, February). Principles of reform and reforming principal training: A theoretical perspective. *Educational Administration Quarterly, 31*(1), 11–37.

Cambron-McCabe, N. H. (1999). Confronting fundamental transformation of leadership preparation. In J. Murphy, & P. B. Forsyth (Eds.), *Educational administration: A decade of reform* (pp. 217–227). Thousand Oaks, CA: Corwin Press, Inc.

Creighton, T. B., & Jones, G. D. (2001). *Selection or self-selection? How rigorous are our selection criteria for education administration preparation programs?* Paper presented at the annual conference of the National Council of Professors of Educational Administration. Houston, TX.

Fusarelli, L. D., & Smith, L. (1999). Improving urban schools via leadership: Preparing administrators for the new millennium. *Journal of School Leadership, 9*(6), 534–551.

Griffiths, D. E., Stout, R. T., & Forsyth, P. B. (Eds.). (1988). *Leaders for America's schools.* Berkeley, CA: McCutchan Publishing Corporation.

Hart, A. W., & Pounder, D. G. (1999). Reinventing preparation programs: A decade of activity. In J. Murphy, & P. B. Forsyth (Eds.), *Educational administration: A decade of reform* (pp. 115–151). Thousand Oaks, CA: Corwin Press Inc.

Jacobson, S. L., Emihovich, C., Helfrich, J., Petrie, H. G., & Stevenson, R. B. (1998). *Transforming schools and schools of education: A new vision for preparing educators.* Thousand Oaks, CA: Corwin Press Inc.

Leithwood, K., & Steinbach, R. (1995). Improving the problem-solving expertise of school administrators. In K. Leithwood, & R. Steinbach (Eds.), *Expert problem solving: Evidence from school leaders* (pp. 281–309). New York: SUNY Press.

McCarthy, M. M. (1999). The evolution of educational leadership preparation programs. In J. Murphy, & K. S. Louis (Eds.), *Handbook of research on educational administration,* 2nd ed. (pp. 119–139). San Francisco: Jossey Bass.

McCarthy, M., Kuh, G., Newell, L., & Iacona, C. (1988). *Under scrutiny: The educational administrations professorate.* Tempe, AZ: University Council for Educational Administration.

Milstein, M. N., Bobroff, B. M., & Restine, L . N. (1991). *Internship programs in educational administration.* New York: Teachers College Press.

Murphy, J. (1992). *The landscape of leadership preparation: Reframing the education of school administrators.* Newbury Park, CA: Corwin Press Inc.

Murphy, J. (Ed.). (1993). *Preparing tomorrow's school leaders: Alternative designs.* University Park, PA: University Council for Educational Administration.

Murphy, J. (1999a). The quest for a center: Notes on the state of the profession of educational leadership. [Monograph]. Columbia: MO: *University Council for Educational Administration,* 1–88.

Murphy, J. (1999b). Changes in preparation programs: Perceptions of department chairs. In J. Murphy, & P. B. Forsyth (Eds.), *Educational administration: A decade of reform* (pp. 170–191). Thousand Oaks, CA: Corwin Press Inc.

Murphy J., & Forsyth, P. (Eds.). (1999). *Educational administration: A decade of reform.* Thousand Oaks, CA: Corwin Press Inc.

National Association of Secondary School Principals. (1992). Developing school leaders: A call for collaboration. *A special report of the NASSP Consortium for the performance-based preparation of principals.* Reston, VA: Author.

National Commission for the Advancement of Educational Leadership Preparation. (2002). *Anchoring statement for the National Commission for the Advancement of Educational Leadership Preparation.* Online: http://www.ncaelp.org

Neville, K. S., & Robinson, C. J. (2003). *The delivery, financing and assessment of professional development in education: Pre-service preparation and in-service training.* Stanford, CA: The Finance Project.

Norton, J. (2002). *Academies in the lead: State academies must prepare school leadership teams with the skills and staying power to raise achievement.* Atlanta, GA: SREB.

Owens, R. G., & Steinhoff, C. R. (1992). Beyond the administrative internship: A proposal for the 1990's. In F. C. Wendel (Ed.), *Reform in administrator preparation: Myths, realities and proposals.* University Park, PA: University Council for Educational Administration.

Pitner, N. J. (1988). School administrator preparation: The state of the art. In D. E. Griffiths, R. T. Stout, & P. B. Forsyth, (Eds.), *Leaders for America's schools* (pp. 367–402). Berkeley, CA: McCutchan Publishing Corporation.

Shipman, N. (2001). Educational leadership professors and the politics of education. *Educational Leadership Review, 1*(1), 11–18.

Short, P. M. (1997). Reflection in administration preparation. *Peabody Journal of Education, 72*(2), 86–99.

Thompson, S. D. (1999). Causing change: The National Policy Board for Educational Administration. In J. Murphy, & P. B. Forsyth (Eds.), *Educational administration: A decade of reform* (pp. 93–114). Thousand Oaks, CA: Corwin Press Inc.

Young. M. D. (2002). *Ensuring the university's capacity to prepare learning focused leadership: Report of the National Commission for the Advancement of Educational Leadership Preparation.* Columbia, MO: UCEA.

Young, M. D. (2004, January). *Reorienting the preparation of school and school district leaders.* Keynote delivered to the Texas Principal Preparation Network. Austin, TX.

Young, M. D., & McLeod, S. (2001). Flukes, opportunities, and planned interventions: Factors affecting women's decisions to enter educational administration. *Educational Administration Quarterly, 37*(4), 462ff.

Young, M. D., Petersen, G. J., & Short, P. M. (2001). The complexity of substantive reform: A call for interdependence among key stakeholders. Paper Commissioned for the National Commission for the Advancement of Educational Leadership Preparation. Columbia, MO: UCEA.

Young, M. D., Petersen, G. J., & Short, P. M. (2002). The complexity of substantive reform: A call for interdependence among key stakeholders. *Educational Administration Quarterly, 38*(2), 137–175.

How Adequate Are the ISLLC Standards and the Educational Testing Service's School Leaders Licensure Assessment?

Louis Wildman

HOW ADEQUATE ARE THE ISLLC STANDARDS?

Many states have now adopted the Interstate School Leaders Licensure Consortium (ISLLC) Standards. California adopted them with only one minor change, substituting the phrase "modeling a personal code of ethics and developing professional leadership capacity" for "acting with integrity, fairness, and in an ethical manner."

According to the Missouri Professors of Education Administration Web site (2003):

> The ISLLC standards were designed to capture what is essential about the role of school leaders—what makes a difference in whether a school community can provide experiences that ensure all students succeed. They were intended to capture what research and practitioners have said are the critical components of effective leadership; the essential aspects of leadership, defined in relation to student success. The standards are designed to help transform the profession of educational administration and the roles of school administrators.

Hence it is appropriate to examine the adequacy of the ISLLC Standards.

Upon examination of the ISLLC Standards, one immediately notices that there is no mention within the Standards of the problems associated with the administration of special education, and just brief mention of large areas vital to the knowledge of a school leader such as school finance and school facilities management. There is much attention given to school public relations.

Each of the six ISLLC Standards includes "knowledge," "disposition," and "performance" components. One "knowledge" component in the sixth standard states that, "The administrator has knowledge and understanding of the role of public education in developing and renewing a democratic society and an economically pro-

---

Louis Wildman, California State University Bakersfield

ductive nation." That is the only mention of "public education" within the ISLLC Standards. While the dispositions state that "The administrator believes in, values, and is committed to: . . . taking risks to improve schools . . . trusting people and their judgments . . . involving stakeholders in management processes . . . [and] a safe environment," the ISLLC Standards do not include a disposition which states that 'the administrator believes in, values, and is committed to public education.' On the other hand, one performance component states that, "The administrator facilitates processes and engages in activities ensuring that the school acts entrepreneurially to support continuous improvement." This may suggest that the authors of the ISLLC Standards thought that education should be part of the economic sector (which justifies inequality), rather than the political sector (which guarantees equality), but we really don't know because the ISLLC Standards have been presented without a philosophical base.

The philosophical premises upon which the ISLLC Standards rest are not explicated. The closest the ISLLC Standards come is in the "knowledge" component to Standard 5:

The administrator has knowledge and understanding of:

• The purpose of education and the role of leadership in modern society.
• Various ethical frameworks and perspectives on ethics.
• The values of the diverse school community.
• Professional codes of ethics.
• The philosophy and history of education.

But, "The purpose of education and the role of leadership in modern society" is left unexplained. The philosophical perspectives from which we are to view "the philosophy and history of education" are not identified. Is the "purpose of education" to prepare students for citizenship or organizational slavery? Are we to view the history of education from the perspective of the oppressed or the oppressors? How should knowledge be obtained or organized? What knowledge is of most worth? These questions are not addressed.

On the other hand, the "disposition" component to Standard 5 is much more specific with regard to ethical premises: The administrator believes in, values, and is committed to:

• The ideal of the common good.
• The principles in the Bill of Rights.
• The right of every student to a free, quality education.
• Bringing ethical principles to the decision-making process.
• Subordinating one's own interest to the good of the school community.
• Accepting the consequences for upholding one's principles and actions.
• Using the influence of one's office constructively and productively in the service of all students and their families.
• Development of a caring school community.

This specificity, along with some related principles, allows the ISLLC Standards to address the area of "student discipline" without directly mentioning "student discipline" within the ISLLC Standards. These related principles include:

- The administrator facilitates processes and engages in activities ensuring that the vision shapes the educational programs, plans, and actions.
- The administrator believes in, values, and is committed to a safe and supportive learning environment.
- The administrator has knowledge and understanding of principles and issues relating to school safety and security.
- The administrator believes in, values, and is committed to a safe environment.
- The administrator facilitates processes and engages in activities ensuring that barriers to student learning are identified, clarified, and addressed.
- The administrator treats people fairly, equitably and with dignity and respect and examines and considers the prevailing values of the diverse school community.
- Expects that others in the school community will demonstrate integrity and exercise ethical behavior.
- Applies laws and procedures fairly, wisely, and considerately.
- The administrator believes in, values, and is committed to using legal systems to protect student rights and improve student opportunities.

Notice the emphasis upon "safety." Safety is mentioned in three separate component standards.

What is lacking is any mention of what should be taught. Just as there is no mention of the academic disciplines, neither is there mention of the curriculum content which students should learn. The ISLLC Standards speak of "learning goals," "high standards of learning," "ensuring that students have the knowledge, skills, and values needed to become successful adults," "curriculum design, implementation, evaluation, and refinement," "curriculum decisions . . . based on research, expertise of teachers, and the recommendations of learned societies," "high-quality standards, expectations, and performances," and "public policy . . . shaped to provide quality education for students," but never specify what content should be taught nor what content-specific pedagogical knowledge administrators should possess.

Not only is there no mention of the specific curriculum objectives or standards that students should learn, there is also no recognition of the concept that students should take over more and more responsibility for their own learning as they develop, along with the notion that education partly teaches students pre-determined objectives and partly facilitates student initiated investigatory pursuits.

On the other hand, the ISLLC Standards are particularly good in recognizing that school leaders must possess appropriate knowledge and dispositions in order to perform adequately. This integration of knowledge, belief, and practice is emphasized throughout, and specifically in the following component: The administrator facilitates, processes, and engages in activities ensuring that the core beliefs of the school vision are modeled for all stakeholders.

What is lacking is a certain humility in the "prescription." The ISLLC Standards recommend that administrators utilize "effective conflict resolution skills" and "effective communication skills," to cite just two examples. But we all know that even the best of these "skills" often fail, and there is no mention in the ISLLC Standards of that possibility.

In sum, the ISLLC Standards provide a good summary of the human relations, school/community relations, and political context of school leadership, but they only touch upon the essential areas of school law, finance, special education, facilities management, personnel, and curriculum.

HOW ADEQUATE IS THE EDUCATIONAL TESTING SERVICE'S SCHOOL LEADERS LICENSURE ASSESSMENT?

At the October 18–19, 2002, conference of the California Association of Professors of Educational Administration, a representative of the Educational Testing Service presented their *School Leaders Licensure Assessment*. Since that presentation did not include any background information on the reliability or validity of that test, I sought that information to appraise whether the state licensing commission—the California Commission on Teacher Credentialing—should utilize this test to accredit school administrators. However, without this information, the California Commission on Teacher Credentialing announced that they had

> . . . adopted the School Leaders Licensure Assessment (SLLA), administered by the Educational Testing Service, as the examination option for obtaining a California Preliminary Administrative Services Credential. Individuals who pass this assessment and meet the following prerequisites will quality for a Preliminary Administrative Credential or Certificate of Eligibility:
> • Possession of an appropriate teaching or services credential;
> • A minimum of three years of successful teaching or school services experience in public schools or private schools or equivalent status;
> • Passage of the California Basic Educational Skills Test (CBEST);
> • Fingerprint and character and identification clearance;
> • Application to the California Commission on Teacher Credentialing and submission of appropriate fees and support documentation.

After having now studied information provided by the Educational Testing Service, I have concluded that the *School Leaders Licensure Assessment* instrument should be required of candidates for administrative certification, but only those who have completed an approved educational administrator preparation program should be allowed to take the examination.

This, incidentally is also the personal opinion of Richard Tannenbaum, the primary Educational Testing Service researcher of the *School Leaders Licensure Assessment*. In personal e-mail correspondence of December 2, 2002, I wrote to him as follows:

> The high stakes testing presently going on in the public schools of California is having the effect of severely narrowing the elementary curriculum to math and reading. I am

wondering if a similar narrowing of the curriculum will occur if educational administrator licensing comes down to the passage of your licensure test without any previous educational requirements? Is it possible to become a licensed architect or licensed physician without completing professional educational preparation in a university school of architecture or school of medicine? My fear is that this high stakes test in educational administration will simply overwhelm legitimate educational preparation programs and that we may see either a significant narrowing of the curriculum or test-preparation clinics springing up, or both.

Later that day he answered as follows:

> I am sure you are much better versed with the status of CA regarding educational administration/leadership than I. In other states, however, it is my understanding that there are educational requirements that must be fulfilled as part of the licensure process—so while the SLLA may be the final requirement, it is not the sole requirement for licensure; graduation from an accredited educational administration/leadership program, for example, may be another. . . . Leadership programs should, in my personal opinion, continue to prepare future educational leaders broadly and with a future vision, to address the question of "what should educational leaders be expected to know and be able to do to be effective—now and in the future?" This is not incompatible with licensure—it's just that licensure taps much more the "necessary now" aspects of readiness to engage in independent practice. (personal communication, Tannenbaum, December 2, 2002)

To understand my thinking with regard to the SLLA, some background is necessary: Back in the fall of 1990, I worked with a group of California professors of educational administration to identify the major sub-fields within educational administration. A survey was first given to a small sample of practicing administrators and faculty in California. The results were studied, and throughout the 1990–91 school year, additional administrators and faculty were sampled. Eventually we concluded that the results were coalescing around the following 17 knowledge base sub-fields and that further sampling was not necessary:

1. The practical, educational administrative implications of major cultural and historical/philosophical perspectives.
2. Research methods (including design, quantitative, qualitative, historical and ethnographic issues).
3. Learning theory (including theories and ideas pertaining to human growth and development, personality and intelligence).
4. Curriculum (decision-making, content, instructional methodology, student evaluation, and curriculum change processes).
5. Student services (counseling, career guidance, student discipline, dropout prevention strategies).
6. Administration of special programs (special education, bilingual education, migrant education, compensatory education).
7. Personnel (certification, recruitment, selection, assignment, academic freedom, compensation, collective bargaining processes, formative and summa-

tive teacher evaluation, teacher rights, counselor evaluation, administrator evaluation, classified employee evaluation, staff development).

8. Educational management (administrative theories, decision-making theories).
9. Educational leadership (theories, processes, and skills).
10. Human relations (conflict resolution, team building, inter-personal and inter-group relations).
11. Systems analysis and design (organizational structure, flow charts, strategic planning, computer spreadsheets/databases, quality control).
12. Site-based leadership (participatory vs. top-down decision making, empowerment).
13. School law and policy development (legal system, church and state, compulsory attendance, student rights, torts).
14. School finance (local, state, and federal roles, budgeting and accounting, equity and equality issues).
15. School public relations (developing and evaluating public support for education).
16. School facilities (planning facilities and grounds, educational specifications, energy and conservation, health and safety, maintenance and operation).
17. District/community leadership (board/superintendent roles, relations, and evaluation; district governance models).

However, it should be pointed out that the sampled practicing administrators and educational administration faculty agreed on the importance of all the sub-fields except one. The practitioners did not agree on the importance of "research methods." But one of the purposes of higher education is to promote deeper understanding and the pursuit of knowledge. Hence we were not persuaded by this data, and research methods was included as one of the sub-fields.

Once the 17 sub-fields were identified, standards sub-committees within each area were established. These sub-committees, in consultation with practicing administrators, enumerated a draft set of sub-topics within each sub-field. Again, after the initial draft, the outline was extensively debated and improved by both practicing administrators and professors of educational administration. To view this work, see Wildman et al. (1993), *A Knowledge Base in Educational Administration*. The chapters in that first NCPEA yearbook were chosen to update members of the profession on recent research in those 17 sub-fields.

With that background, we now consider how the SLLA was written. The *Journal of Personnel Evaluation in Education* (September 1999) contains two excellent articles, written from a measurement and evaluation perspective, describing the job analysis study and the content validation (linkage) study conducted to develop the SLLA: *Laying the Groundwork for a Licensure Assessment* by Richard J. Tannenbaum, and *Gathering Content-Related Validity Evidence for the School Leaders Licensure Assessment*, by Clyde M. Reese and Richard J. Tannenbaum. The Educational Testing Service has identified those two articles as containing a summary of the research evidence for this assessment. I was impressed with the careful methodology utilized and the linkages established between the assessment exercises and the performance each was designed to measure. Only a large testing organization, such as the Educational Testing Service, could afford to hire expert external panels and advisory groups for several day periods to analyze, review, and pilot test such an examination. From a test construction perspective, the Educational Testing Service has done a good job. However, from an educational administration perspective, I have some criticism.

Work on the School Leaders Licensure Assessment began with a literature review "to identify major categories of professional practice for school administrators" (Tannenbaum, 1999, p. 229). Here are the eight documents which the Educational Testing Service staff identified as most relevant to the preparation of this test:

1. *Effective Principal Behaviors*. (Research for Better Schools, 1987)
2. *Principal's Training Simulator in Special Education: Indices of Performance*. (Burrello & DiOrio, 1990)
3. *Developing School Leaders: A Call for Collaboration—A Special Report of the NASSP Consortium for the Performance-Based Preparation of Principals*. (National Association of Secondary School Principals, 1992)
4. *Keys to Success: Critical Skills for the Novice Principal*. (McGrevin & Schmieder, 1993)
5. *Educational Leaders: Professionals or Moral-Social Agents*. (Chen, Goldring & Addi, 1994)
6. *A Job Analysis of Chicago School Principals*. (Nelson, 1982)
7. *A Report on Proposed Specifications for a Performance Assessment of School Principals*. (Murphy, 1995)
8. *Proposed NCATE Curriculum Guidelines for Advanced Programs in Educational Leadership*. (National Policy Board for Educational Administration Educational Leadership Constituent Council, 1995)

None of the documents utilized were mentioned by respondents in a survey I recently conducted, asking members of the National Council of Professors of Educational Administration to list the key books and articles in the field.

Based on a content analysis of the above eight documents, the advice of a number of external expert panels, and the ISLLC Standards, the Educational Testing Service staff eventually came up with 11 responsibility and knowledge areas:

1. Leadership
2. Strategic Planning
3. Facilitating Student Learning
4. Developing, Implementing, and Evaluating Curriculum and Instruction
5. Selecting, Supervising, and Evaluating Faculty and Support Staff
6. Relationships with Faculty and Support Staff
7. Professional Development

8. Community Relations
9. Management
10. Maintaining the Physical Security of Students, Faculty, and Support Staff
11. Operations

If we compare these 11 "responsibility and knowledge areas" with the 17 sub-areas in the knowledge base which I described above, one sees a number of major holes.

Following this comparison, a job-analysis survey was then sent to a stratified, random national sample of 10,034 elementary, middle, and secondary school principals. 2,460 surveys (24.6%) were returned. The purpose of the job-analysis survey was "to identify responsibility statements and knowledge statements . . . important for the competent performance of beginning principals" (Tannenbaum, 1999, p. 235). While this may seem like a reasonable purpose, no information is presented on how respondents distinguished between the "competent performance of beginning principals" and competent performance of experienced principals, or if this is a meaningful distinction.

In preparing this review, I took the practice assessment exercises, and then I scored my responses using the rubrics provided, as suggested in the *Study Kit* (2002, p. 6) for those preparing for the actual SLLA. I found the six-hour assessment exam mentally exhausting and not easy, and I certainly wouldn't criticize the test on that account. However, while I received an almost perfect score, experience will tell whether an intelligent person could pass without having taken courses in educational administration. A lot will depend upon how high a passing score is required.

Table 1.   Comparison of Knowledge Base and ETS/SLLA

Ed. Admin. Knowledge Base	*SLLA Responsibility & Knowledge Areas*
1. Cultural Perspectives	
2. Research Methods	
3. Learning Theory	*Facilitating Student Learning
4. Curriculum	*Curriculum & Instruction
5. Student Services	*Maintaining the Physical Security of Students, Faculty, and Support Staff
6. Special Programs	
7. Personnel	*Selecting, Supervising, and Evaluating Faculty and Support Staff; and * Professional Development
8. Educational Management	*Management
9. Educational Leadership	*Leadership
10. Human Relations	*Relationships with Faculty and Support Staff
11. Systems Analysis	*Strategic Planning
12. Site-based Leadership	*Operations
13. School Law and Policy	
14. School Finance	
15. School Public Relations	*Community Relations
16. School Facilities	
17. District/Community Leadership	

For example, in one sample question a school is described where the "bathrooms are not being cleaned at night and . . . some of the toilets do not flush." One of the ISLLC Standards says that "A school administrator is an educational leader who promotes . . . a safe . . . learning environment," and obviously a school administrator should place a high priority on getting the toilets fixed. But does it take a course in educational administration to know this? Surely not, and I am sure that in my 18 years of teaching educational administration I have never taught this!

On the other hand, another sample question required knowledge of the research on staff development. I wish the test included more questions which required such professional administrative knowledge. (For example, administrators should know that interviews are not good predictors of on-the-job performance.) But the reason it doesn't is because the SLLA is intended to measure just the minimum knowledge and skills necessary for competent school administration. Further, it specifically does not claim to measure the "dispositions" associated with each ISLLC Standard. Those are certainly better appraised throughout an administrator preparation program.

In sum, in the State of California there are many accredited university programs preparing school administrators. There is great strength in their diversity. If the School Leaders Licensure Assessment (SLLA) were only administered to those candidates who had completed an accredited program in educational administration (as is the case in most states that have adopted use of this test), I believe this examination would do much to improve the quality of licensed school administrators in California. However, if the CCTC continues to license anyone that just passes this test, it may narrow the content and scope of administrator preparation.

Use of this assessment instrument alone is not an appropriate way to reduce the fictional shortage of administrative candidates because the shortage is only in a few districts, and, by itself, this test is not intended to be the sole criterion for making employment decisions (*Study Kit*, 2002. p. 6)

HOW WILL THIS TEST CHANGE
EDUCATIONAL ADMINISTRATOR PREPARATION?

In December, 2002, the California Commission on Teacher Credentialing passed a motion allowing candidates for an administrative credential to take and pass the Educational Testing Service's School Leaders Licensure Examination as an alternative to completing an accredited university educational administration program. The first administration of the test occurred on January 11, 2003.

At California State University—Bakersfield, I have taken the following steps in response to this development.

First, as a professor teaching school personnel courses, I have talked more about the preparation of educational professionals within my course. Paradoxically, I find that many teachers and administrators do not value education, and do not see the difference between *training* and *education*. We would not be discussing this problem if there was a greater shared belief in education among educators.

Second, as Coordinator of the Educational Administration Program at California State University—Bakersfield, I have informed all of our alumni about the test. I wanted them to hear about it first in a newsletter from their university. That gave me an opportunity to also provide them with an analysis of the test. We need an informed constituency who understand what this testing option does to our profession.

Third, in cooperation with our county superintendent of schools, I met with all area superintendents to obtain an informal agreement from them that they would not hire individual administrators who had just passed this test without having gone through a regular program. The district superintendents in our area are concerned about a growing movement toward deregulation—including charter schools and vouchers—so I received considerable support from this group.

Fourth, I have tried through correspondence to persuade the California accrediting body (the CCTC), to consider the likely consequences of their actions.

Finally, I have continued to serve on a committee composed of representatives from the state administrator association (ACSA) and the state association of professors of educational administration (CAPEA). There are some indications, for example, written and verbal communication to educational administration faculty from the president of the state administrator association, that the association would try to stop the certification of administrative candidates who only pass a written test. Nevertheless, the state administrator association has been quick to offer a $250 two-day workshop designed to teach individuals how to pass the School Leadership Licensure Assessment, completely bypassing university preparation programs.

So, will the state administrator association and the state accrediting body recognize the importance of quality educational administration preparation programs? Will members of the profession recognize that a test-only credential alternative devalues the worth of every administrative credential? Will superintendents and personnel directors hire administrator applicants who have only passed a written test which does not sample content in the fields of special education, school law, school finance, educational philosophy, and social justice? The jury is still out.

NOTE

This paper was presented at the 2003 Annual Conference of the National Council of Professors of Educational Administration, Sedona, AZ.

REFERENCES

About ISLLC: The ISLLC standards (February, 2003) Retrieved April 26, 2004, from Missouri Professors of Education Administration Web site: http://www.umsl.edu/~mpea/Pages/AboutISLLC/AboutISLLC.html

Interstate School Leaders Licensure Consortium: Standards for School Leaders. (1996). Council of Chief State School Officers, State Education Assessment Center.

Reese, C., & Tannenbaum, R. (1999). Gathering content-related validity evidence for the school leaders licensure assessment. *Journal of Personnel Evaluation in Education, 13*, 3.

Study kit: Book 1. (2002). Ewing, NJ: Educational Testing Service.

Tannenbaum, R. (1999). Laying the groundwork for a licensure assessment. *Journal of Personnel Evaluation in Education, 13*, 3.

Tannenbaum, R. (December 2, 2002). Personal communication.

Wildman, L., Blair, B. G., Cuellar, A., Daugherty, R., Fischer, C., Land, K., Parker, J., Swartz, S., Townley, A., & Zachmier, W. (1993). A knowledge base in educational administration. In J. R. Hoyle & D. M. Estes (Eds.), *NCPEA: In a new voice. The first yearbook of the National Council of Professors of Educational Administration* (pp. 35–60). Lancaster, PA: Technomic Publishing Co.

Wildman, L. (Ed.). (1997). *The fifth yearbook of the National Council of Professors of Educational Administration.* Lancaster, PA: Technomic Publishing Co.

Wildman, L. (December 2, 2002). Personal communication.

II

KNOWING THE WAY

Still in Search of a Knowledge Base for Educational Administration: 2004 and Counting

James E. Berry

In 1996 standards for the preparation of school leaders were endorsed and disseminated nationally by the Council of Chief State School Officers (CCSSO). The standards represented the work of 24 state and professional organizations that came together under the CCSSO umbrella as the Interstate School Leaders Licensure Consortium (ISLLC) to frame "a common core of knowledge, dispositions, and performances that will help link leadership more forcefully to productive schools and enhanced educational outcomes" (CCSSO, 1996, p. iii).

At issue for many professionals—practitioners and professors alike—was the incomplete nature of the ISLLC standards. They became widely recognized as the source document for what school leaders should know and be able to do. Yet they reflected standards for administrative behavior, specifically the role of principal, and not a knowledge base for understanding the field of educational administration. There was a gap between what the standards expected from a principal and what the preparation program expected from an informed professional. Even more troubling was that they were adopted by states as a single source document that defined the entire profession of educational administration. Although the standards were intended to be focused on the school leader embodied by the principal they were applied more liberally to educational leadership at all levels of K–12 and, even, higher education.

These standards also became the foundation for courses and content in university preparation programs in educational administration. The National Council for the Accreditation of Teacher Education (NCATE) adopted ISLLC standards by utilizing them as the measuring stick against which educational administration programs were evaluated. NCATE's embrace of the ISLLC standards served to standardize programs of preparation. The intent was to ensure quality preparation for principals,

James E. Berry, Eastern Michigan University

but the outcome was a regression to standards for driving program improvement in educational leadership. Standards derived from a common core of knowledge, dispositions, and performances did not reflect a knowledge base for the profession. These minimal standards that were intended as entry level expectations for principals soon were more broadly interpreted as expectations for all educational leaders.

STANDARDS AREN'T A KNOWLEDGE BASE

An immediate challenge for educational administration is to identify a knowledge base in order to develop standards for principal preparation. It may be obvious to those in the profession to say leadership in educational administration goes beyond principal preparation. However, the ISLLC standards have managed to reduce the scope and breadth of educational administration in a way that harms the profession, principals, schools, and children.

Designing standards for principal preparation would seem to be a straightforward process. The consortium of professional organizations that developed the ISLLC standards wanted to improve leadership preparation that made a difference in student achievement. There was a need to move the profession beyond the inconsistent quality of university programs. Training, it was believed, was shallow and lacked rigor. The thinking was, define leadership outcomes and program improvement at the university-based program level would result. The intent of the consortium of professional organizations involved in developing the ISLLC standards was to derive from research "the linkages between educational leadership and productive schools, especially in terms of outcomes for children and youth" (CCSSO, 1996, p. 5). Another goal of the consortium was to identify "significant trends in society and education" that shaped leadership at the school level (p. 5). The effort to develop these standards resulted in further discussion about the use and value of an educational administration knowledge base. Although these standards may not reflect a complete and thorough understanding of an educational administration knowledge base their publication did accomplish:

1. Framing of the accreditation process for educational administration programs in NCATE affiliated universities;
2. Some measure of curriculum alignment for university preparation programs around ISLLC standards;
3. Discussion of the ISLLC standards as representative of the field and profession in the training and development of principals and building level leaders.
4. Discussion of a knowledge base as a source for better standards at all levels of educational administration training.

The ISLLC standards offered a starting point for the task ahead. The standards generated discussion, programming, and thinking about the principalship. They also generated renewed interest in developing an educational administration knowledge base for the very reason that the very same standards were limited and incomplete. The ISLLC standards represented leadership preparation at the school level but did not represent the depth and breadth of the broader profession of educational administration.

OVERCOMING THE ADMINISTRATIVE PAST IN EDUCATIONAL ADMINISTRATION

Payne (1875) wrote *Chapters on School Supervision* to address the lack of background and preparation for school administrators in the late 1800's. Educational administration had not been organized as a field or profession and the need for organizing, managing, and operating the rural common school gave way to the more urban age-graded school as the 19th century progressed. After receiving an appointment as a faculty member at the University of Michigan in 1879 Payne incorporated his thoughts about administration into a course for aspiring administrators. The course, *School Supervision*, reviewed such topics as general school management, the art of grading and arranging courses of study, and the powers and duties of a superintendent (Payne, 1886, p. 343). It is the first recognized attempt in America to train aspiring schoolmen for the role of superintendent or principal. There were no standards and the discussion of a knowledge base was not yet on the horizon. Educational administration was emerging as a profession because there was a need to get the job done of organizing and managing schools.

Adams (1880), a contemporary of Payne, wrote disparagingly about school supervisors of the day. He described the pressing need to train supervisors who had skill and ability beyond that of teaching. He wrote that being a supervisor required more than teaching skill and argued for university programs to train administrators. He indicated that education should develop within the profession something that was "a distinctly higher walk of the profession" (p. 940).

A need for supervision of the school enterprise grew into a profession. The complexity of the system grew beyond the teacher as the one room school house grew into a complex bureaucratic organization. Educational administration had very humble beginnings. There was little during the 1800's to attract a person to the position of administrator. In many schools the teacher and principal were one and the same. In some school districts the superintendent took on the role of supervisor and primary administrator. Often the superintendent rode a circuit to oversee a loosely connected system of one room school houses within a region.

When one considers the necessary skills and abilities required to supervise and administer an1800's school there was little to commend a person to the position of principal or superintendent. Adams (1880) described the foremost responsibility of a late 19th century supervisor was having the ability to secure resources and repair the school. Finding money to purchase slate boards and making repairs to buildings, stoves, and outhouses defined a good supervisor. As an evolutionary step in administration Adams saluted the work of these men (and they were men). "Cleanliness," he indicated "is next to godliness; and those who introduced cleanliness, light, and order into the beastly old common school deserved well of their successors" (p. 936). Thus, it appears that one of the earliest standards for a school administrator consisted of the ability to work with tools, fix things, do custodial work, maintain the building, and keep the stove working and the outhouse functional.

No matter what the standards are today for school administration one cannot escape the past. What is now considered quaint was once considered a necessary quality. A school administrator without carpentry skills was ill-suited to the job of 1880. One would concede, however, that this standard has evolved into a much more complex expectation for anyone aspiring to the position of principal. Mastery of carpentry skills is a far removed expectation for principals and not a fixture of educational administration preparation programs. Standards for educational administration are dynamic and change as the times and needs change.

THE STIRRING OF A PROFESSIONAL EDUCATIONAL ADMINISTRATOR

It was because the supervisory role was ill-defined and there was an obvious need to organize for learning that Adams (1880) advocated a new role for schoolmen. He argued that other professions had been elevated to a higher status by becoming disciplines for professional study. Agriculture and law, for example, had become subjects worthy of in-depth study, "But when it comes to the educational development of those who are to constitute the future state, though we spend millions on millions upon it, the universities turn their heads away, and class them as something less than the grass in the field" (p. 939). He believed universities should develop programs to teach the right kind of scientific skill to these men who would become educational leaders. According to Adams (1880),

> They must create a class, individual members of which are already at work—a class which shall be to the teacher what the staff officer of the army is to the line officer, what the jurist is to the attorney, what the physician is to the pharmacist. They must be imbued with the science of their calling. (p. 942)

It wasn't until 1905 that the profession of educational administration graduated its first doctoral students—Elwood Cubberly and George Strayer—who then served as the first professors of educational administration. Teachers College, Columbia University, became the first university to recognize educational administration as an academic discipline worthy of advanced study and it was during the early 20th century that the field of educational administration became an accepted university preparation program. By the end of WW II Silver (1982) wrote that educational administration had achieved program status at 125 colleges and universities across the United States. It is at this time that educational administration began to seek a more complete place in education.

THE MORE THINGS CHANGE THE MORE THEY STAY THE SAME

Although educational administration during the first half of the 20h century was a recognized discipline through the 1950's most faculty members in educational administration "appeared to be recruited from the ranks of former school administrators and reportedly they taught largely by anecdote and prescription" (Campbell & Newell, 1973, p. 1). The field of educational administration evolved into a profession during the 20th century, but it couldn't find its footing as a recognized discipline. By the

1950's it had evolved to the point that it needed to establish itself as an academic field worthy of advanced study and professional status. The quest for a knowledge base and acceptance as an academic profession began in earnest.

The National Council of Professors of Educational Administration (NCPEA) was founded in 1947 and the University Council for Educational Administration (UCEA) ten years later in 1957. Both organizations can trace their origins to the desire for more substance, prestige, and coordination of the discipline. As Culbertson (1995) noted in the discussions leading up to the founding of UCEA, the principle tests for membership in UCEA should be based upon a university's interest, effort, and commitment to devote significant resources to research in educational administration (p. 48). NCPEA did not have the same kind of scholarly or research orientation and its mission would remain closer to the practitioner. Thus, UCEA was organized to move educational administration into a scholarly and academic realm while NCPEA sought a niche for those professors focused on the training of a more practical nature. Both organizations, however, were dedicated to advancing the profession as an academic discipline that informed educational leadership and practice.

The knowledge base quest helps explain the founding of the National Council of Professors of Educational Administration and the University Council for Educational Administration. Elevating the profession became a serious goal for each organization. With the advent of the two professional organizations and a higher profile for educational administration there soon followed theory-based and scientifically validated scholarship to redefine educational administration as an academic discipline grounded in the applied world of schooling and supervision. The field of educational administration was being advanced, the theorists believed, through research and knowledge discovery about the leadership, organization, administration, and management of schools.

Because educational administration lacked a knowledge base to develop programs and a standardized curriculum to serve as a framework for teaching about school administration, the National Council of Professors of Educational Administration undertook in 1954 "a three-year writing project designed to synthesize existing knowledge and suggest new directions" for the profession (Campbell & Gregg, 1957, p. 1). The publication of *Administrative Behavior in Education* in 1957 outlined a framework to advance the field of Educational Administration. In the foreword Campbell and Gregg wrote:

> From the beginning the authors have sought to prepare a volume which would synthesize and interpret research and experience dealing with the factors affecting administrative behavior. It was early agreed that the book should not only bring together what is now known, but also it should look to the future. There was a particular desire to place educational administration on a firmer professional footing by suggesting significant research directions and next steps in theory building. Finally, the implications of this total effort for the improvement of basic preparation programs for administrators and programs for the continued professional development of administrators on-the-job, were to be drawn. (1957, p. x)

Miller (1957) explained the need to identify credible criteria by which effective educational administration could be measured. It was no longer acceptable to generate research in the field to certify the scholarship and professional ability of students working on doctoral degrees. The field needed to link scholars, existing research, and future research to identify a comprehensive knowledge base. It was necessary to develop theories, test them, and generate new knowledge. The field would define itself if professors of educational administration devoted themselves to serious research about the profession:

> In addition to the criteria for effective administration, the professional investigators in the field would work to greater advantage if a comprehensive research design were developed. This is necessary if research studies are to complement each other and if general progress in understanding of educational administration is to be made. So long as accomplishment of a research study serves mainly as initiation to the professional ranks via master's or doctor's degree programs, the stress can well be on the merit of research techniques. But a point has been reached where scholarship is needed not simply for proving individuals scholarly but for defining and developing the field of educational administration. (p. 521)

It was, Miller (1957) claimed, the responsibility of professors of educational administration to study, develop, and advance the field of educational administration. "For the professors of educational administration, development of the field is their primary area of scholarship" (p. 522). Thus, the quest for a knowledge base in educational administration was given a strong send off during mid century. The field had taken a place within colleges of education, sought legitimacy through research, and charted a course for the future. Educational administration was organizing and the profession sought academic absolution by grounding itself in theory, research, and informed practice.

THE QUEST FOR A KNOWLEDGE BASE

Students graduated from programs crammed with theories about leadership and organizations yet found research about schools, children, organizations, and adults lacking in utilitarian knowledge about practical matters of schooling. What is more, the field itself became broadly defined within education.

According to Donmoyer (1999) educational administration employed the big tent approach to knowledge base discovery. That is, every movement—theory, postmodern, post-structural, feminist, social science, scientific, utilitarian, etc.,—that had been discussed within the field of educational administration was embraced because of the difficulty in coming to consensus around a definitive source of professional knowledge. Donmoyer (1999) was not optimistic that coming to agreement around a knowledge base was at hand when he wrote:

> Indeed, if I were a betting man, I would bet that most members of the field would be quite reluctant to abandon the comfort and civility of the "big tents" in order to talk

(even in utilitarian terms) about seemingly intractable problems with those who think and talk differently than they do. Furthermore, even if members of our field are willing to engage in discussion and debate, it will be hard for them not to re-enact the sort of adversarial scripts employed in the past, despite the fact that such scripts did little to promote understanding of a rival's position and functioned primarily to reassure each debater and his (or, in a few instances her) supporters of the correctness of their a priori point of view. (p. 40)

Educational administration has been on a quest to define its knowledge base approaching 200 years with a decidedly quickened pace in the last 50 years. Some progress has been made; however, in 2004 the closest the profession has come to identification of a knowledge base is the ISLLC standards. Donmoyer's statement rings true because educational administration is still in search of a knowledge base. What has educational administration done to close the gap between leading and learning? Why isn't there something better than standards for principal leadership to inform the profession, school leaders, and the greater community? What can the profession do to solidify its place in preparing educational leaders for the future?

DEVELOPING A KNOWLEDGE BASE

The field of educational administration has made the development of a knowledge base a priority for almost 50 years. If one thing is evident, talking about the lack of a knowledge base hasn't helped in defining a knowledge base. It is suggested that the approach to knowledge base development needs to reflect the realities of higher education, K–12 education, the evolving educational field, the politics of change, and commitment from those who claim educational administration as their practice and discipline. It is also time to rethink the heavy commitment to the theoretical and abstract and get practical. Certainly the field can't abandon its accumulated knowledge, but it should organize it in a way that improves educational administration and learning. The challenge is to bring the many voices together.

The effective 21st century school administrator has come a long way from a skill set that began with repair and maintenance. Still, the elusive knowledge base—and the standards derived from it—were yet to be brought together to improve the preparation of school leaders even though the knowledge base was like shifting sand. It still existed . . . somewhere (Achilles, 1994, p. 172). Though some progress has been made, educational administration still programs its discipline around incomplete standards. The same question exists in 2004 as in 1957. How can educational administration improve educational administration?

KNOWLEDGE BASE DEVELOPMENT 2004

What is clear in 2004 is that a knowledge base in educational administration is still a quest. Achilles and Price (2001) wrote about the lack of an educational administration knowledge base and argued for a framework to develop one. "Sources of a professional KB in field include research, theory, and consensually validated exemplary professional practice, or informed professional judgment (IPJ). Local knowledge, legal knowledge, and experience are part of IPJ" (p. 9). Hoyle, English, and Steffy (1994) took the position that an applied approach to knowledge base development was critical for the acceptance of an educational administration knowledge base. "The university programs emphasize intellectual development and the research base, but the applied skills must be learned largely in a field setting" (p. 11). NCPEA itself sponsored the development of the text *Administrative Behavior in Education* almost 50 years ago with the specific goal of placing educational administration "on a firmer professional footing by suggesting significant research directions and next steps in theory building" (Campbell & Gregg, 1957, p. x).

Research conducted by scholars over the past 50 years in a wide range of disciplines has helped educational administration gain a greater understanding of the field and discipline. Today, more than ever before, educational administration has gained an understanding about what makes for an effective school administrator. For example, Waters, Marzano, and McNulty (2003) compiled three decades of research about educational leadership and its effect on student achievement. According to the authors, "21 leadership responsibilities that are significantly associated with student achievement" were identified through a meta-analysis of the data (p. 4). It is fair to say that a clearly identified knowledge base in educational administration is on the horizon because so much of what is known about the discipline has been researched, written about, and disseminated. If nothing else, the first 100 years of common sense administrative practice serves as the foundation for educational administration. It would seem that putting the pieces together to frame a knowledge base is a large part of the task to define a knowledge base.

One must also pause to point out an opposing point of view about the whole field and the folly of chasing down a knowledge base. Haller, Brent, and McNamara (1997) claimed graduate programs in educational administration had "little or no influence on the attributes that characterize effective schools" (p. 222). The profession has to look at its impact on teaching and learning and recognize that, in some quarters, training programs in educational administration are not well regarded. Confronting the place educational administration has within colleges of education and its status as a profession is certainly linked to the credibility of a knowledge base.

ENGAGING THE PROFESSION TO DEFINE A KNOWLEDGE BASE

Perhaps no aspect of educational administration preparation has shaped the profession as dramatically as the theory movement of the 1950's. The effort to develop a more academic discipline was intended to elevate thinking and research about educational administration in order to likewise elevate the practice of administrators. What it did was distance the practitioner from the professor. Griffiths (Campbell & Gregg, 1957) summarized the importance of theory development as a way to inform good practice: "Unless a theory can provide guidance for the administrator when he needs to act, it is a poor theory indeed. The educational administrator should be able to use the theory in much the same way as a practicing doctor should be able to use the theory developed by researchers in biological laboratories" (p. 364). The theory movement was an attempt to ground the field of educational administration and elevate its status at the same time. However, educational administration did not gain acceptance as a science nor achieve the desired effect of turning good theory into better practice. Theories did engage practitioners in thinking about school operation and leadership but the gap between theory and practice remained intractable. Almost 50 years after a serious effort to elevate educational administration as an academic discipline commenced, questions continue to linger about the field as a source of knowledge about leadership and administration.

The science of educational administration that came out of the theory movement in the 1950's has only helped to accentuate the distance between the practitioner and those who teach about practice at the university. How can the profession put in place a knowledge base that has escaped definition for almost 50 years? What has kept the profession sidestepping the problem of a knowledge base?

CHARTING KNOWLEDGE BASE DEVELOPMENT

After reviewing the effort to elevate educational administration to a recognized discipline over the last 50 years it seems reasonable to conclude that the effort to define an educational administration knowledge base has fallen well short of the goal. It is time to rethink the approach taken to gain credibility and acceptance as a profession. If one of the measures for achieving this goal was to compile a knowledge base, the profession has unfinished work. Following are some issues that need careful consideration by the professional organizations committed to developing leaders within education.

If educational administrators make a difference in schools, professors of educational administration are in a position to prove this point to the public and other educators. What is remarkable is that the profession has not come together around the aspects of training and administration to support the basic premise that certain skills and abilities can be learned. Thus, how the profession does come together to develop a knowledge base is a significant first step toward actually obtaining a knowledge base. Following are some issues that need to be addressed to take the final step toward an accepted knowledge base in educational administration:

1. Education must consider an educational administration knowledge base a compendium of information that emanates from many fields. Professors of educational administration must compile data and define the core knowledge important for success. A knowledge base will be utilized as a source for training future educational leaders who practice in the many varied educational organizations in this and other nations.
2. The knowledge base is dynamic and incomplete. It must be addressed and understood as an ongoing field of knowledge with no end, only iterations.
3. Determining a process to define the knowledge base is as important as the work on a knowledge base. Educational administration has approached development of core knowledge as an extension of each educational administration professor's scholarly contribution over the course of a professional career. The total accumulation of knowledge about educational administration published since 1875 has become the "all things under the tent" knowledge base.

4. The University Council for Educational Administration and the National Council of Professors of Educational Administration must lead in the development and acceptance of a generally accepted knowledge base that serves education. They are the only two organizations that have the professional resources to accomplish, and continue, the task.

5. This must be a collaborative project with practitioner and professional organizations. The process to develop a knowledge base must include an ongoing participation of organizations that represents the view of practitioners.

6. The quest for a knowledge base is 50 years and counting. The ISLLC standards are a nationally recognized starting point and offer a foundation toward the development of a knowledge base.

SUMMARY

A sustained effort to refine a knowledge base will only help the profession of educational administration. It isn't that the discipline doesn't have a knowledge base, it is that consensus hasn't been reached on what matters most. Perhaps the discipline should be broad and inclusive. Perhaps it should be narrow and exclusive. Perhaps it should have more of a practitioner orientation. Perhaps it should lean to the scholarly. Perhaps is perhaps the problem?

It is time for NCPEA and UCEA to come together with other professional/ practitioner educator organizations to clearly articulate an educational administration knowledge base. This is not a problem of knowledge, but a problem of process. Building collaboration and linkages to work together for the common good appears to be a major failing of past efforts to define an educational administration knowledge base. An immediate task is to figure out how to improve upon what already exists by working together.

REFERENCES

Achilles, C. M. (1994). The knowledge base for education administration is far more than content. In J. Burdin & J. Hoyle (Eds.). *Leadership and diversity in education: The Second Yearbook of the National Council of Professors of Educational Administration* (pp. 164–173). Lancaster, PA: Technomic, Inc.

Achilles, C. M., & Price, W. J. (2001, Winter). What is missing in the current debate about education administration (EDAD) standards! *AASA Professor, 24*(2). American Association of School Administrators.

Adams, C. F. (1880, November). Scientific common-school education. *Harper's Monthly Magazine, LXI*(366), 934–942.

Campbell, R. F, & Newell, L. J. (1973). *A study of professors of educational administration.* University Council for Educational Administration. Columbus, OH: UCEA.

Campbell, R. F., & Gregg, R. T. (1957). *Administrative behavior in education.* New York: Harper & Brothers.

Council of Chief State School Officers. (1996, November). *Interstate school leaders licensure consortium standards for school leaders.* Washington, DC: CCSSO Publications.

Culbertson, J. (1995). *Building bridges: UCEA's first two decades.* University Park, PA: UCEA.

Donmoyer, R. (1999). The continuing quest for a knowledge base 1976–1998. In J. Murphy & K. Louis (Eds.). *Handbook of Research on Educational Administration* (pp. 25–43). San Francisco: Jossey Bass.

Griffith, D. E. (1957). Toward a theory of administrative behavior. In R. Campbell & R. Gregg (Eds.). *Administrative behavior in education* (pp. 354–390). New York: Harper & Brothers.

Haller, E. J., Brent, B. O., & McNamara, J. H. (1997, November). Does graduate training in educational administration improve America's schools? *Phi Delta Kappan, 79*(3), 222–227.

Hoyle, J. R., English, F. W., & Steffy, B. E. (1994). *Skills for successful school leaders*, 2nd ed. Arlington, VA: American Association of School Administrators.

Miller, V. (1957). Assessment and projection. In R. Campbell & R. Gregg (Eds.). *Administrative Behavior in Education* (pp. 513–527). New York: Harper & Brothers.

Payne, W. H. (1875). *Chapters in school supervision*. Cincinnati, OH: Wilson, Hinkle & Co.

Payne, W. H. (1886). *Contributions to the science of education*. New York: Harper & Brothers.

Silver, P. F. (1982). Administrator preparation. In H. E. Mitzel (Ed.). *Encyclopedia of educational research,* 5th ed. Vol. 1 (pp. 49–59). New York: Free Press.

Waters, T., Marzano, R. J., & McNulty, B (2003). *Balanced leadership: What 30 years of leadership tells us about the effect of leadership on student achievement.* Mid-continent Research for Educational Learning: http://www.mcrel.org/PDF/LeadershipOrganizationDevelopment/5031RR_BalancedLeadership.pdf

A Model for Building Knowledge
for Professional Practice

Rodney Muth, G. Thomas Bellamy, Connie L. Fulmer,
and Michael J. Murphy

In educational leadership, as in other professions, the field's accumulated knowledge is directly related to the success of individual practitioners, the confidence of policy makers in the profession, the ability to prepare new practitioners in reliable ways, and the professional status that school leaders attain. The central importance of the growing knowledge base in educational administration has been a consistent theme in efforts to advance the professional status of school leaders (Hoy, 1994; Thompson, 1993), just as the weaknesses in the same knowledge base are cited by opponents of professional approaches to improving school leadership (Hess, 2003). Despite the importance of organizing the field's knowledge, such efforts have struggled to include emerging forms of knowledge while maintaining coherence and relevance to practice (Donmoyer, 1999).

This chapter is part of a larger project examining how professional knowledge for educational leadership might be organized around the major challenges that principals face and investigating how such an organization of knowledge might support professional practice and preparation (Bellamy, Fulmer, Murphy, & Muth, in preparation). We conceptualize the challenges faced by school leaders as positive *accomplishments*, those intermediate results (Gilbert, 1978) of a school's actions through which schools strive to support student learning. For schools, these accomplishments include such results as the learning goals that are defined to challenge students and teachers, the instruction actually provided toward meeting such challenges, and the development and maintenance of parent partnership to support both students and teachers. These intermediate results have value because they contribute to valued school outcomes, particularly student learning.

Rodney Muth, University of Colorado at Denver
G. Thomas Bellamy, University of Colorado at Denver
Connie L. Fulmer, University of Colorado at Denver
Michael J. Murphy, University of Colorado at Denver

Our proposal for defining a set of accomplishments that needs to be realized in practically all schools is illustrated in Figure 1, the Framework for School Leadership Accomplishments. The Framework identifies nine accomplishments through which schools support student learning and shows how those accomplishments are also intended to support and reinforce the efforts of individual students, parents, and professionals. These accomplishments focus on student learning, placed in the center as the overarching outcome. As the first tier shows, student learning is supported initially by student effort, over which the school has only indirect control. The next tier, however, identifies those accomplishments—learning goals defined, instruction provided, student climate sustained, and related services supplied—that bolster student effort. In addition, family support, family-community partnerships, and family involvement all undergird both student effort and the professional effort invested through the inner tier of accomplishments. The outer tier focuses directly on the principal's effort—school renewal encouraged, staff efforts supported, school operations organized, and resources obtained and used—all essential to realizing results that stimulate student learning. Organizing knowledge in this way emphasizes the results that the principal's daily actions are intended to promote. The familiar problems that principals face are the day-to-day issues or concerns that arise and need to be solved. All of these, however, occur within a larger framework as a principal leads a school community toward realizing the positive accomplishments necessary to meet the primary goal of a school: student learning.

To organize knowledge around accomplishments, we propose a straightforward structure. Knowledge is important as it answers two questions about each accomplishment. First, what constitutes quality in the accomplishment? That is, what indicators are needed to assure that an accomplishment meets local and other relevant standards? Second, what strategies are potentially useful in a principal's and school's pursuit of excellence in each accomplishment? That is, what knowledge about effective strategies is needed to ensure that actions taken will facilitate the ends sought? Answering these questions requires a broad knowledge base that includes traditional resources—social science research and ethical, critical, and legal reasoning—as well as the craft knowledge that emerges from practice and the individual knowledge that principals gain from personal experience.

While the profession has many publications that support sharing of individual school successes and stories, it does not have an organized way to capture, organize, disseminate, and analyze craft knowledge. This gap is significant, for craft knowledge often precedes more formal research, fills in gaps between studies, and points to dilemmas of practice that require disciplined, critical investigation (Lindblom & Cohen, 1979). This chapter describes our preliminary recommendations for making craft knowledge a more usable part of the profession's knowledge base.

THE IMPORTANCE OF PRACTICE-BASED KNOWLEDGE

In the 1970s, professor of educational administration R. Jean Hills took a sabbatical from his academic assignment. On his sabbatical, he took the year-long job of an elementary school principal in Wyoming. Following this year, he reflected and wrote

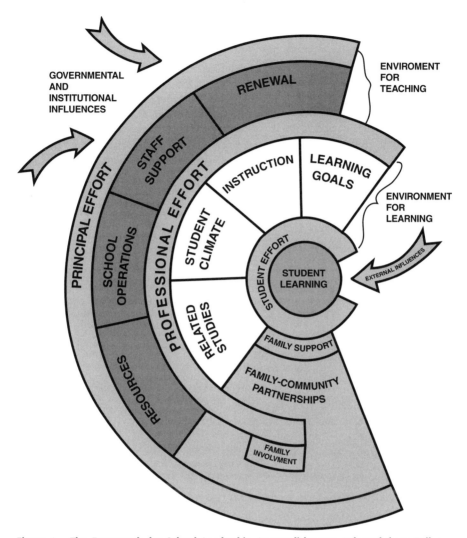

Figure 1. The Framework for School Leadership Accomplishments (adapted from Bellamy, 1999; copyright G. T. Bellamy, 2003)

about this experience (1978). Particularly, he wrote about how formal knowledge, as it was then organized, figured in his success as a school principal. He determined that his vast knowledge of theories from the various disciplines used in educational administration was not very helpful to him in making decisions as a school principal or in determining how to improve the school.

What Hills (1978) concluded from this experience was that theories as learned were not helpful because they were not organized around problems of practice and, therefore, were not useful to practitioners. Medicine, he observed, had organized its

knowledge around the problems that medical practitioners confront. It did so by using organ systems and delving into the physiology and pathophysiology of these systems, the things that doctors needed to know to practice effectively. He advocated
that the organization of knowledge in education follow a similar pattern and be organized around problems of administrative practice.

But Hills was a lone voice in the wilderness. The "Theory-Research Movement,"
under the leadership of the University Council for Educational Administration, was
at its peak. And legitimate theories that most thought helpful to practice came from
the social and behavioral science disciplines—sociology, political science, psychology, economics, and so forth (cf. Culbertson, 1964, 1995; Griffiths, 1959; Halpin,
1968). A strong belief shared at the time was that infusing these theories into practice was essential for improving practice and raising professional status, and Hills
was considered by many to be the leading authority in educational administration on
the work of Talcott Parsons. Hills was intimately familiar with the many prominent
theories of the day and was a participant in what was called the "Theory-Research
Movement" in educational administration. Even so, following his sabbatical he realized that discipline-based theory is not enough and championed a focus on problems of practice.

Kennedy (1987), in her seminal article on the acquisition of expertise, pointed out
that a great difficulty with the theory-research approach to preparation lay in the
transfer of knowledge. Most fields that used the theory-research approach relied on
extensive internships to connect theory and practice, but the transfer often remained
incomplete. This is exactly what Hills (1978) determined.

Much later, Donmoyer (1999) arrived at much the same conclusion as Hills
(1978) and advocated that knowledge should be judged by the criterion of utility, not
its source in social or behavioral science. To this end, Kennedy (1987) developed a
typology to show how knowledge can be used as the basis of "deliberation," the
process of creating mental models and assessing the consequences of various alternatives before they are implemented.

AN EXPANDED VIEW OF A PROFESSIONAL KNOWLEDGE BASE

Taking Hills's (1978) position that knowledge should be organized narrowly around
problems of practice as a starting point, we contend that practitioners depend (and
must depend) on an eclectic knowledge base. Using this base, they want useful
knowledge, knowledge that will help them lead a school community toward increased student learning. Although the criterion of utility is now gaining currency in
educational administration, men and women of philosophy and science have written
extensively about utility and personal ownership of knowledge for a long time. See,
for example, Polanyi (1962), *The Tacit Dimension*, and Lindblom and Cohen (1979),
Usable Knowledge.

Five important components that undergird this eclectic knowledge base are critical to principal decision-making: ethical and critical reasoning, legal reasoning, social science research, ordinary or craft knowledge, and personal knowledge. These
bases of knowledge are listed and briefly defined in Table 1.

Table 1.   An Expanded, Eclectic Knowledge Base

Knowledge Base	Definition
Ethical and Critical Reasoning	Ethical and critical reasoning is an important part of the knowledge base for school principals. Principals are expected to do the right and the good thing and be able to negotiate conflicting community values (see Heifitz, 1994, *Adaptive Leadership*). Ethical reasoning provides the basis. Education's importance in today's diverse and complex world makes it a place where values intersect and conflict. For instance, education is the path toward upward mobility—yet schools as institutions are expected to preserve social privilege in many communities. Curriculum and instructional methods have value overtones. Ethical reasoning seems to have grown in significance as the authority of science has diminished. Nearly all standards for principals and administrators call for knowledge about ethics and ethical reasoning (see, for example, the Colorado Standards for Principals and Administrators).
Legal Reasoning	Laws that empower and constrain principals come from many sources: constitutions, statutes, administrative law, local board policy decisions, and common law (Valente & Valente, 2001). The law reflects judgment—the political consensus of policy makers and the accumulated wisdom or incremental consensus over time of judges (Polanyi, 1962). School administrators are public officials whose duties and authority are assigned civilly. They are always limited by and accountable within a legal framework. Legal reasoning deals with more than constraints, however. It is the basis of justice and the protection and promotion of rights.
Social Science Research	Research from the social and behavioral sciences has been the "go to" source for definitive information teaching and learning, leadership, and organization. Dewey wanted teachers to be trained in "laboratory" rather than "apprenticeship" settings because he believed that they would internalize the latest scientific knowledge (Shulman, 1998). Griffiths (1959) wrote that educational administration needed to focus on the development and use of rigorous, theory-based research and made it clear that qualitative and action-research approaches did not count. By 1991, he had changed his view and was accepting of a much wider scope of methods (Griffiths, 1991). Griffith's transformation reflects the field. Now, we have pretty broad agreement that many approaches can yield useful knowledge.
	Despite the broadening of the list of legitimate social science methods, one cannot doubt that much of the knowledge which undergirds practice will come from this source. The NRC recently advocated that schools use scientifically based practices. That admonition has found its way into the recent ESEA reauthorization language.Craft or Ordinary Knowledge. Few doubt that principals often base their actions on the

(continued)

Table 1.   An Expanded, Eclectic Knowledge Base (*Continued*)

Knowledge Base	Definition
	knowledge and beliefs common to the field. Lindblom and Cohen (1979) observe that social problem solvers rely much more on "ordinary knowledge" for the solution of problems than on social science research. Merton (1959) came to the same conclusion, but for a different reason. By ordinary knowledge Lindblom and Cohen mean knowledge that derives from "common sense, casual empiricism or thoughtful speculation and analysis" (p. 12). While we use the term craft knowledge, we mean the ordinary knowledge of principals. Craft or ordinary knowledge seems to be what is called clinical knowledge in medicine and other professions. Hills (1978) observed that medicine made great strides when efforts were made to codify and organize the ordinary or craft knowledge base of doctors.
Personal Knowledge	Here we take our cue from Polanyi (1962) whose influential book, *Personal Knowledge*, introduces the importance of tacit knowledge or inarticulate knowledge in acts of problem solving. Psychologists have long been interested in how people operate on knowledge that they cannot articulate. Clearly, principals operate on personal or tacit knowledge in the solution of problems they face. Although it is discouraged, some believe that this may be fundamental to principal behavior. Another view of personal knowledge comes from organizational economists. House (1998), in *Schools for Sale*, points out that teachers (and presumably principals) build a set of "specific assets" which includes knowledge and skills that they acquire to do the job well. This is personal knowledge as we mean it here in that principals invest in acquiring these assets and they are not easily transferred to others without loss of value.

How Accomplishments Vitalize Useful Knowledge

An eclectic knowledge base alone is insufficient for a principal to lead a school community toward greatness. First, each school is unique and the mix of knowledge that is useful varies from place to place. Second, principals need some way to organize and prioritize the vast array of knowledge contained in this eclectic knowledge base. Hills (1978) claimed that knowledge should be organized around problems of practice. To most, problems of practice—those often pesky situations that take up so much time and require principal intervention—refer to the daily issues with which a principal deals. While these problems are important and no principal could survive for long without managing them effectively, we contend that principals must solve daily problems within a framework of larger accomplishments. The accomplishments selected for action should derive from careful study of a school's data and needs and a deep understanding of what can and should be done to raise student learning to higher levels.

Rather than focusing on "micro problems" of daily school operations (Spillane, Halverson, & Diamond, 2001), the accomplishment perspective reframes the challenges of practice to create conditions and results that support the efforts of students, staff, and parents. To establish and sustain these conditions, school leaders work over more extended periods, selecting problems for attention and deciding what might constitute a solution (Robinson, 1996), all the time balancing and focusing the school to improve some accomplishments while sustaining others. This long-term process can be conceptualized usefully in the annual cycle that characterizes much of the work of a school.

The focus on accomplishments also points to the need for comprehensive knowledge. School leaders respond one way or another to the challenges that they face, sometimes drawing on formal knowledge, but using whatever information is available to guide their work. Because research and theory are necessarily incomplete in relation to the challenges that principals face (Lindblom & Cohen, 1979), craft knowledge assumes particular importance in the effort to organize the profession's knowledge around school accomplishments. Given that both craft knowledge and personal knowledge are critical to effective principal practice, the question is how the perspectives of Hills (1978) and others can be realized such that this knowledge can be codified, shared, and used effectively in practice and in preparation.

AN ANNUAL-CYCLE APPROACH TO SCHOOL IMPROVEMENT

Annual processes for school improvement planning and accountability are familiar parts of school leaders' roles. District policies and state legislation have required annual planning for some time, and annual testing requirements of the federal No Child Left Behind Act foreshadow an even greater emphasis on annual planning for school change. Like many external mandates, annual-school-improvement processes can easily become matters of bureaucratic compliance. While exceptional leadership may be required for annual plans to be an integral part of a school's priorities and culture, the possibility clearly exists to frame important school changes and support the development of strong school communities in the context of these annual planning processes (Bellamy, Holly, & Sinisi, 1999). In fact, whatever its relationship to formally required plans, school improvement generally is an annual processes, bookended by prior success and failures and future expectations.

Viewing the work of school leaders as accomplishments and framing an instance of principals' work as an annual cycle in the life of a school has two potential benefits for the formal and informal processes of school improvement. As we discuss below, these perspectives first suggest a way of thinking about principals' work that recognizes its complexity while simplifying its structure enough for analysis and reflection. An orientation to the annual cycle helps to frame the separate domains of leadership within which the principal operates as well as the ways that those separate domains can form a coherent annual picture of school leadership. Second, an annual-cycle approach structures a natural time for documentation, reflection, and collegial interaction between school years, at a time when this is feasible in the incredibly busy lives of principals.

Connecting the Dots of Principal Leadership

Daily life in the principalship involves responding to a constant stream of problems and issues—and defining some other things as problems because they block paths to important school goals. Problems are rapid-fire, complex, and messy; solutions require judgment, moral choices, and sensitivity to the interests of many different local constituents. However, problems are always solved in an effort to achieve larger purposes: creating school conditions that promote student learning. And of course, those conditions have different importance in different settings. In addition to keeping the goals in mind as daily problems are encountered, principals must be "master diagnosticians" who identify which aspects of a school most need improvement at any given time (Portin, Schneider, DeArmond, & Gundlach, 2003).

To influence the context in which problems are identified and to solve those problems in ways that move the school toward its goals, principals exercise leadership in three different but related domains. *Leadership for sustainable purposes* requires a principal to understand the competing values and priorities within a school's community, find a working balance among these views, and lead discussions that sharpen and develop sustainable commitments to school purposes. *Leadership for strategic focus* engages the principal in issues of what to emphasize to achieve school purposes. In this domain, a principal's challenge is to focus the school on those accomplishments that have the greatest potential for improving student learning. *Leadership for effective action* is day-to-day problem solving. Here, a principal's challenges are to determine which problems should receive attention, what results are desired, what actions would most likely produce these results, and how to mobilize others to act.

An annual view of how these three domains of leadership interact can improve practice because effectiveness in each leadership domain depends on the others. Figure 2 illustrates these connections. The annual cycle of school leadership begins well before school begins as a principal (working in the domain of sustainable purposes) frames an understanding of a community's priorities and values and uses this information to make decisions about local criteria for quality in student learning and school accomplishments. The principal and other school leaders work simultaneously in the domain of strategic focus, making sense of annual student learning data, evaluating various aspects of the school's functioning (how well it is doing on the various accomplishments), and setting goals or priorities for the year. Structural changes to implement the goals at the start of the year are followed by the ongoing process of selecting and solving problems in ways that move the school toward its goals. The same problems serve as the basis for conversations during the year, to increase participation, commitment, and clarity in the school's goals and in the entire community to increase participation, commitment, and clarity associated with the school's purposes. Annual measures of student learning provide a way to assess the school's strategies and successes at the end of the year and begin planning for the next cycle. Whether or not one uses an accomplishment perspective for analyzing the details of these parts of a school's annual cycle of operations and improvement, the annual-cycle structure can provide a way of identifying important components and highlighting their relationship to each other.

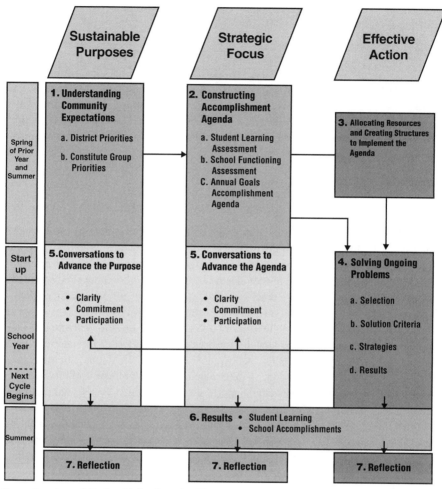

Figure 2. Annual Cycle of School Leadership

A Time for Documentation and Reflection

The annual cycle also emphasizes what is done between school years—preparing the case, evaluating results, reflecting on what did and did not work, and planning for the future. While it is easy to argue from a distance that this analysis and reflection should be ongoing aspects of any leader's work, the constant press of daily issues in schools makes time for reflection a real luxury for most principals (Public School Forum of North Carolina, 1987). The summer between school years is a natural time for such work. It recognizes the longer time frames that are involved in some of the most important aspects of principals' roles—those involved with establishing the cultural and organizational context within which daily work occurs. Using summer months to prepare, share, and reflect on annual outcomes might well bring coherence to the many different processes for school planning, data analysis, and principal evaluation that typically occur between school years.

USING AN ANNUAL-CASE METHOD FOR CODIFYING PRACTICE-BASED KNOWLEDGE

Developing a readily usable practice-based knowledge base is not an easy task, and current efforts to gather cases (cf. UCEA, 2003) as teaching tools fall short of the needs of principals in the field. They do so because they tend to be a-contextual, limited in scope, and representative of specific problems which ordinarily are not generalizable. The annual case, as outlined here, takes the annual cycle of events in a school—and thus a principal's time frame—as the unit of analysis instead of specific, isolated problems.

Benefits

Cases that focus on the annual cycle of professional actions and results have several benefits. First, they can extend the profession's knowledge base through the explicit inclusion and honoring of practitioner knowledge as a source of important information. Second, such cases of professional action can provide hypotheses and questions for social science research, helping to bridge the gap between practitioner knowledge and more formal research results. For example, in medical fields cases serve as the accumulated "professional text" which confirms or questions treatment prescriptions. Third, these "professional cases" can facilitate leadership succession in schools. For instance, case notes in law are so standardized that attorneys can quickly learn the background of a case when transfer of responsibility occurs. Fourth, professional case notes can support communication with a school administrator's many constituencies just as case notes in architecture (plans and models) help regulators, clients, neighbors, and others envision what is planned and what its impact might be. Finally, professional cases serve as bases for professional learning and development. While professional cases often are quite different from teaching cases, case development and sharing can provide insights about decision processes in schools and their short- and long-term effectiveness.

Requirements for Useful Professional Cases

To serve these many purposes, professional cases should meet several standards:

1. be public, sharable, and stored for access by others (Hiebert et al., 2002)
2. reflect a useful unit of analysis of the profession's work (Hiebert et al., 2002)
3. provide sufficient description of context to facilitate analyses and comparisons across cases
4. support sharing critical, ethical, and legal reasoning as well as procedural knowledge

For the principalship, an annual case of a year in the life of a school appears to meet these criteria, and the annual cycle of schooling appears to be the most relevant time span in which to conceptualize and act on problems of practice faced by school principals. In this time frame, day-to-day problem solving can be contextualized both in the macro-variations that affect the course of schooling during a school year and within the Framework for School Leadership Accomplishments (FSLA). The FSLA provides a convenient set of categories for organizing knowledge, actions, and outcome evaluations in a continuous, reciprocal stream that builds on prior years toward coming years. The annual-case method or process is a means by which the annual cycle can be organized and appreciated as well as a means of continuous data collection across multiple sites, events, and years to improve knowledge *of*, *in*, and *for* practice (Jenlink, 2001).

The Annual Case
The annual case is based on the annual cycle of school leadership, and this annual cycle of events, aimed at improving practices and outcomes in a school given a particular year's problems of practice, is directly related to longer-term issues that extend beyond any single year's boundaries. Each selected accomplishment is composed of micro-problems, each of which must be addressed for the larger, longer-term outcomes to be achieved. Further, the purposes a school serves—both those valued by the public and those pursued by private interests (Bellamy et al., in preparation)—are a significant part of the context of practice and school improvement.

Within these multiple contexts, the types of knowledge needed to address school problems, the framework in which they are lodged, and the array of school purposes provide heuristics for selecting and bounding problems annually. The annual cycle generally works well, too, because the annual calendar for most schools provides natural beginning, ending, and reassessment periods. Each year, then, is a substantive "case history" in the continuous improvement and renewal cycle through which schools proceed annually.

The Annual Case and Preparation for the Next Cycle
Clearly, the annual-case process is ongoing. One year's case provides a foundation for the next, and planning for the next requires analysis of data, plans, and results from past cases. Each year, then, is a successive approximation of the idealized state that a school's leadership and the school's community desires for the children who attend the school over time.

Developing Processes
How one engages in preparing an annual case will vary from school to school, based largely on the leadership of the principal, the experience and capacity of the staff, the expectations of the community, the resources available, and the nature of the students. Whatever the varying conditions—the public and private purposes; the level of achievement of a school currently and over time; or the types, quality, or abundance of resources accessible—explicit and consistent processes for data collection, planning, community involvement, feedback processes, and the like are

fundamental to successful, continuous improvements in student learning. An initial outline of a case format might include some of the following information:

1. location and participation information (who has been involved)
2. the year of the case (for context across comparisons)
3. characteristics of the community (for local context)
4. a list of the defined accomplishments pursued during the case year
5. the success criteria developed for each accomplishment to specify the quality-performance indicators
6. the important problems addressed
7. the data collected, the ways in which they were collected, and the methods used to analyze them
8. the results that attended each accomplishment
9. plans for the next annual cycle
10. a list of documents that support the annual-case process

Doing Action Research
Action research (Stringer, 1996) is the logical methodology for most school-based, data-collection processes. While action research has gained credence in the last decade or so as a legitimate way to understand schools and schooling processes, it still remains a "second fiddle" in the orchestra of research in university settings. This is not so, however, in settings where more formal and often slow research processes need to give way to the press for quick, useful, and targeted information that can lead to immediate improvements in classroom learning.

Key to effective action research in gathering data for an annual case is participation, collaboration, and observation. In particular, action research is more likely to be implemented if those involved in the change process also are involved in the research and decision making based on the research. In this regard, action research facilitates "action learning" (McGill & Beaty, 1995; Morley, 1989), a process through which close collaboration among the "researchers" and the "researched" builds learning-based relations that are mutually respectful and trusting (Rehm & Muth, 1998). Ideally, the subjects of action research become partners in intentional change that is specific and local. In schools, this means that students, most often the subject of action research, themselves would become knowledgeable participants in the action-learning process as would teachers and other stakeholders.

Analyzing a School
The development of sound cases that have use beyond their immediate environment requires full disclosure of contextual information, starting with the characteristics of the community and the school. This context should include local support and expectations, nature of staff, and so forth. Further, how the school functions—what works and what does not—needs to be examined carefully.

Selecting Types of Data

A good case marshals student data from the past through the present to establish comparative bases for future efforts and improvements. The types of data needed in any year depends heavily on the type of accomplishments selected for an upcoming year. While data sources may vary by district or state, organizing them according to the Framework for School Leadership (FSLA) would facilitate analyses while adding to knowledge of practice in consistent ways.

Recording and Displaying School and Community Characteristics

As a principal and school-leadership team begins a school-level analysis, the initial goal is to determine how to adjust the school's emphasis on the purposes of public education. For instance, what community characteristics and politics require a strong emphasis on education for school safety, economic participation, and so on? What values are associated with the various purposes important to the community? Which stakeholders are most invested in these values, and what assets do they have that can assist—or impede—the school in achieving its goals?

Questions for Case Analysis

1. How is the community served by the school, including its economic, linguistic, and ethnic demographics and its population changes?
2. What patterns in the community's political activism are related to education, and how do these patterns establish conditions or constraints on the school's actions?
3. Do particular orientations at the district level emphasize some purposes and values above others?
4. Which values held for the role of public schools by the public require special attention?

Beginning the Process

The following questions can help develop a rich description of the principal's annual process of setting goals for improving learning.

Questions for Rich Description

1. What has been the learning and achievement of the students served by the school?
2. What are the results of analyses and the disaggregation of statewide and other testing data?
3. In what groups, ages of students, and subject areas is the school succeeding?
4. Where are the problems and achievement gaps?
5. What needs to be done?
6. What action strategies are possible?
7. Who should be involved to what ends?
8. How can it all get done?

Developing an Agenda

As responses to such questions determine a principal's agenda, they establish bases for school improvement that take into account community characteristics and preferences. The focus becomes what should be changed to achieve the student learning (and other goals) for the school.

Questions for School Improvement

1. Using the components of the FSLA as an outline, what does the beginning-of-the-year evaluation say about the school's strengths and weaknesses?
2. What criteria are necessary to decide which areas were strong and which were weak?
3. What is the agenda for change during the year, and which aspects of the FSLA need to be targeted for improvement in the coming year?
4. Why are the accomplishment areas chosen the most important points to attack?

Implementing an Agenda

During the year, the principal and the school's leadership team will handle many critical problems that advance or threaten the annual agenda. To contextualize these action issues, a principal could analyze problems during the year that provide a particular opportunity or challenge to the school's improvement agenda.

Questions for Problem Analysis

1. Why was this problem important?
2. How was the problem defined?
3. What constraints (solution requirements, objectives) were used to define the outcome needed to resolve the problem?
4. What strategies were used to act on the problem?
5. What happened?
6. How did the result advance or retard the agenda?
7. What were the unanticipated consequences on other aspects of the school?

Ending the Process

Especially in schools, all good things must come to an end—in order to being anew. The annual-case process provides data and perceptions on what changed during the year related to both the annual agenda and specific goals for student learning.

Questions for Concluding the Annual Case

1. What were the student-learning results for the year?
2. What progress was made on the goals identified at the beginning of the year?
3. What new problems are apparent that now need to be addressed?
4. What evidence shows progress on the agenda?

5. Did accomplishments selected for improvement actually change outcomes for the better?

Getting Ready for Next Year
Finally, the annual-case process provides the opportunity for a principal to reflect on what was learned from the year and consider how that learning might lead to different leadership, management, and action strategies during the next year.

Questions for Reflecting on the Annual Case

1. Looking back on the year, what was learned about setting goals, developing an agenda, selecting problems for attention, establishing solution constraints (Robinson, 1996), or choosing action and leadership strategies?
2. What kinds of events or problems can the school now anticipate that it did not anticipate before?
3. Who else should be involved?
4. What should be done differently—and how?

When such questions are detailed satisfactorily, a final case can be written and "published" with appropriate privacy safeguards as a historical record, an assessment of progress, a foundation for decisions for the coming year, and a sample for distribution to other principals and preparation programs. Also, the case could be archived online, again with the appropriate safeguards, for student and faculty use and distributed through workshops as a "learning case" for professional development and practice improvement.

Reflecting on Accomplishments and Practice
Integral to the annual-case process is reflection on what is being learned, how, and to what ends. Such reflections can be facilitated in multiple ways to assist principals and aspiring principals to become deliberative practitioners (Kennedy, 1987). The first way of encouraging reflection is through the case analysis process in which principals—and others—are asked to analyze their role in the case process, think critically about the consequences of their actions, and ask questions about alternatives and their likely outcomes and effects. These reflections can be developed as journal entries, as part of the regular debriefing process, and as part of the case-writing process.

The Multiple Uses of Annual Cases
Annual cases can serve multiple ends, all of which cry for the systematic development of craft or practice-based knowledge. In particular, the annual case can provide principals and staff an annual process for systematically, regularly, and continually examining goals, trends, and outcomes to refine plans, practices and results. Such cases can, as well, systematically gather data in a common framework that can be used for professional development and preservice preparation. Further, annual cases

can provide researchers in educational administration with a ready supply of authentic practice settings that are at once more complex, contextual, and complete than most cases currently available for teaching (cf. Ashbaugh & Kasten, 1991; Snowden & Gorton, 1998). Moreover, researchers can do cross-case analyses to develop theory based in successful practices. Finally, such cases can be used to strengthen the overall knowledge base in educational administration, adding over time a potentially vast body of practice-based knowledge to the field's already strong knowledge bases in social science, ethics, critical-reasoning, and law.

Generating and Codifying Knowledge

Systematically undertaken with a common structure, annual cases can provide a consistent framework for developing, collecting, and codifying practice-based craft knowledge. While case texts abound (Ashbaugh & Kasten, 1991; UCEA, 2003; Snowden & Gorton, 1998), the range and types of data are limited and the specifications for what constitutes a "case" are inconsistent and sparse. One purpose of the annual-case process is to provide explicit and systematic procedures for gathering and organizing data about decision processes and outcomes in schools. This also makes comparisons possible across schools and districts to support the continuous enhancement of practice-based knowledge about effective practice.

Eventually, members of the educational administration research community might want to determine the types of assessments necessary to establish whether particular practices are successful in specific situations. Data from systematically organized annual cases could provide researchers with cross-case data that could lead to multiple insights about practice.

Dissemination of Cases: Supporting Principals and Aspiring Administrators

The University Council for Educational Administration has developed an online journal of cases, *The Journal of Cases in Educational Leadership*, designed to articulate current issues for school leadership preparation (UCEA, 2003). Annual cases, developed by practitioners, practitioners with students, and practitioners and university faculty, could serve similar purposes. In addition, annual cases also could become a source of professional-development activities for principals and other school leaders in and across school districts, a means of developing insights about practice and generalizations across cases, and a way of developing and codifying craft knowledge. It is this last development that we see as most germane to the improvement of professional-leadership practice in schools. Currently, rich practice-based knowledge is simply not available systematically to practitioners, to those who study practice, or to those who prepare or are preparing to be future practitioners.

A Note on "Case Teams"

It is well recognized that principals are busy people, immersed in often frenetic activities in pursuit of success for children and youth in schools. To ask them to add one more task to their already overloaded plate is, perhaps, folly. Yet, if the annual-case process were embedded in expectations for school improvement, used to assess school and principal performance, and viewed as a means of continuous reflective practice, then it is likely that the annual-case process would become part of the "normal" expectations for principal work. To facilitate such a culture change, case teams—composed of faculty, doctoral students, and preservice students—might work with practicing principals to implement the annual-case process over time. Each case team might have a case manager, and students in preparation would be expected to work closely with the principal, developing the case over the course of the year, and adding the results to the students' portfolio. Doctoral students might evolve dissertation topics that both satisfy their program requirements and help accumulate data about effective practice.

A case team could meet periodically with a principal to work through the design, implementation, and assessment processes necessary to install the processes to support the work of the principal and the school's leadership team while facilitating the continuous improvement of student learning. Initially, the team could simply debrief the principal, seeking data about a school's successes and challenges while assisting the principal in developing plans to address current problems as well as those on the horizon. The team could also develop with the principal ways to collect and process data that speak to the problems, eventually contextualizing them in a longer time frame and within a larger framework. Preliminary case write-ups could be discussed and critiqued regularly as part of case-team visits out of which consistent procedures for data collection and analysis, the involvement of relevant stakeholders, and the development of an annual accomplishment agenda might emerge.

Accomplishments to be pursued could be selected by the principal with the team according to success criteria important to the school at that time, and success criteria could be established initially according to known or desired practices. The processes could be broadened to include other constituents over time as the principal and school become comfortable with the processes and find the outcomes useful for involving a school's leadership team and faculty in problem solving for improving student engagement and learning.

USING THE ANNUAL-CASE METHOD TO PREPARE SCHOOL LEADERS

Engaging preservice students in authentic work with practicing principals through the annual-case process could only add to the capacity of future principals to understand and anticipate the problems of practice that they will have to address in their leadership roles. Reading cases, helping to write one as part of a team working with a school, and analyzing cases across similar problems to determine successful practices would add significantly to the authenticity of the principal-preparation experience.

Uses of Cases

For over a hundred years, cases have been used to bridge the theory-practice gap in law, business, and medicine (Ashbaugh & Kasten, 1991). In the 1940s, cases were used to "relate concepts and theories to the practice of administration" (p. 3) by describing administrative situations that commonly involve a decision or problem

(Erskine, Leenders, & Mauffette-Leenders, 1981). They can be used additionally to help students develop skills in critical thinking, problem solving, decision making, and reflective practice as well as for research, evaluation, or policy analysis (Kowalski, 1991, 1995). Kowalski distinguishes the *case method* as the use of cases as a teaching method, and several texts have been published for this purpose (Ashbaugh & Kasten, 1991; Hanson, 2000; Kirschmann, 1995; Konya Weishaar & Borsa, 2000; Kowalski, 1991, 1995, 2002; Merseth, 1997). The electronic journal, *Journal of Cases in Educational Leadership,* published by UCEA, is comprised entirely of teaching cases.

Today, most case-teaching and problem-based-learning approaches in principal education deal with micro-level problems (Spillane, Halverson, & Diamond, 2001), generally without information about the macro-level context. While these micro-cases may help principals lead single-loop learning in their schools, cases that address the broader issues in annual planning should produce the double-loop learning that is fundamental to organizational learning and change (Argyris, 1982).

One of the benefits of the FSLA and the accomplishment perspective is the use in preparation programs of annual cases developed by and with practicing principals. For us, the annual case is more than a leadership tool. It represents a "defining component of practice" (Spillane, Halverson, & Diamond, 2001, p. 26) that guides the principal in linking the *macro functions* and the *micro tasks* of school leadership. As such, the annual case is an essential element for developing knowledge and facilitating knowledge acquisition in preparation programs so that principals can use the FSLA (or another inclusive model) and become accomplishment-minded principals. Thus, the annual case could serve learners in three important ways: as content, as protocol, and as a defining component of professional practice.

The Annual Case as Content
The annual case could be introduced to students first as content. Students could study annual cases to learn about the work of the principal, the annual cycle in which it occurs, the yearly goals established by the principal, the key components targeted and strategies selected for improvement in educational outcomes, and the type of data that justifies those decision and provides evidence of goal achievement and agenda completion.

The Annual Case as Protocol
In addition, the annual case could be a protocol, a format, a series of steps, or a process used by students to get an intimate perspective on planning processes that principals use to prepare annual agendas for their practice. Working in groups, students could support a principal in preparing an annual case using the annual-case format. Students could interview, collect data, and write the text required for construction of the annual case. Such work would contribute to the creation of an annual agenda with and for the specific school and the upcoming year and becomes the source of continuing conversations between the students and the principal about practice. In this process, students would gain skills in using the format to

identify goals, select improvement strategies, and collect evidence-bearing data for the strategies implemented.

The Annual Case as Defining Component of Practice

Finally, after acquiring the knowledge and skills embodied in the preceding stages, students would come to understand the annual case as a framework for reflective practice, school improvement, and professional development. The following steps and stages could be used to introduce principal candidates to the annual case format.

1. View the scope and sequence of their work in the time frame of the annual cycle
2. Capitalize on the structure of the FSLA to organize and prioritize the elements of an annual agenda based on focused analysis of relevant school data
3. Appreciate the power that local community values and purposes have over the success or failure of an annual agenda by comparing and contrasting distinctive annual cases and the choices made by principals and the consequences
4. Learn the structure of the annual case format by first reading annual cases written by expert principals
5. Ease into annual-case writing by working with other principal candidates and a principal to record the process of determining annual goals and micro-tasks to achieve those goals, collecting and constructing the body of evidence required for the assessment, reflection, evaluation, and inevitable repurposing for the next cycle
6. Engage in dialog with university faculty, clinical faculty, and student colleagues about critical tension points in the annual case, decisions made or not pursued, any misreading of community values or purposes, or any displacement of primary goals with those less importance
7. Engage in critiquing annual cases and proposing changes in specific elements in annual agendas, yearly goals, or reanalysis of data
8. Adopt the annual case format as a defining component of their professional practice

By reading and critiquing existing cases, by working with principals to develop annual agendas, and by writing or participating in the writing of several annual cases, prospective principals can develop the generalized skills needed for leadership in constantly changing school circumstances. In addition, they can develop the reflective skills that support continuous learning from practice and analyze and apply such experiences in the larger context of the cases and the need for improvement of learning outcomes for all students.

SOME NEXT STEPS

While the FSLA and the annual case provide two means for reorganizing the knowledge base in educational administration and facilitating its use in professional development at all levels, they also provide new ways to organize, think about, and conduct research on practice. The FSLA, the types of principal leadership, and the annual case discussed here also suggest that, by using systematic processes for school improvement, the field and practice of educational administration can be professionalized and schools can ensure that all children learn and succeed.

REFERENCES

Argyris, C. (1982). How learning and reasoning processes affect organizational change. In P. Goodman & Associates (Eds.), *Change in organizations: New perspectives on theory, research, and practice.* San Francisco: Jossey-Bass.

Ashbaugh, C. R., & Kasten, K. L. (1991). *Educational leadership: Case studies for reflective practice.* New York, Longman.

Bellamy, T., Fulmer, C., Murphy, M., & Muth, R. (in preparation). Reshaping the principalship: Knowledge, practice, and preparation.

Bellamy, T., Holly, P., & Sinisi, R. (1999). *Cycles of school improvement.* Oxford, OH: National Staff Development Council.

Culbertson, J. (1964). The preparation of administrators. In. D. E. Griffiths (Ed.), *Behavioral science and educational administration.* 63rd Yearbook of the National Society for the Study of Education, Part II (pp. 303–330). Chicago: University of Chicago Press.

Culbertson, J. (1995). *Building bridges: UCEA's first two decades.* University Park, PA: University Council for Educational Administration.

Donmoyer, R. (1999). The continuing quest for a knowledge base:1976–1998. In J. Murphy & K. Louis (Eds.), *Handbook of research on educational administration* (2nd ed., pp. 25–43). San Francisco: Jossey-Bass.

Erskine, J., Leenders, M., & Mauffette-Leenders, L. (1981). *Teaching with cases.* London, Ontario: School of Business Administration, University of Western Ontario.

Gilbert, T. (1978). *Human competence.* New York: McGraw-Hill.

Griffiths, D. E. (1959). *Administrative theory.* New York: Appleton-Century-Crofts.

Griffiths, D. E. (1991). Special Issue: Nontraditional theory and research. *Educational Administrative Quarterly, 27*(3).

Halpin, A. (1968). The development of theory in educational administration. In A. Halpin (Ed.), *Administrative theory in education.* New York: Macmillan.

Hanson, K. L. (2000). *Preparing for educational administration using case analysis.* New York: Pearson Education.

Heifetz, R. A. (1994). *Leadership without easy answers.* Cambridge, MA: Harvard University Press.

Hiebert, J., Gilmore, R., & Stigler, J. (2002). A knowledge base for the teaching profession: What would it look like and how can we get one? *Educational Researcher, 31*(5), 3–15.

Hess, F. (2003). *A license to lead? A new leadership agenda for America's schools.* Washington, DC: Progressive Policy Institute.

Hills, J. (1978). Problems in the production and utilization of knowledge in educational administration. *Educational Administration Quarterly, 14*(1), 1–12.

House, E. R. (1998). *Schools for sale: Why free market policies won't improve America's schools, and what will.* New York: Teachers College Press.

Hoy, W. (Ed.). (1994). *PRIMUS: The University Council of Educational Administration document base.* New York: McGraw-Hill.

Jenlink, P. M. (2001). Beyond the knowledge base controversy: Advancing the ideal of scholar practitioner leadership. In T. J. Kowalski & G. Perreault (Eds.), *21st century challenges for educational administration* (pp. 65–88). Lanham, MD: Scarecrow Press.

Kennedy, M. M. (1987). Inexact sciences: Professional education and the development of expertise. In F. I. Last (Ed.), *Review of Research in Education, 14* (pp. 133–167). Washington, DC: American Educational Research Association.

Kirschmann, R. E. (1995). *Educational administration: A collection of case studies.* Englewood Cliffs, NJ: Prentice Hall.

Konya Weishaar, M. E., & Borsa, J. C. (2000). *Inclusive educational administration: A case study approach.* New York: McGraw Hill.

Kowalski, T. J. (1991). *Case studies in educational administration.* New York: Longman.

Kowalski, T. J. (1995). *Case studies in educational administration* (2nd ed.). New York: Longman.

Kowalski, T. J. (2002). *Case studies in educational administration* (3rd ed.). New York: Pearson Education.

Lindblom, C. E., & Cohen, D. K. (1979). *Usable knowledge: Social science and social problem solving.* New Haven, CT: Yale University Press.

Merseth, K. K., (1997). *Cases in educational administration.* Boston: Allyn & Bacon.

McGill, I., & Beaty, L. (1995). *Action learning: A guide for professional, management and educational development* (2nd ed.). London: Kogan Page.

Merton, R. K. (1959). *Social theory and social structure.* London: Free Press.

Morley, D. (1989). Frameworks for organizational change: Towards action learning in global environments. In S. Wright & D. Morley (Eds.), *Learning works: Searching for organizational futures* (pp. 163–190). Toronto: ABL Group, Faculty of Environmental Studies, York University.

Polanyi, M. (1962). *Personal knowledge: Towards a post-critical philosophy.* Chicago: University of Chicago Press.

Portin, B., Schneider, P., DeArmond, M., & Gundlach, L. (2003). *Making sense of leading schools: A study of the school principalship.* Seattle: University of Washington, Center on Reinventing Public Education. Retrieved October 1, 2003, from http://crpe.org/pubs.shtml#leadership

Public School Forum of North Carolina. (1987). *The condition of being an educator: An analysis of North Carolina's public schools.* Raleigh: Public School Forum of North Carolina.

Rehm, R., & Muth, R. (1998). Toward a theory of problem-based learning for the preparation of educational administrators. In R. Muth & M. Martin (Eds.), *Toward the year 2000: Leadership for quality schools. Sixth Annual Yearbook of the National Council of Professors of Educational Administration* (pp. 289–299). Lancaster, PA: Technomic.

Robinson, V. M. (1996). Problem-based methodology and administrative practice. *Educational Administration Quarterly, 32*(3), 427–451.

Shulman, L. S. (1998). Theory, practice, and the education of professionals. *The Elementary School Journal, 98*(5), 511–527.

Snowden, P. E., & Gorton, R. A. (1998). *School leadership and administration: Important concepts, case studies and simulations* (5th ed.). New York: McGraw Hill.

Spillane, J. P., Halverson, R., & Diamond, J. B. (2001). Investigating school leadership practice: A distributed perspective. *Educational Researcher, 30*(3), 23–28.

Stringer, E. T. (1996). *Action research: A handbook for practitioners.* Thousand Oaks, CA: Sage.

Thompson, S. (Ed.) (1993). *Principals for our changing schools: Knowledge and skill base.* Lancaster, PA: Technomic.

UCEA (2003). *UCEA Review, 45*(2), 1–2.

Valente, W., and Valente, C. (2001). *Law in the schools.* Upper Saddle River, NJ: Merrill Prentice Hall.

Leading from below the Surface: Expanding the Knowledge Base in Educational Administration

Theodore Creighton

When we think of great effective leaders, names like John Kennedy, Golda Meir, Colin Powell, Margaret Thatcher, and Martin Luther King come to mind. In education, we all can think of a few nationally known figures who are credited with strong educational leadership. Some lead our large urban districts (e.g., former Governor Roy Romer in Los Angeles) and still others are recognized as national policy makers (e.g., Secretary of Education Rod Paige). Certainly a few former U.S. secretaries and assistant secretaries of education should join this prestigious list: Diane Ravitch and William Bennett. These truly great educational leaders can be counted on two hands, but what of the majority of men and women leading our schools today? When looking closely, we realize that today's effective principals and superintendents do not fit the stereotype of courageous, risk-taking, charismatic, and dynamic individuals. I argue that the effective school principal is not highly visible, is not nationally recognized, charismatic, or necessarily out in front of the organization. Don't misunderstand me: some are and they are truly valued in our educational arena. But many of our effective principals are modest and unassuming. They aren't charismatic, but effectively lead schools in a quiet and low-key manner. What does this other low-key, quiet leader look like?

I must admit, that much of my position is based on the recent book of Joseph Badaracco (2002), *Leading Quietly*. As sometimes happens, we run across the writing of a great author, and we say, "That's exactly what I have been trying to say." This has been the case with my exposure to *Leading Quietly*. Though Badaracco talks about leadership in the corporate world, I argue the same is true in situations requiring effective school leadership. Badaracco helped me understand that true leadership is not grand or heroic: It occurs in small steps by people guided by humility, practicality, and common sense. They have the ability to look well below what we see on the surface.

Theodore Creighton, Sam Houston State University

Badaracco (2002), in his unorthodox guide to effective leadership, *Leading Quietly*, points to the great Albert Schweitzer as a person who changed many lives and inspired countless others. Schweitzer wrote these words in his autobiography addressing the role of great individuals reshaping the world:

> Of all the will toward the ideal in mankind, only a small part can manifest itself in public action. All the rest of this force must be content with small and obscure deeds. The sum of these, however, is a thousand times stronger than the acts of those who receive wide public recognition. The latter, compared to the former, are like foam on the waves of a deep ocean. (Schweitzer, 1963, p. 74)

Badaracco goes on to state:

> Here is Albert Schweitzer, a great man, telling us to rethink and even devalue the role of great figures in human affairs. Schweitzer compares their efforts to the "foam" and instead praises "small and obscure deeds." (p. 3)

If we reexamine leadership, and especially the work of effective principals in our schools, we see men and women who are distant from the much praised description of effective leadership in much of the present literature. And they are not highly visible, charismatic, visionary, or out in the front of the charge. But they are effectively leading schools, dedicated to improved teaching and student learning, and having a positive impact on education improvement and reform.

There is a general absence in the present leadership literature of what really sets leaders from below the surface apart from the more traditional courageous, charismatic principal. In Badaracco's research, he did find some different characteristics that do set them apart: it is more a matter of character than tactics. "These men and women relied heavily on three unglamorous virtues: restraint, modesty, and tenacity" (2002, p. 170).

Principals who lead from below the surface, actually consider some of our more traditional and accepted forms of leadership a danger. Much of our leadership preparation and training focuses on: (a) making decisions quickly and aggressively, (b) thinking across the whole organization as we consider problems and decisions, and (c) considering all decisions both important and urgent. For example, a popular leadership theorist suggests that we change the metaphor of "ready, aim, fire" to "ready, fire, aim." It seems to me that this suggestion encourages quick, rapid decision making. In addition, I am not convinced that we all believe some issues are more important than others and that some are urgent and some are not, but when observing and talking with practicing principals, they tell us that a distinction between importance and urgency is not often made in their daily work of leading schools. Perhaps the correct metaphor is "ready, aim, aim, aim, aim, fire."

My work with school principals and superintendents has uncovered the same conclusions as we read in Badaracco's work. Principals who lead from below the surface actually consider the three points above to be dangers in effective leadership. More noticeable and obvious are such characteristics as:

1. Principals who lead from below the surface must be careful of quick decisions and proceeding at a lightning speed.
2. Principals who lead from below the surface don't set out to prove anything or solve the world's problems: they operate slowly, carefully, cautiously, and really just want to do their small part in the grand scheme of things.
3. Principals who lead from below the surface have the ability to distinguish between importance and urgency. And these principals are masters at picking their causes: causes that they care about deeply and see through to the end.

LAYING THE THEORETICAL GROUNDWORK FOR LEADING FROM BELOW THE SURFACE

To thoroughly define "leading from below the surface," I must first of all, review the existing leadership theory to help place leading from below the surface in perspective. The theoretical/conceptual framework that is the primary focus of this article is shaped by the review. This "leading from below the surface" framework serves as a "connect" and adds considerably to our present knowledge base in educational administration. Please trust that the placement of the framework fits best after (rather than before) my review of leadership theory.

Let me now, however, provide a brief overview and specific definition of leading from below the surface.

First, What Is the Surface?

I suggest that for the most part, *surface* is synonymous with the obvious or clearly visible. As we attempt to positively impact teaching and learning, we see teachers delivering instruction is some pretty clear ways: direct instruction, collaborative learning groups, individual learning centers, use of technology to enhance learning, etc., etc. And we spend most of our time observing this teaching in formal classroom situations. We are guided by clear goals, specific objectives, and evaluate teachers systematically. Don't misunderstand me: I agree that much learning takes place in traditional classrooms. But to get below the surface, we must expand our thinking beyond the obvious and visible.

Looking at students and evidence of effective learning, we again focus on the more visible and obvious: test scores, attendance data, discipline referrals, and report card grades. Here lies an inherent danger of staying on or above the surface: we have a tendency to highlight the average and above-average students, missing some of the students who might be considered at risk of educational failure. The real attributes and successes of some students are not clearly revealed by test scores and report card grades. Again, we must look deeper to get at the complete meaning of effective learning.

To further identify the surface, let's revisit our friends' Bolman and Deal (1984). Remember the four frames they suggest as approaches to better understand and manage organizations: (a) structural frame, (b) human resource frame, (c) political frame, and (d) symbolic frame? My below-the-surface model can be better understood if we think of the first two frames representing the surface, and the last two frames helping us to lead from below the surface.

Think for a moment about the first two frames: structural and human resource. If we look closely, we really find that these two frames occur on the surface, or as Deal (1987) explains, "the structural and human resource frames attend primarily to formal structure" (p. 235), and "represent the obvious sides of schools" (p. 234). The structural frame emphasizes the importance of structure: rules, policies, objectives, and management kinds of activities. The human resource frame involves the needs, feelings, and prejudices of teachers, students, and administrators in our schools. The often repeated theme of *principal as instructional leader* is heavily emphasized by structural ideas, and centers on the structural and human resource frames. To better define my leading from below the surface, let me highlight a portion of their discussion of these two frames:

> It is not that either of these perspectives is wrong; they are both quite useful in explaining how schools work or in developing policies and strategies for helping them to improve. The main problem is that each leaves something out; that together they do not highlight significant features of schools as organizations. To capture the *hidden sides of schools,* we need to entertain other *less obvious* perspectives. (p.235)

It is these hidden sides of schools that I suggest we travel to in leading from below the surface.

Now What Does "Below the Surface" Mean?

Let's start with an example. In a recent program evaluation for the Klein Independent School District in Houston, Texas, I was asked to investigate the number of graduating seniors taking advanced math courses. When looking at the existing data, I noticed that 72% of the students graduating from the district's three high schools completed advanced math courses (Pre-Algebra, Algebra 1 & 2, Geometry, Trigonometry, Statistics, Pre-Calculus, and Calculus) during their high school career. The superintendent and board were very proud of this figure. But to the superintendent's credit, he requested that I look into the situation further. We both agreed that sometimes looking at a single statistic does not present the whole story or paint the complete picture.

Obviously, we wanted to look at issues of gender, ethnicity, race, and socioeconomic level. But more importantly, I wanted to investigate the completion rates as they corresponded to each of the individual math courses. Specifically, I wanted to report the highest math course that students completed. Something very interesting and significant surfaced. My findings are shown below.

We're sure glad we did not stop at the first data report, revealing a 72% completion rate. Sure enough, it is accurate, but as you see, does not really complete the picture. This second bit of information suggested that the district needed to attend to some specific courses and specific groups of students.

Table 1.   Percent of Graduating Seniors by Highest
Mathematics Course at Klein High School

Highest Math Course Completed	% Seniors Completing
Pre-Algebra	9%
Algebra 1	13%
Algebra	27%
Geometry	18%
Trigonometry	22%
Pre-Calculus	11%
Calculus	7%
Statistics	9%

In the process of our literature review, we uncovered the results of a similar study completed by the U.S. Department of Education, National Center for Educational Statistics in 1995, representing graduating seniors across the nation. This information, shown in Table 2, was helpful in showing the Klein School District, that there was nothing terribly wrong with their low figures. They were very close to the national figures. Though this was somewhat comforting to them, the superintendent still found his figures unacceptable, and began to look at strategies for increasing the completion rates in Pre-Algebra, Algebra 1, and Algebra 2. His rationale was to improve the base courses, in hopes of improvement naturally occurring in the more advanced courses.

We hear much these days about data-based decision-making. I suggest we use different terminology to describe how principals lead from below the surface: *evidence-based decision-making.* Many times (as in my example above) it is not enough to just look at the clear and obvious data: the data revealed a 72% completion rate. But looking at the evidence requires a broader and deeper (below the surface) investigation. The individual math course completion rate was much more meaningful and truly represented what was happening at Klein's three high schools.

As our visit with Bolman and Deal helped us with understanding the *surface,* let me suggest that they can also help us better understand *below the surface.* Let's go back to their four frames, and focus on the last two: (a) political and (b) symbolic. In their discussion of the hidden sides of schools, they state that political and symbolic theories look at schools quite differently. Rather that advocating rational control exercised through authority, a political view concentrates on a negotiated order achieved through the exercise of power among groups and coalitions (Peterson & Wimpleberg, 1983). From a symbolic perspective (rituals, ceremonies, stories, gossips), the elements of culture form the glue that holds an organization together (Deal & Kennedy, 1982).

Some organizations have tangible products, allowing leaders to focus mostly on Bolman and Deal's structural and human resource frames. But schools are much more complex, with effective teaching and student learning representing more intangible products. And because of this complexity, school leaders must spend considerable time "hanging out" below the surface.

Table 2. Percent of Graduating Seniors by Highest Mathematics Course Completed in High School

Highest Math Course Completed	% of Seniors Completing
Less than Pre-Algebra	8%
Pre-Algebra	6%
Algebra 1	11%
Algebra 2	31%
Geometry	14%
Other advantage math*	21%
Calculus	9%

*Includes Algebra 3, Trigonometry, Pre-calculus, and Probability and Statistics
SOURCE: Department of Education, National Center for Education Statistics (1995), *Vocational Education in the United States: The Early 1990s, Table 49*

In a sense, leading from below the surface involves two significant dimensions: (a) expanding your decision-making beyond the formal and obvious places (i.e., classrooms) and (b) moving from data-based decision-making to a deeper perspective utilizing evidence-based decision-making. Effective principals are those who focus time and attention on each of these two areas. And they realize that very few significant decisions are made in the principal's office or in meetings with the superintendent or board. Effective principals make decisions in hallways with teachers, on school buses with children, in kitchens with cafeteria workers, on the ball field with coaches, and at the Tuesday evening Lion's Club meeting. Though these places are very visible and on the surface in their own right, the principal's presence there is *below the surface* in regard to where traditional leadership preparation suggests leadership takes place.

Let me provide another example to help us understand leading from below the surface. While serving as superintendent of the Westside School District in California, we received word from the State Department of Education that our application for building restructuring monies was approved. This meant that finally we would have the monies to refurbish our classrooms with state-of-the-art technology, new air conditioners (to replace our trusty old "swamp coolers"), fix the leaks with new roofs, new bathrooms, and all the rest of our construction needs. As you know, the superintendent of a small rural district is designated as the owner of a building construction or re-construction project, monitoring architects, contractors, bids, change orders, and building inspectors. This role is all-consuming, requiring early A.M. meetings with architects and contractors, and after-hours meetings with Board members.

In a very real sense, all of one's time in this situation takes place in Bolman and Deal's structural and human resource frames, and consists of the very obvious: working with established plans and procedures, interpreting contracts, inspecting completed work, staying on budget, etc. I think you can begin to sense the difficulty lying ahead for me.

I found myself spending less and less time conferring with teachers and students. Busy with the re-construction project, I began to neglect the more invisible and intangible aspects of leading the district. Often, I would have to designate classroom observations and the handling of staff meetings to the Principal. Obviously, this was a great opportunity for the Principal, as he became more and more responsible for instructional leadership. But, for me, it meant not paying attention to the *political and symbolic frames* (below the surface).

The trouble ahead for me included: (a) frustrated teachers who felt ignored and unsupported, (b) disappointed community members who missed the regular communication and contact with their superintendent, and (c) puzzled education officials who noticed my increased absence from county and state meetings and workshops. Needless to say, I discovered myself in a potentially dangerous situation. Fortunately, for whatever reason, I was able to shift focus and get myself back to the *below the surface issues.* Part of the solution was to pull my principal into some of the decisions and meetings required with the re-construction responsibilities. In addition, I solicited and invited more participation and involvement from individual board members with these duties, allowing me to return to some of the more invisible and intangible matters.

Leadership Is Both Objective and Subjective

A final analogy to help us with the understanding of leading from below the surface is to look at the objective and subjective sides involved. The objective components of *on the surface* are, as stated earlier, visible and tangible. Charged with monitoring the building re-construction, I rarely thought about anything but the visible and tangible: building plans, contracts, inspection codes, and all the other formal aspects of building construction. If we think for a moment of our often quoted paradox of management and leadership, I posit that I was doing a pretty good job of managing.

Leading from *below the surface* requires a principal or superintendent to address the subjective components of leadership: the more invisible and intangible things such as teachers' attitudes and beliefs, community members' feelings, and state and county educators' perceptions. Not until I returned to below the surface did I get back to the real essence of leading a school district.

Allow me to suggest that leading from below the surface can be likened to an iceberg: only 10% of the iceberg is seen above the surface of the water. It is the 90% of the iceberg that is hidden below the surface of the water that most concerns the ship's captain who navigates the water. Like an iceberg, the most meaningful (and potentially dangerous, as I found out as superintendent during re-construction) is the invisible or subjective part that is continually operating at the unconscious level that shapes peoples' beliefs and perceptions (Cushner et al., 2003). It is this aspect of leadership that can be most troublesome and potentially dangerous, and requires the most attention and emphasis in effectively leading schools.

A FURTHER REVIEW OF THE
KNOWLEDGE BASE IN EDUCATIONAL ADMINISTRATION

How would you complete this sentence? "Leadership is . . . ." I suggest there are as many ways to complete the sentence as there are individuals reading this chapter. In the past 50 years, there have been as many as 65 different classifications developed to define the dimensions of leadership (Fleishman et al., 1991, as cited in Northouse, 2004). And within these 65 classifications, there are several specific theoretical forms of leadership. You know—situational leadership, transformational leadership, moral leadership, and on and on and on. And to further cloud the issue, we distinguish between leadership and management. WOW! Where do we go from here? Truly, leadership is a very complex phenomenon.

In taking you through a brief history of leadership theories and approaches, I want to follow a format presented by Peter Northouse (2004) in his recent 3rd edition of *Leadership: Theory and Practice.* This format follows the classifications of leadership mentioned above, and obviously within each classification there exist several different theories or models.

And be aware that the point I want to make is that from my experience and perspective, I do not see leaders from below the surface following any of the specific theories. I am reminded of a quote from a world-renown statistician related to theories and models:

All models are wrong—but some are useful.

George E. P. Box
Professor Emeritus, University of Wisconsin

I agree that leaders have something to learn from the study of leadership theory. But I am suggesting however, that there are large numbers of effective school leaders who pay attention to and exhibit characteristics far removed from any of our established theories. Let me go on with my brief review of the literature.

In the early 1800s, leadership characteristics or "traits" were studied to determine what made certain people great leaders. For example, if we could identify the traits possessed by an Abraham Lincoln, we could perhaps duplicate it in others. This "trait approach" was based on the belief that leaders were born with certain characteristics that made them great leaders and were different than others who were more passive followers. Examples of some of these traits were: intelligence, self-confidence, self-determination, integrity, and sociability.

In the middle of the century, many researchers (e.g., Stogdill, 1948) argued that no identifiable set of traits separated effective leaders from ineffective leaders. Leadership now began to emerge as a relationship between people and situations. This actually was the beginning of a theory now called, situational leadership." Though first surfacing in 1948, it is interesting to observe that we now in 2004 are revisiting the notion of situational leadership.

Behavioral Leadership

Researchers, after realizing that trying to identify leadership traits or characteristics was not dependable, began to study leadership *behavior.* In other words, they wanted to observe individuals as they were actually leading an organization or group of people.

During the '60s and early '70s, two major research studies looked at the behavior of leaders: (a) The Ohio State Studies and (b) The University of Michigan Studies.

The first study focused on asking employees to report the number of times their leaders displayed certain types of behavior. Two specific types of leadership behaviors surfaced: (a) behavior centered on structure and (b) behavior based on consideration. In other words, leaders provide *structure* for employees and leaders *consider or care* about the people under them. The University of Michigan study revealed similar results, identifying two specific types of leadership behavior: (a) production oriented and (b) employee oriented. Production orientation involved completion of tasks and getting work done, paralleling the structure behavior found in the Ohio study. Employee orientation involved the display of strong human-relations skills, and relationships with employees, aligning with the consideration behavior of the Ohio study.

In essence, these two studies indicated that effective leaders had to concern themselves with both task orientation and relationship orientation. And, some organizations might need leaders more focused on tasks while others might benefit from leadership with strong human-relations skills.

Situational Leadership

Hersey and Blanchard (1993) are credited with the development of the theory of situational leadership. In essence, situational leadership involves a different form of leadership for a variety of situations. The contention is that effective leaders must adapt his or her style to the requirements of different situations. Interestingly, the two components of situational leadership (directive behavior and supportive behavior) again parallel the structure and consideration constructs identified in the Ohio State study and the production orientation and employee orientation of the Michigan study. Figure 1 shows such an alignment.

As you may notice, we are beginning to see the distinction between what we now consider as management behaviors (structure, production, directive) and leadership behaviors (consideration, employee orientation, supportive). Directive behaviors involve giving directions to organizational members, outlining goals and timelines, and methods of evaluation. On the other hand, leaders use supportive behaviors to help organizational members to feel good about themselves, and giving them social and emotional support.

As popular as the Hersey/Blanchard theory is, little research has been completed giving evidence that the theory really does improve performance. And critics argue

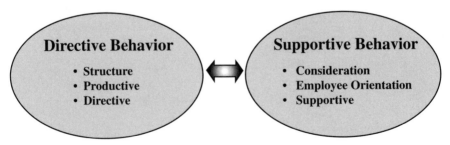

Figure 1.   Directive and Supportive Behavior

that the model does not adequately address "developmental levels" of subordinates. In addition, situational leadership theory does not fully address one-to-one versus group leadership in an organizational setting (Northouse, 2004, pp.62–63).

Contingency Leadership Theory

About a decade after Hersey and Blanchard presented the situational leadership theory, Fiedler and Chemers (1984) developed the contingency leadership theory. This theory is also related to what the literature refers to as "leader-match theory" (Fiedler & Chemers, 1984), where leaders are matched to differing situations. So, we are basically talking about a match between a leader's style and various situations.

Fiedler suggests that a leader's style is either task motivated or relationship motivated. Task-motivated leaders deal mostly with goal setting and accomplishment while relationship-motivated leaders concentrate more on closer interpersonal relationships with employees. Interesting—these styles will fit nicely into our Figure 2 and are more toward management and leadership behaviors.

Fiedler was the first to specifically categorize situational variables: (a) leader-member relations, (b) task structure, and (c) position power. Leader-member relations involve the confidence and loyalty workers have for their leader. Leaders with appropriate task structure are very clear and specific with relating goals and objectives to members of the organization. Position of power is simply the amount of authority a leader has in making decisions.

Path-Goal Theory of Leadership

In the early '70s, House and Dressler (1974) popularized the *path-goal theory.* This theory focuses more on what motivates members of the organization to perform well, and whether or not they feel appropriately rewarded for their work. So the challenge for the leader is to implement a leadership style that best meets the motivational needs of the worker.

House and Dressler (1974) suggest that effective leadership requires making the "path to the goal" clear to all in the organization, and involves (a) appropriate coaching, (b) removal of the obstacles that make reaching the goal difficult, and (c) making work satisfying to all.

Within the path-goal theory are four distinct styles of leadership: (a) directive leadership, (b) supportive leadership, (c) participatory leadership, and (d) achievement-oriented leadership. Do you not agree that we could easily add the components of the path-goal theory to our Figure 2?

It is interesting to note that the path-goal theory is the first model to address the issue of motivation. It is also the first theory to come along that begins to address "practicality" and points to the real purpose of leadership being to guide and coach members of the organization toward the achievement of goals and objectives.

Transformational Leadership Theory

Transformational leadership theory surfaced quite recently and is credited to the work of James MacGregor Burns (1978). Burns presents two types of leadership: *transactional and transformational.* He considered transactional most of the previous models presented in this chapter, that focus on what happens between leaders and their followers. Principals who offer bonuses to teachers who successfully raise student test scores exhibit transactional leadership. Teachers who routinely give students a grade for work completed are practicing transactional leadership. In both of these examples, the "exchange" between the leader and follower is quite simple: you do this, and I will give you this.

Leaders who practice transformational leadership, on the other hand, pay special attention to the needs and desires of the followers, and try to help members achieve their highest potential. Basically, the theme is to give more attention to the follower's needs rather than the leader's needs. Transformational leaders often exhibit strong values and ideals and can motivate people to act in ways that support the organization above their own self-interests (Kuhnert, 1994). Please see Figure 2 below.

A Theoretical Framework for Leading from below the Surface

Let me suggest that the leaders I will begin to describe (below the surface) do not fit into any of the formal leadership theories presented in this chapter. I do agree, that many of the individual traits and behaviors are evident. But I contend that truly effective school leaders possess and passionately pursue a third group of traits/behaviors.

One of the purposes of presenting the historical look at leadership over the last half century is to demonstrate that *leading from below the surface* is not so much a theory in itself, but rather a product of the progression of leadership theory. Its time has come. Just as the work of the Ohio and Michigan studies in the 1960s and 1970s drew attention to the differences between structure and consideration, we have progressed to a point that we now realize the difference and importance of such things as: (a) evidence-based decision-making, (b) collaboration as opposed to cooperation, (c) the importance of strategy, and (d) looking beyond the obvious. Figure 2 displays the framework that helps us with our further discussion of leading from below the surface.

I agree that school leaders can benefit from the work of Stoghill, Hersey and Blanchard, Fiedler, House, and MacGregor Burns. But the quiet, less visible, non-charismatic leaders I discuss in these pages, really spend more time and effort in this third area displayed in Figure 3. We will investigate these leadership qualities in the conclusion ahead.

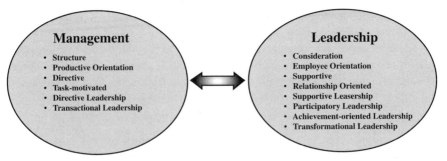

Figure 2.   Management and Leadership Behavior

Figure 3.   Theoretical Framework for Leading below the Surface

CONCLUSION

This author argues that our students with special needs (limited English speaking, students of color, students with disabilities) are "below the surface." On and above the clearly visible surface are the majority of our students: the average and above average student. But, getting to the needs of our special populations requires leaders to "investigate and practice" effective strategies that take us below the visible surface.

It is no exaggeration to state that our politicians and legislators are obsessed with the accountability of schools and especially obsessed with the way/s we measure success. The very recent federal legislation, No Child Left Behind, requires that we focus more attention on "previously marginalized students." Though our many critics argue that education has failed these students, I contend that many of our principals and superintendents do an admirable job of providing high-quality instruction to all students. And in doing so, they regularly and intentionally "look below the surface" for factors and phenomena causing any disparity in the teaching and learning domains.

Think of any current dialogue or discussion of education: Has accountability ever been mentioned *without* the inclusion of the word *testing?* Though some might argue that the words *accountability* and *testing* should not be used interchangeably, "testing" without question, serves as the centerpiece of many, if not most, accountability systems (Waite et al., 2001, p. 184). It is beyond the scope of this article to discuss in detail the pros and cons of using tests to hold schools (and ultimately principals) accountable for student success. But suffice it to say, little research exists addressing the merits of tests and their appropriate applications (AERA, 2001). This is the very critical reason why successful leaders MUST look below the surface, to ensure that all students receive fair, equitable, rigorous, and appropriate instruction in our schools.

Below the Surface: Data or Evidence Based?

As I state repeatedly, a critical component of leading from below the surface is a principal's practice (and willingness) to investigate below the existing data. To further emphasize my point, I want to share with my readers the results of a study conducted earlier in my career as a teacher for the Los Angeles Unified School District. This study is presented in greater detail in *Schools and Data: The Educator's Guide to Using Data to Improve Decision Making* (Creighton, 2001), but a brief overview here will provide another example of leading from below the surface and emphasize the importance of reaching below existing data.

When I was working as a sixth-grade teacher for the Los Angeles Unified School District in the early 1980s, the Los Angeles Police Department implemented the now famous and nationally recognized D.A.R.E. program. As you know, the program's purpose is to educate students about the dangers of drugs, alcohol, tobacco, and gang violence.

As teachers, we were pretty convinced that students' attitudes toward drugs and alcohol changed for the better during their sixth-grade year when they were involved in the D.A.R.E. program. The existing data showed a positive effect on our students' attitudes. But our real question and concern was: Did students begin to revert back to their negative attitudes as they moved up into the junior-high grades?

We administered a student attitudinal survey to a fifth-grade class to get an idea of their attitudes before D.A.R.E. involvement. We administered a similar survey to the same class in sixth-grade after they completed the D.A.R.E. training. Finally, we administered the attitudinal survey to the same group of students after the completion of seventh-grade—1 full year after receiving D.A.R.E. training.

The results may not be that surprising: Scores noticeably went from low in fifth-grade, to medium/high in sixth-grade, only to fall back down significantly in seventh-grade. Here is where many folks might stop and interpret the existing data, without investigating further below the surface.

We need to be careful that we do not create a cause-and-effect interpretation here. Some might argue that D.A.R.E. causes negative attitudes regarding drugs because the students' attitudes declined after the first year. No, not necessarily! Perhaps the results are due to other societal factors (junior-high school environment, the transition from elementary school to junior-high, etc.) that caused this change in attitudes.

The finding does not indicate that the program is ineffective, but it does indicate to us that the efforts must continue for more than 1 year. As you know, since that time, the program has been expanded down to fifth-grade and up through seventh-grade. I suspect the reason for this expansion is related to our earlier findings. Also, the contact time with the D.A.R.E. officer consists of 1 or 2 hours per week. We suspected that this short amount of time produced short-term attitudinal effects. So you see, the "culprit" may not be the D.A.R.E. program itself but the extremely limited amount of time spent on activities and instruction.

My point is that with the heavy emphasis on principals making data-based decisions, and the unending pressure from the state and federal governments for accountability, there is a tendency to just look at existing data. I can think of no situation that does not benefit from a much deeper and thorough investigation. The most recent findings related to student dropout rates in our larger urban cities (e.g., New York, Chicago, Houston, Los Angeles) are a case in point. Existing data indicate rates in the range of 2–8%, but school leaders willing and committed to investigating below the surface find rates really approximate 25–50%. In addition, we suspect large numbers are actually "pushed out" by our school districts and administrators. This is a very complex issue, and beyond the scope of this article to settle: but, suffice it to say, "we desperately need principals and other school leaders who are willing to "look below the tip of the iceberg."

Data-Driven vs. Evidenced-Based Decision-Making
Let me first make a distinction between these two terms. Data-based decision-making is the current buzz term in education circles today. We have entire courses in our preparation programs devoted to the use of data to improve decision-making in our schools. This author himself has spent considerable time and effort on the subject (Creighton, 2001). To help make the point that perhaps we have "gone astray" with this emphasis on data, let me provide a couple of examples that seem to illustrate this point.

Many of my examples come from the Houston Independent School District. Part of the reason for this is the fact that I currently work for Sam Houston State University, an hour's drive north of Houston. In addition, the students who enroll in our Master's and Doctoral Program come from the Houston and North Houston area schools. But beyond these reasons, another is somewhat significant. In Linda McNeil's powerfully written *Contradictions of School Reform* (2000), she states in the author's preface:

> The setting for this book is Houston, Texas. This is extremely significant. Houston has the fifth largest public school system in the United States. More than 150 home languages are spoken by the children in its public schools. For a simple and powerful reason, what happens in Houston can quickly affect the entire nation: Texas is the second largest state in the United States, and its political power increasingly sets the national agenda. (p. xxi)

Though Linda McNeil is a professor at Rice University, I consider her to be one of the great educators who "lead from below the surface." And I make the point that leaders come from all corners. I will return later to an example of her research and work, that will again demonstrate a distinction between data-based decision-making and evidence-based decision-making.

Attendance Rates vs. Absence Rates
You are obviously familiar with the term *average daily attendance* (ADA). We collect these data for several reasons, but primarily to calculate the number of dollars

we receive in state and federal monies. Simply, if students are present, we receive additional funding to help educate them. In addition, and again in Texas, schools are also given accountability ratings based upon ADA. So, principals and superintendents give heavy emphasis to implementing strategies that keep attendance rates high.

Many of the schools receiving the highest accountability rating (Exemplary) report ADA in a range of 92—98%. A 92% sounds pretty good, even has a connotation of a grade of A—right? So we report that on average, we have 92% of our students in attendance.

John Barrera, a principal at Las Americas School in Houston is a leader who looks "below the surface" and asks a different question: One not perhaps related to state funding so much, but certainly related to quality instruction. If the ADA is 92%, what about the absence rate? That's simple—8%. So John brings a different question to the surface: On average, how many of our students are absent? Investigating a little further below the surface, John comes up with this important issue related to "evidence-based" decision-making.

If on average, 8% of the students are absent, and based on the year of 180 days of instruction, these students are missing approximately two weeks of school per year (2% of 180 days equals 14.4 days). John concludes that his school's Exemplary Rating based on a 92% attendance rate is one thing, but students missing two weeks of school per year is quite another. You may argue that focusing on attendance is no different that focusing on absence. Well, it is all a matter of perspective, and reflects a characteristic of leaders from below the surface. John cares deeply for the marginal students—and believes that looking at the absence rate rather that the attendance rate gives him a better chance of focusing on students at risk of educational failure. Yes, he concerns himself with data, but digs deeper for further *evidence* to more effectively lead his school.

Here is the grand paradox of accountability and the standards movement—undermining quality and creativity and increasing discrimination (McNeil, 2000).

Narrowing of the Achievement Gap

Here is another example where simply making decisions based on existing data does not work for the benefit of students at risk of educational failure. Again we turn to the Houston Independent School District for our example, but I suggest this could (and perhaps does) happen in any school district across the nation.

During the 2000 Presidential Debates (Commission on Presidential Debates, 2000), George Bush and Al Gore tossed much rhetoric back and forth related to school accountability and student testing programs. The argument continued to focus on whether the Clinton Administration or the state of Texas had a better understanding of accountability. Governor Bush at that time (and now President Bush) was (and still is) fond of pointing to the "narrowing of student achievement gaps" in the state of Texas. The same claim was presented by Rod Paige (then Superintendent of Houston School District) and continues to be heard from the current Secretary of Education. Figure 4 displays data we often saw referred to by both politicians.

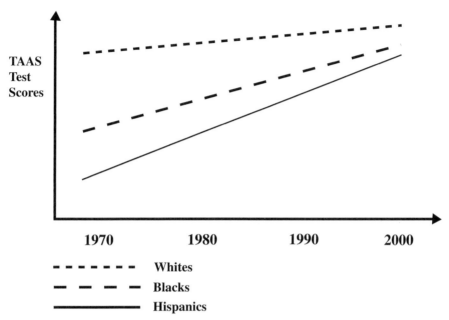

Figure 4.   Narrowing the Achievement Gap

Sure enough! The data reported were basically correct and accurate. But certain area superintendents and principals began to investigate "below the surface." The data in Figure 4 represents test scores of students tested. This sounds like a "no brainer," but wait a minute! Who were the students not being tested? In other words, let's look closely at the students represented (and not represented). The answers to this question illustrate the danger in making decisions on existing data only.

Turns out that approximately 28% of the African American and Hispanic students had dropped out from the time they enrolled in school to the time these tests were administered. Paralleling this important evidence, in a national study Waite et al. (2001) found that only 50% of African American and Hispanic students enrolled in our nation's public schools have actually progressed to high school graduation. Is it unreasonable to assume that this large number of minority students dropping out of school were eliminated and not included in the testing pool reported in Figure 4? And if they were not in the testing pool, that the academic performance (test scores) of these particular groups would likely rise?

Looking below the surface further, our principals found other factors that might have accounted for this "narrowing of the gap" in student achievement. The number of students identified as special education students, and thus qualified for exemption from taking these reported standardized tests, nearly doubled between 1994 and 1998. This finding also seems likely to have narrowed the gap only on the surface. Most alarming is an additional finding by Waite et al. (2001) that reports only 70% of students in Texas actually graduated from Texas in the 1990s—a below-the-surface missing student rate of 30%, or approximately 700,000 children. I am not questioning the increase in special education students or the importance of providing services to them: I am only pointing to the importance of including ALL the *evidence* that lies below the surface that are required in addition to data when making wise education decisions.

I also repeat my finding in looking at effective school leaders, that many are more concerned with the "below-the-surface" characteristics displayed in the theoretical framework we looked at in Figure 3. As did John Barrera in our earlier example, a few principals now are focusing more on the missing students and reasons for their absence, than they are in the claims of politicians who tout huge gains in test scores and the narrowing of the achievement gap.

As I am currently writing this article, a few courageous "leaders from below the surface" in the Houston School District have uncovered evidence indicating school and district administrators have actually held students back a grade to prevent them from entering the testing pool. In other words, testing currently takes place in tenth grade: some students who are not expected to do well on the state standardized test are temporarily held as ninth graders, thus keeping them from the testing pool.

Drop-Out Rate—2% or 28%?

Over the past few years, the Houston School District has reported unusually low percentages of student drop-outs in the district. City and state reports reveal an impressive 1–2% drop out rate for Whites, and an equally impressive 2–3% for Black, Hispanics, and other minority populations. In addition, the state of Texas designated the Houston district as above average or "Exemplary" in its Academic Excellence Indicator System (AEIS). This rating is based on several factors, one of which is low student drop-out rates. Another factor is the student achievement of minority groups, drawing more attention to the evidence I present above related to the narrowing of the gap.

In summer 2003, the Houston School District was awarded the outstanding urban school district in the nation by the Eli Broad Foundation, partially based on the reported narrowing of the achievement gap and the low drop-out rates.

Recent evidence has surfaced indicating that the district may have falsely reported drop-out data. Daily reports in the *Houston Chronicle* point to poor record keeping and some falsification of data at various schools in the district. Actual drop-out rates seem to be closer to 20–30% for minority populations. As I am writing this, review teams from the Texas Education Agency (TEA) are investigating the dilemma further and are contemplating the removal of the "exemplary rating" to one of "below average."

I return for a moment to Joseph Badaracco (2002) and his popular book, *Leading Quietly*.

> If we look at leadership with a wide-angle lens, we can see men and women who are far from heroes and people from the top of organizations, but are yet solving important problems and contributing to a better world. (p. 5)

The vast majority of difficult, human problems—both inside and outside organizations— are not solved by a swift, decisive stroke from someone at the top. What usually matters are careful, thoughtful, small, practical efforts by people working far from the limelight. In short, quiet leadership is what moves and changes the world. (p. 9)

Somewhere, below the surface and out of the limelight, are leaders challenging the claims of the Houston School District's claims of narrowing achievement gaps and low drop-out rates. Though they are not yet identified or highly visible, I suspect these leaders are building-level principals and teachers who are guided by a willingness and commitment to look below the surface in the name of social justice, equity, and fairness for all children, especially those at risk of educational failure.

Concluding Thoughts

A new model of school leadership is emerging. Whether we call it "leading from below the surface," or choose some other label, is not important. Fletcher and Kaufer (2003) state that this emerging model "depends less on individual, heroic leaders, but rather on leadership practices imbedded in a system of interdependencies at different levels within the organization"(p. 21).

The assessment committee of the President's Advisory Committee on Educational Excellence for Hispanic Americans (as cited in Waite et al., 2001) reported that more than 2 million Hispanic students have been underrepresented or ignored because they may have been excluded from state testing programs. Critics have also reported that the pressure on low-achieving and minority students has been so intense that it has caused many of them to drop out of school (McNeil, 2000).

I believe we are currently at a "Y' in the road. If we continue to focus mostly on the surface, huge numbers of minority and at risk students will continue to fall further and further behind and worse, out of the learning organization altogether. On the other hand, if we can learn and practice "below the surface strategies," our education system has a chance to turn around. Someone once said, "leadership cannot be learned, leadership *is* learning."

REFERENCES

American Educational Research Association (2001). *AERA position statement concerning high-stakes testing in preK–12 education.* Retrieved 2/20/01: www.aera.net/about/policy/stakes.htm

Badaracco, J. (2002). *Leading quietly: An unorthodox guide to doing the right thing.* Boston: Harvard Business School Press.

Bolman, L., & Deal, T. (1984). *Modern approaches to understanding and managing organizations.* San Francisco: Jossey-Bass.

Burns, J. (1978). *Leadership.* New York: Harper & Row.

Commission on Presidential Debates (2000). *The first 2000 Gore-Bush presidential debate*: October 3, 2000. Retrieved 1/24/01: www.debates.org/pages/trans2000a.htm

Creighton, T. (2001). *Schools and data: The educator's guide to using data to improve decision making.* Thousand Oaks, CA: Corwin Press.

Cushner, K., McClelland, A., & Safford, P. (2003). *Human diversity in education: An integrative approach* (4th ed.). New York: McGraw-Hill.

Deal, T. (1987). Effective school principals: Counselors, engineers, pawnbrokers, poets . . . or instructional leaders? In W. Greenfield (Ed.), *Instructional leadership: Concepts, issues, and controversies* (pp. 230–245.) Boston: Allyn & Bacon.

Deal, T., & Kennedy, A. A. (1982). *Corporate cultures*. Reading, MA.; Addison-Wesley.

Fiedler, F., & Chemers, M. (1984). *Improving leadership effectiveness: The leader match concept* (2nd ed.). New York: Wiley.

Fletcher, M., & Kaufer, D. (2003). *Accountability in action*. New York: Princeton Press.

Hersey, P., & Blanchard, K. (1993). *Management of organizational behavior: Utilizing human resources* (5th ed.). Englewood Cliff, NJ: Prentice Hall.

Hersey, P., & Blanchard, K. H. (1969). *Management of organizational behavior: Utilizing human resources*. Englewood Cliffs, NJ: Prentice Hall.

House, R., & Dressler, G. (1974). The path-goal theory of leadership. *Journal of Contemporary Business, 3,* 81–97.

Kuhnert, K. (1994). Transforming leadership: Developing people through delegation. In B. Bass & B. Avolio (Eds.), *Improving organizational effectiveness through transformational leadership* (pp. 10–25). Thousand Oaks, CA: Sage.

McNeil, L. (2000). *Contradictions of school reform: Educational costs of standardized testing.* New York: Routledge.

Northouse, P. (2004). *Leadership: Theory and practice* (3rd ed). London: Sage.

Peterson, K., & Wimpleberg, R. (1983). *Dual imperatives of principals' work*. Paper presented at the meeting of the American Educational Research Association, Montreal.

Schweitzer, A. (1963). *Out of my life and thought*. New York: New American Library.

Stogdill, R. (1948). Personal factors associated with leadership. A survey of the literature. *Journal of Psychology, 25,* 35–71.

Waite, D., Boone, M., & McGhee, M. (2001). A critical sociocultural view of accountability. *Journal of School Leadership, 11,* 182–201.

Corporate Solutions to Public School Effectiveness: A Comparison of Modern Business Practices with Acts of Competent School Leadership

James Smith and Connie Ruhl-Smith

Citizens of the United States are now, more than ever, making the case for educational institutions (P–12 and higher education) to begin operating like for-profit corporate entities. The authors of this work have, for a number of years, carefully examined the myriad parameters that surround such statements. These examinations have focused primarily on the need for school reform to come about in environments almost diametrically opposed to that of the for-profit community. Some of these works, particularly the most recent ones, have centered on the examination of these assertions, especially as they apply to the fervor surrounding standards and standardized testing. Others have directly targeted the banality of the aforementioned statement itself. Toward that end, this paper is constructed to continue the discourse that surrounds an examination of such banality and, furthermore, to allow the reader the opportunity to gain specific insights into the illogical and misguided notion that schools should, indeed, function more like U.S. corporations. Moreover, this work will carefully analyze a specific series of corporate behaviors that, if implemented in schools or school districts, would be disastrous to the well-being of these institutions.

It seems only logical to begin with the report that is most frequently mentioned in any discussion of schools and, concomitantly, the need to reform the organizational and administrative constructs that envelop all that takes place in the school setting. That document, *A Nation at Risk* (U. S. National Commission on Excellence in Education, 1983), is the Holy Grail for those who wish to engage in any discussion of school reform utilizing a corporate model. To paraphrase one of the most powerful (or damning) adages contained within that document, one only need compose a simple sentence: Our nation is at grave risk; once unchallenged as a preeminent power in commerce, industry, science, and technological innovation, we are now being

James Smith, Bowling Green State University-Firelands
Connie Ruhl-Smith, Bowling Green State University

overtaken by competitors from throughout the world. The mantra for those who support the redesign of educational institutions to a business model goes something like this, "If educational institutions functioned more like businesses, our children would surpass those in all other nations on the planet." If such is an accepted tenet of some form of logic, then the authors of this work are truly confused. A mere fifteen years after *A Nation at Risk* was published, the economy of the United States was the strongest in the history of modern civilization. If educators and educational institutions were the cause of a national crisis in 1983, would schools not be the center of the success that brought the economy to its apex in 1998? As Peter Sacks (1999) notes in his work, *Standardized Minds*,

> I know of no economist who would attribute the current vigor in the U.S. economy to any "reforms" brought forth by the school accountability movement . . . Perhaps the best thing educational policymakers can do for the American economy is to promote policies that improve Americans' opportunities to get more education. (p. 86)

Although the economic largess of the United States was the envy of the entire industrial world in the late 1990s, the authors of this paper agree with Sacks in stating that no economist or politician would openly suggest that schools (reformed or otherwise) were the driving force behind the tremendous economic growth. But is it not illogical to assume that a floundering economy is the result of weak schools and/or school systems, while, conversely, not the same driving force when the economy vastly improves? Is this sort of recognition or affirmation not the case, as Boutwell (1997) posits, simply "because the real culprit for the downturn was not education at all and top executives knew that" (p. 100).

As we moved from the 1980s into the early 1990s, the Chrysler Chairman at that time, Lee Iococca, told a gathering of educators "your product needs a lot of work, and in the end, it's your job to fix it" (Moffett, 1994, p. 587). He continued his diatribe by stating: "Your customers don't want to hear about your raw material problems" (p. 587). Certainly, Chairman Iococca was correct. Schools in the early 1990s did need massive reform. The infrastructure of many urban schools was crumbling. Cities like East St. Louis had high schools with raw sewage leaking into their cafeterias (Kozol, 1991). As recently as 1990, many urban and rural schools had no computer facilities. In 1993, nearly 411,000 children in Chicago could not begin school on time because the school district did not have adequate funding to open the schoolhouse doors. This action, delaying the beginning of the academic year in Chicago, was the fifth such action in a ten-year period (Ohanian, 1999, p. 117). Without question, Lee Iococca was right; schools were in need of reform. However, it seems more than moderately ironic that the reform initiative not suggested by Mr. Iococca was one involving a massive federal bailout of all under-funded school districts in the country, something similar to the taxpayer bailout that of which his corporation, Chrysler, was once the beneficiary. If schools were operating in a manner that seemed to border on intellectual bankruptcy, why would Chairman Iococca not recommend the same type of specialized treatment for which he lobbied Congress in order to save his bankrupt corporation? Was the economic impact of the potential failure of Chrysler more detrimental than the failure of hundreds of thousands of children who toil in school facilities that are, by any professional's determination, substandard? Is it possible that Chairman Iococca did not recollect the power of the federal government to provide solutions to massive public problems? Had he forgotten the power of the GI Bill (The Serviceman's Rehabilitation Act of 1944) to provide additional educational opportunities that resulted in unmatched prosperity during the postwar decades? Had he forgotten the importance of federally funded TRIO Programs that have guaranteed college scholarships to low-income students (i.e, on a much more pronounced scale than the highly touted Eugene Lang Scholarships provided by the public sector)? Had he overlooked the long-demonstrated success of TRIO, limited only by funding that is inadequate to reach more than a small percentage of the currently eligible students (Lowe, 2002)? The authors doubt that Mr. Iococca overlooked any of the aforementioned; rather, it seems obvious that he ignored such information with the hope that an average citizen might not join Clinton Boutwell (1997) in the following line of thought:

> Whenever a nation as large and diverse as the United States has a common purpose—whether it is war, depression, poverty, or encouraging industrial growth or agricultural policy—it has turned to the federal government. Then why shouldn't the government have an important role as we wrestle with the transformation to the New Economy? It is time for the federal government to take action again. (pp. 140–141)

Another example of questionable corporate behavior from the early 1990s, was the sixty-week tenure of Michael Ovitz, former President of the Disney Corporation. This situation brings to light an additional set of questions and concerns (i.e., related to the disconnect between corporations and public school organization and operation) that simply cannot or, at the very least, should not be overlooked. Ovitz, by all internal and external accounts, was not a successful senior corporate executive for Disney. After only sixty weeks, he was asked to leave his position with the Disney Corporation. Given an estimated $70,000,000 departure allowance (i.e., severance package), Mr. Ovitz was, in essence, granted a severance package equal to approximately $29,167 per hour of work conducted as a Disney senior executive (Masters, 2001). As Susan Ohanian notes in her work, *One Size Fits Few*:

> In 1995, a third of all children in the U.S. lived in homes with incomes of less than $25,000, less than one hour of Michael Ovitz's bonus pay for unsatisfactory work. One in five children was [residing] in a home with an income below $15,000. When we're talking about what standards are required for children growing up in America, shouldn't we consider household income? (1999, p. 115)

Although the aforementioned Chrysler Chairman, Lee Iococca, was correct in his assertion that education professionals must not fixate on the "raw materials" that enter their classrooms, it is obvious that Michael Ovitz's children and grandchildren will enter a classroom setting with significantly more advantages than the children who come to school from a home with an aggregate yearly family income equal to scarcely one hour of severance compensation he received from Disney.

This notion of inequality of experience brings us to the year 2000 and beyond. Without question, the standards and standardized testing movement that has swept this nation is largely predicated upon the belief that any successful business must test and retest the end product. This test and retest practice is now replicated in thousands of classrooms from Maine to California. Students, some as young as six years of age, are forced to prove that, as an end product, they are worthy of passing inspection. However, the proponents of such standardization seldom share the full picture regarding such test/retest actions. As Alfie Kohn notes: "Research has repeatedly found that the amount of poverty in the communities . . . accounts for the great majority of the difference in test scores from one area to the next" (2000, p. 7). Fortifying the notion that wealth or poverty can be a powerful predictive measure of outcomes on standardized tests, as well as other elements of academic "competence," Iradshie (1995) notes:

> When you have a child poverty rate that is four times the average of western European countries that are our principal industrial competitors, and when those children are a significant part of our future work force, you have to worry about the competitive effects as well as the social fabric effects. (pp. A1, A4)

Although seldom openly discussed or debated in the mainstream media, is it possible that this utilization of standardized instruments for promotion and measure of overall performance is not to bring forth educational change at all? Could it be that what is masqueraded as a device for social and economic change is nothing more than a way to solidify the existing social and economic divisions of our society? Peter Sacks posits the following as reification of this possibility:

> Indeed, if social engineers had set out to invent a virtually perfect inequality machine, designed to perpetuate class and race divisions, and that appeared to abide by all requisite state and federal laws and regulations, those engineers could do no better than the present-day accountability systems already put to use in American schools. (1999, p. 158)

As we advance to 2002 and beyond, the authors of this paper continue to question the belief that adherence to a business model is or ever could be good for schools. Certainly, such actions can be good for some students. However, for others, the lack of success in meeting certain standards or gaining a specific "cut score" will, in all probability, not serve as a motivator to learn more or do better. In fact, McNeil and Valenzuela (2000) found that the Texas Assessment of Academic Skills (TAAS) increased minority student dissatisfaction with schooling and, ultimately, resulted in the escalation of overall minority dropout rates for such youngsters throughout the state. Although no evidence exists of an organization called Rich Parents Against Equalitarian School Reform, Jeannie Oakes has been known to refer to those individuals most interested in the sorting and measuring movement as Volvo vigilantes

(Ohanian, 1999). Oakes and her colleagues have provided one of the most compelling insights into the motivation and methodologies, as internalized by these Volvo vigilantes:

> The dominant order of concern about schooling [at present] has been that if my own child does well, the community will do well (not . . . my own child will only do well in a strong community). The century's end has brought the ascendance of policy makers and social theorists who argue that only a reemergence of individual morality, accountability, and volunteerism can mitigate the hard edge of self-interest. How far this is from collective work to create educative, socially just, caring, and participatory schools to raise all of the community's children! . . . We think it will take something else to fan the flames of the nation's civic soul. (2000, p. 325)

RECENT EXAMPLES OF BUSINESS/CORPORATE MISMANAGEMENT

As has been discussed, grave concerns exist on the part of the authors with respect to the utilization of business models for overall educational reform. Specific examples of corporate mismanagement seem to be the most powerful mechanism to bring into focus the illogical use of for-profit business practices as a template for school reorganization or reinvention. The first, and most telling, example is Enron. In December 2001, the seventh-largest publicly traded corporation in the United States declared bankruptcy. This once-proud $100 billion corporation, with more than 200,000 employees worldwide, could no longer maintain the "shell game" that was carefully created to disguise losses via a shifting of deficit spending to partnership corporations owned or managed by then Enron Chief Financial Officer, Andrew Fastow. The end result of this corporate debacle was the loss of retirement funds and life-long savings for countless thousands of Enron employees and investors.

The demise of this energy trading corporation, because of executive mismanagement, board of director greed, and accounting malpractice (The Financial Collapse of Enron, 2002), shocked a national audience of investors and stock analysts who, just months earlier, listed Enron as a truly tremendous investment opportunity. The saga that surrounds Enron, Arthur Andersen, and the Board of Directors appointed to serve the best interest of all Enron stockholders, has been a prominent discussion item in virtually every element of popular culture. The excesses of former CEO Kenneth Lay, who was provided a multi-million dollar personal line of credit by the Board of Directors, was exceptionally well documented. That each member of the Enron Board of Directors was paid nearly $350,000 annually (in cash and equity compensation) has become a discussion item for dinner conversations throughout rural, urban, and suburban communities. The now legendary statement by Mrs. Kenneth Lay regarding the quest of her family for liquidity (Hale, 2002) provides many with a quixotic mix of humor and sadness. To paraphrase the words of a late night talk show host, one wonders if liquidity and stupidity rhyme for a specific reason.

Enron is just one example of the massive deceit and dishonesty that surrounded virtually all of a corporation's daily business practices. Another prominent for-profit example that might serve as a similar model for such unethical business practices is

ImClone. A small Manhattan biotechnical corporation, ImClone was on the verge of bringing to market the colorectal cancer drug, Erbitux. This was a publicly traded stock selling for approximately $75 per share in early December of 2001. On December 6, 2001, Harlen Waksal, brother of ImClone CEO, Samuel Waksal, sold nearly $50 million worth of ImClone stock. That sale, transpiring only two days after it appeared evident that the FDA would not approve Erbitux, was well in advance of the public notice of the FDA action. By late December, still in advance of any public announcement of the lack of approval by the FDA, Waksal's father and daughter sold $9.3 million of ImClone stock. And, finally, long-time friend of CEO Waksal, Martha Stewart (now convicted for her involvement in the ImClone scandle), unloaded 3,928 shares of ImClone stock just one day before the FDA released public notice that Erbitux would not be reviewed, for final approval, due to inadequate clinical trial data. By June 12, 2002, ImClone stock was trading (on Nasdaq) at a mere $7.83, nearly one-tenth of its peak price; the price at which the stock was aggressively purchased just months earlier (Appleby, Knox, & O'Donnell, 2002).

On that same June date, Mr. Waksal was met at his $2 million Manhattan loft by four FBI agents and, subsequently, was delivered to a New York courtroom to face charges of conspiracy to commit securities fraud and perjury (Appleby, Knox, & O'Donnell, 2002). As was the case with Enron, those most damaged by these illegal actions were individuals who believed that ImClone was an honest and legitimate company. Their beliefs, in turn, caused grave loss of retirement dollars and equally dire losses of individual and collective personal savings. Again, is this the model that best reflects a democratic nation? If such is the case, possibly we all need to heed the words of Michael Apple (2001):

> For neoliberals [individuals deeply committed to markets and individual choice], the world in essence is a vast supermarket. In effect, education is seen as simply one more product like bread, cars, and television. By turning it over to the market through voucher and choice plans, education will be largely self-regulating. Thus, democracy is turned into consumption practices. In these plans, the ideal of the citizen is that of the purchaser. The ideological effects of this position are momentous. Rather than democracy being a political concept, it is transformed into a wholly economic concept. The message of such policies is what might best be called "arithmetical particularism" in which the unattached individual—as a consumer—is deraced, declassed, and degendered. (p. 39)

Yet a third prominent outline of corporate fraud, greed, and executive isolation is WorldCom. On July 17, 2002, officials at WorldCom, the second-largest long distance provider in the United States, agreed to freeze a specified set of corporate assets in order to halt a group of bank executives from attempting to recover $2.5 billion in recent loans made to the company. Just six weeks after obtaining the aforementioned loans, WorldCom executives admitted to U.S. District Judge Jed Rakoff and members of the Securities and Exchange Commission that loan dollars were, indeed, received without admission of $3.85 billion in unreported/misreported expenses (Beltran, 2002). Facing the largest Chapter 11 bankruptcy in U.S. history (directly on the heels of Enron), the agreement to freeze assets was only a short-term strategy to purchase time prior to the formal filing of a bankruptcy statement. On July 23, 2002, WorldCom filed the largest Chapter 11 bankruptcy in U.S. history. This filing was nearly twice the size of the Enron filing and three times larger than earlier large-scale bankruptcies by Texaco and Financial Corporation of America.

In an era where state and federal legislators are touting the power of corporate efficiency and measurement to improve school operations, are these internationally recognized failures not visible to elected officials? Or, is it the simple fact that tangible issues, such as additional amounts of school funding producing real gains in student performance (every $100 per pupil spent will increase student achievement by one-fifth of a standard deviation), are too threatening to most legislators (Hedges, Laine, & Greenwald, 1994; Greenwald, Hedges, & Laine, 1996). Have the scant and unreliable data on school choice and vouchers been accepted and the more robust findings with regard to reduced class size ignored (Molnar & Achilles, 2000a) because of the same degree of threat to a preconceived notion of paradigmatic change? To quote Molar and Achilles (2000b): "Good public policy should be constructed using the most powerful data available to actually help the schools provide a high quality education to the students they serve. When it comes to the evidence on vouchers and the evidence on class size, the policy choice is clear" (p. 3).

Are we, as a society, so blinded by the hopes and desires of consumerism that we have lost sight of the egalitarian mission of public schooling in American (i.e., actually providing high quality education to all students served)? In the collective opinion of the authors of this work, a combination of these issues may indeed be the essence of the ignorance (or pabulum) that is generally presented by political leaders with respect to genuine school reform. As Timothy Hacsi states in his highly thought-provoking text, *Children as Pawns: The Politics of Educational Reform,*

> It would be wishful thinking to expect politicians to make evidence a leading determinant in the policies they choose to advocate. Being reelected drives most politicians, not the public good; or to be somewhat less cynical, politicians define the pubic good largely in the terms espoused by those who voted for them, by the stand of their political party, and by those who fund their campaigns. In either case, evidence about what works is usually well down the list of factors influencing policy. (2002, p. 209)

The words of Hacsi appear to support the lack of logic regarding the continued legislative defense of charter schools in the state of Ohio; this support exists, even in light of the dismal scores by charter school students on statewide proficiency tests. *The Cincinnati Enquirer*, on June 11, 2002, reported that only 6 percent of fourth and sixth grade students enrolled in Ohio Charter Schools passed all five tests mandated by the Ohio Legislature. In comparison to traditional public school students, these charter school youth performed with far less success. Traditional public school students passed all five tests at a rate of 43 percent at both the fourth and sixth grade levels, evidencing more than seven times greater success on said examinations (Welsh-Huggins, 2002). Nonetheless, legislators, many of whom are avid supporters of statewide high-stakes examinations (and support the perceived relationship of examination outcomes to intellectual capability), continue to advocate strongly for the continued development of charter schools throughout the state, again a perfect example of Dr. Hacsi's contention.

Another example from the ever-popular world of business might bring some additional light with respect to the absolute levels of disingenuousness that exist on the part of most right-leaning politicians (i.e., with regard to such concerns). Albert J. Dunlap, a self-described darling of the for-profit establishment and author of a best selling business text, *Mean Business*, agreed to pay a $500,000 civil penalty in September 2002 related to unfair business practices while serving as CEO of Sunbeam Corporation. This personal payment of $500,000 is the largest penalty ever levied in the United States against an individual for corporate financial fraud. With a misstatement of more than $60,000,000 in earnings as chief executive of Sunbeam, Mr. Dunlap was instrumental in the collapse of investments on the part of thousands of individuals who had faith in his leadership to bring Sunbeam back to prominence, much like he did at Scott Paper and Consolidated Press Holdings. Mr. Dunlap, frequently known as "Chainsaw Al" for his tenacity in eliminating employees and improving a company's financial profile at any cost, has been barred by the Securities and Exchange Commission from ever holding a position as senior officer or member of a board of directors for any U.S. Corporation (Farrell, 2002). Although Dunlap neither admitted nor denied mismanagement or fraud, the settlement reached on behalf of the class-action shareholders appears to validate the contention made by Harrison and Bluestone (1988) in their seminal work, *The Great U-Turn: Corporate Restructuring and the Polarizing of America*, that CEOs, often for very personal reasons, have developed short time horizons and adaptive strategies that have allowed their shareholders to realize quick financial returns by attempting to squeeze more and more profit from any process possible. Furthermore, as Boutwell (1997) has described, the myopic actions of the above mentioned "squeezing" has produced business entities that can now only flourish as a result of searching for more and more ways to eliminate costs:

> Having [a] short-range strategic view, CEOs [have] passed over modernization investments that required longer developmental periods before showing profits. But that approach was at the expense of the capital investment, innovation, and development of more effective management processes that were needed for corporate growth. It was a self-satisfied approach that took the rewards of the moment as an indication that all was well. (p. 101)

A simple question must be asked: What business practices outlined in this work are transferable to schools? What lessons can school superintendents learn from the behaviors of an individual like Chainsaw Al? Is it possible that the lesson most notably learned here is that greed and misbehavior can lead to wealth, fortune, and fame? Readers must know that Kenneth Lay still (at time of this publication) remains free from incarceration. His spectacular homes remain as part of his family's overall wealth portfolio. Could Giroux (2002) be correct in his assessment that business modeling for P–12 schools rests with the belief that privatization will lead to personal and familial enhancement equal to that found in the examples provided above? As Giroux so cogently states:

> The corporatizing of public education has taken a distinct turn approaching the 21st Century. No longer content to argue for the application of business principles to the organization of schooling, the forces of corporate culture have adopted a more radical agenda for public education. Central to this agenda is the attempt to transform public education from a public good, benefiting all students, to a private good designed to expand the profits of investors, educate students as consumers, and train young people for the low-paying jobs in the new global marketplace. (2002, p. 106)

THE MOST PROMINENT CALL FOR BUSINESS PRACTICE IDENTIFICATION IN PUBLIC SCHOOL SETTINGS

As Giroux notes, numerous examples of for-profit initiatives can be found in the redesign of public schools to meet a corporate model of increased profit and increased effectiveness. Voucher initiatives, charter schools, Channel One, the Edison Project, Education Alternatives Inc., Cover Concepts Inc., and Pizza Hut Book-it Awards are all examples of corporate actions or corporate leadership designed to reform pubic schools for the betterment of all children. However, the data simply do not support such claims or prognostications. Allen Greenberg (2001), Editor of the *Philadelphia Business Journal*, reported that Edison Schools Inc. had cumulative losses of nearly $220 million with little sign of this financial downturn relenting. In filings with the Securities and Exchange Commission during that same year, Edison executives were forced to make the following statement regarding overall financial viability and potential for future stockholder success: "We have not yet demonstrated that public schools can be profitably managed by private companies and we are not certain when we will become profitable, if at all" (Miner, 2002, pp. 135–136). Although this sort of acknowledgment is an obvious blow to those who have supported previously noted contentions to the contrary, the most damaging blow for Edison can be found in an overall assessment of effectiveness. As Dallas Independent School District Superintendent Mike Moses stated in the *American School Board Journal*: "We looked at their seven schools against seven comparable schools, and truthfully, Edison's performance was not superior. It was not inferior, either. We just didn't see much difference" (Cook, 2001, p. 8). Similar responses have been noted in San Francisco (i.e., where an Edison School produced the lowest test scores in the district) and in New York City (i.e., where local voters rejected an Edison bid to manage five local schools), the site of Edison's corporate headquarters.

Given the focus of this work and, concomitantly, the paucity of "hard data" to support claims of corporate improvement of public schools across this nation, it would be irresponsible of the authors to overlook the most significant development in business principle application to the public school environment. At the center of this monumental shift in operational practices and operational behaviors is the use of standardized testing to assess student performance, teacher effectiveness, and school improvement. Legislators, local politicians, and thousands of members of the educational community have successfully argued that increased focus on academic measurement will, almost without question, produce improved results with regard to student achievement. Prominent educational consultants, like Michael Schmoker (1999), argue that standardized testing can be properly aligned with instructional actions and student practice, thus producing significantly increased levels of student performance. Schmoker contends that such efforts are a truly "promising development" in education (1999, p. 74). This point of view is clearly becoming the dominant one in the United States. Books, articles, and monographs on instructional alignment, teaching to the test, and aligning instructional activities to test bank questions pervade the educational landscape. Some authors even contend that the alignment of teaching and testing will, once and forever, end the belief that race, poverty, and other social issues hamper overall opportunities for educational success (Gorman, 1999).

As many politicians and educational consultants move forward with their vigorous support of the teaching and testing alignment, others forcefully question the efficacy of such actions (Hudson, 1998; Kohn, 2000; McNeil, 2000; McNeil & Valenzuela, 2000; Nevi, 2001; Ohanian, 2002; Popham, 2001; Smith & Ruhl-Smith, 2002a; Smith & Ruhl-Smith, 2004). A 1998 study indicated that students in states with mandatory high school graduation tests performed less effectively on a neutral measure of academic performance than did students from states with lower-stakes assessment systems (Neill & Schaeffer, 1998). Furthermore, these same examinations are under fire for their inability to produce the results that the test construction experts claim to be the only purpose for the test. In the case of the SAT, the College Board claims that this test is designed solely to predict students' first year college grades. However, men continue to outscore women on the SAT, while women continue to outpace men on grade reports during their first year of college (The National Center for Fair and Open Testing, 2000a). With more than 1.75 million young people taking the SAT each year, is it a concern to the U.S. public that this test does not even produce the basic results claimed by the test construction experts? Obviously, the answer is a resounding "no." Just two years ago, the Hudson Institute commissioned a report entitled, *On Shaky Ground*. This report is a basic diatribe against all that is done in public P–12 educational institutions in Indiana (Bracey, 2000). The report, authored by Garber, Heet, and Styring (2000), repeatedly provides reference to the importance of using the SAT to make comparisons between students in Indiana and their counterparts throughout the country. In one instance, the report includes a graphic of SAT scores reported by average family income; the authors then chose to make the following assertion:

> Indiana's public education system fails students everywhere, whether their trip to school winds through the newest suburbs in an SUV or through cornfields in a pick-up truck or through urban streets on public buses. (p. 21)

Obviously, the fact that the SAT does not offer the predictive validity that the test construction experts maintain it should is of little or no consequence to the authors of that report. Furthermore, the fact that the test is designed solely to predict first-year college success seems to be unobserved by the Hudson Institute authors. Possibly, the real concern for those involved with the creation and distribution of *On Shaky Ground* was the fact that the following phenomena, as reported by Berliner and Biddle (1995), was not observed:

> at present the average SAT score earned by students goes down by fifteen points for each decrease of $10,000 in family income. This means, of course, that whenever colleges use the SAT for making admissions decisions, they are also discriminating against students from poorer homes. And it means that aggregate SAT scores will also fall when more students from poorer families choose to take the test. (p. 19)

How is it that such a large percentage of the U.S. public seems to endorse the use of standardized testing even though these tests do not offer the intended results? First, one must take into account the immediate access to the media by those voices speaking in favor of standardized tests (e.g., politicians, state superintendents, and corporate leaders). Second, it must be noted that the powerful presentation of ideas by pedagogical conservatives like E. D. Hirsch, Jr. and Diane Ravitch has allowed the political right to link U.S. culture with phrases such as efficient, effective, and necessary school reform. Third, a considerable number of neoliberal educators have accepted such testing practices as a means of assuring equal opportunity, diversity, and progressive modes of curricular and instructional practice. Furthermore, some moderate-to-liberal educators have simply accepted this standardization process as a means of precluding noneducators from taking total control of U.S. schools (Vinson, Gibson, & Ross, 2000).

This odd mix of neoliberal, conservative, and mainstream political power has allowed a few major corporations to flourish because the U.S. public has been led to believe that testing is, indeed, an efficient and effective way of assessing what is truly occurring in modern U.S. schools. The authors of this work believe it is important to display the tremendous financial results that this skewed collective perception has provided for certain corporate entities. According to Sacks (1999), Harcourt General Incorporated was in 1997 a $3 billion-per-year company; the Houghton Mifflin Company recorded $529 million dollars in sales of testing materials during that same year; the Educational Testing Service, from 1980 to 1996, grew in overall sales by 256 percent, recording a sales volume of $380.6 million (triple that of the 85 percent rise in consumer prices over the same period). Without question, testing in the U.S. is now a big business. Upon the backs of children and adolescents, corporate executives, members of their boards, and the respective corporate shareholders to whom they report, have made huge profits. Schools and school districts (and their taxpayers) have invested heavily in this standardized testing phenomenon. However, the simple question of testing to what end seems to be so frequently overlooked. As Glasser notes in a section of his landmark work, *The*

Quality School (1990), teachers can and do facilely articulate the dissatisfying paradox that this national obsession with standardized testing reifies for them on a daily basis. The following words of a classroom teacher epitomize the thoughts of hundreds of thousands of educators across the country:

> If I teach conceptually and challenge them [students] to think and defend their ideas, which is the way I know is right, my students have a chance to succeed in learning something worthwhile, but they may not do well on the tests that measure fragments and I will be labeled a troublemaker and a failure. On the other hand, if I teach the way I am told, my students will fail to learn anything that I, and most of them, believe is worthwhile, but I will be praised as a successful team player and they will be blamed as incompetent. (Glasser, 1990, p. 23)

Why do the thoughts of teachers, like those expressed above, so often fail to be reported by the mainstream media or discussed in statehouses from Maine to Hawaii? Is it because, as Audrey Thompson (1996) believes, political pragmatism is such an interwoven aspect of our culture that politicians are incapable of examining the educational system in new and different ways? Has this type of political pragmatism become so ingrained in our everyday life that we can accept only solutions that appear to revert back to the status quo? Do we simply accept race, gender, and socioeconomic power indicators as "the way things must be" and, thus, continue to search for sorting mechanisms that reify the hegemonic needs of our preconceived notions? The authors of this work are truly troubled by these questions because it seems virtually impossible to reject the darkness that surrounds the many answers they evoke.

The struggle for civic virtue, the engagement in broad-based intellectual thought, and the creation of environments that portray an emancipatory message are some of the essentials that will allow education to be both real and meaningful to the 21st century student. However, these are clearly educational constructs that will never appear as part of a multiple-choice format. Therefore, it must be asked—is there support for real educational reform or are we forever mired in the Frederick Winslow Taylor notion of schools as places of standardized effectiveness, efficiency, and order? Should there be any doubt that Taylor's thoughts and ideas are alive and well in the standards/standardization movement, one only need reflect on the words of Tucker and Codding (1998):

> In education, every minute counts, and everything one does should be tested against one criterion: whether it is more likely than anything else you could do in that minute to get your students to the standards. This applies with special force to technology, because of its expense as well as its power. (p. 99)

THE BUSINESS MODEL FOR
ACCOUNTABILITY AND STUDENT PERFORMANCE

As has been discussed in prior sections of this work, much confusion seems to exist with respect to the topics of standardized testing, professional accountability, and student performance. Given the apparent seamlessness that the media utilizes to portray a direct correlation between standardized test scores and teacher accountability, there can be little wonder why considerable bewilderment exists both within and outside the educational community. Authors, such as Wiggins (1994), exacerbate this problem when they posit notions such as the following: "It is not [standardized] tests per se but the failure of classroom teachers . . . to be results focused and data driven" (pp. 17–18). Again, this type of statement would lead the average reader to believe that results focused and data driven educators must utilize standardized tests in order to be successful in their quest for overall increases in student performance. However, authors like Wiggins certainly must have failed to read and understand the words of Cornell West (1993) and the earlier words of Carter Godwin Woodson (1933) that urge educators to consider the relevance of Eurocentric schooling in relation to the Black experience in the United States. If standardized tests measure only isolated elements of the Eurocentric curriculum, and if Eurocentric schooling is at best irrelevant to Blacks and at worst a lie and a cheat to their children, why would professional educators want to rely on such tests to make data driven decisions? Possibly, those most driven by data and standardization have forgotten that our democracy was constituted, for many, in ways that were truly the antithesis of democratic action:

> it is true that the United States is constituted by people from all over the world—and that this is one of the things that makes it so culturally rich and vital—such a perspective constitutes an erasure of [true] historical memory. For some groups came in chains and were subjected to state-sanctioned slavery and apartheid for hundreds of years. Others suffered what can only be called bodily, linguistic, and cultural destruction. (Apple, 2001, p. 50)

Given the words of Apple, Woodson, and West, the National Center for Fair and Open Testing openly challenges these commonly held assumptions about standardization with the following statement: "No test is good enough to serve as the . . . primary basis for important educational decisions" (The National Center for Fair and Open Testing, 2000b, p. 1).

The question of accountability with respect to racial fairness and relevance is only one segment of the debate that is seldom unearthed by the mainstream media. Another significant element of this debate can be found in the area of curricular narrowness. Teachers have been urged to adjust their instructional focus to test items and test formats. As was reported by the classroom teacher (cited earlier in this work), many other educators have simply acquiesced in order to be seen as good educators and fine team players. Possibly, these team players do not understand nor have they internalized the thought-provoking words of William Ayers in his text, *To Teach: The Journey of a Teacher*:

> Standardized tests can't measure initiative, creativity, imagination, conceptual thinking, curiosity, effort, irony, judgment, commitment, nuance, good will, ethical reflection, or a host of other valuable dispositions and attributes. What they can measure and count

are isolated skills, specific facts and functions, the least interesting and least significant aspects of learning. (Ayers, 1993, p. 59)

Berliner and Biddle (1995) question the belief that most citizens of the United States are interested in accepting and promoting an education system that results in instruction directed specifically toward "learning that is narrow, test-specific, standardized, superficial, and easily forgotten" (p. 197). This doubt for prevailing support of such testing has been cited, although not widely quoted, in works like *Choosing Excellence* (Merrow, 2001). Here popular journalist John Merrow documents, through results of a national survey, that 68 percent of all respondents and 71 percent of public school parents opted for "classroom work and homework" rather than standardized "test scores" (p. 44) as evidence for overall learning. Given this data, why, then, would politicians so anxiously accept standardized tests as the panacea for educational ills and the cornerstone for accountability? Could it be that we are again seeing members of the dominant society and the educational elite vigorously striving to maintain their positions of power and prestige? As Patricia Kusimo (1999) notes in her essay, "Rural African Americans and Education: The Legacy of the Brown Decision," it seems more than coincidental that in the 623 counties in eleven Old South states (Alabama, Arkansas, Florida, Georgia, Louisiana, Mississippi, North Carolina, South Carolina, Tennessee, Texas, and Virginia), where some of the highest percentages of African Americans reside, more than half (54 percent) of all Black adults, age 25 or older, do not possess a high school diploma. Further evidence of this nature is offered by Hill, Campbell, and Harvey (2000):

> In the largest cities, over 30 percent of all children live in poverty, compared to less than 20 percent elsewhere. Teacher salaries are seldom as high as in wealthier suburbs, so city schools often lose their best teachers. As a result, schools in the lowest-income neighborhoods are often staffed by shifting casts of new and provisionally certified teachers. City children are more likely than children elsewhere to have teachers who lack field-specific training, and the discrepancies are greatest in the most challenging fields, mathematics and science. (pp. 10–11)

What must educators do, then, to be accountable, but likewise professionally responsive, in their quest for accountability? Many outstanding educators would argue that they are accountable each and every day that they walk into the classroom. These individuals are accountable to their students. They are accountable to their principals. They are accountable to their professional colleagues. They are accountable to curriculum directors who, in collaboration with other teaching professionals, create the curriculum guides that are the essence of their daily instructional activities. These men and women passionately teach the curriculum assigned to them. They test in accordance with that curriculum. They design units that expand the basic curriculum and create opportunities for in-depth discussions and far-reaching experimentation. They design both simple and complex measures of student success. They report these successes (and the corresponding failures) to their students and to parents and guardians of these students. These men and women have the ability to design, on a localized basis, extremely robust measures of student success. As Berliner and Biddle (1995) note

> Given commitment, leadership, and support, many teachers are quite capable of designing creative, authentic assessment programs; and when such programs are explained to parents, many parents will choose them over standardized multiple-choice tests. Traditional, standardized tests are clearly hampering efforts to improve the schools. If we are to hasten change we must develop and experiment with more performance tests. Performance and portfolio assessment are not yet in widespread use, largely because they are so different from past visions of what assessment ought to be. But they are surely an important part of the school-improvement effort. As our vision of curricular aims are expanded to promote greater thoughtfulness, self-awareness, and competence in students, we will also need a lot more testing procedures that are authentic, performance oriented, and locally evaluated. (p. 320)

How would or could efforts of this nature be funded? The simple answer to this query rests with a rather elementary accounting analysis of the dollars spent on state and national test endeavors. If the Educational Testing Service was documented as producing a sales volume of $380.6 million in 1996, greater sales magnitudes certainly exist today. Recent news publications have indicated that the present sales volume for this one testing construction organization exceeds $600 million (Monastersky, 2002). The surplus earnings reported by this not-for-profit organization in June 2001 were $34,000,000. So robust were these earnings that eleven employees were given bonuses in excess of $97,000 and seven were given one-time payments exceeding $150,000. One employee, Kurt Landgraff, accepted a bonus of $366,000 for just eleven months of corporate labor (Monastersky, 2002).

Schools and school districts are, without question, contributing heavily to such increases in sales and the accompanying increases in corporate wealth. If the outflow of such dollars were kept locally (i.e., in districts or multi-district collaboratives), many of the authentic assessment measures noted above could be developed. Furthermore, dollars could be redirected from the governmental largess back to educational professionals employed within a specific state or region. Clearly, examples like that found in the state of Mississippi indicate that this redistribution could and should prove more reasonable in both a real-use and real-outcome sense:

> Mississippi . . . signed a $4.4 million contract with McGraw Hill/CTB, partly on the strength of the company's promise to deliver test results in early July, two months after the first test [was to] be given. That would allow low performing schools to regroup, to change their practices, to retrain teachers . . . But then McGraw Hill/CTB announced that it would not be able to provide test results until mid-November, long after the window for making changes had closed, and only five months before the second round of testing. Did the state leadership take this into account and postpone the high-stakes decision . . . In a word, no. Mississippi was determined to hold educators accountable, even if it . . . [meant] not giving them a chance to use what they learned from the first round's results . . . the public was hell-bent for "accountability." (Merrow, 2001, pp. 32–33)

This redistribution of state dollars could move testing beyond the banality of the aforementioned example and allow for increased opportunities for teachers to extend the restricted nature of their professional contracts (i.e., beyond the current nine or ten month barrier). It could, likewise, provide the opportunity for the creation of authentic measures that would actually serve as benchmarks for genuine accountability. Organizational actions of this type would move beyond the power-coercive strategies that have been outlined above and would, conversely, incorporate much of the best elements of professional empowerment, as described below:

> Empowerment involves the sense people have that they are at the center of things, rather than the periphery. In an effectively led organization, everyone feels he or she contributes to its success. Empowered individuals believe what they do has significance and meaning. Empowered people have both discretion and obligations. They live in a culture of respect where they can actually do things without getting permission first from some parent figure. Empowered organizations are characterized by trust and system-wide communication. (Bennis, 2000, p. 29)

It seems only prudent to share here a powerful statement made by a former North Carolina teacher of the year, James Rogers, who is now employed by the elite Phillips Academy in Andover, Massachusetts:

> I have a unique experience in that I taught in a public school and now I teach in a private school. We talk about standards and accountability. No one comes and asks us, "What did you do in that class?" We give our test, and our students come out of those classes. We have a reputation: If you come to our school, you're going to get a good education. And so the public has nothing to say about it. I don't worry about meeting someone else's standards in my classroom. I have standards. The whole history department has standards. (Henry, 2000, p. D5)

As we have noted in previously published works (Smith & Ruhl-Smith, 2002a), if this interpretation of accountability is acceptable in one of the most elite high school academies in New England, is it not possible to replicate this same belief in public school environments throughout the fifty states? Undoubtedly, educators at private academies seem to be given greater levels of freedom and autonomy to define standards and standardization for themselves; thus, creating a more meaningful definition and more aligned outcomes—students with the ability to think and perform academic tasks in powerful and appropriate ways.

THE INABILITY TO DENY THAT WHICH IS OBVIOUS

Studies cited throughout this work have provided findings that are clearly counter to the commonly held notion that a business model or business approach can or will improve public education in the United States. Such is true for other countries as well. For example, Boaler (1998) examined traditional versus nontraditional mathematics instruction in Great Britain. Her findings were in keeping with numerous others noted throughout the corpus of this paper, demonstrating a lack of success by students in classrooms or schools that had heightened attention toward standardized testing and organized instruction around a restricted curriculum. Furthermore, Boaler found the negative effects of this attention and focus to be even greater among youngsters with a working class heritage; particularly disadvantaging young women, even those previously identified as the brightest in their respective classes. Data of this nature force the authors to speculate that these results could be providing precisely the types of outcomes most desired by those who refuse to observe or accept that which we have defined as "obvious."

As we continue to examine the rather apparent counter-effects of the standardized testing movement, it seems rather logical, at this point in the work, to refer to findings posited by Donald H. Graves (2002), an individual who draws upon decades of experience in reading instruction and teacher education. Dr. Graves openly states that it is not only improbable but impossible to access the following learner qualities that are essential for skilled reading to be a part of any individual's learning profile. These qualities include: curiosity, initiative, sensitivity, self-regulation, expressiveness, ability to pose the right problem, and the ability to discriminate. Graves continues with his assessment of the inability of standardized tests to produce useful evaluative data with the following words:

> Currently, we are testing what we value, quick thinking. But what about long thinking? Can we discern thinkers like Thomas Jefferson, Albert Einstein, and Charles Darwin, who were self-professed long, slow thinkers? Can we identify and encourage the children who can formulate a question, fine the information, design an evaluation, and know whether they have answered their original question? The problems of a democracy are not solved through a single, quick answer but by thorough-minded thinkers who sustain thought on one problem for days, months, or years. In short, computers assess very well when there is only one right answer, but fall short when student formulate their own question or write longer essays to show their thinking. (p. 34)

There are myriad conclusions that a researcher can draw from this quotation. However, the most frightful ones, in the collective opinion of these authors, rest with the belief that quick thinking (as coined by Graves) is desired by those who most support standardization because quick thinking will be required of many youngsters as they assume low-wage and low-skill occupations in the growing U.S. service economy. If Aronowitz and DiFazio (1994) are correct, the future of high-paying and challenging occupations in the United States will exist for less that 20 percent of all college graduates within the very near future. Will the remainder of these individuals, then, use their quick thinking skills to perform mundane low-wage jobs? As Boutwell so cogently inquires: "Could it be that building a large labor pool from which to select applicants—that is, a large supply of workers—is part of Corporate America's plan?" (1997, p. 19).

It is difficult, if not impossible, to overlook the ramifications of this model of transforming schooling into a business/corporate structure without making mention of the financial gain to be garnered by those who so easily appear to overlook the issues and considerations outlined throughout this paper. First, the reader must be reminded that education in the United States is estimated to be, at present, a $700 billion enterprise. Michael Apple refers to this $700 billion venture as the "next health care—that is as a sphere to be mined for huge profits" (2001, p. 7). The afore-mentioned examples of profits made by the Educational Testing Service, Harcourt General, and Houghton Mifflin are excellent illustrations of Apple's contention that great financial gain can be made by those who, in real or perceived ways, meet the needs of those leaders most supportive of the business/corporate model of educa-tion. Wyatt (1999) reported significant illustrations of such greed when he described the goal of many business/corporate enthusiasts as merely being desirous of trans-forming large portions of publicly controlled educational institutions into a "con-solidated, professionally managed, money-making set of businesses that include all levels of education" (p. A1). Possibly, this explains the continued calls for charter schools and for-profit schools, even when performance data are documented as be-ing below that of traditional P–12 public institutions. Additionally, as Metcalf (2002) illustrates, the line between corporate desire and governmental leadership has, on the topic of education, recently become so blurred, it is impossible to deter-mine what entity is truly driving the other:

> The amount of cross-pollination and mutual admiration between the [Bush] Adminis-tration and the [educational assessment] empire is striking: Harold McGraw Jr. sits on the national grant advisory and founding board of the Barbara Bush Foundation for Family Literacy . . . The McGraw Foundation awarded current Bush Education Secre-tary Rod Paige its highest educator's award while Paige was Houston's school chief; Paige, in turn, was the keynote speaker at McGraw-Hill's "government initiatives" con-ference last spring. Harold McGraw III was selected as a member of President George W. Bush's transition advisory team, along with McGraw-Hill board member Edward Rust Jr. . . . An ex-chief of staff for Barbara Bush is returning to work for Laura Bush in the White House—after a stint with McGraw-Hill as a media relations executive. John Negroponte left his position as McGraw-Hill's executive vice president for global mar-kets to become Bush's ambassador to the United Nations. (pp. 52–53)

Finally, if all of the data contained within this work are not significant enough to convince the reader of the duplicitous and disingenuous nature of many of the claims made by those most ardently supporting the transformation of schools into corporate-like organizational structures—and if claims that those individuals with the most to gain are indeed the most vociferous on this topic are less than convincing—then, possibly, the words of Ohanian (2002) will help clarify the "circle of deceit" that sur-rounds much of what is reported, locally, regionally, and nationally, as legitimate re-search surrounding educational reform:

> These days, private policy organizations play an increasingly important role in shaping education policy, but the public hasn't a clue about either their agenda or the incestuous ties among them. In April 2000, for example, the Thomas B. Fordham Foundation is-sued The State of State Standards, giving every state a grade, but the casual reader doesn't have a clue about the particular bias behind the D+ for Vermont and the B for Texas. And to get more bang for the buck, a Fellow at one conservative think thank

promotes and praises the work of Fellow at another . . . Here is how it work: Marci Kanstoroom, director of research at Fordham, publishes an article on the miracle of Texas in *Education Next*, a publication of the Hoover Institution. *Education Next* is sponsored by the Thomas B. Fordham Foundation, Manhattan Institute for Policy Research, and the Program on Public Policy . . . Chester E. Finn, Jr., senior editor at *Education Next*, is president of the Thomas B. Fordham Foundation . . . Fellow at the Hudson Institution . . . [and] now designated "scholar" at the Manhattan Institute . . . Simply put, when Finn writes a paper at Fordham, he can act as outside reviewer at Manhattan, and then get it published at Hoover . . . When a newspaper runs an article about a report published in the *American Journal of Medicine* or *Educational Researcher* or *Physical Review*, the reader knows that report was subject to external review before it was published. With all the inbreeding and crossbreeding in the private policy operations, maybe the newspapers that cover the goings-on at these organizations should include a truth-in-disclosure statement. (pp. 192–193)

CONCLUSION

This paper was written, as is noted prominently in the introduction, to carefully analyze the rhetoric and assertions made by a wide variety of proponents for school reform via the business/corporate model. The data to support success utilizing such reform initiatives, however, simply do not exist. For those willing to carefully investigate the claims most commonly made in favor of these reform efforts, it is obvious that "the emperor has no clothing." Actions of corporate leaders have created absolute disarray in the major financial markets. For-profit schools are, in no significant ways, outperforming their public P–12 counterparts. Standardized instruments for the assessment of student learning toward specific outcomes are frequently unable to document evidence of "true" learning. Corporations that produce such standardized instruments and supporting preparation documents have proven unable to meet "guaranteed timelines" but, nonetheless, continue to generate profits at rates astronomically greater than the growth in virtually any other sector of the U.S. economy. In fact, these corporations seem to be among the very few which are truly growing and expanding in today's shrinking economy.

So, then, what have we learned from early attempts at "corporatizing" (Giroux, 2002) public schools? Students, particularly students of color, are increasingly exiting secondary schools without hope of attaining a high school diploma. Organizations like the Edison Project are unable to substantially increase the ever-important test scores that so dominate their instructional focus. States continue to invest massive amounts of scarce financial resources in testing programs (and supporting materials for said programs) that have little hope of ever accurately assessing anything more than basic skill development. It is virtually impossible for these tests to assess curiosity, initiative, sensitivity, self-regulation, expressiveness, ability to pose the right problem, and the ability to discriminate (Graves, 2002). Those on the political right continue to loudly and boldly state that increased investment of public monies is not the answer to school reform, while senior executives at the Educational Testing Service are granted bonus checks ranging from $150,000 to $366,000. All the while, as these bonuses are being offered, research findings document that increased public monies do make a difference—not when applied to testing programs or vouchers, but when dedicated to class size reduction and general fund augmentation (Hedges, Laine, & Greenwald, 1994; Greenwald, Hedges, & Laine, 1996; Molnar & Achilles, 2000a; Molnar & Achilles, 2000b). Therefore, in our opinion, only one substantive conclusion can truly be made. That conclusion is a rather simple charge or command that we hope will be spoken or shouted on a daily basis in schools as well as state and federal office buildings: "Let us move beyond hyperbole and disingenuousness and carefully examine the real issues that face schools, school districts, educational professionals and the children these professionals serve. The youth of today deserve at least that much!" (Smith & Ruhl-Smith, 2002b, p. 16).

NOTE

Sections of this work appeared previously in Standardized testing and educational standards: Implications for the future of emancipatory leadership in U.S. schools. In G. Perreault & F. C. Lunenburg (Eds.), *The changing world of school administration* (pp. 44–59). Lanham, MD: Scarecrow Press.

REFERENCES

Apple, M. W. (2001). *Educating the "right" way: Markets, standards, God, and inequality.* New York: Routledge Falmer.

Appleby, J., Knox, N., & O'Donnell, J. (2002). ImClone ex-CEO faces insider-trading charges. *USA Today* [on-line]. Retrieved July 31, 2002, from http://www.usatoday.com/money/covers/2002-06-13imclone.htm

Aronowitz, S., & DiFazio, W. (1994). *The jobless future.* Minneapolis, MN: University of Minnesota Press.

Ayers, W. (1993). *To teach: The journey of a teacher.* New York: Teachers College Press.

Beltran, L. (2002). WorldCom bankruptcy looms. *CNNMoney* [on-line]. Retrieved July 31, 2002, from http://money.cnn.com/2002/07/18/news/worldcom/index.htm

Bennis, W. G. (2000). *Managing the dream: Reflections on leadership and change.* Cambridge, MA: Perseus.

Berliner, D. C., & Biddle, B. J. (1995). *The manufactured crisis: Myths, fraud, and the attack on America's public schools.* Reading, MA: Addison-Wesley.

Boaler, J. (1988). *Experiencing school mathematics.* Philadelphia: Open University Press.

Boutwell, C. E. (1997). *Shell game: Corporate America's agenda for schools.* Bloomington, IN: Phi Delta Kappa.

Bracey, G. W. (2000). *Bail me out!* Thousand Oaks, CA: Corwin Press.

Cook, G. (2001). Searching for miracles. *American School Board Journal* [on-line]. Retrieved February 3, 2003, from http://asbj.com/2001/12/1201coverstory.html

Farrell, G. (2002). Chainsaw Al Dunlap to pay $500,000 SEC fine. *USA Today* [on-line]. Retrieved January 31, 2002, from http://www.usatoday.com/money/industries/manufacturing/2002-09-04-sunbeam_x.html

Garber, M. P., Heet, J. A., & Styring, W. (2000). *On shaky ground.* Indianapolis: Hudson Institute.

Giroux, H. A. (2002). Schools for sale: Public education, corporate culture, and the citizen-consumer. In A. Kohn & P. Shannon (Eds.), *Education, Inc.: Turning education into a business* (pp. 105–118). Portsmouth, NH: Heinemann.

Glasser, W. (1990). *The quality school: Managing students without coercion*. New York: Harper & Row.

Gorman, L. (1999). An end to educational racism. *Independence Institute: Independence Feature Syndicate* [On-line]. Retrieved July 31, 2002, from http://i2i.org/SuptDocs/OpEdArcv/Gorman/AnEndtoEducationalRacism.html

Graves, D. H. (2002). *Testing is not teaching: What should count in education*. Portsmouth, NH: Heinemann.

Greenberg, A. (2001). Edison's risk factors. *Philadelphia Business Journal* [on-line]. Retrieved February 3, 2003, from http://philadelphia.bizjournals.com/philadelphia/stories/2001/11/26/editorial1.html

Greenwald, R., Hedges, L. V., & Laine, R. D. (1996). The effect of school resources on student achievement. *Review of Educational Research, 66*(3), 361–386.

Hacsi, T. A. (2002). *Children as pawns: The politics of educational reform*. Cambridge, MA: Harvard University Press.

Hale, B. (2002). Kenneth Lay: A fallen hero. *BBC News* [on-line]. Retrieved July 31, 2002, from http://news.bbc.co.uk/1/hi/business/1779445.stm

Harrison, B., & Bluestone, B. (1988). *The great u-turn: Corporate restructuring and the polarizing of America*. New York: Basic Books.

Hedges, L. V., Laine, R. D., & Greenwald, R. (1994). Does money matter? A meta-analysis of studies of the effects of differential school inputs on student outcomes. *Educational Researcher, 23*(3), 5–13.

Henry, T. (2000, May 15). Educators stand and deliver: Top teachers provide the lesson plan for improving schools. *USA Today*, p. D5.

Hill, P. T., Campbell, C., & Harvey, J. (2000). *It takes a city: Getting serious about urban school reform*. Washington, DC: Brookings Institution Press.

Hudson, W. E. (1998). *American democracy in peril: Seven challenges to America's future* (2nd ed.). Chatman, NJ: Chatman House.

Iradshie, K. (1995, April 17). Gap in wealth in U.S. called the widest in the west. *Los Angeles Times*, pp. A1, A4.

Kohn, A. (2000). *The case against standardized testing*. Portsmouth, NH: Heinemann.

Kozol, J. (1991). *Savage inequalities: Children in America's schools*. New York: Crown.

Kusimo, P. S. (1999). *Rural African Americans and education: The legacy of the Brown decision*. Charleston, WV: ERIC Clearinghouse on Rural Education and Small Schools (ERIC Document Reproduction Service No. ED 425 050).

Lowe, R. (2002). The hallow promise of school vouchers. In A. Kohn & P. Shannon (Eds.), *Education, inc.: Turning education into a business* (pp. 119–130). Portsmouth, NH: Heinemann.

Masters, K. (2001). *The keys to the kingdom: The rise of Michael Eisner and the fall of everybody else*. New York: Harper.

McNeil, L., & Valenzuela, A. (2000). The harmful impact of the TAAS system of testing in Texas. Beneath the accountability rhetoric. *The Civil Rights Project: Harvard University* [On-line]. Retrieved July 31, 2002, from http://www.law.harvard.edu/civilrights/conferences/testing98/drafts/mcneil_valenzuela.htm

McNeil, L. M. (2000). *Contradictions of school reform: Educational costs of standardized testing*. New York: Routledge.

Merrow, J. (2001). *Choosing excellence: "Good enough" schools are not good enough*. Lanham, MD: Scarecrow Press.

Metcalf, S. (2002). Reading between the lines. In A. Kohn & P. Shannon (Eds.), *Education, inc.: Turning education into a business* (pp. 49–57). Portsmouth, NH: Heinemann.

Miner, B. (2002). For-profits target education. In A. Kohn & P. Shannon (Eds.), *Education, inc.: Turning education into a business* (pp. 131–139). Portsmouth, NH: Heinemann.

Moffett, J. (1994). On to the past: Wrong-headed school reform. *Phi Delta Kappan, 75*(8), 584–590.

Molnar, A., & Achilles, C. (2000a). Voucher and class-size research. *Center for Education Research, Analysis, and Innovation* [On-line]. Retrieved February 7, 2003, from http://asu .edu/educ/epsl/EPRU/point_of_view_essays/cerai-00-28.htm

Molnar, A., & Achilles, C. (2000a). Letter to Mr. Tim Russert, NBC. *Center for Education Research, Analysis, and Innovation* [On-line]. Retrieved February 7, 2003, from http://www .asu.edu/educ/epsl/EPRU/letters_to_editors/cerai-00-29.htm

Monastersky, R. (2002, November 25). ETS paid large bonuses to 11 employees, document shows. *The Chronicle of Higher Education Daily Report*, pp. 1–2.

Neill, M., & Schaeffer, B. (1998). High-stakes testing fails to improve student learning. *Fairtest Press Release* [On-line]. Retrieved February 7, 2003, from http://www.fairtest.org/ pr/naeppr.html.

Nevi, C. (2001). Saving standards. *Phi Delta Kappan, 82*, 460–461.

Oakes, J., Quartz, K. H., Ryan, S., & Lipton, M. (2000). *Becoming good American schools: The struggle for civic virtue in education reform.* San Francisco: Jossey-Bass.

Ohanian, S. (2002). *What happened to recess and why are our children struggling in kindergarten.* New York: McGraw Hill.

Ohanian, S. (1999). *One size fits few: The folly of educational standards.* Portsmouth, NH: Heinemann.

Popham, W. J. (2001). *The truth about testing: An educator's call to action.* Alexandria, VA: Association for Supervision and Curriculum Development.

Sacks, P. (1999). *Standardized minds: The high price of America's testing culture and what we can do to change it.* Cambridge, MA: Perseus.

Schmoker, M. (1999). *Results: The key to continuous school improvement* (2nd ed.). Alexandria, VA: Association for Supervision and Curriculum Development.

Smith, J. M., & Ruhl-Smith, C. (2004). Corporate answers to public school problems: A call for counteraction. *NCPEA Leadership Review, 4*, 1–7.

Smith, J. M., & Ruhl-Smith, C. (2002a). Standardized testing and educational standards: Implications for the future of emancipatory leadership in U.S. schools. In G. Perreault & F. C. Lunenburg (Eds.), The *changing world of school administration* (pp. 44–59). Lanham, MD: Scarecrow Press.

Smith, J. M., & Ruhl-Smith, C. (2002b, August). *Examining corporate solutions to public school effectiveness: The power of hyperbole and the essence of disingenuousness.* Paper presented at the annual meeting of the National Council of Professors of Educational Administration, Burlington, VT.

The financial collapse of Enron: Hearing before the Subcommittee on Oversight and Investigations of the House Committee on Energy and Commerce, 107th Cong., 1 (2002).

The National Center for Fair and Open Testing. (2000a). Gender bias in college admissions tests. Fairtest [On-line]. Retrieved February 7, 2003, from http://fairtest.org/facts/ genderbias.htm

The National Center for Fair and Open Testing. (2000b). How standardized testing damages education. Fairtest [On-line]. Retrieved February 7, 2003, from http://fairtest.org/facts/ howharm.htm

Thompson, A. (1996). Political pragmatism and educational inquiry. *Philosophy of Education Yearbook* [On-line]. Retrieved November 15, 2002, from http://x.ed.uiuc.edu/EPS/ PES-Yearbook/96_docs/thompson.htm.

Tucker, M. S., & Codding, J. B. (1998). *Standards for our schools: How to set them, measure them, and reach them.* San Francisco: Jossey-Bass.

United States National Commission on Excellence in Education. (1983). *A nation at risk: The imperative for educational reform.* Washington, DC: U.S. Government Printing Office.

Vinson, K. D., Gibson, R., & Ross, E. W. (2000). *High stakes testing and standardization: The threat to authenticity* [On-line]. Retrieved February 4, 2003, from http://www.pipeline .com/~rgibson/HighStakesTesting.htm.

Welsh-Huggins, A. (2002). Charter schools perform poorly on state proficiency tests. *The Cincinnati Enquirer* [On-line]. Retrieved July 31, 2002, from http://enquirer.com/editions/ 2002/06/11/loc_charter_schools.htm

West, C. (1993). *Keeping faith: Philosophy and race in America.* New York: Routledge.

Wiggins, G. (1994). None of the above. *The Executive Educator, 16,* 14–18.

Woodson, C. G. (1933). *The mis-education of the Negro.* Washington, DC: The Associated Publishers.

Wyatt, E. (1999, November 4). Investors see room for profit in the demand for education. *The New York Times,* A-1.

The Endangered Knowledge Base of School Administration and Supervision: Educational Leadership Becomes an Oxymoron

Richard Fossey and Angus MacNeil

Educational leadership as an academic field is in trouble. The public, as well as practicing school administrators, are questioning the usefulness—both the methods and results—of school leadership programs (Bottoms & O'Neill, 2001; Institute for Educational Leadership, 2000). Educational leadership professors need to change the way they see their jobs. Otherwise the entire business of preparing school principals and superintendents may leave the universities entirely (McCarthy, 1999, p. 135).

A GROWING TENDENCY TO HIRE
NONTRADITIONAL SCHOOL LEADERS

What are the signs of crisis? First, school districts are beginning to look outside the traditional education community for executive leadership. In particular, more and more districts are choosing superintendents who have no training in educational administration. For example, the Los Angeles school district hired Colorado's former Governor, Roy Romer, to be its new superintendent in 2000 (Purdum, 2000; Miller, 2001). Although Governor Romer had been involved in educational policy issues for many years, he had never run a school system and had no formal training in educational administration.

In San Diego, Alan Bersin, former U.S. Attorney, heads the city school system. Until recently, Paul Vallas, Chicago's former budget director, served as the Chicago school superintendent (Brownstein, 2002). Vallas recently left Chicago to be the Philadelphia schools chief. New Orleans and Seattle both chose former military officers to lead their school districts a few years ago. Neither military man had any former educational administration training or experience.

Richard Fossey, University of Houston
Angus MacNeil, University of Houston

In New York City, Joel Klein, a former federal prosecutor, is in charge of a school system of more than one million children (Steinhauer, 2002). Klein became chancellor of the New York school district in 2002, shortly after Harold Levy stepped down from the post. Levy also is an attorney.

As a final example, Rod Paige, now U.S. Secretary of Education, became superintendent of Houston Independent School District in 1994, without any formal training in school administration (McAdams, 2000, pp. 104–121). Although Paige had been dean of the school of education at Texas Southern University prior to becoming HISD's schools chief, he did not hold a Texas superintendent certificate at the time he was selected, and he had no experience as a public school district administrator. A University of Houston professor declared Paige to be "the least prepared person to become superintendent in the history of HISD" (McAdams, 2000, p. 115). Yet Paige, who eventually became U.S. Secretary of Education, is considered to be one of the most successful urban school superintendents in recent history.

These examples illustrate a point of view that is emerging about school leadership in the United States, particularly among the nation's business and political leaders. Specifically, the sentiment is growing that the best educational leadership comes from outside the field of education. Business people, lawyers, political leaders, and finance experts—not educators trained in colleges of education—may be best suited to attack the ills of public education, particularly in the inner-cities. As Donald McAdams put it while reflecting on Rod Paige's tenure as HISD superintendent:

> A strong leader with broad experience, political and management skills, and enough knowledge of education to face confidently the bureaucracy of a big city school system is more likely to be a reform leader than a traditional superintendent who has spent his or her entire professional life working within the system he or she is trying to reform. (2000, p. 256)

Clearly, this sentiment reflects not only a lack of confidence in traditionally trained school administrators, but also at least an implicit lack of confidence in the educational administration programs that prepared them. If educational leadership departments do not re-establish their credibility as competent preparers of urban school leaders, they will ultimately lose their reason for existing and be shut down.

EDUCATIONAL LEADERSHIP PROGRAMS ARE FACING INCREASING REGULATORY SCRUTINY

Second, we are seeing more and more state legislatures or state education agencies put school leadership programs under tough accreditation, accountability, and regulatory standards. This too signals a lack of confidence in educational leadership departments.

Not long ago, educational administration departments were at the periphery of the accountability movement, with the primary focus being on teacher preparation programs. As long as educational leadership professors taught courses that were prescribed by the state's education agency, no one inquired too closely regarding what was actually being accomplished. That is no longer true. Today, educational leadership programs are scrambling to meet external standards promulgated by outside bodies; and in some states, principal preparation programs have come under tough scrutiny by state regulatory agencies.

Without a doubt, the leading regulatory assault on educational leadership programs has come from the Educational Leadership Constituent Consortium (ELCC), which now reviews educational leadership programs in connection with the NCATE accreditation process for colleges of education. ELCC examines educational leadership programs against standards promulgated by the Interstate School Leadership Consortium (ISLC). These standards were created for the purpose of raising the quality of educational leadership preparation programs in the United States and shutting down programs that are unwilling or unable to comply with the ELCC/NCATE standards (English, 2002).

Although the ELCC review process has been in place only a short time, it already does not seem likely that it will promote better quality in educational leadership programs. Fenwick English argues that the ELCC review process has emerged as a "ruthless drive for the reduction of variance in preparation programs," a drive that ultimately will lead to a "dumbing down" of the educational leadership curriculum at many universities. English also charges the ELCC review process with being "anti-theoretical" and "anti-intellectual." In English's view, the ELCC process could ultimately lead to a standardization of educational leadership programs at a time when the field would greatly benefit from experimentation and diversity in program content.

Our own experience with ELCC/NCATE review leads us to believe that English may be right. Our educational leadership department at the University of Houston prepared a folio for ELCC review in early 2002, a folio that largely consisted of a written narrative, our department's course syllabi, and various examples of student outcomes. All syllabi were tailored to mimic the ELCC standards and to provide documented evidence that our department was meeting each and every standard. ELCC reviewers paid virtually no attention to the quality of scholarship in our department, the quality of our teaching, our links with education constituencies, or whether we were actually doing what our syllabi represented. All in all, our department's ELCC review process resembled a connect-the-dots exercise more than an intellectually rigorous review of our department's educational leadership program.

It is also interesting to note that many of the nation's leading colleges of education—Harvard, Stanford, Teachers College at Columbia, Vanderbilt, and Wisconsin—do not subject themselves to NCATE or ELCC review (English, 2002). Meanwhile, ELCC's list of approved educational leadership programs include some located in the most mediocre colleges and universities in the United States. It is hard to see how ELCC will improve the quality of educational leadership preparation when the country's leading programs don't participate and some of the nation's most lackluster institutions get ELCC's seal of approval.

PRINCIPAL AND SUPERINTENDENT PREPARATION
NO LONGER A UNIVERSITY MONOPOLY

Finally, some states are breaking up the universities' old monopoly in preparing students to become principal and superintendents. In Texas, for example, regional educational service centers and individual school districts can receive permission to develop their own alternative certification programs for superintendents and principals (Alvarado, 2001). This would have been unthinkable just a few years ago.

A look at teacher certification shows how threatening alternative certification could become for educational leadership departments. In Texas, colleges of education have been unable to provide enough teachers to supply the state's 1000-plus local school districts. Regional educational service centers, created by the state legislature to provide various support services for schools, have stepped into the breach.

Last year, the Region IV Educational Service Center, located in Houston, prepared 775 people for alternative teacher certification, an enormous help in alleviating the shortage of teachers in the Houston metropolitan area. In addition, the Houston and Pasadena school districts prepared another 439 teachers for initial certification. Together, these three entities prepared more certified teachers than all four campuses of the University of Houston put together (Texas State Board of Education Certification, 2002).

Just as important, Texas school leaders have watched alternatively certified teachers at work and found that their teaching skills are on par with those of university-trained teachers (Alvarado, 2001). Alternatively certified teachers have no trouble finding jobs, and non-traditional certification programs (mostly regional service centers and school districts) are capturing more and more of the teacher preparation market each year. Last year, non-traditional programs accounted for almost one out of four of the state's new certified teachers (Texas State Board of Education Certification, 2002).

If non-university providers gear up to begin preparing principals in large numbers, school districts may conclude that they can live without the services of educational leadership departments. In Texas, this could happen soon. Region IV Service Center officials estimate that the seven-county Houston metropolitan area needs around 600 new certified school administrators each year. Meanwhile, between 1995 and 2000, the University of Houston's main campus prepared only about 10 percent of that number on an annual basis. Service centers and school districts have the authority to compete with universities in the administrative certification field; and they will surely begin competing aggressively if they conclude that the Houston-area universities cannot meet the region's demands for more certified principals.

Likewise, the business community is expressing a desire for new models for preparing education leaders, ones that produces leaders who look more like corporate CEOs than traditionally trained educators. Perhaps the chief expression of this sentiment is the Broad Center for Superintendents, founded through the efforts of billionaire businessman Eli Broad. The Broad Center recently instituted an Urban Superintendents Academy, which is designed to prepare people with outstanding leadership qualities to be chief executives in urban school districts

(Broad Center for Superintendents, 2002). "The skills necessary to run a huge urban school district have changed dramatically in recent years," Broad said. "They have to know or be trained in management, problem solving, finance, labor relations, systems operations and so on" (Arenson, 2002).

Broad's academy, which lasts about ten months, allows participants to continue working full time while undergoing an intense "boot camp" experience in urban school leadership. Apparently, the Broad program is not intended to substitute for university-based superintendent certification programs, and it does not lead to a formal superintendent credential. Nevertheless, the existence of the Broad Center for Superintendents symbolizes the business community's lack of confidence in mainline universities' educational leadership programs—and a clear sign that many of the nation's business leaders believe that a new way of preparing educational leaders is needed.

HOW DID EDUCATIONAL LEADERSHIP PROGRAMS GET INTO THIS MESS?

Several factors gave rise to this crisis of confidence in the educational leadership professorate. First, the status of public education changed a great deal over the past thirty or forty years. By the end of the twentieth century, it was clear that urban education had severe problems and that many inner-city school systems had collapsed as effective learning organizations all across America. Racial isolation, poor student achievement, high dropout rates, and deteriorating infrastructures became the hallmark of public education in the nation's urban core (Fossey, 2002; Fossey, 2003). And in many urban systems, a culture of corruption, indifference, and mismanagement made reform almost impossible to achieve.

By the 1990s, the nation's business community was fully alarmed at the condition of urban education; business leaders know that the economic health of the cities depends on decent public education. A chorus arose for more effective school leadership, which many business leaders understood to mean school leaders who had the background, experience, and perspective of a corporate CEO executive.

Educational leadership departments have changed substantially over the past thirty years, and most people agree that their preparation programs have improved. Unfortunately, the field has not found a way to reliably produce school leaders who can successfully respond to the urban education crisis. Instead, educational leadership departments have been gradually investing more and more of their energy into theoretical research.

Twenty-five years ago or so, "Ed Ad" professors were often former principals and superintendents who were not scholars but who were closely connected to the public schools. Many of these professors were literally "good old boys." That is, they were usually males, generally retired from school positions, and "good" in the sense that they were genuinely committed to developing public school leaders.

Typically, the good old boys did little scholarly research, and their teaching style often consisted of telling "personal success stories and lively antidotes" (McCarthy,

1999, p. 125, citing Marland, 1960, p. 25) in their educational administration classes. In general, these professors were closely connected to schools and had great influence in the development and selection of public school principals and superintendents.

But the "good old boys" were often an embarrassment to the universities where they worked because they had little regard for research or the scholarly ethos of mainline academe. Moreover, these old-style educational administration professors were frequently criticized for being inattentive to cultural and racial diversity, and for perpetuating school administration as a white male profession.

Within the last thirty years, many universities—particularly the research universities—replaced the good old boys with true scholars whose training more closely aligned with that of other university professors. Many of the new breed professors were social science researchers with narrow academic specialties and a strong commitment to theory development (McCarthy, 1999, p. 125).

By the 1980s, the theoretical scholars had replaced most of the good old boys in the research universities. In general, the new generation of educational leadership professors raised the reputation of their discipline, improved the quality of doctoral level research, and produced a great deal of published scholarship. In the eyes of many, the rise of the social science scholars and the departure of the good old boys greatly improved the quality of educational leadership preparation programs.

On the other hand, the new-style professors seldom had any personal experience as school administrators (Clifford & Guthrie, 1988, p. 338). Perhaps that is why, as Greenfield (1995) noted, educational administration scholars often tend to accept theories developed in non-school contexts as suitable for understanding school leadership. In recent years, educational leadership departments began to evolve into bastions of theoretical research—often disconnected from schools—with faculty members pursuing isolated research agendas and departments having no coordinated sense of program or mission.

The Department of Education at the University of Chicago exemplified this trend. Over time, it lost connection with the world of practice; and in 1996, the University decided to shut it down (Bronner, 1997; Worthington, 1996). Founded by John Dewey in 1895 and once considered one of the premier educational research units in the United States, the University of Chicago's Department of Education closed its doors in 2001.

This evolution in the world of educational administration would not have precipitated a crisis except for the fact that various public constituencies began to demand a different kind of school leader. Often these demands were conflicting and some were simply wrong-headed; but the educational leadership profession was poorly equipped to meet or counter these demands because it had lost sight of its mission, which was to prepare competent and effective school leaders.

A second factor has contributed to the crisis in educational leadership. Because educational administration units are usually fairly small, colleges of education often put educational leadership programs into departments with other small program areas that have unrelated missions. Thus, educational administration faculty might be grouped with school counseling faculty, technology faculty, research methodologists, philosophers, or higher education administration professors. These subunits might share a common sense of mission in the abstract sense, but the faculty members who know and care about school leadership often become a minority voice in departmental decisions about educational administration program adjustments and curriculum changes.

A third factor in the crisis is the increasing difficulty of finding educational leadership professors who are both good researchers and experienced school administrators. School principals and superintendents now command salaries that are higher—and sometimes much higher—than an assistant professor's compensation. Indeed, we are now facing a shortage of school principals (Fenwick, 2000; Steinberg, 2000), at least partly due to the fact that principals' salaries are not high enough given the challenges of the principal's job. If people are unwilling to become principals because of salary concerns, they are surely even more reluctant to enter the educational administration profession, where typical salaries are even lower.

All of these factors have combined to create a crisis in educational leadership, and this crisis has demoralized many of the people in this profession. Again and again we hear about educational leadership departments that are contentious, drifting, and even dysfunctional. Indeed, educational leadership departments have become the perennial "bad boy" units in colleges of education all across the country.

WHAT SHOULD WE DO NOW?

What should we do about this problem? First, we think educational leadership departments should adopt the professional school model and begin seeing themselves much like law schools, business schools, and schools of social work. An educational leadership department's main business is to prepare professional school leaders who are "safe to practice." Scholarly research is important of course, but law and business professors do not neglect scholarship. Instead, in professional schools, research accompanies and grows out of the professional education mission.

Moreover, a substantial segment of the larger education community *wants* educational leadership departments to be professional schools. We hear no public outcry about the need for more education scholars, more "pure" education research, or more social scientists. In fact, Clifford and Guthrie (1988, pp. 330–31), in their study of American education schools, suggested that our nation's universities might be better off if "unproductively focused" colleges of education were closed.

Unfortunately, many educational leadership departments—particularly those located in American research universities—are retreating further and further into the bastion of theoretical research. At one time, the Ed.D. degree was thought to be an avenue for countering this trend. The Ed.D. is, after all, a professional degree, not an academic degree, and thus an appropriate degree for programs that develop educational leaders on a rigorous professional school model. Alas, many of the universities that offer Ed.D. degrees have turned their Ed.D. programs into Ph.D. programs under another name. In other words, many Ed.D. programs place a heavy emphasis on research methodology with only minimum attention paid to developing school leadership expertise.

Second, we think educational leadership departments need to be wholly dedicated to school leadership and perhaps to college and university leadership as well. Scholars with purely theoretical research agendas perform valuable work, but they need to do it in other academic units. The nation needs more and better school leaders—especially in the inner cities—and it needs them now. Scholars who are clueless about the realities of urban education should not be involved in shaping educational leadership programs and curriculum.

Third, educational leadership professors need to modernize the way they offer their programs. Non-university providers of alternatively certified teachers have already shown that they can be produce certified teachers faster and often cheaper than colleges of education. Some educational leadership departments have streamlined their programs, organized off-campus cohorts, and adapted their teaching schedules to be more convenient to working professionals. In general, these departments have managed to maintain their enrollment levels. Departments that have not have seen their enrollments decline.

Finally, we think educational leadership professors need to articulate a clearer vision of what we do and who we are so that we can counter external pressure to move the whole notion of school leadership in the wrong direction. Increasingly, legislatures, regulatory bodies, and the business community express the view that school principals should be more like chief executive officers, business managers, and corporate leaders. There is some sense in this talk. In general, the public correctly perceives that private industry operates more efficiently than public education and that corporate leaders are often more decisive and more flexible than school leaders. Unlike public education, private industry operates under intense market pressures in a ruthless accountability environment.

Nevertheless, schools are where children learn and are nurtured. Learning communities require a different kind of vision and leadership than corporations. One need only look at the inner-city parochial schools, which eschew any notion that education should be structured on business principles. Research has shown that the Catholic schools often do a better job of educating inner-city children than their secular counterparts.

In our view, the field of educational leadership has not done a particularly good job in preparing school leaders, and that is why the field is under pressure. For example, educational leadership scholars have produced mountains of research on school dropout rates. Indeed, it is hard to imagine that any more can be said about this problem. Yet high school graduation rates remain shockingly low in the inner cities—hovering around 50 percent (Fossey, 1996; Green, 2001). Decades of research on school dropout rates have contributed almost nothing to solving this problem.

Likewise, principal preparation programs have been almost totally ineffective in reducing the practice of corporal punishment in the schools. If educational leadership professors were effectively communicating a vision of schools as safe and nurturing school communities, no student would leave a principal preparation program without an abhorrence of corporal punishment.

CONCLUSION

"Since the 1980s," Martha McCarthy wrote in 1999, "there have been calls for reform in nearly every aspect of the preparation of school leaders and admonitions that universities may be replaced in this regard unless their programs are substantially transformed (p. 135, citing Achilles, 1984; Griffiths, 1988; Murphy, 1993). So far, the nation's school leadership programs have been sluggish in responding to growing signs of frustration.

Today, educational administration as a discipline is in a *fine mess*, and practitioners are expressing *diminished confidence* in university preparation programs. Deans of Education spend their time being *almost candid* as they *vigorously ignore* the *accurate rumors* that educational leadership programs are *found missing*. It is our *unbiased opinion* (if *subtly exaggerated*) that the *harmonious discord*, *enthusiastic indifference*, and *happy apathy* that characterize educational administration will ultimately create a *history of the future* that will end in a *planned exodus*. Our preparation programs have an *extended deadline* to make changes that will result in something other than *meaningful nonsense*. Our efforts to be responsive to the field have been *enormously small* and *mighty weak* as our programs *float to the bottom* in importance and are declared *genuine fakes*.

As the reader has probably noticed, the italicized phrases in the paragraph above are oxymorons, and yet are strangely appropriate for discussing the educational leadership discipline. And that is our point. If *Educational Leadership* does not change, our field will become an oxymoronic term.

REFERENCES

Achilles, C. M. (1984). Forecast: Stormy weather ahead in education administration. *Issues in Education, 2*(2), 127–135.

Alvarado, R. (2001). *Teacher preparation effectiveness of an alternative certification program as perceived by campus administrators in the education service center, Region 2, Texas.* Ph.D. dissertation, Texas A&M University.

Arenson, K. W. (2002, July 30). The new schools chancellor: Other cities; trends of noneducators leading schools. *New York Times* [online]. Available at: <nytimes.com>.

Bottoms, G., & O'Neill, K. (2001). *Preparing a new breed of principals: It's time for action.* Atlanta, GA: Southern Regional Education Board.

Broad Center for Superintendents (2002*). The Broad Center Opportunity* [online]. Available at: http://www.broadcenter.org/nsite/opportunity/index.shtml.

Bronner, E. (1997, September 17). End of Chicago's Education School stirs debate. *New York Times* [on line]. Available at: <nytimes.com>.

Brownstein, R. (2002, June 24). Ailing school systems prescribed an injection of leadership. *Los Angeles Times* [online]. Available at the Broad Foundation's web site: http://www .broadcenter.org/nsite/press/index.shtml.

Clifford, G. J., & Guthrie, J. W. (1988). *A brief for professional education: Ed school.* Chicago: University of Chicago Press.

English, F. W. (2002, September 30). *About the policing functions of ELCC/NCATE and the standardization of university preparation programs in educational administration* (Unpublished memorandum to Ted Creighton, Executive Director of National Council of Professors in Educational Administration, and Michelle Young, Executive Director of the University Council of Educational Administration [online]. Available at: <NCPEA.org>.

Fenwick, L. T. (2000). *The principal shortage: Who will lead?* Cambridge, MA: The Principal's Center, Harvard Graduate Education.

Fossey, R. (1996, October). High school dropout rates: Are we sure they are going down? *Phi Delta Kappan, 78,* 140–144.

Fossey, R. (2002). *Urban school systems: An overview and assessment.* Houston, TX: Center for Reform of School Systems. (Unpublished paper).

Fossey, R. (2003). School desegregation is over in the inner cities: What do we do now? In L. F. Miron & E. St. John (Eds.), *Reinterpreting urban school reform* (pp. 15–32). Albany, NY: SUNY Press.

Greene, J. P. (2001). *High school graduation rates in the United States.* New York: Manhattan Institute.

Greenfield, W. D. (1995). Toward a theory of school administration: The centrality of leadership. *Educational Administration Quarterly, 31*(1), 61–85.

Griffiths, D. E. (1988). *Educational administration: Reform PDQ or RIP* (UCEA Occasional Paper No. 8312). Tempe, AZ: University Council for Educational Administration.

Institute for Educational Leadership. (2000). *Leadership for student learning: Reinventing the principalship.* Washington, DC: Author.

Marland, S. P. (1960). Superintendents' concerns about research applications in educational administration In R. F. Campbell & J. M. Lipham (Eds.), *Administrative theory as a guide to action* (pp. 21–36). Chicago: University of Chicago, Midwest Administration Center.

McAdams, D. R. (2000). *Fighting to save our urban schools . . . and winning!* New York: Teachers College Press.

McCarthy, M. (1999). The evolution of educational leadership preparation programs. In J. Murphy & K. Louis (Eds), *Handbook of Research on Educational Administration. 2nd ed.* (pp. 45–72). San Francisco, CA: Jossey-Bass.

Miller, M. (2001, June). The super: L.A. superintendent Roy Romer may be the most talented man ever to run a big-city school district. *Washington Monthly* [online]. Available at: <wysiwyg://doc.68/http://www.washingtonmonthly.com/features/2001/0106.miller.html>.

Murphy, J. (1993). Ferment in school administration: Rounds 1–3. In J. Murphy (Ed.), *Preparing tomorrow's school leaders: Alternative designs* (pp. 1–38). University Park, PA: University Council for Educational Administration.

Purdum, T. S. (June 8, 2000). Ex-Gov. Romer embraces his mission: Running Los Angeles schools. *New York Times,* p. 20.

Steinberg, J. (September 2, 2000). Nation's schools struggling to find enough principals. *New York Times,* p. 1.

Steinhauer, J. (2002, July 30). The new school chancellor: Overview; Bloomberg picks a lawyer to run New York schools. *New York Times* [online]. Available at: <http://nytimes.com/>.

Texas State Board of Education Certification (2002). *Number of teachers obtaining initial certification from educator preparation programs (1993–2002)* [online]. Available at: <http://www.sbec.state.tx.us/resrchdata/texas_teacher_production_1993%20to%202002.pdf>.

Worthington, R. (1996, August 24). Review puts U. of C. education department in peril: Older faculty, weak commitment cited. *Chicago Tribune* [online]. Available at: <http://www.chicagotribune.com/>.

Connecting Superintendents with the Technical Core of Teaching and Learning: A Synthesis of Research Findings

Steven P. Shidemantle and John R. Hoyle

THEORETICAL FRAMEWORK FOR THE TECHNICAL CORE AND SUPERINTENDENTS

Superintendents in the United States are charged with overseeing the design of curriculum focused on the instruction and learning in multiple school contexts. Researchers, however, have gained tacit knowledge, but little empirical evidence that directly links these instructional leadership responsibilities of superintendents to actual student performance on a variety of measures. According to Björk (1996) the education reports that burst on the scene beginning in 1983 identified superintendents as pivotal to the success of school improvement and highlighted their role as instructional leaders to enhance student learning. Although a CEO of schools has multiple roles to fill each day, instructional leadership has become a top priority as an indicator of executive performance (Björk, 1993; Bredeson, 1996). Research findings indicate that superintendents with successful districts exhibited high levels of involvement in instructional matters (Cuban, 1984; Hoyle, 2002). These CEOs used their managerial skills and power to influence the behavior of principals and teachers who are more closely linked to student achievement. Research on Instructionally Effective School Districts (IESD) identified superintendents' instructional leadership skills including staff recruitment of outstanding educators to improve learning and teaching and influence the quality of instructional programs (Cuban, 1984; Hoyle, Björk, Collier, & Glass, 2004). The literature confirms that CEOs not only help create the conditions and set the tone for instructional design and assessment, but also rally their staffs around the technical core of teaching and learning.

School district chief executives face growing challenges related to decreased funding, rising education costs along with growing demands for meeting higher student achievement standards, and intensifying concerns about effective leadership.

Steven P. Shidemantle, Katy Junior High School, Katy, Texas
John R. Hoyle, Texas A&M University

Teaching and learning—education's *technical core*—constitute the axis upon which education systems revolve. Hoyle (1991) asserted that the school superintendent must be competent in the technical-core processes, coupled with the other effective leadership and management processes that "transmit a common core of knowledge and skills indigenous to the role of district CEO" (p. 23). School finance, political issues, media relations, human resources, and long-range planning efforts are vital to the support of a district's vision for academic excellence and ultimately student learning and achievement. The focus of executive leadership is centered upon the system of organizational actions where the actual products of teaching and learning are formed (Hoy & Miskel, 2001). From this tug-of-war of explicit requirements and implicit core actions evolves the question of how to meet educational demands; maintain the focus of the financial responsibilities, politics, media relations, human resources, and planning; and remain centered on the improvement of teaching and learning. Scholars strive to provide answers by adding to educational administration's knowledge base through new targeted investigations.

As Achilles (1996) stated, however, "When building something substantial or important, a person usually starts with a solid, firm, strong foundation. A classic example of architects, engineers, and builders not heeding this axiom can be found in the gravity-defying tower of Pisa" (p. 1).

The role of the school superintendent has been built on the expanding knowledge base of educational administration (Hoyle, 1991). If those in research, however, neglect educational administration's knowledge base in their investigations, then the structure of education could begin to lean.

The knowledge base of educational administration has developed, expanded, and matured since its birth in the late 1800s. Practicing superintendents and scholars, William Payne and William Harris, developed the first scientific basis upon which educational administration's knowledge base was to be built (Culbertson, 1988). Realizing that the education of students in school settings was dependent upon the development of educational organization and management, Payne drew from the social, political, and legal fields to propose that educational administration use the principles of these sciences to explain systems of education. These early leaders of learning and scholars of educational administration, agreed that superintendents must be masters of teaching and learning, i.e., of the technical core.

The works of Payne and Harris (Cubberly, 1927) contributed to the science surrounding the development of education administration and its knowledge base. The attention now becomes connecting the core knowledge of education administration with the core actions of the superintendency. Over the past decades school superintendents have come under great scrutiny in the effort to improve American education. These system executives have been forced away from student learning to satisfy the needs they face in managing budgets, personnel, politics, human resources, and long-range planning. Their role has indeed been greatly expanded beyond the roots established by scholars such as Payne, Harris, Rice, Dewey, and others. The core of educational administration's knowledge base, however, has been reinforced throughout its history.

This responsibility of ensuring and maintaining a highly refined technical core is reflected in the AASA superintendent standards. The standards developed by Hoyle, Glass, and Oates (1992), adapted by the American Association of School Administrators (Hoyle & AASA Commission on Standards for the Superintendency, 1993), and later adapted in the Interstate School Leaders Licensure Consortium (ISLLC) and the National Council for Accreditation of Teacher Education (NCATE), reflect the high level of responsibility that is placed on the superintendent concerning teaching and learning. The standards that directly address the technical core demonstrate this priority by stating that educational leaders will:

- Standard 5: Design curriculum and a strategic plan that enhance teaching and learning in multiple contexts; provide planning and future methods to anticipate occupational trends and their educational implications; identify taxonomies of instructional objectives and validation procedures for curricular units, using theories of cognitive development; align and sequence curriculum; use valid and reliable performance indicators and testing procedures to measure performance outcomes; and describe the proper use of computers and other learning and information technologies. (p. 9)
- Standard 6: Exhibit knowledge of instructional management by implementing a system that includes research findings on learning and instructional strategies, instructional time, advanced electronic technologies, and resources to maximize student outcomes; describe and apply research and best practice on integrating curriculum and resources for multicultural sensitivity and assessment strategies to help all students achieve at high level. (p. 10)
- Standard 7: Develop a staff evaluation and development system to improve the performance of all staff members; select appropriate models for supervision based on adult motivation research. (p. 11)

Curriculum design, instructional leadership strategies, assessment strategies, staff performance evaluation, and student achievement indicated in the above standards are vital to the core success of schools. Although these standards address the direct responsibilities of the superintendent for the technical core, all the standards serve as benchmarks to guide the health and vitality of teaching and learning through all aspects of superintendent performance.

The purposes of this paper are (a) to discuss education administration's research framework that connects the actions of the school superintendent with the technical core of teaching and learning, (b) to explore the connection between the superintendency and the technical core through a representative synthesis of research published in two top-tier educational administration journals, and (c) to propose a call for new research investigations that link the actions of school superintendents with the technical core through instructional leadership and improved student learning.

SCHOOL SUPERINTENDENTS' CONNECTION
WITH THE TECHNICAL CORE

Efficacious leadership of school executives is at the center of American school restructuring and reform. A key factor that indicates the effective nature of educational reform is the school superintendent's direct emphasis on the technical core (Bridges, 1982; Björk, 1993; Bredeson, 1996; Bredeson & Johansson, 1997; Cuban, 1984; Herman, 1990; Petersen, 1999; Petersen & Short, 2001; Wirt, 1990). The school superintendent historically has been known to be the instructional leader of the school system (Bredeson, 1996). Although the role has clearly expanded over the past 150 years, Björk (1993) maintained that instructional leadership of the technical core continues to be an essential factor in district success. The superintendent's connection with classroom learning, though somewhat removed and infrequent, is necessary for district success and improvement (Wimpelberg, 1988). How then do school superintendents maintain connection with the technical core through instructional leadership?

Herman (1990) implied that notable weaknesses are found in the knowledge base concerning the technical core in educational administration. In a research presentation at the Conference of the Southern Regional Council on Educational Administration, Herman's findings affirm a framework of fundamental behaviors that superintendents exhibit as instructional leaders:

- Allocating instructional personnel (personnel)
- Organizing instructional program (curriculum)
- Activities supporting the instructional program (curriculum/budget)
- Developing instructional personnel (personnel)
- Planning for the instructional program (budget, curriculum, and personnel) (p. 7–8)

Herman related budget, personnel, and curriculum as three executive management areas that are key to the success of superintendents' instructional leadership skills. The coupling of leadership competencies and school management areas shows the importance of integrating both capacities to effectively guide district success.

How can effective teaching and learning be cultured and matured if school superintendents do not practice efficacious instructional leadership? Later research that built upon Herman's work were the technical core investigations completed by Petersen (1999). Much of the groundbreaking information concerning instructional leadership has come through Petersen's investigations of superintendents. He explored the relationship between the core actions and behaviors of five superintendents who were perceived to have a strong focus on instructional leadership. The selection criteria were based on peer recognition, demographics, and student test scores.

Peterson (1999) administered a 52-item survey to 45 building principals and 31 school board members who had worked at least two years with the five superintendents mentioned above. His results revealed the following essential instructional leadership characteristics of the five superintendents:

- Creation and active promotion of an instructionally oriented vision;
- Creation of an instructionally supportive organizational structure;
- Assessment and evaluation of personnel and instructional programs;
- Full organizational adaptation of the instructional program and its leadership. (p. 17)

These characteristics are central to superintendents' connection with teaching and learning through instructional leadership. Petersen noted that school board support was unusually high in each of these districts. Board support of the superintendent was a key variable in student scores found on the Texas Assessment of Academic Skills (TAAS) in a study conducted by Hoyle, Ealy, Skrla, & Hogan (2001). Superintendents given the freedom to make personnel decisions for leadership positions have better control over instructional program success. These findings support the theory that instructional leadership remains a primary quality that school boards look for in prospective superintendents (Björk, 1993; Cuban, 1984; Kowalski & Oates, 1993; Petersen & Short, 2001).

Rowan (1995b) found that until 1985 issues surrounding the core work of learning and teaching were not central elements of preparation or practice in education administration. In citing the National Policy Board for Educational Administration (1989), Rowan reports that "after a decade of sustained efforts to reform instruction in American schools, administrator preparation programs . . . rarely require extensive course work on learning, teaching, or instructional management" (p. 115). This gap, however, appears to be closing since standards driven superintendent preparation programs place increased emphasis on instructional processes and student assessment (Hoyle, Björk, Collier, & Glass, 2004).

The work of Rowan, Petersen, Short, and others intensified the focus on educational administration research efforts to examine the issues that directly link administrative practice with educational administration's fundamental knowledge base of the technical core. These observers recommend a delicate balance among all CEO leadership responsibilities to assure strong instructional focus. This balance of the other skill domains to support student learning has been given limited attention in the research literature. Superintendents are charged to help create and refine curriculum that respects all culture and lifestyles without losing the focus of a unified curriculum for all learners in their schools. Foriska (1998) says it best about the complex curriculum challenges faced by CEOs. He writes that superintendents must administer the many components and responsibilities of the district, yet model ways to "develop curriculum and instructional systems that teach students to prepare for an information and service based society, and equip them with the skills for dealing with the complex problems to which there are no easy answers" (p. 1). This balance is precarious when policy makers—i.e., legislators, state departments of education and professional administrator associations lobby for leaner standards—driven, and test-monitored curricula. Under the current climate of government, all CEOs feel pressure to model their instructional systems, including reading and math curriculum, after the No Child Left Behind (NCLB) guidelines. CEOs faced with these federal and state mandates and guidelines are concerned about the overall balance of the learning options for all students and about the preoccupation by policy makers with achievement based on pre-specified outcomes that can narrow the curriculum and stifle student creativity, problem solving and critical thinking. Elliot Eisner (1998), a leading advocate for stronger humanities education, writes, "To ameliorate our discomfort with subjectivity, we employ assessment methods that are characterized by precision, certainty, and attention to fragmented content" (p. 299). This caveat is among the reasons that CEOs strive for balance in the technical core. The following is a synthesis of research on the progress that educational administration researchers have made in connecting the profession's technical core with the practice of the school superintendent.

SYNTHESIS OF RESEARCH

Articles published in recent years in the *Educational Administration Quarterly (EAQ)* and the *Journal of School Leadership (JSL)* were examined to explore research findings concerning school superintendents' connections to the technical core. The criteria for selection includes articles either titled or focusing on instructional leadership, curriculum development, teacher effectiveness, student outcomes, learning communities, and accountability. Once the articles were selected according to the criteria, the authors analyzed the research procedures and methods, and theoretical base for appropriate sorting.

Educational Administration Quarterly Research

EAQ published 368 research-related articles between 1990 and 2002. The results of the analysis produced only two articles that related to superintendents' activities with the technical core. The two superintendency articles that met the above criteria were qualitative in nature. Six general theoretical essays were found to mention the outlined criteria, but addressed education administration in general, and differentiation between superintendency and principalship roles was ambiguous.

Descriptive Findings

The articles related to the superintendency did not directly address the criteria outlined above; rather, they described elements that supported a functional relationship between the superintendency and the technical core. Both qualitative studies, conducted in California school districts, provide few insights to the executive functions of the school superintendent and the technical core.

Davis (1998) investigated superintendents' views of why principals are relieved of their positions. This qualitative study was frameworked through telephone interviews of non-randomly selected California school superintendents. The questionnaire addressed core questions and was aligned with the Yukl Multiple Linkage Model of effective leadership. Davis found only a weak relationship between the technical core-related issues and involuntary departure of principals. Strong links, however, were found with communication and relationships, decision-making and judgment, lack of trust and confidence, ineffective political management, and involuntary departure. As a superintendency weathervane, the research data indicated that superintendents view social and political issues as predominate factors of importance in the success of school administrators. The research did not elaborate on this perspective, but the data showed definite possibilities that the superintendents' views were a reflection of their own professional framework. This perspective warrants further detailed research.

Mitchell and Beach (1993) investigated the views and actions of district superintendents through the encumbering task of organizational restructuring. Through interviews with 21 district superintendents and selected district staff, technical core-related functions were described in terms of needed changes through reform efforts to improve teacher effectiveness and curriculum development. The study found three emergent themes:

1. Superintendents focus their thinking using a generalized conceptual framework (i.e., related to institutional, organizational, or operational type issues).
2. Superintendents tended to approach educational problems from a social community perspective rather than an educational effectiveness perspective.
3. Superintendents viewed restructuring as an opportunity to create links in building stronger socially supportive school/community relationships and charge the professional staff with the responsibility of instructional program development and the maintenance of the technical core.

The observed themes, as stated in this study, seem to disconnect the role of the superintendency rather than couple it with the technical core. Perhaps there is an unintended gap in the research that overlooks the superintendents' actions that precipitate their perceived disconnectedness with the core. Possibly the concept that forms the idea that the superintendent is the instructional leader of the school district is so broad and complex that educational administration research divides the overall concept into manageable fragments that can be examined in depth. Through the author's search for articles related to this topic, numerous articles were found concerning superintendent evaluations, job perceptions, social and political issues, feminist and post-modernist critique studies, and school board relations, and yet none of the articles researched mentioned the core concept that anchors education to its knowledge base—learning and teaching. The major issue with either analysis is that the profession (both in research and practice) appears to minimize the importance of valid connections of superintendent actions to the core—learning and teaching. In sum, qualitative research presents a strong need for instructional leadership and presents rationale for the leadership to emerge, but minimal empirical evidence about the role of the CEO and his or her impact on teaching and learning is available.

Journal of School Leadership Research
JSL published approximately 415 research related articles between 1990 and 2002. Three articles related to superintendents' active engagement with the technical core.

Descriptive Findings
Dillon and Halliwell's (1991) quantitative survey investigation explored the responses of 250 randomly selected New York superintendents' and school board presidents' (N = 500) views of superintendent evaluation purposes, weaknesses, and strengths. One hundred seventy-eight of the 250 selected superintendents (71.2%) and 128 of the 250 selected school board presidents (51.2%) responded to the survey.

The overall response rate was 61.2%. This presents limitations because of internal and external validity threats resulting in little meaning drawn from the study.

The investigation, however, is worth reporting and its results lay possible groundwork for future investigations. The summary findings as they relate to the purposes of this paper are:

- School board presidents (65.48%) view improvement of instructional (technical core) leadership as the most important purpose of superintendent evaluation, whereas superintendents do not share this view (12.83% viewed it as important).
- Superintendents (43.01 %) view school board members not possessing the evaluation skill required to appropriately perform evaluations as the main weakness of superintendent evaluations, whereas school board presidents do not share this view (16.28% viewed it as a weakness).
- Managing and evaluating personnel, improving student outcomes, and curriculum (technical core) leadership are ranked in the top four functions of a superintendent by both board presidents and superintendents.

Although promising, the findings yield only directional groundwork for future targeted investigations. This study could have added more to the research knowledge base by probing statistical relationships among instructional goals, processes and student achievement records.

Bredeson (1996) investigated superintendents' engagement with curriculum development as instructional leaders. In this empirical study, Bredeson employed qualitative and quantitative methods to gather and analyze data from a three-page questionnaire. Data were collected from 326 of the 397 randomly selected Wisconsin superintendents (81.2%).

The investigation found that superintendents' engagement with curriculum and instruction was within the context of their instructional leadership characteristics. Preliminary analyses revealed nine important areas of administrative tasks as reported by the respondents: budget and finance, communications/public relations, personnel administration, working with school boards, leadership and vision, instructional leadership and curriculum, general administration, working with staff and others, and planning. Results showed that instructional leadership and curriculum were ranked fourth by superintendents when asked about their level of importance. In contrast, however, when ranked by the amount of time committed to administrative tasks, instructional leadership and curriculum dropped to seventh. Budget and finance remained first in both analyses. The analyses also revealed four principal types of roles in which superintendents are categorized: instructional visionaries, instructional collaborators, instructional supporters, and instructional delegators. The results showed that most superintendents characterized themselves as instructional supporters (36.1 %), then as instructional delegators (26.0%), instructional collaborators (25.4%), and instructional visionaries (12.5%).

Bredeson concluded his study by integrating the preliminary investigations to examine the relationship between levels of importance and time commitment to each type of instructional leader. Instructional visionaries and collaborators placed the highest priority on instructional leadership compared to instructional supporters and delegators. Instructional supporters and delegators both ranked instructional leadership eighth in the amount of time committed. Consistent rankings of time commitment between all types of instructional leaders were budget and finance (first), personnel administration (second), community/public relations (third), and working with staff (ninth).

The framework of Bredeson's (1996) findings imply:

- Superintendents placed high value on technical core engagement.
- Superintendents were not able to commit an equating amount of time to technical core engagement.
- Superintendents consistently give budget and finance issues higher priorities of importance and time commitment than technical core issues.
- Superintendents' description of their engagement with instructional leadership can be categorized into four main types: visionary, collaborator, supporter, and delegator.
- Instructional visionaries and collaborators place a higher level of importance on engagement with the technical core than do instructional supporters and delegators.
- Superintendent actions are dictated by available time commitment rather than level of importance.

The synthesis of articles in two leading journals in educational administration reveals a dearth of targeted quality research that focuses on superintendents' directed engagement with education's main purpose—teaching and learning. If the superintendent is the instructional leader of the district and all responsibilities are extensions of his or her role as the executive leader, then prior research should provide evidence derived from statistical and other methods to help school executives refocus and maintain the relationship with the technical core of teaching and learning. Research on this technical core connection is directional at best, but does challenge researchers to deepen investigations about how school superintendents balance their time and expertise to assure that the technical core of teaching and learning is the main purpose.

A CALL FOR NEW INVESTIGATIONS

The discord between the logic and theory behind the connection of the superintendent with education's technical core through instructional leadership and the limited field of research on this phenomenon is the foundation upon which the authors' posit both a need for research that seeks evidence about the role of school superintendents in actually improving student achievement. This research agenda could provide powerful guidance in the preparation and professional development of CEOs in education.

Rowan (1995a) argued that increased research is needed to understand the links between educational administration and the technical core. Significant research that answered Rowan's 1995 call examined the relationship between technical core issues and the school principal (see e.g., Blase & Blase, 1999, 2002; Hoy, 1994; Hoy & Sweetland, 2001; Leithwood, 1994, 2002; Leithwood & Jantzi, 1999; Leithwood, Steinbach, & Raun, 1993). A concentration of targeted research linking the technical core with school superintendent actions by the profession has yet to be undertaken. To enhance educational reform efforts, scholars in the profession could initiate a call for a specialized research agenda that explores school superintendent engagement activities with the core of education administration's knowledge base. From the synthesis of the minimal research found, the authors of this article suggest three main areas for research.

First, investigations into superintendent engagement activities with the technical core should be conducted. The pressures of politics, finance, community partnerships, media relations, and legal functions continue to place enormous pressures on the district executive leader who can easily be distracted from the primary roles of teaching and learning. Twenty years ago, Campbell, Fleming, Newell, and Bennion (1987) stated, "If educational administration ever had a central core or intellectual cohesion, that era seems to be past" (p. 199). Since that time, researchers realize that learning and teaching constitutes the central core that brings intellectual cohesion to education leadership. An analysis of the divergence of research agendas through the 1970s and 1980s (Achilles, 1994) indicated that the era does seem to have passed. The formation of the National Policy Board (NPB) was an effort to reunify administrator groups who diverged in the late 1960s. Pressures surrounding the superintendency are attractive areas for research (Hoy, 1994). Hoy asserted that the tensions among the traditionalists, constructivists, structuralists, feminists, and postmodernists serve to increase the complexity of gaining a clear view of the technical core. Nevertheless, the core focus of educational administration—learning and teaching— has maintained the significance of its knowledge base from Harris and Payne's generation.

Second, further investigations are needed to define effective instructional leadership behaviors in the superintendency. Research performed by scholars in the profession supports the significance of the superintendent as the instructional leader of the education system (see Björk, 1993; Bredeson & Johansson, 1997; Kowalski & Oates, 1993; Murphy & Hallinger, 1988; Wirt, 1990). The superintendent has both the legal and moral obligation to ensure that students achieve at the highest levels (Wimpelberg, 1997). As Björk (1993) posited, "Improving education, however, requires district level leadership. Research studies indicate that superintendents who serve as instructional leaders contribute to the instructional effectiveness of their school districts" (p. 249). Furthermore, Murphy and Hallinger (1988) asserted that "curriculum and instruction, the consistency of technical core factors, [and] the strong instructional leadership role of the superintendents . . . set these districts apart" (p. 180). Investigations that aid in defining effective superintendent instructional leadership behaviors could reveal previously hidden paths that lead to increased student learning and achievement. Mixed model research designs, for instance, could show if, how, and why instructional leadership varies with district size, culture, beliefs, attitudes, economics, and learning communities. These investigations could yield essential untapped insights into superintendent technical core behaviors that impact student learning and achievement.

Third, a meta-analysis of research that connects superintendent actions with the technical core through instructional leadership might couple smaller investigations that may be limited by sample size, significance, effect size, power, low survey return rates, or other threats to internal or external validities. First, exploratory (hypothesis generating) meta-analyses that ask general research questions that guide research syntheses would generate specific hypotheses for confirmatory (hypothesis testing) meta-analysis (McNamara, Morales, Kim, & McNamara, 1998). Whether exploratory or confirmatory, meta-analytic investigations can determine moderator and mediator variables that often reveal answers to conflicting study results and irreconcilable differences between investigations (Hunt, 1997). Verstehen evaluations that illuminate emerging themes through naturalistic research syntheses (Light & Pillemer, 1984) could be allied with traditional meta-analytic measures to provide a more complete understanding of such complex and confounding concepts as executive instructional leadership. These *quanti-narrative* measures call upon researchers to incorporate all ways of knowing when conducting scholarly research. By connecting smaller investigations, more accurate and consistent meaning could be drawn from the studies' collective influences and provide key insights to increased student learning.

GUIDANCE FOR INVESTIGATIONS

The review of the research findings of Herman (1990), Bredeson (1996), and Petersen (1999) revealed common threads within the research fabric that give rise to behavior characteristics and competencies necessary for successful instructional leadership by superintendents. Although the scholars discussed the generalizable limits and alternative explanations of their findings, they collectively provide promising insights into solidifying a framework that researchers can use to directly investigate school superintendents' engagement with the technical core through instructional leadership. The following guidelines for further investigations of superintendent engagement with the technical core and instructional leadership are a starting point:

- Articulation of an instructional vision to promote and maintain district, school board, and community adaptation;
- Organization of the instructional program;
- Support (financial and organizational) of the instructional program;
- Collaboration with school administration, faculty, and community in developing a district instructional plan;
- Development and evaluation of instructional program personnel;
- Assessment and evaluation of instructional programs;
- Axiomatic priority toward instructional program success;
- Clear knowledge of the research relating to schooling and student achievement.

CONCLUSION

Throughout the evolutionary histories of research and practice in medicine, law, and the clergy, the core attention on the patient, the client, and the parishioner have remained steadfast in these respective professions. Researchers in educational administration continue their activities: the development and refinement of knowledge about teaching and learning and educational leadership. Growing demands detract from the main issue of teaching and learning. Practicing and aspiring superintendents need a stronger research base to expand their expertise in curriculum theory and purpose, and to add to their skill base in the delivery, assessment and value of what is taught and tested. Tools forged in scholarly research enable school superintendents to construct and maintain an active vision that answers the whats, hows, and whys of school administration (Achilles, 2001), and ultimately keep student improvement in the spotlight. If researchers jointly concentrate on forging the right tools to connect school superintendents with the technical core of the profession and reinforce education administration's knowledge base, then increased student learning could become an expectation rather than an exception. Finally, researchers in school administration could redirect their efforts to seek answers to the following questions:

1. Are instructional programs and student learning a result of school superintendents' skills in organizing staff and allocating financial resources?
2. Do NCATE, AASA, and ISLLC standards-driven preparation programs produce superintendents with superior instructional leadership skills and dispositions?
3. What skills and leadership dispositions propel some superintendents toward greater success than others in improving instruction and student performance?
4. Do leadership practices of school superintendents as measured by the Leadership Practices Inventory (LPI) by James Kouzes and Barry Posner, and other self-report leadership measures, relate to the quality of instruction and student performance?

REFERENCES

Achilles, C. (2001). What is missing in the current debate about education administration (EDAD) standards. *The AASA Professor, 24*(2), 8–14.

Achilles, C. (1996, Spring). *If we're rebuilding education, let's start with a firm foundation.* Paper presented at the annual meeting of the University Council for Educational Administration, Louisville, KY.

Achilles, C. (1994). Searching for the golden fleece: The epic struggle continues. *Educational Administration Quarterly, 30*(1), 6–26.

Blase, J., & Blase, J. (2002). The micropolitics of instructional supervision: A call for research. *Educational Administration Quarterly, 38*(1), 6–44.

Blase, J., & Blase, J. (1999). Principal's instructional leadership and teacher development: Teachers' perspectives. *Educational Administration Quarterly, 35*(3), 344–378.

Björk, L. (1996, April). *The implication of school restructuring on university-based professional preparation programs.* Paper presented at the Annual Conference of the American Educational Research Association, New York.

Björk, L. (1993). Effective schools—effective superintendents: The emerging instructional leadership role. *Journal of School Leadership, 3*(3), 246–259.

Bredeson, P. (1996). Superintendent's roles in curriculum development and instructional leadership: Instructional visionaries, collaborators, supporters, and delegators. *Journal of School Leadership, 6*(3), 243–264.

Bredeson, P., & Johansson, O. (1997). *Leadership for learning: A study of the instructional leadership roles of superintendents in Sweden and Wisconsin.* Eric Clearinghouse, Educational Management [EA028616, 34 pages]. Available: Doc. No. ED411583.

Bridges, E. (1982). Research on the school administrator: The state-of-the-art, 1967–1980. *Educational Administration Quarterly, 18*(3), 12–33.

Campbell, R., Fleming, T., Newell, L , & Bennion, J. (1987). *A history of thought and practice in educational administration.* New York: Teachers College Press.

Cuban, L. (1984). Transforming the frog into a prince: Effective school research, policy, and practice at the district level. *Harvard Educational Review, 54*(2), 129–150.

Cubberly, E. (1927). *State school administration.* Boston: Houghton-Mifflin.

Culbertson, J. (1988). A century's quest for a knowledge base. In N. J. Boyen (Ed.), *Handbook of research on educational administration* (pp. 3–36). New York: Longham.

Davis, S. (1998). Superintendents' perspectives on the involuntary departure of public school principals: The most frequent reasons why principals lose their jobs. *Educational Administration Quarterly, 34*(1), 58–90.

Dillon, R., & Halliwell, J. (1991). Superintendents' and school board presidents' perceptions of the purposes, strengths and weaknesses of formal superintendent evaluations. *Journal of School Leadership, 1*(4), 328–337.

Eisner, E. (1998). *The enlightened eye: Quantitative inquiry in education.* (2nd ed.). New York: Merrill Publishing Co.

Foriska, T. (1998). *Restructuring around standards.* Thousand Oaks, CA: Corwin Press.

Herman, J. (1990) *Instructional leadership skills and competencies of public school superintendents: Implications for preparation programs in a climate of shared governance.* Paper presented at the Conference of the Southern Regional Council on Educational Administration, Birmingham, AL.

Hoy, W. (1994). Foundations of educational administration: Traditional and emerging perspectives. *Educational Administration Quarterly, 30*(2), 178–198.

Hoy, W., & Sweetland, S. (2001). Designing better schools: The meaning and measure of enabling school structures. *Educational Administration Quarterly, 37*(3), 296–321.

Hoy, W., & Miskel, C. (2001). *Educational administration: Theory, research and practice.* New York: McGraw-Hill.

Hoyle, J. (2002). *Superintendents for Texas school districts: Solving the crisis in educational leadership.* Fort Worth, TX: Sid W. Richardson Foundation Forum.

Hoyle, J. (1991). Educational administration has a knowledge base. *Record in Educational Administration and Supervision, fall/winter, 21*–27.

Hoyle, J., & AASA Commission on Standards for the Superintendency. (1993). *Professional standards for the superintendency.* Arlington, VA: American Association of School Administrators.

Hoyle, J., Björk, L., Collier, V., & Glass, T. (2004). *The superintendent as CEO: Standards-based performance.* Thousand Oaks, CA: Corwin Press.

Hoyle, J., Ealyk, C., Skrla, L., & Hogan, D. (2001). Superintendent performance and the relationship to district student performance. In T. Kowalski & G. Perrault (Eds.), *21st century challenges for school administrators* (pp. 272–285). Lanham, MD: Scarecrow Press.

Hoyle, J., Glass, T., & Oates, A. (1992, February). *Professional Standards for the Superintendency.* Paper presented to the American Association of School Administrators, Arlington, VA.

Hunt, M. (1997). *How science takes stock: The story of meta-analysis.* New York: Russell Sage Foundation.

Kowalski, J., & Oates, A. (1993). The evolving role of superintendents in school-based management. *Journal of School Leadership, 3*(4), 380–390.

Leithwood, K. (2002). School leadership and teachers' motivation to implement accountability policies. *Educational Administration Quarterly, 38*(1), 94–119.

Leithwood, K. (1994). Leadership for school restructuring. *Educational Administration Quarterly, 30*(4), 498–518.

Leithwood, K., & Jantzi, D. (1999). The relative effects of principal and teacher sources of leadership on student engagement with school. *Educational Administration Quarterly, 35*(5), 679–706.

Leithwood, K., Steinbach, R., & Raun, T. (1993). Superintendents' group problem-solving processes. *Educational Administration Quarterly, 29*(3), 364–391.

Light, R., & Pillemer, D. (1984). *Summing up: The science of reviewing research.* Cambridge, MA: Harvard University Press.

McNamara, J., Morales, P., Kim, Y., & McNamara, M. (1998). Conducting your first meta-analysis: An illustrated guide. *International Journal of Educational Reform, 7*(4), 380–397.

Mitchell, D., & Beach, S. A. (1993). School restructuring: The superintendent's view. *Educational Administration Quarterly, 29*(2), 249–274.

Murphy, J., & Hallinger, P. (1988). Characteristics of instructionally effective school districts. *Journal of Educational Research, 8*(3), 175–181.

National Policy Board for Educational Administration. (1989). *Improving the preparation of school administrators: An agenda for reform.* Charlottesville, VA; University of Virginia, Curry School of Education.

Petersen, G. (1999). Demonstrated actions of instructional leaders: An examination of five California superintendents. *Education Policy Analysis Archives, 7*(18). [Online]. Available: epaa.su.edu/epaa/v7nI 8.html.

Petersen, G., & Short, P. (2001). The school board president's perception of the district superintendent: Applying the lenses of social influence and social style. *Educational Administration Quarterly, 37*(4), 533–570.

Rowan, B. (1995a). Research on learning and teaching in K–12 schools: Implications for the field of educational administration. *Educational Administration Quarterly, 3*(1), 115–133.

Rowan, B. (1995b). Learning, teaching, and educational administration: Toward a research agenda. *Educational Administration Quarterly, 31*(3), 344–354.

Wimpelberg, R. (1997). Superintending: The undeniable politics and indefinite effects of school district leadership. *American Journal of Education, 105*(3), 319–345.

Wimpelberg, R. (1988). Instructional leadership and ignorance: Guidelines for the new studies of district administrators. *Education and Urban Society, 20*(3), 302–310.

Wirt, F. M. (1990). *The missing link in instructional leadership: The superintendent, conflict, and maintenance.* Eric Clearinghouse, Educational Management [EA022602, 84 pages]. Available Doc. No. ED327945.

SHOWING THE WAY

Careful Selection of Aspiring Principals: An Exploratory Analysis of Leadership Preparation Program Admission Practices

Tricia Browne-Ferrigno and Alan Shoho

Research on high-performing schools shows a direct link to effective principal leadership (Educational Research Service, National Association of Elementary School Principals, & National Association of Secondary School Principals [ERS, NAESP, & NASSP], 1998; National Commission for the Principalship, 1990). Current complexities of educational reform and paradigm shifts suggest that administrators of 21st century schools have broader expectations placed upon them than in the past (Calabrese, 2002; Colon, 1994; Elmore & Fuhrman, 2001; Marsh, 1997; Short & Greer, 1997). Recent reform efforts require dramatic changes in the core technology of schools and in the leadership required for the resulting restructured schools (Murphy, 1992). Today's school principals need adeptness at addressing multiple — often confusing — issues that require appropriate responses to external change forces (Hargreaves & Fullan, 1998; Leithwood, Jantzi, & Steinbach, 1999) and simultaneous initiation and maintenance of internally driven renewal processes (Barth, 2001; Fullan, 1999; Schlechty, 1997, 2001). Despite daunting challenges, the outcomes of reform and renewal efforts must be classrooms, schools, and school districts where human energy "is transformed into desired student academic and social growth" (Grogan & Andrews, 2002, p. 234).

In response to the new demands on school administration, the principalship is being re-conceptualized (Murphy, 1998, 2002), changing from a traditional authoritarian, top-hierarchical position to dynamic leadership models or management tasks dependent upon contexts or challenges (Council of Chief State School Officers [CCSSO], 1996; Portin, Schneider, DeArmond, & Gundlach, 2003). The effective principal of today is one who can address a daily stream of diverse issues needing immediate attention, while concurrently creating school cultures and communities that optimize opportunities for learning (Gordon, 2004; Lunenburg & Ornstein,

Tricia Browne-Ferrigno, University of Kentucky
Alan Shoho, University of Texas at San Antonio

2004; Ubben, Hughes, & Norris, 2001). Conforming to this new vision of educational leadership leaves many principals "feeling that they are being pulled in many different directions simultaneously" (Leithwood, 2001, p. 19).

A contemporary principal may be required at one moment to assume the role as facilitator of empowered school governance teams (Lambert, 1998; Sergiovanni, Burlingame, Coombs, & Thurston, 1999) and at another moment as leader of a learning community (DuFour & Eaker, 1998; Senge et al., 2000; Sergiovanni, 1994, 2001). Expanded school functions based upon changing student populations and learner needs create additional demands on the skills and expertise of school leaders (Deal & Peterson, 1999; Gordon, 2004; Levine, Lowe, Peterson, & Tenorio, 1995; Sergiovanni, 1992). Novice principals often report difficulty in balancing technical and managerial tasks while also performing as visionary leaders who meet the expectations of superintendents and school board members (Daresh, 2002; Daresh & Playko, 1997). According to Ripley (1997), today's principals are "pulled in different directions and some are breaking under the stress" (p. 55), a fact not unnoticed by teachers and other educational practitioners who comprise the major supply of new entrants into school administration.

Filling vacant principalships is becoming problematic because the pool of qualified candidates willing to assume positions as school leaders grows smaller (ERS, 1998; McAdams, 1998; Young, Petersen, & Short, 2002). Trends indicate that filling open principalships will become more difficult in the next decade as retirement rates of experienced principals increase, high percentages of current principals move to non-administrative positions, and numbers of qualified applicants choosing to become school leaders decrease (ERS et al., 2000; Newton, 2001). Reasons for the shrinking pool of principal candidates are interrelated and confounding (Grogan & Andrews, 2002; Usdan, 2002; Winter, Rinehart, & Munoz, 2001), but nonetheless connect to the "harsh realities of being school principals" (Browne-Ferrigno & Muth, 2001, p. 1) in public schools today. Thus, replacement of exiting educational leaders requires concerted efforts to attract and select quality applicants to the field. But are university-based principal preparation programs using appropriate selection criteria to select students who are ready and willing to face the seemingly daunting challenges of school administration?

This chapter draws together findings from multiple sources that reflect current admission standards and selection criteria to principal preparation programs and explores their implications in the initial phase of educational leadership development. The sources include (a) reviews of current state regulations for administrator credentials, (b) reviews of selected literature about reform of preparation programs, and (c) findings from recent studies of admission practices. Implications and recommendations include the use of alternative performance assessments for student selection, rather than only the traditional quantitative measures currently used as admission requirements in most programs.

ADMINISTRATOR LICENSURE: CONTROLLING THE PROFESSION
State licensure mandates represent the "most profound government influence on leadership preparation" (McCarthy, 1999) and those who enter the principalship.

Control of administrator credentials is predicated on the notation that "only well-prepared and qualified individuals are provided licenses to lead" (Young et al., 2002, p. 153). The adoption of new standards for school leaders by nearly 40 states required many university-based programs to revise content and deliver instruction beyond traditional classroom settings (CCSSO, 1996; Murphy, 1999; National Policy Board for Educational Administration [NPBEA], 2002a; Young et al., 2002). In most cases, completion requirements for university programs link directly to state licensure or certification requirements. Additionally, new standards for the accreditation for leadership programs have further expanded program changes (NPBEA, 2002b).

Zimmerman (2002) compiled a handbook that displays requirements for school administrator certification in all 50 states and notes that "qualifications vary dramatically from state to state" (p. v) because nationally accepted requirements have not been developed. According to Zimmerman's findings, Michigan is the only state to date that no longer requires state-approved administrator credentials. However, applicants for administrator positions and incumbent administrators must complete state-approved professional-development hours within specified time periods in order to be employed.

The remaining 49 states continue to issue P–12 administrator credentials. At least 40 of the 49 states require initial applicants to complete an approved principal preparation program, hold a graduate degree (often in educational administration), and provide evidence of two to five years of full-time teaching experience or work in P–12 schools. Some states require all three conditions be met, while others only one or two in various combinations. Additionally, applicants for administrator licenses or certifications in some states also must hold valid teaching credentials (sometimes for the same state that issues the administrator credential), attain qualifying scores on specified professional examinations, complete monitored preservice clinical practicums or internships, or complete first-year practice induction programs. An intriguing finding is that 12 states require applicants to complete full-time experiences in school-administrative positions for specified time periods before becoming professionally certified as school principals (Zimmerman, 2002).

At least 43 states require successful completion of a state-approved administrator preparation program, and some of those states identify specific content or standards to be covered. Additionally, a recent review of state department of education Web sites indicate that several have links to related sites that announce policy changes for credentialing or information about school districts. A few Web sites specifically mention the Interstate School Leadership Licensure Consortium (ISLLC) Standards (CCSSO, 1996) as the guiding force in credential requirements.

Over the past two decades "business and political influentialists" (Usdan, 2002, p. 303) have played key roles in stimulating and expanding the standards-and-accountability reform movement. The strength of non-educational leaders in determining entrance into the practice of school administration is evident through changes in state licensure requirements, linked to standards developed by some individuals far removed from the realities of P–12 schools. Usdan (2002) asserts that the "field of educational leadership preparation desperately needs to be transformed as expeditiously as possible" (p. 306), including attention to the critical issue of student quality.

RECRUITMENT AND SELECTION:
IMPROVING LEADERSHIP PREPARATION

For more than four decades, improving the recruitment and selection of new candidates for the principalship has been a call for change. In 1960 the American Association of School Administrators cited the practice of using "*admission* rather than *selection* procedures" (p. 83) as damaging to the field of educational leadership. Thirteen years later the University Council for Educational Administration (UCEA) published a monograph commissioned by the Educational Resources Information Center that defines *New Approaches to Recruitment and Selection of Educational Administrators* (Stout, 1973) within the parameter of educational change.

According to Stout (1973), redesigned admission processes used by university professors in the selection of students—and eventual principals—can contribute to needed changes in American schools "by training, preparing, or simply certifying men and women who are different from those trained in the past" (p. 15). Such a deliberate shift in thinking about the relationship between admission to professional training and future administrator placement requires "a shift in recruiting mechanisms" (p. 28) in which universities no longer rely upon candidate self-selection to programs. Instead, Stout asserted that admission criteria need to be "implicitly designed to select for job performance, not for training program success" (p. 33) in order to "produce better quality administrators than those now in the schools" (p. 39).

The most recent call to improve educational leadership preparation and practice began in response to the work by the National Commission on Excellence in Educational Administration published in 1987 and the 1989 report by the NPBEA. A flurry of responses by leadership educators and non-educators resulted. But despite these new calls for action to improve leadership preparation, Murphy posited in 1992 that "little progress has been made in resolving the deeply ingrained weaknesses that have plagued training systems for so long" (p. 79). In particular, the recruitment and selection processes for entry into university programs remain "informal, haphazard, and casual" (Murphy, 1992, p. 80), with the most prevalent practice being candidate self-selection. According to Tyack and Cummings (1997), the only criteria for entrance into an educational leadership program in the middle of the 20th century was a "B.A. and the cash to pay the tuition" (p. 60), a widespread practice continuing today. Despite evidence of some proactive efforts toward careful recruitment and selection of students (Crow & Glascock, 1995; Murphy, 1999; Pounder & Young, 1996), most program admission processes have changed little as the following literature review indicates.

FINDINGS FROM UCEA-BASED STUDIES

The publication of *Leaders for America's Schools* (Griffiths, Stout, & Forsyth, 1988) is often highlighted as the impetus for recent innovations of preparation programs, particularly among University Council for Educational Administration (UCEA) members. Several major changes were recommended, including the need to "recruit quality candidates who have the potential to become future leaders" and "encourage minorities and women to enter the field" (Milstein, 1992, p. 2). With support from the Danforth Foundation, UCEA launched a series of case studies that explored the dynamics of changing traditional preparation programs that are "deeply entranced" (p. 5) into experimental training models. Admission processes were included in these studies.

In his review of five programs, Milstein (1992) found that restructured programs made changes in the determination of who participated. All five institutions moved away from candidate self-selection and emphasis on academic potential (i.e., traditional approaches linked to quantitative measures) and modified selection processes to include district leader nominations based upon perceived leadership potential. Field leaders agreed to sponsor candidates and provide release time and other resources to assist the candidates in successfully completing the programs. Application documents often included essays on leadership and values, in addition to the traditional sources of academic potential.

As a result of his findings, Milstein (1992) outlined critical elements in the selection process that need changing. First, purposeful selection of candidates, with focus on leadership potential, needs to be a partnership activity involving school district leaders and university faculty members. Through purposeful selection, attention to recruitment and support of minority candidates can be made. Second, admission processes need to move from an emphasis on selection based upon academic potential (e.g., scores on nationally normed test, grade point averages, letters of recommendation) to criteria establishing potential as leaders. Program selection criteria need revising to reflect the reality that

> the more important intent of preparation is to produce leaders, not scholars. Leaders are measured by their sense of purpose, ability to get others engaged with them as they translate purposes, manage the enterprise, and intervene when required to keep the system on target. These are qualities that are best measured by *past leadership behaviors*, and through clear communication of purposes, and demonstration of the *ability to respond adequately in situations that require leadership behaviors* [emphasis provided by author of report]. (p. 10)

The final selection strategy connects to placement following completion of the program, a responsibility commonly left to individual graduates. Milstein asserts that selecting quality candidates for reformed programs and preparing them to become school leaders is not enough, but instead, only the first two steps in assuring schools are led by effective principals. "Nomination and selection to participate in preparation programs is the first step toward controlling entrance to the profession. Effective preparation is the second step. Purposeful involvement in the placement process is the third step" (Milstein, 1992, p. 10). In other words, the quality of entering students and exiting graduates and their placements as school leaders are all important standards of measuring the success—and effectiveness—of principal preparation programs.

Restructuring of admission processes, however, appears to have occurred sparingly, based upon findings from an UCEA-initiated study of student selection practices used by its member institutions during 1991. The purpose of the investigation was to access current recruitment and selection practices and explore implemented strategies aimed at attracting minorities and women to educational administration programs (Murphy, 1999). Forty of the then-50 UCEA member institutions participated. Based upon respondents' weighted answers, the criteria perceived to be most important for admission to leadership preparation programs were (a) Graduate Record Examination (GRE) scores, (b) grade point averages (GPA), (c) letters of recommendation, (d) writing samples, and (e) performance during personal interviews.

In a more recent survey, Murphy (1999) found evidence of greater focus on purposeful recruitment to ensure diverse student bodies. Responses by chairpersons at 44 UCEA-member institutions indicated that approximately 25% claimed efforts of greater selectivity of students, particularly through raised standards on GRE scores and grade point averages. Writing samples, documentation of previous leadership experiences, and use of personal interviews were other strategies sometimes used in candidate selection (Murphy, 1999).

Findings from Nationwide Web-Based Study

To expand and update the research base about selection criteria, Creighton and Jones (2001) explored student admission practices used by 450 leadership preparation programs. They reviewed each university's Web site to access graduate school admissions criteria and any requirements specific to educational administration programs. The sample included representative programs across all geographic regions within the United States. A purposeful sample (N=45) of universities was used to verify Web-based findings through communication with deans of graduate schools, department chairs, and other department personnel.

Findings indicate that the prevailing practice for acceptance to leadership preparation programs continues to be use of (a) GRE scores, (b) GPA, and (c) letters of recommendation. Cut-off score standards or score-combination standards used in assessing the quality of applicants' GRE and GPA data, however, varied considerably from program to program. Based upon their findings and those of the Educational Testing Service, the researchers assert that special care in interpreting GRE scores is required especially for "students who may have had educational or cultural experiences somewhat different from those of the traditional majority" (Creighton & Jones, 2001, p. 14). Low performance on GRE individual subtests can result in barring admission to female and minority applicants.

An interesting finding by Creighton and Jones was that, although all 450 programs required that applicants had earned an undergraduate degree from an accredited university, "only 3% (15) required the degree to be in education or one strong in the liberal arts" (p. 10). Somewhat surprising is the finding that only 180 programs (40%) required applicants to hold a teaching credential or have P–12 teaching experience. Even more perplexing is the fact that 270 university-based programs

(60%) allow students to complete graduate programs in educational administration without first satisfying the minimum years of teaching experience required for state certification as an administrator.

Creighton and Jones believe this finding is alarming and posit that students with only a year or two teaching experience lack the "first-hand knowledge and understanding of the school setting, students, teachers, administrators, and instruction" (p. 24) to make sense of their learning. The practice of admitting applicants to principal preparation programs without sufficient teaching experience is a "disservice to the candidates themselves . . . [and] a disservice to the teachers, students, and community members in the schools these aspiring principals will someday attempt to lead" (p. 24).

Further, allowing new teachers to complete administrator certification requirements early in their career results in excessive numbers of administrator-certified candidates who either remain in positions as classroom teachers or seek principalships several years after completing leadership preparation. Some states are addressing this problem by placing time limits between provisional certification upon completion of a graduate degree and professional certification upon placement as a school administrator. Additional research is needed to determine if "a relationship exists between effective school leadership and a limited amount of classroom teaching experience or other school-site experience" (Creighton & Jones, 2001, p. 25).

Findings from Leadership Educator Survey

Expanding upon previous research about student characteristics, Creighton and Shipman (2002) surveyed faculty and administrators of leadership preparation programs through listserv databases used by the National Council of Professors of Educational Administration (NCPEA) and UCEA. The purpose of the study was to access attitudinal data about student characteristics that were perceived to be indicators necessary for successful and lifelong learning. The researchers used the same constructs and indicators identified in a Delphi study conducted by Nadeau, Donald, Konrad, and Tremblay (1990, as cited in Creighton & Shipman, 2002).

The Likert-scale survey asked respondents to assess the importance of 20 indicators perceived to measure student quality within four major constructs: (a) general academic preparedness; (b) verbal and written communication skills; (c) ability to analyze, synthesize, and think critically; and (d) commitment to learning. The five highest-scoring indicators (i.e., applies learning to real-life situations; can put things into context; defines the essence of a problem; conceives, plans, and executes goals; considers all sides of an argument and makes an independent judgment) are in the *ability to analyze, synthesize, and think critically* construct. Faculty ranked basic written and verbal communication skills, evidence of independent study and efforts beyond basic course requirements, and classroom teaching experience as the next five indicators of success in educational leadership preparation.

Eight of the nine least important indicators of student quality (i.e., letters of recommendation; degrees, diplomas, certificates; college transcripts; performance on GRE verbal; GPA; performance on GRE combined; performance on GRE analytical; performance on GRE quantitative) are in the *academic preparedness* construct. Yet these criteria—judged by leadership educators to be least indicative of student quality—are used extensively as admission standards for leadership preparation programs (Creighton & Shipman, 2001).

Findings from Other Studies

In a study involving 25 administrators who participated in one of five different programs, new entrants into educational leadership positions did not feel fully prepared for the reality of the tasks required in their jobs (Kraus & Cordeiro, 1995). The new assistant principals and principals found the workload, immediacy of issues, time demands, and politics of the job overwhelming at times. All 25 administrators, however, identified classroom teaching experience and previous leadership responsibility as extremely helpful in their new careers. Participants cited previous learning experiences both inside and outside education as being instrumental in their preparation as school leaders: (a) committee and group work, (b) on-the-job administrative experience, and (c) life experiences. For some, mentoring and encouragement by administrators were important in their decision to become school leaders. The researchers recommend that program selection processes "value the varied experiences and non-traditional backgrounds of program applicants" (p. 25). Myriad experiences, such as community leadership, corporate work, and even single parenthood, provide broader vision and expanded perspectives that help school leaders initiate and sustain educational change (Kraus & Cordeiro, 1995).

Crow and Glascock (1995) examined the influence of role conceptualization on candidates' socialization into educational administration during a non-traditional principal preparation program aimed specifically at recruiting women and minorities. The recruitment and selection process included six rarely used strategies:

1. Nomination by superintendents with emphasis on identifying excellent teachers among women and minorities.
2. Rigorous application process requiring nominees to reflect on career history, experiences as a teacher/learner, and vision of leadership.
3. Reference letters from superintendent, principal, and peer along with documentation of work with adults and children
4. First-cut selection by advisory committee consisting of (college) faculty and board of education staff members.
5. Videotaped sessions with semifinalists in small groups to assess abilities to communicate, work co-operatively, influence group opinion, and facilitate group task completion.
6. Final selection by a panel of recognized experts unaffiliated with the college who viewed videotapes and read applications. (p. 27)

The rigorous selection process helped to create an *esprit de corps* perception within the cohort that inspired candidates' ability to effect important changes within schools. At the end of the program, however, the school system that partnered with the university faced a severe budget crisis that resulted in personnel cutbacks. Only 9 of the 17 candidates received placements as school or district administrators (Crow & Glascock, 1995), and thus, the long-term results of the rigorous selection process are unknown.

Research suggests that candidates' career aspirations may play a significant role in the recruitment and selection of program participants and the identification of future principals. Several studies indicate important connections between career aspirations and career paths in educational administration (Begley, Campbell-Evans, & Brownridge, 1990; Browne-Ferrigno, 2003a; Merrill & Pounder, 1999; Pavan, 1987; Whitcombe, 1979). The decision to seek state credentials to become a school administrator occurs at different career stages for women and men. Additionally, many viable candidates for preparation programs never apply because they question their ability to lead; thus, encouragement from others before and during program participation appears to increase placement rates as administrators after completion of preservice training (Hamilton, Ross, Steinbach, & Leithwood, 1996).

Need for Robust Candidate Selection

Careful recruitment and selection of candidates are cited often as necessary elements in the restructuring or reform of preparation programs (Achilles, 1987; Barnett & Caffarella, 1992; Coleman, Copeland, & Adams, 2001; Hill & Lynch, 1994; Murphy, 1993; Schmuck, 1992; Smith, 1990). Yet in light of recent national studies (Creighton & Jones, 2001; Creighton & Shipman, 2002), selection procedures used by departments of educational administration remain unsystematic and unstructured, and maddeningly frustrating in light of the past decade-plus attention to reforming university-based administrator preparation programs.

Robust recruitment and selection processes are critically important because haphazard, laissez-faire approaches to student admission processes are destructive to the profession and the reputation of programs (Milstein & Krueger, 1997; Murphy, 1992). Leadership educators may be contributors to underachieving P–12 schools because of our failure to select carefully new entrants to the field of administrative practice. Have our laissez-faire approaches to recruiting and selecting students for principal preparation programs contributed to the problems of ineffective school leadership? Has open admission to preparation programs generated not only too many administrator-certified educators who never seek placement as school leaders, but also marginal principals who selected educational administration as a career path for the wrong reasons?

Robust selection processes in administrative preparation programs are needed as the initial step in selection of quality school leaders. Recruiting quality candidates may require expanded use of distance learning, alternative certification, reciprocal certification and portable retirements, and greater collaboration with districts and state departments (Keedy & Achilles, 2001). Evaluating leadership potential of candidates requires alternative assessments (e.g., writing samples, interviews) and performance demonstrations (e.g., auditions, group decision making) in conjunction with higher standards on traditional admission criteria required by graduate schools (Creighton, 2001; Keedy & Achilles, 2001).

For many years administrator-preparation programs have played a "cash cow" role at universities where high expectations for high enrollments (i.e., generating large amounts of semester credit hours) and low levels of resources are the norm (Murphy, 1993; Twombly & Ebmeier, 1989). The result has been continued open enrollment through candidate self-selection and admission to preparation programs based upon traditional graduate school requirements—rather than the careful selection of potential future school leaders. Muth and Barnett (2001) warned if accountability policies are enacted that measure the effectiveness of principal preparation programs based upon placement rates of graduates and their subsequent performance on the job as school leaders, then issues of candidate recruitment and selection become critical. That warning has credence today based upon the recent changes in program accreditation processes (NPBEA, 2002b). Hence, university-based preservice principal development may no longer be able to meet the conflicting demands as both "cash cow" generators and nationally approved preparation programs.

PROGRAM INPUT-OUTPUT ISSUES: DEVELOPING EFFECTIVE SCHOOL LEADERS

Effective administrator preparation requires not only quality programs based upon standards and proven practices, but also quality students who have the potential and desire to become effective school leaders. The recruitment and selection of "capable and talented individuals to participate in leadership programs" (Playko & Daresh, 1992, p. 21) is a critical first step in preparing future school leaders. Thus, the reconceptualization of administrator preparation programs requires reconceptualization of selection criteria that ensure graduates able to meet the challenges and complexities of leading 21st century schools.

Mapping Backwards for Desired Outcomes

Efforts to improve the effectiveness of leadership preparation programs begin by careful consideration of desired student outcomes and use of futurist perspectives to answer such questions as, What are the key identifiable traits of effective school leaders? What do graduates of today's leadership preparation programs need to know and be able to do as successful leaders of tomorrow's schools? What desired leadership skills can be developed through professional training? What previous experiences, personal attitudes and dispositions, and career aspirations—that cannot be developed through professional training but can be measured—link to desired leadership ability? Responses to questions like these form the framework for improved recruitment and selection strategies.

Assessing Potential for Role-Identity Transformation

Because leadership preparation fundamentally is about transformation, a changed orientation from a teacher mindset to an administrator mindset (Browne-Ferrigno & Muth, 2001; Crow & Glascock, 1995; White & Crow, 1993), the seeds of transformation need to be present. Personal purpose and vision—qualities that do not emerge from quantitative measures such as GRE scores or GPA—are critical influences in the transformative journey from classroom teacher to school administrator. Thus, alternative assessments that measure leadership potential, such as performance activities during group interviews or observations of applicants in their current work settings, are needed in tandem with required graduate school admission requirements in the selection of candidates for administrator training. Alternative performance assessments provide what is needed: more and better information about each applicant's "attributes or capabilities" (Ortiz, 1982) or "emotional intelligence" (Goldman, 1998) as an adaptive school leader.

Using Alternative Selection Strategies

Many innovative programs—both initial preparation for aspiring principals and intensive professional development for practicing principals—use unique selection criteria linked to school leadership standards, administrative practice, and placement as school leaders (e-Lead, 2003). Various existing tools and strategies for accessing leadership traits and skills, evaluating adaptive intelligence, and guiding career planning (Gagnon, 2003; Kowalski, 2003; Lunenburg & Ornstein, 2004) are available that could be modified for use as admission selection criteria.

For example, the NASSP utilizes ten ISLLC-based skills under four broad areas for "selecting and developing the 21st century principal" (NASSP, 2003, p. 3) during long-term professional development of aspiring and practicing principals. These skills-development topics include (a) *educational leadership* (setting instruction direction, teamwork, sensitivity); (b) *resolving complex problems* (judgment, results orientation, organizational ability); (c) *communication* (oral, written); and (d) *developing self and others* (development of others, understanding own strengths and weaknesses). This model could serve as the basis for developing alternative selection criteria for university-based preparation programs. Furthermore, several projects have already successfully implemented performance-based selection assessments crafted to meet diverse site and program requirements (Browne-Ferrigno, 2003b; Creighton, 2001; Crow & Glascock, 1995; Milstein, 1992) that could potentially be used in other settings.

Another possible framework for developing authentic selection assessments could be the "school critical functions and action" model developed by Portin et al. (2003, p. 18). In-box questions, role-playing activities, and professional reflections could be based upon seven critical leadership functions (i.e., instructional, cultural, managerial, human resource, strategic, external development, micropolitical) and their corresponding actions. Use of this framework, both during admission selection activities and preservice training, would help aspiring principals assess their strengths and limitations and determine appropriate placements for them following program completion (Portin et al., 2003).

Creating ISLLC-Based Alternative Performance Assessments

At this writing, 40 states have adopted the ISLLC Standards, the accompanying licensing assessments, or some variation of the two as the framework for the preparation, certification, and evaluation of principals. A careful analysis of the nearly 200 indicators within the six ISLLC Standards suggest four recurring themes (Hessel & Holloway, 2002, p. 21):

- A Vision of Success
- A Focus on Teaching and Learning
- An Involvement of all Stakeholders
- A Demonstration of Ethical Behavior

If visionary, instructional, collaborative, and ethical practices are hallmarks of the effective contemporary principal, then why not use these themes as the foundation for developing standards for admission to administrator preparation programs? Several strategies can be used in the selection process.

Presentation of an education platform and a career-goal statement could measure an applicant's visioning skill, ethical stance, and writing ability. Previous experiences as an instructional or collaborative leader could be presented through a resume that highlights an applicant's participation on school or district committees that develop curriculum or examinations, select textbooks, conduct student transitioning activities from one school level to another, or create professional development activities. An applicant's resume could also provide evidence of professional engagement through membership in professional associations, attendance at professional conferences, participation in professional development activities, and commendations and awards for teaching and learning achievements. Additionally, evidence of school leadership potential can be provided through evidence of publications of teacher inquiry or comprehensive action research findings, demonstration of skills in using information technology, or involvement in community activities or advocacy groups.

Group assessment activities and performance auditions (i.e., responses to in-box messages, role-played telephone conversations, small-group activities) for semifinalists could provide evidence of candidates' skills in communication, analysis and problem solving, and collaboration and teamwork. Use of authentic assessments linked directly to administrator standards orient leadership preparation programs toward future practice and frame relevance of program participation toward a specific career objective—becoming a school leader.

Taking Immediate Action

Reconceptualized admission requirements require more time and energy in the selection of students for programs in educational administration. Nonetheless, action is needed to address the growing problem created by too few applicants for principalships and too many administrator-certified educators never seeking placements. Many typical preparation programs may see at least 50% of their graduates delay entering school administration, while many other graduates never become school administrators (ERS et al., 2000; Grogan & Andrews, 2002; McAdams, 1998; Young et al., 2002). What keeps these graduates from entering the profession? And what are the costs to university programs, states, and especially districts now desperately in need of high-quality administrators? These questions are critical in a time of shortage of quality applicants (Muth & Browne-Ferrigno, 2003; Painter, 2003), particularly for the most challenging assignments (Roza, Cello, Harvey, & Wishon, 2003).

The problem of non-placement by program graduates will need to be addressed because new program accreditation standards require evidence of "program outcome effectiveness" (NPBEA, 2003b, p. 31). In addition to providing evidence of graduates' passing rates on state-required licensing exams, university-based programs may also be asked to provide evidence of program effectiveness based upon

1. Surveys of job placement rates;
2. Surveys of employer satisfaction as related to the standards;
3. Summaries of internship evaluations conducted by professionals with whom, or for whom, students worked while an intern;
4. Summaries of probationary evaluations of graduates by employers;
5. Program of self-assessments based on the standards by graduates three years after completion of the program. (p. 31)

Although not all programs are accredited by NCATE, the new Educational Leadership Constituent Council now used in the evaluation of many university-based programs may well be the catalyst that forces major changes in the selection process for aspiring principals.

Stout recognized back in 1973 that "the adoption of new selection criteria probably carries with it the necessity to restructure recruitment, training, and placement" and perhaps "even restructuring the university and the professorship" (p. 42). Despite the costs in time and energy, attention must be directed toward changing admission practices to university-based programs in order to select quality leadership entrants to the field of educational administrative practice.

REFERENCES

Achilles, C. M. (1987, November). *Toward a model for preparation programs for education's leaders.* Paper presented at the annual meeting of the Southern Regional Council for Educational Administration, Gatlinburg, TN.

American Association of School Administrators. (1960). *Professional administrators for America's schools* (Thirty-eighth AASA yearbook). Washington, DC: National Educational Administration.

Barnett, B. G., & Caffarella, R. S. (1992, October–November). *The use of cohorts: A powerful way for addressing issues of diversity in preparation programs.* Paper presented at the annual meeting of the University Council for Educational Administration, Minneapolis, MN.

Barth, R. S. (2001). *Learning by heart.* San Francisco: Jossey-Bass.

Begley, P. T., Campbell-Evans, P., & Brownridge, A. (1990, June). *Influences on the socializing experiences of aspiring principals.* Paper presented at the annual meeting of the Canadian Society for Studies in Education, Victoria, BC.

Browne-Ferrigno, T. (2003a). Becoming a principal: Role conception, initial socialization, role-identity transformation, purposeful engagement. *Educational Administration Quarterly, 39*(4), 468–453.

Browne-Ferrigno, T. (2003b, November). *Principals Excellence Program: Advanced professional development for administrator-certified leaders.* Paper presented at the annual meeting of the University Council for Educational Administration, Portland, OR.

Browne-Ferrigno, T., & Muth, R. (2001, November). *Becoming a principal: Role transformation through clinical practice.* Paper presented at the annual meeting of the University Council for Educational Administration, Cincinnati, OH.

Calabrese, R. L. (2002). *The leadership assignment: Creating change.* Boston: Allyn and Bacon.

Coleman, D., Copeland, D., & Adams, R. C. (2001). University education administration program development: Administrative skills vs. achievement standards as predictors of administrative success. In T. J. Kowalski & G. Perreault (Eds.), *21st century challenges for school administrators* (pp. 53–61). Lanham, MD: Scarecrow Press.

Colon, R. J. (1994, October). Rethinking and retooling for the 21st century: A must for administrators. *NASSP Bulletin,* 84–88.

Council of Chief State School Officers. (1996). *Interstate School Leaders Licensure Consortium: Standards for school leaders.* Washington, DC: Author.

Creighton, T. (2001). Lessons from the performing arts: Can auditioning help improve the selection process in university administration preparation programs in the 21st century? In T. J. Kowalski & G. Perreault (Eds.), *21st century challenge for school administration* (pp. 101–112). Lanham, MD: Scarecrow Press.

Creighton, T., & Jones, G. (2001, August). *Selection or self-selection? How rigorous are selection criteria in education administration programs?* Paper presented at the annual meeting of the National Council of Professors of Educational Administration, Houston, TX.

Creighton, T. B., & Shipman, N. J. (2002, Fall). Putting the H.O.T.S. into school leadership preparation. *Education Leadership Review, 3*(3), 26–31.

Crow, G. M., & Glascock, C. (1995). Socialization to a new conception of the principalship. *Journal of Educational Administration, 33*(1), 22–43.

Daresh, J. C. (2002). *What it means to be a principal: Your guide to leadership.* Thousand Oaks, CA: Corwin Press.

Daresh, J. C., & Playko, M. A. (1997). *Beginning the principalship: A practical guide for new school leaders.* Thousand Oaks, CA: Corwin Press.

Deal, T. F., & Peterson, K. D. (1999). *Shaping school culture: The heart of leadership.* San Francisco: Jossey-Bass.

DuFour, R., & Eaker, R. (1998). *Professional learning communities at work: Best practices for enhancing student achievement.* Bloomington, IN: National Educational Service.

Educational Research Service. (1998). *Is there a shortage of qualified candidates for openings in the principalship? An exploratory study.* Alexandria, VA and Reston, VA: National Association of Elementary School Principals and National Association of Secondary Principals.

Educational Research Service, National Association of Elementary School Principals, & National Association of Secondary School Principals. (1998). *The principal, keystone of a high-achieving school: Attracting and keeping the leadership we need.* Arlington, VA: Educational Research Service.

e-Lead. (2003). *Leadership for student learning.* Programs database. Retrieved November 28, 2003, from http://www.e-lead.org

Elmore, R. F., & Fuhrman, S. (2001). Holding schools accountable: Is it working? *Phi Delta Kappan, 83*(1), 67–72.

Fullan, M. (1999). *Change forces: The sequel.* Philadelphia: Falmer Press.

Gagnon, W. L., Jr. (2003). *Complete interview procedures for hiring school personnel.* Lantham, MD: Scarecrow Press.

Goldman, D. (1998). *Working with emotional intelligence.* New York: Bantam Books.

Gordon, S. P. (2004). *Professional development for school improvement: Empowering learning communities.* Boston: Pearson.

Griffiths, D. E., Stout, R. T., & Forsyth, P. B. (Eds.). (1988). *Leaders for America's schools.* Berkeley, CA: McCutchan.

Grogan, M., & Andrews, R. (2002). Defining preparation and professional development for the future. *Educational Administration Quarterly, 38*(2), 233–256.

Hamilton, D. N., Ross, P. N., Steinbach, R., & Leithwood, K. A. (1996). Differences in the socialization experiences of promoted and aspiring school administrators. *Journal of School Leadership, 6*(4), 346–367.

Hargreaves, A., & Fullan, M. (1998). *What's worth fighting for out there?* New York: Teachers College Press.

Hessel, K., & Holloway, J. (2002). *A framework for school leaders: Linking the ISLLC Standards to practice.* Princeton, NJ: Educational Testing Service.

Hill, M. S., & Lynch, D. W. (1994). Future principals: Selecting educators for leadership. *NASSP Bulletin, 78*(565), 81–84.

Keedy, J. L., & Achilles, C. M. (2001). The intellectual firepower needed for Educational administration's new era of enlightenment. In T. J. Kowalski & G. Perreault (Eds.), *21st century challenges for school administrators* (pp. 89–100). Lanham, MD: Scarecrow Press.

Kowalski, T. J. (2003). *Contemporary school administration: An introduction* (2nd ed.). Boston: Allyn and Bacon.

Kraus, C. M., & Cordeiro, P. A. (1995, October). *Challenging traditions: Re-examining the preparation of educational leaders for the workplace.* Paper presented at the annual meeting of the University Council for Educational Administration, Salt Lake City, UT.

Lambert, L. (1998). *Building leadership capacity in schools.* Alexandria, VA: Association of Supervision and Curriculum Development.

Leithwood, K. (2001). School leadership and educational accountability: Toward a distributed perspective. In T. J. Kowalski & G. Perreault (Eds.), *21st century challenges for school administrators* (pp. 11–25). Lanham, MD: Scarecrow Press.

Leithwood, K., Jantzi, D., & Steinbach, R. (1999). *Changing leadership for changing times.* Philadelphia: Open University Press.

Levine, D., Lowe, R., Peterson, B., & Tenorio, R. (Eds.). (1995). *Rethinking schools: An agenda for change.* New York: New Press.

Lunenburg, F. C., & Ornstein, A. C. (2004). *Educational administration: Concepts and practices* (4th ed.). Belmont, CA: Wadsworth/Thomson Learning.

Marsh, D. D. (1997, March). *Educational leadership for the 21st century: Integrating three emerging perspectives.* Paper presented at the annual meeting of the American Educational Research Association, Chicago, IL.

McAdams, R. P. (1998). Who'll run the schools? The coming administrator shortage. *The American School Board Journal, 29*(8), 37–39.

McCarthy, M. M. (1999). The evolution of educational leadership preparation programs. In J. Murphy & K. S. Lewis (Eds.), *Handbook on research on educational administration* (2nd ed., pp. 119–139). New York: Longman.

Merrill, R. J., & Pounder, D. (1999, October). *Attraction and retention of high school principals.* Paper presented at the annual meeting of the University Council for Educational Administration, Minneapolis, MN.

Milstein, M. M. (1992, October–November). *The Danforth Program for the Preparation of School Principals (DPPSP) six years later: What we have learned.* Paper presented at the annual meeting of the University Council for Educational Administration, Minneapolis, MN.

Milstein, M. M., & Krueger, J. A. (1997). Improving educational administration preparation programs: What we have learned over the past decade. *Peabody Journal of Education, 72*(2), 100–106.

Murphy, J. (1992). *The landscape of leadership preparation: Reframing the education of school administrators.* Newbury Park, CA: Corwin Press.

Murphy, J. (Ed.). (1993). *Preparing tomorrow's school leaders: Alternative designs.* University Park, PA: University Council for Educational Administration.

Murphy, J. (1998). What's ahead for tomorrow's principals. *Principal, 78*(1), 13–14.

Murphy, J. (1999). Changes in preparation programs: Perceptions of department chairs. In J. Murphy & P. B. Forsyth (Eds.), *Educational administration: A decade of reform* (pp. 170–191). Thousand Oaks, CA: Corwin Press.

Murphy, J. (2002). Reculturing the profession of educational leadership: New blueprints. *Educational Administration Quarterly, 38*(2), 178–191.

Muth, R., & Barnett, B. (2001). Making the case for professional preparation: Using research for program improvement and political support. *Educational Leadership and Administration: Teaching and Program Development, 13,* 109–120.

Muth, R., & Browne-Ferrigno, T. (2003, August). *Why don't our graduates take administrative positions? And what's the cost?* Paper presented at the annual meeting of the National Council for Professors of Educational Administration, Sedona, AZ.

National Association of Secondary School Principals. (2003). *Selecting and developing the 21st century principal.* Reston, VA: Author.

National Commission on Excellence in Educational Administration. (1987). *Leaders for American's schools.* Tempe, AZ: University Council for Educational Administration.

National Commission for the Principalship. (1990). *Principals for our changing schools: Preparation and certification.* Fairfax, VA: Author.

National Policy Board for Educational Administration. (1989, May). *Improving the preparation of school administrators: The reform agenda.* Charlottesville, VA: Author.

National Policy Board for Educational Administration. (2002a). *Standards for advanced programs in educational leadership for principals, superintendents, curriculum directors, and supervisors.* Retrieved April 12, 2002, from http://www.npbea.org/ELCC

National Policy Board for Educational Administration. (2002b). *Instructions to implements standards for advanced programs in educational leadership for principals, superintendents, curriculum directors, and supervisors.* Retrieved November 24, 2003, from http://www.npbea.org/ELCC

Newton, R. M. (2001, Summer). A recruitment strategy: Retooling the principal's role. *The AASA Professor, 24*(4), 6–10.

Ortiz, F. I. (1982). *Career patterns in education: Women, men and minorities in public school administration.* New York: Praeger.

Painter, S. B. (2003, November). *Higher admissions standards for principal preparation: A contrarian view.* Paper presented at the annual meeting of the University Council for Educational Administration, Portland, OR.

Pavan, B. N. (1987, April). *Aspiration levels of certified aspiring and incumbent female and male public school administrators.* Paper presented at the annual meeting of the American Educational Research Association, Washington, DC.

Playko, M. A., & Daresh, J. C. (1992, October-November). *Field-based preparation programs: Reform of administrator training or leadership development?* Paper presented at the annual meeting of the University Council for Educational Administration, Minneapolis, MN.

Portin, B., Schneider, P., DeArmond, M., & Gundlach, L. (2003, September). *Making sense of leadership schools: A study of the school principalship.* A report prepared under a grant from The Wallace Foundation. Seattle: University of Washington, Center on Reinventing Public Education.

Pounder, D. G., & Young, I. P. (1996). Recruitment and selection of educational administrators: Priorities for today's schools. In K. Leithwood, J. Chapment, D. Corson, P. Hallinger, & A. Hart (Eds.), *International handbook of educational leadership* (pp. 279–308). Boston: Kluwer.

Ripley, D. (1997). Current tensions in the principalship: Finding an appropriate balance. *NASSP Bulletin, 81*(589), 55–65.

Roza, M., with Cello, M. B., Harvey, J., & Wishon, S. (2003). *A matter of definition: Is there truly a shortage of school principals?* Seattle: Center for Reinventing Public Education, Daniel J. Evans School of Public Affairs, University of Washington.

Schlechty, P. C. (1997). *Inventing better schools: An action plan for educational reform.* San Francisco: Jossey-Bass.

Schlechty, P. C. (2001). *Shaking up the schoolhouse: Show to support and sustain educational innovation.* San Francisco: Jossey-Bass.

Schmuck, R. A. (1992). Beyond academics in the preparation of educational leaders: Four years of action research. *OSSC Report, 33*(2), 1–10.

Senge, P. M., Cambron-McCabe, N., Lucas, T., Smith, B., Dutton, J., & Kleiner, A. (2000). *Schools that learn: A fifth discipline fieldbook for educators, parents, and everyone who cares about education.* New York: Currency Doubleday.

Sergiovanni, T. J. (1992). *Moral leadership: Getting to the heart of school improvement.* San Francisco: Jossey-Bass.

Sergiovanni, T. J. (1994). *Building communities in schools.* San Francisco: Jossey-Bass.

Sergiovanni, T. J. (2001). *The principalship: A reflective practice perspective* (4th ed.). Boston: Allyn and Bacon.

Sergiovanni, T. J., Burlingame, M., Coombs, F. S., & Thurston, P. W. (1999). *Educational governance and administration.* Boston: Allyn and Bacon.

Short, P. M., & Greer, J. T. (1997). *Leadership in empowered schools: Themes from innovative efforts.* Upper Saddle River, NJ: Prentice Hall.

Smith, J. M. (1990, April). *The redesign of principalship preparation programs: Rhetoric or substantive reform.* Paper presented at the annual meeting of the Ohio Council of Professors of Educational Administration, Columbus, OH.

Stout, R. T. (1973). *New approaches to recruitment and selection of educational administrators.* Columbus, OH: University Council for Educational Administration.

Twombly, S., & Ebmeier, H. (1989, December). Educational administration programs: The cash cow of the university? *Notes on Reform.* Charlottesville, VA: National Policy Board for Educational Administration.

Tyack, D. B., & Cummings, R. (1977). Leadership in American public schools before 1954: Historical configurations and conjectures. In L. L. Cunningham, W. G. Hack, & R. O. Nystrand (Eds.), *Educational administration: The developing decades* (pp. 46–66). Berkeley, CA: McCutchan.

Ubben, J. C., Hughes, L. W., & Norris, C. J. (2001). *Creative leadership for effective schools* (4th ed.). Boston: Allyn and Bacon.

Usdan, M. D. (2002). Reactions to articles commissioned by the National Commission for the Advancement of Education Leadership Preparation. *Educational Administration Quarterly, 38*(2), 300–307.

Whitcombe, J. E. (1979, December). *A comparison of career patterns of men and women teachers: Teacher career and promotion study.* Paper presented at the national conference of the New Zealand Association for Research in Education, Wellington, New Zealand.

White, E., & Crow, G. M. (1993, April). *Rites of passage: The role perceptions of interns in the preparation for principalship.* Paper presented at the annual meeting of the American Educational Research Association, Atlanta, GA.

Winter, P. A., Rinehart, J. S., & Munoz, M. A. (2001, November). *Principal certified personnel: Do they want the job?* Paper presented at the annual meeting of the University Council for Educational Administration, Cincinnati, OH.

Young, M. D., Petersen, G. T., & Short, P. M. (2002). The complexity of substantive reform: A call for interdependence among key stakeholders. *Educational Administration Quarterly, 38*(2), 137–175.

Zimmerman, S. (2002). *Handbook of certification requirements for school administrators.* Lanham, MD: University Press of America.

Design Elements for Meaningful Clinical Practice Experiences: The Core of Principal Preparation Programs

Connie L. Fulmer, Rodney Muth, and Kenneth F. Reiter

One of the most perplexing problems facing those who prepare future school leaders is how to provide these future leaders with realistic and useful exposure to their future roles in educational organizations. History shows that this has not been an easy task. As a result, the scope and type of these transitional experiences too often were "left either to the students, or to the first employer" (Kennedy, 1987, p. 153).

Both past and current efforts of NCATE and the work of the Danforth Foundation (Millstein & Associates, 1993) and others (Cooper & Boyd, 1987; Heller, Conway, & Jacobson, 1988; Holifield & King, 1993; Jackson & Kelley, 2002; Moore, 1964; Murphy, 1992; National Policy Board, 1989, 2002) have pushed programs to develop full-time, long-term, intensive internship or clinical-practice experiences. In this tradition, this paper reviews early, current, and future perspectives of clinical-practice experiences and outlines the design elements undertaken by the principal-licensure program at the University of Colorado at Denver to address the field's long-standing concerns. Design elements discussed here include clinical-practice tracks, the role of standards in self-assessment, criteria for authoring clinical-practice goals, and a program-long perspective of clinical-practice activities.

EARLY, CURRENT, AND FUTURE PERSPECTIVES ON CLINICAL PRACTICE

Early perspectives on clinical-practice experiences in the 1900s suggested "the administrator could learn his profession effectively on the job by trial and error" (Gregg, 1969, p. 993). According to Frank Spaulding in 1910, "the training of the administrator emphasized the practical aspects of the job" (Callahan & Button, 1964, p. 81). Some of the first courses were described as being summaries of the

Connie L. Fulmer, University of Colorado at Denver
Rodney Muth, University of Colorado at Denver
Kenneth F. Reiter, University of Colorado at Denver

"concrete practical experiences of some former successful school superintendent, now turned teacher in some newly established chair or department of education" (Cubberly, 1924, pp. 182–183). More recent perspectives on clinical practice have included the following criticisms: (a) a general lack of attention paid by preparation programs to any "field-related substance dealing with current problems, needed skills, and administrative tasks" (Culberston & Farquhar, 1971, p. 9); (b) most programs suffer from an "absence of robust clinical experiences" (Murphy, 1992, p. 91); and (c) inattention to clinical practice in preparation programs.

Probably more school administrators fail because of poor skills than any other single reason, yet program and faculty in educational administration fail to do anything about it. It's as though a baseball team in spring training gave the player books to read and lectures on the theory of baseball and did not have the player practice hitting and fielding. Administrators have to perform, and in order to perform well they must have the basic skills of administration (Griffiths, 1988, p. 71). Further, learning experiences required by existing programs have been found to be "irrelevant to the jobs trainees assume" (Mulkeen & Cooper, 1989, p. 1) or have failed to provide future administrators with the "kind of experiences or knowledge that practitioners need" (Muth, 1989, p. 5). Moreover, current administrator training programs do not adequately reflect the realities of the work place (Murphy, 1992, p. 88). Because institutions often base their programs on theory, social sciences, and the processes of rational decision making, they are "well off the mark as effective preparation for the chaotic life of a principal or superintendent" (Crowson & McPherson, 1987, p. 49). Again, "school administration as practiced by superintendents and principals bears little resemblance to school administration as taught in graduate schools of education" (Peper, 1988, p. 360).

Training programs continue to be driven by books, lectures, and examinations. Many of them place only marginal emphasis on what administrators actually do on the job. Clinical experiences in schools are often perfunctory. Practicing administrators are generally not used in a meaningful way in the teaching process. Schools are infrequently used as learning laboratories. Reality-based training situations and materials are not regularly emphasized . . . in short, we have not progressed very far in our efforts to bridge theory and practice (Murphy & Hallinger, 1987, p. 257).

Cooper and Boyd (1987) highlight the problem well: "How often do classes, workshops, or seminars actually take on a school as a laboratory organization, looking, learning, and helping" (p. 21)? Similarly, Sergiovanni (1989) argues that the issue goes beyond merely missing the mark: current preparation programs may actually provide future candidates with perspectives that may be dysfunctional in practice.

Others suggest that clinical-practice activities should be central to the purposes and design elements of preparation programs, recommending that trainers of administrators (a) "must look to modify the system, to make training more rigorous, more interesting, more enticing, and more integrated with real school problems" (Cooper & Boyd, 1987, p. 22), (b) must emphasize that administration is a way of thinking and acting and that more attention should be paid to the doing, convincing, exploring, and thinking about problems in schools (Peterson & Finn, 1995), (c) must emphasize the need to develop more effective strategies to bridge research and practice (Murphy & Hallinger, 1987, p. 278), and (d) must point to the balance needed in preparation programs, while neither being "restricted to the development of skills" nor systematically excluding skill instruction (p. 255).

Peper (1988) prefaces his recommendations on clinical practice by positing, "clinical education is the coordinated teaching and learning of skills that are based on an established philosophy of pedagogy and predetermined learning theory and are correlated with an assessment of job-related requirements"(p. 362). In addition, he offers five levels for an effective clinical practice experience (pp. 365–366). Peper's vision of clinical practice and recommendations for levels of skill development (see Table 1) are followed by an admonition, "clinical practice cannot be bootstrapped or shoehorned successfully" into an existing program (p. 366). Additionally, he reminds us that the type of internship described above would require funding and added responsibility for state legislators, professional organizations, and university-level administrators. Nevertheless, Peper asserts, "the payoff is improved leadership of American schools and school systems" (p. 366).

Pounder, Reitzug, and Young (2002) spoke to the importance of clinical-practice experiences when they recommended, "although often relegated to a secondary role, field and clinical experiences might well serve as the core of the educational leadership preparation experiences" (p. 282). According to the authors, the following possibilities existed: (a) field experiences might be sequenced before, during, and after content coursework, (b) field experiences could begin with an intensive experience, and (c) field experiences could include service learning experiences (pp. 283–284). For Pounder, Reitzug, and Young (2002), field experiences should provide students with opportunities to "serve as apprentice administrators, educational leaders, inquirers, and change agents" (p. 282). Field experiences should be those in which students not only can practice but also initiate and facilitate school improvement activities that involve change for "equity, social justice, democracy, and community" (p. 282). They recommend that students engage in learning activities focused on shadowing, participation, advocacy, and critical reflection in more than one location.

Further, Pounder, Reitzug, and Young (2002) pose the following "ideals" for clinical-practice design: (a) participation in a non-school social service agency or

Table 1.   Peper's Recommendations for Levels of Clinical Practice

Level	Recommendations
Level One	Awareness and Exploration of Skills
Level Two	On-site Observations by candidates of others who held leadership role in businesses, state departments, school districts, or citizen groups.
Level Three	Demonstration Laboratories—prepared cases and practice techniques for low-risk/success-prone experiences (equipped with computers and video feedback materials).
Level Four	Structured Internship—under the supervision of accomplished adjunct clinical professor, students should undertake projects, and develop advanced skills.
Level Five	Consultation— in the art of practice with a new principal or superintendent until candidate develops full professional status.

other education-related community agency or initiative, (b) participation in a school setting in a cultural context that is different from that with which the student is most familiar, (c) participation in work for a cause that is a significant long-term initiative about which the student feels passionately and that works to change educational or social practice in a school district, community or state, (d) participation in inquiry and planning that address real problems identified by a school district, and (e) interaction among a variety of school leaders at all levels of administration in the district, region, and state.

These early, current, and future perspectives on clinical-practices experiences guided the design efforts in our own program. With the help of principal partners who co-deliver cohort learning experiences, we have been able to base our assessments of students' clinical-practice experiences and their other performance tasks in the ELCC-NCATE (National Policy Board for Educational Administration, 2002) standards. The remainder of this paper outlines these design elements and key processes used in developing the Administrative Leadership and Policy Studies (ALPS) clinical-practice experience, the core of our principal-licensure program.

THREE TRACKS

The first design element specifies three clinical-practice tracks. These tracks define the types of clinical practice experiences that students are required to complete. Track-one activities include those specifically tied to performance-based assessments conducted within a school context. Track-two activities are common-event experiences required of all students in all cohorts. Track-three activities are those associated with each student's individual clinical-practice experience. Each track or type of clinical-practice activity is described below.

Track One

The thinking behind track-one activities is the need to ground what students are learning in their classes within the context of schools. Track-one activities include all clinical-practice activities tied to program-wide performance assessments. Because many of the performance assessments are long term, track-one activities take place over the entire program. These activities supplement the work required by projects associated with content typically present in traditional courses (e.g., supervision, evaluation, curriculum design, the budget cycle, school improvement, legal audits), and are designed and carried out by the students in the context of real school settings. Students acquire content from seminar settings and program reading lists but develop and apply their skills in school contexts.

Track Two

Track-two activities are designed to provide common clinical-practice experiences in which all students in all cohorts are required to participate. These experiences include but are not limited to leadership team meetings, special education staffing meetings, school improvement team meetings, accountability team meetings, crisis management team meetings, referendum meetings, school board meetings, bond-hearing meetings, staff hiring meetings, curriculum development meetings, data mining workshops, and visits to various community service agencies that support the ongoing work of schools. This list is customized for each cohort, and students are required to select a pre-specified number of common events for their clinical practice. The power of track-two activities has been evidenced in the rich dialog that resulted around the commonalities and differences of the activities across districts. Students discuss the differences created by resource disparities, size of districts, the type and style of leadership, and the developmental level of event participants in specific districts. Track-two activities help students gain a range of leadership experiences during the program.

Track Three

Track-three clinical-practice activities are designed by student-practitioners following an extensive self-assessment process (based on state and national standards) in concert with each student's site supervisor. These activities represent the heart of the program's clinical-practice experience, are driven by clinical-practice goals, must be integrated throughout the program, and cover three or more major standards per goal. The process of authoring clinical-practice goals, detailed in a later section of this paper, is one of the most important learning experiences in the principal-licensure program.

These clinical-practice tracks provide students with (a) projects in which they had differential experiences due to the unique nature of the school districts in which they worked and learned, (b) common events that all school districts required of their leadership staff, and (c) highly individualized and intensive clinical-practice experiences based on the unique learning needs of each student and learning opportunities available in a particular school district.

THE ROLE OF STANDARDS AND SELF-ASSESSMENT

A second design element of the clinical-practice experience is the role that standards play in the self-assessment process undertaken by students before they attempted to author their clinical-practice goals. The ELCC-NCATE standards are performance based and therefore perfect for students to use as the basis for their self-assessment activities. By doing so, students develop a clear picture of where they have skill strengths and areas in which they are experience poor.

Students score themselves on each standard element as (a) having little knowledge about the area, (b) knowing about it but having no literature base or direct experience, (c) having conceptual knowledge of the area and the ability to describe strategies and skills related to the standard in the context of schooling, or (d) having direct experience as a leader with a particular standard in the context of a school and knowledge of the literature and strategies associated with the content of the standard. The self-assessment process linked the skills of the students with the standards of the field as the starting place for designing meaningful clinical practice experiences.

AUTHORING CLINICAL PRACTICE GOALS

Building on their self-assessments, students are required to create clinical-practice projects that provide service to their school districts in the form of leadership, management, and observation activities. Based on their self-assessments, students are encouraged to outline the types of activities that could build strengths in their areas of weakness and in areas with which they have little familiarity. In those areas in which they have strength, they are encouraged to outline activities that not only build upon strengths but also give them opportunities to grow and lead. Before beginning their clinical-practice experience, students develop goals and tasks related to the standards. For most, authoring their clinical-practice goals is a challenging task. It is a *process*, not an event.

Students are asked to view their goals and tasks from the perspective of a principal, and the initial form is not as neat and tidy as a stand-alone performance standard. Because the process is iterative, requires dialogue with site and university supervisors, and involves writing and rewriting, it takes time and creates some anxiety for students. Our instructional team views this authoring process as critical to the development of administrator perspectives. It represents one of the first real tests of whether student practitioners have the capacity for developing administrator perspectives. Since instituting this three-track clinical-practice process, we have received outstanding feedback from field-site supervisors on the authenticity, depth, and breadth of our student-practitioners' clinical-practice activities.

Central to each successful clinical-practice experience is a student's work in authoring and then pursuing a set of relevant, appropriate, and challenging clinical-practice goals. The process of authoring an acceptable set of goals typically takes place during a three to four week period and includes frequent instances of dialogue between the student and the university clinical-practice supervisor. During the process, students learn that the process of writing and rewriting also involves discussions and negotiations with the site supervisor. This interactive process ensures that student-authored goals meet the following criteria.

Criteria for Authoring Clinical-Practice Goals

1. Goals must be relevant to the context of a student's clinical-practice environment while meeting program standards (and/or state standards).
2. Goals must be written to provide service to the school site rather than simply to meet the needs of the student practitioner. Those needs are met when they successfully complete the goals and tasks that they authored.
3. Goals must provide an appropriate mix of demanding *leadership* and *managerial* experiences with less demanding *observation* experiences.
4. Goals must provide challenging assignments that require the development of skills that are relatively new to the student and experiences that cause the student to move outside of a personal comfort zone. Students are not permitted to use their typical job functions as clinical-practice activities.

Specific Strategies for Authoring Clinical-Practice Goals

Typically, students are asked to author five to six goals that include approximately 10 carefully defined supporting tasks. The format for writing goals is guided by students' choices of specific *leadership-management-observation* verbs. Students are required to construct clinical-practice goals from each of the three verb categories described above. The substance of any particular clinical-practice goal depends on the student's level of experience and the school-site supervisor's level of comfort in allowing the student to engage in student-specified, clinical-practice activities. While students are required to author an appropriate number of goals from each verb list, they are asked to start with about six goals, using two verbs from each category.

The next step in the goal-authoring process requires students to develop supporting *tasks* that facilitate their achievement of each of the six goals. In the task-authoring process, students are encouraged to use a variety of verbs from all three columns. As the goals and tasks are completed, students review the state performance standards, analyze and enumerate how those standards might be met by their clinical-practice goals. In many cases, students find that they have the opportunity to meet a great number of the program standards through this process. Many students reported to us that they used the standards as a catalyst for developing a goal area.

As part of the process, students are asked to identify the standards associated with each of their clinical-practice goals. Table 3 provides an example of one goal and two related tasks. More tasks were associated with this particular goal, but only two are offered here as examples. It is during this portion of the process that students either acknowledge that their goals are broad and deep enough to meet with both school-site and university supervisors' approval, or they realize that they have more work to do in this authoring process.

The process outlined above moves students away from a check-list approach to meeting standards through thoughtful, assessment-based analyses. Without such guidance, students wrote goals that were limited in scope and minimally connected to the broader processes taking place within a school or district. Writing high-quality goals is increasingly important with the emphasis that is now being placed on the school improvement process.

Another strategy used with students during the goal-authoring process is to coach each student through the construction of a clinical-practical goal and brainstorm the

Table 2.   Examples of Leadership, Management, & Observation Verbs for Clinical-Practice Goals

Leadership Verbs	Management Verbs	Observation Verbs
Conduct	Analyze	Shadow/Follow a Process
Direct	Develop	Follow a Process
Chair	Write Reports	Interview
Implement	Collaborate	Attend
Evaluate	Facilitate	Observe
Lead	Analyze Data	Participate

Table 3.   Sample Goals and Task Format for Authoring Clinical-Practice Goals

Goal 4	*Participate in Personnel Actions*
Major Tasks	
1.	In conjunction with the principal, participate in the selection and hiring process of a new teacher and provide coaching, observation, and evaluation for her/his effective classroom instruction. Participate in the coaching, observation, and evaluation of a non-probationary teacher. (At least one of the two teachers will teach a different subject and/or grade level than I have taught.)
	Colorado Performance Standards: 2.1; 3.3; 7.1; 7.2; 7.3; 7.4; 7.6; 7.7; 7.8
2.	Meet with the principal to gather information and suggested guidelines that will allow me to author a "memorandum of understanding" that explains the purpose of my being involved in the evaluation process and denotes the use and (if need be) disposal of all data and observations that are gathered by me.
	Colorado Performance Standards: 2.1; 3.3

related tasks. If the stated goal is too narrow or too broad, the university supervisor coaches that student through the process of broadening the goal or paring it back. This same coaching process is used to help students see that goals should be stated as a benefit to the school community. For example, a goal states, "I will attend budget meetings to learn about the budget process" would need to be rephrased, "I will serve on the school budget advisory committee." The coaching process helps the student redirect energy toward leading, managing, or observing activities that benefit the efforts of the principal and the larger school environment. Coaching is critical during the early stages of the program when the clinical-practice, goal-authoring process takes place. The very act of having to change one's perspective from teacher to school leader is difficult in the beginning. The sooner the student is able to make this shift, the easier the goal-authoring process becomes. The time invested in the initial stages of the clinical-practice experience yields worthwhile benefits to the student and for their clinical-practice experience.

PROGRAM-LONG NATURE OF THE CLINICAL-PRACTICE EXPERIENCE

Another design element of this clinical-practice experience is that it begins with a student's entry into the program and ends when the program is completed. Much of our program was designed to be project based and lead directly to portfolio artifacts generated through performance assessments. By the time students complete clinical activities related to these projects (track one), attended common events required by partner districts (track two), and complete their goal authoring activities (track three), they already have taken major steps toward developing an administrator perspective. From these early experiences, students continue their work on their clinical-practice goals over the entire 16-month, or 4-semester, span of the program. This program-long design was our response to the criticisms lodged by the field and summarized at the start of this paper. The activities created by students help them make sense (Louis, 1980) of school contexts from the perspective of a principal rather than that of a teacher. These sense-making activities from all three tracks provide opportunities for the transfer of knowledge that Kennedy (1987) claims is so often difficult when students try to transition from academic contexts to professional practice.

SUMMARY

The paper presented a review of literature focused on early, current, and future perspectives of clinical-practice experiences in educational leadership programs. Using both criticisms and recommendations, faculty identified and used four design elements as tools to revise the clinical-practice requirements of the principal licensure program. These elements included the use of (a) three clinical-practice tracks, (b) the role of standards in self-assessment, (c) criteria for authoring clinical-practice goals, and (d) a program-long perspective of clinical-practice activities. Types of clinical-practice activities were outlined in tracks. The first track included activities related to performance assessments required by the program. Second-track activities had students attending common events and sharing those experiences with students from other districts and across cohorts. Track-three activities were authored by students themselves and made up the individualized portion of the clinical-practice experience. Since these structures were implemented, instructional faculty have reported that students appear to have more confidence in their ability to be successful in their first administrative position. Our next step is to collect evidence that may support this hypothesis.

REFERENCES

Callahan, R. E., & Button, W. H. (1964). Historical change of the role of the man in the organization:1865–1950. In D. E.Griffiths (Ed.), *Behavioral science and educational administration. 63rd National Society for the Study of Education Yearbook* (Part II, pp.73–92). Chicago: University of Chicago Press.

Cooper, B. S., & Boyd, W. L. (1987). The evolution of training for school administrators. In J. Murphy & P. Hallinger (Eds.), *Approaches to administrative training* (pp. 3–27). Albany: State University of New York Press.

Crowson, R. L., & McPherson, R. B. (1987). The legacy of the theory movement: Learning from the new tradition. In J. Murphy & P. Halllinger (Eds.), *Approaches to administrator training in education* (pp. 45–64). Albany: State University of New York Press.

Cubberly, E. P. (1924). *Public school administration*. Boston: Houghton Mifflin.

Culbertson, J. A., & Farquhar, R. H. (1971). Preparing educational leaders: Methods employed in administration preparation. *UCEA Newsletter, 12*(4), 11–14.

Gregg, R. T. (1969). Preparation of administrators. In R. L. Ebel (Ed.), *Encyclopedia of educational research* (4th ed., pp. 993–1004). London: Macmillan.

Griffiths, D. E. (1988). *Educational administration: Reform PDQ or RIP*. (Occasional paper, No. 8312). Tempe, AZ: University Council for Educational Administration.

Heller, R., Conway, J., & Jacobson, S. (1988). Here's your blunt critique of administrator preparation. *Executive Educator, 10*(9), 18–22.

Holifield, M., & King, D. L. (1993). Meeting the needs of beginning school administrators: Report of a professional induction project. *Journal of School Leadership, 3*(3), 321–328.

Jackson, B. L., & Kelley, C. (2002). Exceptional and innovative programs in educational leadership. *Educational Administration Quarterly, 38*(2), 192–212.

Kennedy, M. M. (1987). Inexact sciences: Professional education and the development of expertise. In F. I. Last (Ed.), *Review of research in education, 14* (pp. 133–167). Washington, DC: American Education Research Association.

Louis, M. R. (1980). Surprise and sense making: What newcomers experience in entering unfamiliar organizational settings. *Administrative Science Quarterly, 25,* 226–251.

Moore, H. A. (1964). The ferment in school administration. In D. E. Griffiths (Ed.), *Behavioral science and educational administration. 63rd National Society for the Study of Education yearbook,* (Part II, pp. 11–32). Chicago: University of Chicago Press.

Milstein, M., & Associates (1993). *Changing the way we prepare educational leaders: The Danforth experience.* Newbury Park, CA: Corwin Press.

Mulkeen, T. A., & Cooper, B. S. (1989, March). *Implications of preparing school administrators for knowledge-work organizations.* Paper presented at the annual meeting of the American Educational Research Association, San Francisco.

Murphy, J. (Ed.). (1992). *The landscape of leadership preparation: Reframing the education of school administrators.* Newbury Park, CA: Corwin Press.

Murphy J., & Hallinger, P. (1987). New directions in the professional development of school administrators: A synthesis and suggestions for improvement. In J. Murphy & P. Hallinger (Eds.), *Approaches to administrative training in education.* Albany: State University of New York Press.

Muth, R. (1989, October). *Reconceptualizing training for educational administrators and leaders: Focus on inquiry.* Notes on Reform, No. 2. Charlottesville, VA: National Policy Board for Educational Administration.

National Policy Board for Educational Administration. (1989). *Improving the preparation of school administrators: An agenda for reform.* Charlottesville, VA: Author.

National Policy Board for Educational Administration. (2002). *Standards for advanced programs in educational leadership for principals, superintendents, curriculum directors, and supervisors.* Arlington, VA: Author.

Peterson, K. D., & Finn, C. E. (1985). Principals, superintendents, and the administrator's art. *Public Interest, 79,* 42–62.

Peper, J. B. (1988). Clinical education for school superintendents and principals: The missing link. In D. E. Griffiths, R. T. Stout, & P. R. Forsyth (Eds.), *Leaders for America's schools* (pp. 360–366). Berkeley, CA: McCutchan.

Pounder, D., Reitzug, U., & Young, M. D. (2002). Preparing school leaders for school improvement social justice, and community. In J. Murphy (Ed.), *The educational leadership challenge: Redefining leadership for the 21st century* (pp. 261–288). Chicago: University of Chicago Press.

Sergiovanni, T. J. (1989). Mystics, neats, and scruffies: Informing professional practice in educational administration. *Journal of Educational Administration, 27*(2), 521–526.

Kentucky's Female Superintendents: Implications for Accountability and Reform

Youlanda C. Washington, Stephen K. Miller, and Jeanne R. Fiene

Research on women in educational administration over the past several decades has illuminated how culture and professional norms have created masculine myths of the best way of leading (Bjork, 2000). In turn, these myths have perpetuated traditions and gender bias in the superintendency. Such dominant assumptions are being challenged by a growing body of feminist research that not only spotlights weaknesses in traditional discourse in the field, but is also filling a gap in the professional knowledge base regarding the effectiveness of women's leadership perspectives.

Issues shaping women's experiences in the public school superintendency are important to educators and researchers (Skrla, Reyes, & Scheurich, 2000), especially as women find themselves in a position where the vast percentage of their colleagues are men. Researchers are piercing the silence that surrounds women in school administration, promoting pro-equity discussion about and among female school leaders at both the individual and professional level.

PURPOSE

With women knocking on the glass ceiling, using a leadership style that is highly connective, deriving its strength from empowering others, the question remains, why are there still so few women in the superintendency? Addressing this general void, the purpose of this study was to investigate the experiences of women superintendents in the state of Kentucky. Helgesen (1990) suggests the feminist style of leadership takes on different appearances, different shapes, and different directions as a web in constant redesign. This study supplements the knowledge base on those patterns.

The significance of this study lies in the fact that Kentucky is a rural state that leads the nation in educational reform. Under the Kentucky Education Reform Act

Youlanda C. Washington, Oldham County Schools, Buckner, KY
Stephen K. Miller, University of Louisville
Jeanne R. Fiene, Western Kentucky University

of 1990 (KERA), the state has implemented a new governance structure, modified leadership practices, increased emphasis on curriculum and instruction, and raised expectations for achievement and equity. In a southern state where cultural under-pinnings play a major role in the socialization process, 16 women may have altered the perceptions of women in a male-dominated occupation. Yet their insights and ex-periences have not been recorded, their voices not heard. Accordingly, the re-searchers explored the leadership perspectives of these female superintendents within the milieu of an historically low achieving state undergoing comprehensive reform, the center point of which is a high stakes value-added accountability system.

WOMEN IN SCHOOL ADMINISTRATION

Women are under represented in the superintendency of public schools (Shakeshaft, 1989). A problematic issue is that leadership traditionally has been studied using male norms as the standard for behaviors (Chliwniak, 1997). The prevailing model defined the professional manager as a person who had an "internal decision-making monopoly and authority over others" (Kanter, as cited in Adkison, 1981, p. 313) and relied on a rigid hierarchical structure, competition, and control to bring about re-sults (Ortiz & Marshall, 1988). Rost (1994) asserted that the white male leadership paradigm has no relevance for the post-industrial age. Naisbitt (1985) suggested that organizations are becoming less hierarchical, more responsive and innovative—meaning there should be fewer levels of administration in school organizations. His implication was that the human element is far more important than structural and/or organizational considerations.

Traditionally, K–12 education is a female-dominated profession; however, the peo-ple who fill the leadership role of the superintendent are predominately men (Konnert & Augenstein, 1995). Typical school leaders come from the American middle class, a white middle-aged male from a small town with a rural background (Glass, 1992). Glass found that 6.6% of the nation's superintendents were women or members of a racial or ethnic minority group. According to Glass (2000), the percentage of women superintendents had nearly doubled from 6.6% to 13.2% with the greatest increase found in suburban and urban areas rather than in rural school districts. Of the nation's 13,728 superintendents, 1,984 are women; 16 of those were found in the rural state of Kentucky (B. Isnko, personal communication, January 30, 2000).

Women in school administration inhabit a traditionally male profession that has evolved from the male managerial, command-and-control model of the early 20th cen-tury. At that time, schools were organized into bureaucracies where male principals and superintendents supervised female teachers who, in turn, directed the students (Or-tiz & Marshall, 1988). The educational system has been organized as a traditional home where gender structure has remained relatively stable throughout the century. Because society has viewed the ideal leader as displaying forceful masculine qualities, these beliefs have translated into having men in formal positions of authority.

Women have historically had the fewest employment opportunities in the area of K–12 educational administration (Restine, 1993), and the selection of a woman su-perintendent still remains a rarity in public education. Yet Pavan (1987) indicated that women were well prepared and obtained the necessary certification to hold the top executive position. Naisbitt and Aburdene (1990) indicated that women would provide the leadership to move organizations into the next century because (a) the dominant principle of organization has shifted from management to leadership and (b) being a leader today no longer requires one to have been socialized as a male.

Although some women have negotiated the male culture, and interest in women gaining access to top administrative posts is increasing, women have largely been excluded from key administrative roles. Both educational administrative theories and practice have contributed to this status (Shakeshaft, 1995). The traditional literature in school administration was based on theories derived strictly from male experiences. Gallos (1992) indicated that women were asked to learn the experiences of men and accept them as representative of all human experiences. However, men and women in educational administration have not had identical experiences or shared histories due to the legacy of discrimination and exclusion that has shaped the world (Shakeshaft, 1987).

Researchers and educators concur that much of the problem stems from subtle notions of gender and leadership as well as from outright discrimination (Keller, 1999). Gender bias constitutes a primary set of beliefs or attitudes, gendered expectations for people's abilities and interests (Sadker & Sadker, 1985). The concept encompasses "culturally-determined cognitions, attitudes, and belief systems about females and males. Furthermore it varies across cultures, changes through historical time and differs in terms of who makes the observations and judgments" (Worell & Remer, 1992, p. 9). Patterson (1994) indicated that white men define and legitimate the dominant culture, therefore shaping the observations and judgments of society. Moreover, societal constructions of perceived gender differences biased the treatment of women in the educational setting (Hackney, 1994), from the way women were hired for a job to how people viewed women in leadership roles. Thus, women's experience in school administration includes attitudinal and institutional barriers to advancement that are nonexistent for men (Shakeshaft, 1989).

Discriminatory attitudes and institutional barriers for women continue to be prevalent today. Researchers blame women's inability to advance in administration on attributes that are not compatible with the traditional leadership styles (Helgesen, 1990). Society views the tough, logical, hierarchical approach as behaviors needed in leading school districts. Consequently, the practice of placing men in administrative positions becomes reinforced. Because women remain in the minority in management circles, the male stereotype endures (Powell, 1988).

Patterson (1994) stated that it is tacitly assumed that the white-male-defined standards for what constituted effective leadership. People tend to hire people like themselves; therefore white males hire white males (Shakeshaft, 1989), thus locking women into low-power, low-visibility positions with very little chance for advancement (Hansot & Tyack, 1981). Consequently, women seeking advancement in school administration generally can progress only up to the point of the superintendency where they hit the "glass ceiling" (Shakeshaft, 1989). Estler (1975) suggested that preferential sponsoring and promotional practices explain the sexist imbalance in education administration and described how male hegemony characterizes our social world (cf. Hansot & Tyack, 1981), thus excluding women from the power structure that controls appointment to administrative positions.

Other researchers and scholars indicate that women themselves are the reason for their under representation in the superintendency. Researchers cite the "individual perspective" (Schmuck, 1980, p. 242), a set of concepts related to "internal barriers" (Hansot & Tyack, cited in Shakeshaft, 1989, p. 82), and "person-centered explanations" (Ortiz & Marshall, 1988, p. 130) as keys for the persistent and continuing gender segregation in the profession (Tallerico & Burstyn, 1996). The researchers look to women themselves for the "cause": personal traits, characteristics, abilities, or qualities. Schmuck (1980) indicated attitudes that focus on poor self-image and a lack of confidence, motivation, and low aspirations were cited as the causes for women not advancing to the top educational positions.

Ortiz and Marshall (1988) indicated it is not that women have poor self-image or lack aspirations; rather women direct their emphasis to the job at hand as their major source of satisfaction and self-esteem. Shakeshaft (1989) indicated that women tend to have experiences in the private-sphere domain and thus have more self-confidence in this area. On the other hand, men have experiences in the public-sphere arena and have more self-confidence there. Since women and men have different levels of experiences, attitudes are formed based on the experiences of men because they are the ones who are visible.

Lougheed (1998) indicated that these attitudes were formed at an early age and were reinforced by prevailing traditions and society's socialization processes. Men and women need to be aware of the attitudes held toward women leaders and the extent that gender bias influences attitudes and reinforces institutional barriers. Shakeshaft (1989) concluded that the ideology of patriarchy resulted in a recentric society, explaining why men, and not women, occupy the formal leadership position in school districts and society even though there is a growing preference for female approaches to school leadership.

Although much has been written on the topic of gender and leadership, the issue remains important because no significant change has occurred. The predominant pattern of women teaching and men managing America's schools still holds (Bell & Chase, 1993; Glass, 2000). To deny women's ability to hold administrative positions is to deny women's experiences and the extant research about discriminatory practices (Tallerico & Burstyn, 1996). Shakeshaft (1989) contended that studying leadership from the perspective of women and their experiences is an initial step in an attempt to bring about a transformation of leadership. A closer examination of women superintendents' experiences could shed insight on the changes that could be made to support women in this male-dominated world. Wesson and Grady (1994) indicated that educators should re-conceptualize the dimensions of educational leadership to achieve a better understanding of the behavior and experiences of women superintendents, because women have always been an important factor in educating our youth and creating a rich legacy for leadership.

According to Konnert and Augenstein (1995), the face of the superintendency will literally change as the number of women and minorities in leadership increases. There will be significant transformations in the educational process, curriculum content, organizational structure, and role definition. These paradigm shifts will require a new understanding of and commitment to visionary leadership on the part of the superintendent.

METHODOLOGY

The study utilized qualitative methods of data collection and analysis to understand the complex factors of female leadership. Examined were the development of a professional identity and the strategies that facilitated and contributed to attaining the superintendency. These female interpretations and perceptions were critical to the investigation. However, the researchers did not depend only on the insiders' emic accounts to uncover reality. The analysis also included cross-checking through etic perspectives to address the extant power distribution.

The development of the interview guides and pre-interview questionnaire was based on questions written by the researchers and borrowed from similar instruments in previous studies. The document analysis protocol was developed specifically for this study. The data representing the experiences of the superintendents were derived from the combination of these instruments. A preliminary pilot study was conducted to refine the measures and procedures used. A purposeful sample of women was selected based on their knowledge about gender in educational leadership and their availability and willingness to participate.

Of the 16 districts with female superintendents, only 12 participated. The instruments (pre-interview questionnaire, interview guides, and document analysis protocol) were designed to retrieve pertinent information (see Appendices in Washington, 2002). The specific items on the different instruments were mapped to the research questions to facilitate analysis. This qualitative study unfolded with a pre-contact letter mailed to the superintendents, followed by a contact letter and the questionnaire. For each district, interviews were arranged with the superintendents as well as a central office administrative team member and a school board member who served on the initial interviewing team that hired the superintendent (if possible). Each interview session lasted between one to two hours with follow-up occurring when needed. Sessions were audio taped and transcribed. The researchers critically analyzed and reported the meaning of the different data streams, revealing the nature of the role of women superintendents in the state of Kentucky.

RESULTS AND DISCUSSION

The findings in this study frequently parallel the results of previous work in this field. This statement is important when considering the overall validity of the study. Although the adequacy of qualitative research is typically judged by different criteria than traditional quantitative studies (cf. Marshall & Rossman, 1995), generalizability is still relevant. Traditionally internal validity is the strength of the study itself (its credibility or sense of believability). This is strengthened in the current study by triangulating the interviews with the female superintendents themselves with additional interviews with central office personnel and school board members from the same district, as well as the document analysis of materials from each district.

Traditional external validity refers to the "reach" of the study beyond the subjects and the context in which they work. This consideration is limited because of the small number of female superintendents, by the rural nature of Kentucky, and the specific comprehensive reform policies under KERA. However, the study does contribute to the external validity of the field of women in leadership positions because the current findings largely mirror previous studies (different state context, similar results). In turn, the similar findings across previous studies increase confidence in the internal strength of the current research. At the same time, some of the data here suggest different interpretations. These conclusions will require subsequent studies for corroboration.

Consistent with the qualitative approach, findings and discussion are combined, organized by the five research questions.

Research Question 1

What Patterns, Themes, or Trends Characterize the Professional Work of Female Superintendents?

Four patterns emerged from the data—surveys, interviews, and mined documents— as related to the professional work of female superintendents: (a) an instructional focus for the district; (b) knowledge and experience; (c) putting children first, and (d) being a change agent.

All participants saw the superintendents as an instructional leader who was a teacher at heart. One commonality was the superintendent's ability to use experience as a teacher to assist the organization in growing professionally. Each superintendent was described as still able to teach and model effective teaching strategies. Their abilities to lead the organization and promote student achievement were evident as the administrative personnel and board members shared how the superintendents organized retreats and workshops and even taught parent sessions.

The superintendents had a strong background in the Kentucky Education Reform Act (KERA). This knowledge assisted them in developing a strategic plan and goals that would support students and district outcomes. These women were very proficient in orchestrating from the background, enhancing participation, and managing reform. Their accomplishments were consistent with Murphy's (1994) work on the changing role of the superintendent in Kentucky's reform movement, i.e., becoming a district instructional leader.

Each superintendent articulated a "children first" attitude. They indicated their motivation to serve as superintendent was to make improvements so children could be successful. They all displayed a high level of confidence in their ability to make changes for students. Ultimately, these women saw themselves as being proactive guardians for children, extinguishing any fires that could diminish the possibility of success for all students. They explained they were teachers at heart and wanted to share a vision of support for children. The administrative personnel and board members confirmed that the superintendent kept the concept of "children first" at the forefront of every decision made within the district, even when it required that the superintendent go against the cultural grain and dismiss/fire an employee. All meetings, retreats, and conferences reportedly began with "What is best for children?"

The superintendents viewed themselves as change agents. They had the ability to mold a district by using web-like leadership skills (Helgesen, 1990). They saw themselves as risk takers who initiated changes to support student success, facilitating change to insure employee growth as well as student achievement. This pattern (being a change agent) dovetails with the instructional leadership pattern just discussed. The initial change in their new tenure came as they reorganized central office to align with instruction. The other subgroups indicated that the superintendents' instructional leadership was grounded in the articulation of their vision of the future and their sense of the district's mission for increased student achievement.

Part of being a change agent was having relational skills. The superintendents described themselves as valuing people and empowering them to make the best decisions for children. They believed in being listeners, sensitive to the people within the organization. The other two role groups depicted the superintendents as being able to delegate, build capacity, empower, collaborate, communicate effectively, reflect, and respect people for their decisions and their right to disagree. The central office administrators and board members saw the superintendents as genuinely caring for employees and treating each challenge as an opportunity to communicate both the district's vision and its mission. This concept of change was inclusive, relating back to earlier themes, e.g., being knowledgeable in various areas and capitalizing on situations because of varied experiences.

These four patterns are consistent with themes from other studies of leadership (Brown & Irby, 1993; Heller, 1992; Shakeshaft, 1995; Wesson & Grady, 1994). The women's instructional focus carried over from their days as a teacher, including seeing themselves as learners. The instructional focus was reflected in their career choices and experiences (curriculum centered). The overlapping of these patterns can be seen in the drive to put children first, a hallmark of these women as they moved up the ranks. Finally the superintendents learned how to effect change and carried this skill with them to the superintendency.

The patterns of professional priorities that emerged from this study were also consistent with the rhetorical themes of Owen (1986). Overall, the superintendents believed that leadership was distinct from management in that leaders set the example, build capacity, and share the responsibility for student success. These attributes were so entwined within the data that the participants articulated them as being inseparable, i.e., it is impossible to be an effective school district CEO in today's society without utilizing these priorities to enact needed changes.

Research Question 2
What Strategies Do Female Superintendents Use in Establishing Their Professional Identity?
The women superintendents in this study commented that the keys to their professional identity involved (a) personal characteristics and (b) leadership traits. Inner

characteristics provided the strength needed to continue their climb to the superintendency and sustain them in the position. The women indicated that these personal qualities represented a solid foundation that emerged during the challenges of their role as CEO. Among these qualities, integrity was deemed the highest priority, a value characterized as the linchpin of their personal identity. Other character traits round out and complement integrity. Instances of all these characteristics were found throughout the interviews from all three role groups.

Although the superintendents identified sterling inner values as the most important aspect of professional identity, leadership traits were also mentioned frequently. However, the factors discussed by the superintendents under this topic virtually repeated the characteristics of professional work described under *Research Question 1* (a focus on professional practice, instructional leadership, priorities for children, and bringing about change by leading and empowering people).

That these women identified their basic values and principles (their personal identity) as the foremost part of their overall professional identity is not surprising. This finding is consistent with Dorn, O'Rourke, and Papalewis (1989) who conducted a qualitative study seeking the leadership qualities found in women in administrative positions. Of the nine qualities identified, five were mentioned by the female superintendents in the current study. Similarly, the general consensus of Ortiz (1991) and Shakeshaft (1995) was that these inner qualities are a primary strength of female superintendents.

The leadership traits that were discussed by the participants of this study (explicated in R*esearch Question 1* above) are consistent with other studies such as Morris (2000), Glass (2000), Brunner (1997), Dorn et al. (1989), and Wesson and Grady (1994). These women created a vision that supported student achievement; focused the mission through leadership—teaching, modeling, and supporting instructional changes that were current and consistent with national best practices; facilitated change through consensus; utilized collaboration to promote change; and created a strategic plan which involved more people in the decision-making process.

Research Question 3

What Are the Keys to Successful Entry into the Role of the Superintendent?
The three role groups articulated four factors as important to successful entry into the position: (a) being well prepared, (b) conflict management, (c) ability to address finances, and (d) developing supportive networks.

Preparation included the proper educational background, coupled with relevant experiences. The superintendents' focus on education began at an early age. The importance of obtaining a quality education was taught to them by the adults (parents/guardians) in their lives. Education was defined as the learning of life and was divided into two segments: academic and behavioral (practical lessons). The women revealed their pragmatic bent by demonstrating how their experiences shaped their life, both personal as well as professional, e.g., district committees or professional organizations.

These superintendents relied on their collaborative skills to manage conflict. They saw their ability to listen and engage all parties in productive discussion as a valued tool to solicit support for the school district. The data revealed the women to be good problem solvers because of their intuitive skills, pro-active behavior, and relational skills.

The ability to manage finances once again demonstrated collaborative skills as integral to their professional careers. Because the women understood the importance of managing finances, they sought every opportunity to participate on a committee to learn about the operations of finances. When faced with limits to their knowledge of fiscal management, they used collaboration to bring people to the table to discuss financial issues. Thus the superintendents did not appear to be hindered in any way regarding fiscal matters. They consistently relied upon the support of an advisor within the central office to learn and grow in the arena of finances.

The superintendents in this study developed supportive professional networks in their lives. They recognized the importance of cultivating relationships with their peers while keeping one eye on those in leadership who could serve as sponsors or mentors. The women articulated an intuitive drive as they differentiated between those who were deemed leaders versus managers. Their ability to make this distinction was part of the evolution of the qualities needed to lead a district successfully, as well as facilitating their own upward mobility.

Overall, these women could be characterized as constructing a personalized career agenda for the superintendency, findings consistent with the research of Pavan (1987), Logan (1998), and Grogan (1996) pertaining to the importance of women's preparation for top positions in school districts. In this study those career moves involved earning their certification through a university program, utilizing knowledge gained from serving on committees, participating in leadership activities to enhance their ability to manage conflict, and special efforts to understand fiscal management. Finally, they utilized their networks to strengthen their own leadership skills and opportunities through mentoring relationships. Noteworthy was the focus on formal education (earning a doctorate). According to Glass (2000), over the last ten years the numbers of women earning a doctorate and entering school administration programs have both increased. Thus this study provides additional support for the trend that women are aligning themselves with a primary desire of school boards, that superintendent candidates have experience with tough managerial decisions coupled with advanced degrees in education.

Research Question 4
What Norms, Biases, and/or Barriers Limit the Career Advancement of Women to the Superintendency?
Although everyone faces obstacles in education, the three subgroups all indicated specific challenges were crucial: (a) budget cuts, (b) staffing ratios, (c) personnel issues, (d) school consolidations or improvements, and (e) student achievement.

When asked if these challenges were general to any superintendent, the answer was "yes." When asked if these challenges were gender specific, the individuals from each group indicated "no." Each group explained that the challenges faced were a part of the role and responsibility of any individual in administration. Yet what appeared to surface *indirectly* from within these challenges were the norms, bias, and barriers that were specific to the gender of the superintendent. The superintendents indicated that they did not nor had they ever felt any bias or faced any barriers from the board that hired them, and they commented that their respective boards of education continue to support them. But one superintendent cited difficulty with a central office female, another cited a male principal, and a third cited difficulty with a newly elected female board member. While the specific examples seemed to be limited in nature, all articulated some degree of bias shown throughout their careers.

The interviews revealed that any norms and bias likely originated from deep-rooted tendencies that surfaced at the mere thought of a female in the role of superintendency. The women, as well as the administrative personnel members and board members, indicated that many communities and even their peers were concerned whether women could be tough enough to handle the difficult issues and budget items. This depiction of attitudes displayed toward these superintendents is consistent with the attitudinal studies on school administration by Whitaker and Lane (1990) who found a consistent bias against women compared to men. While women were perceived to be more capable in school-related administration, men were still believed to be the ones who should be making the decisions. More bluntly, males were perceived as better at personnel issues (discipline, firings) and finances.

According to the participants in this study, this bias was very subtle in the beginning but manifested itself quickly, becoming overt and pointed. The superintendents indicated that other women appeared to question their ability to lead, while men questioned their ability to make the tough decisions. Several board members articulated that they had dealt with this same type of bias from community members. It appeared that females attempted to discriminate against these women prior to their appointment as well as during their tenure. Men appeared to discriminate after the superintendent was appointed. This type of subtle discrimination is consistent with Gupton and Slick (1996), who reported that the literature is replete with claims of sex-role stereotyping as one of the major barriers to women in educational administration.

The tendencies of other females to use manipulative tactics with boards of education in an attempt to halt or alter their decision to hire the best candidate, who just happened to be a female, appears to be rooted in a societal perception that men are the ones who should be serving in the role of superintendent. Likewise, the insubordinate actions displayed by some males, after women were appointed to the position, appear to be linked to widespread attitudes about gender and role. These external barriers articulated here were consistent with the research pertaining to the women's place model (Estler, 1975) and other studies by Wesson and Grady (1994), Shakeshaft (1989), Skrla et al. (2000), and Brunner (2000).

While the superintendents indicated in their questionnaire that they were not sure if a good ol' boy network existed, their responses during the interviews reflected that some form of such a network did exist. The administrative personnel and board members likewise indicated the existence of these networks, actually more strongly then the superintendents themselves. These other two role groups believed that it manifests as a cultural overtone within state and regional meetings and even in offices that oversee the hiring of a superintendent, e.g., the board of education itself or related agencies that guide boards in the process (Chase & Bell, 1994). The perception was that large numbers of local boards are *not* progressive in their search for women leaders, a condition strongly rooted in the good ol' boy network. It was as though there is an unwritten code (you can't join our circle), that the entrance to the position is closed to women. The result is *covert* behaviors (lack of progress, hires not made, opinions not respected) as well as the *overt* forms of discrimination that surfaced after the hiring.

This distinction between covert and overt forms of bias can perhaps explain the somewhat contradictory statements of these women superintendents regarding barriers and prejudice. While they consistently stated they had not run into barriers, particularly in the hiring process and from their own boards of education, their anecdotes reflected the after-the-fact overt incidents from subordinate personnel or at statewide meetings. Why the disconnect? The answer lies in how the good ol' boy network operates: a deeply engrained set of structures and attitudes that change slowly and operate primarily through denial of opportunity. This is covert, widespread, and prevents many female candidates from ever being taken seriously, let alone being hired. Yet this group of 12 female superintendents indicated they had not run afoul of this covert network.

What needs to be recognized here is the status of these 12 women. They represented the *only* 16 districts in the state of Kentucky with a female superintendent. (For a variety of reasons, the other four did not participate in the study.) Thus they were, at the time, a pioneering group. Not only are they atypical, but the boards that hired them are unusual. According to Rogers and Schumacher (1971), these boards are innovators with respect to the S-curve of adoption of innovations across institutions. It is very likely that these women did not and have not experienced the covert denial of opportunity during the hiring process because their boards were among the first to break with old traditions and customs. There are 176 school districts in Kentucky. The 16 districts that had female superintendents represent only 9% statewide. That these women may not have themselves experienced the covert denial of opportunity does not equate to the demise of the good ol' boy network. Its continued operation is more accurately reflected in the percentage of positions where females have yet to be given a chance, in the majority of districts where attitudes and behaviors remain solidly within the influence of traditional sex role structures.

It should be noted that the distinction between covert bias or discrimination and overt prejudice is not widely utilized. To the authors' knowledge, this differentiation has not been described in the literature on women in school leadership, but is common in the sociological literature on racism. Here the scholarly interpretation is on why so many whites generally deny the existence of racism in today's society and, even more strongly, deny that they personally have ever discriminated. The answer is that most whites equate "racism" with personal overt acts of prejudice. Scholars, theorists, and persons of color, on the other hand, equate racism with institutionalized inequality where the injustices are embedded in the very fabric and structures of society, involve the exercise of power, and frequently occur at a taken-for-granted, unconscious level (Bell, 1989; Wilson, 1987; Tilly, 1998). The parallel for women's studies is that the covert denial of opportunity is institutionalized sexism while the overt discriminatory anecdotes are part of the "I haven't and wouldn't do that" realm.

Research Question 5
What Insight Can Be Gained from the Demographic Data Pertaining to the Superintendents?
The demographics pertaining to the women superintendents focus on personal data, which capture age, family structure, social origin, and childhood leadership activities. These factors represent the demographics that shape their leadership behavior as superintendent. These women collectively had traditional family backgrounds. Nine of the 12 had local roots (seven were Kentucky natives). Their households were intact (11 of 12 had dual-parent families). They had primarily middle-class homes (9 of 12) in which business was the most common for fathers and homemaker for mothers. All had active childhoods with lots of activities and opportunities for leadership —recreational, 58%, school-related, 29%, and the rest church activities. Finally 75% were in the two age brackets 47–51 and 52–57. Together, these personal data revealed that their path to success in working with or serving others was developed at an early age in life.

Overall, these demographic findings support other studies related to the feminine leadership model. The success of these women depended in part on their social origins and educational achievements. These female superintendents have incorporated their social and educational development into their professional careers. This is consistent with Maienza's (1986) study that indicated that women leaders learn to react to opportunity and power very early in their lives, and they continue to utilize significant opportunities for upward mobility in the organizations surrounding them.

Study Implications
This study provides strong evidence on the ability of women superintendents to lead successfully. Yet the findings also suggest the continued existence of male dominance as a major impediment to women aspiring to the superintendency. The cultural overtones of the good ol' boy network are deeply ingrained in the thought processes of those who have been raised within this milieu. Concepts embedded and formed at an early age may trigger fears or insecurities that surface when the structural arena (associations, clubs, etc.) of white males is threatened. The image of a glass ceiling barring progress for women administrators suggests the subtlety of existing networks of power. Yet even the most dominant forms of privilege can be weakened when conditions change. Different challenges require a different mode of leadership. The new leadership style must respond to school reform, a new emphasis on student achievement, curriculum and instruction as the preeminent focus of schools, more diverse student bodies and faculty, and utilization of talent so that the district and schools *improve* their functioning and outcomes. This is in stark contrast with schools as stasis organizations, in which top-down hierarchical control functioned

well to preserve discipline and stability. The new aims for schools require nuanced, collaborative leadership and the skills to relate to people, traits long associated with women.

As noted above, these aspects of leadership are widely perceived to be the strength of women. In contrast, the hierarchical, traditional leadership of males seems to have been better suited to a time when schools operated under a different system with achievement presumably determined by the individual abilities of the students, not the quality of teaching and learning. Instead, schools were evaluated on "keeping things quiet," success in extracurricular activities (particularly sports), and keeping problems and complaints at bay (see Meyer & Rowan, 1978; Miller, 1992).

Clearly times are changing. Previous studies have indicated that females consistently demonstrate the collaborative leadership and nurturing of human potential that are called for as education moves into the 21st century (see Aburdene & Naisbitt, 1992; Hoyle, 1989). It is likely that subsequent research as well as some existing work (cf. Murphy, 1994) will demonstrate that these traits of leadership are not the sole domain of females. Nonetheless, the specific results of this research indicate that the 12 women superintendents (and their districts) do reflect this instructionally focused leadership style.

ACCOUNTABILITY AND SCHOOL ADMINISTRATION

This in-depth study addresses the question, "What is distinctive about women in the role of the superintendent in the state of Kentucky?" Findings reveal that the 12 women may well be changing the path for future women in the state of Kentucky based on their "feminist leadership," a style consistent with effective schools research and a larger body of literature directed toward understanding the ways women fit into educational organizations, their leadership style, and biases toward women school administrators (Bjork & Rogers, 1999).

The findings suggest that all of these women had a fundamental commitment to offer the best to and for children as they began their administrative careers. Through sheer determination to improve life for students, these women created their professional identity. The use of their feminine qualities, coupled with a strong knowledge base, ushered them into a reform period in which their leadership style is consistent with the changing image of the superintendency in Kentucky. Their "children first" focus is clearly consistent with KERA's value-added accountability model (cf. Miller, 1992).

The data, collected and analyzed to address the five research questions (women's professional work, professional identity, strategies for successful entry into the superintendency, norms and/or barriers faced, and demographic information), are consistent with previous work in the field. Dorn et al.'s (1989) qualitative study pertaining to female administrators' leadership, Ortiz's (1991) work on the strengths of women superintendents, Gupton and Slick's (1996) research on the trends toward participatory style leadership, and Murphy's (1994) examination of the role of the superintendent in Kentucky since the passage of KERA are all precursors to the findings in the current study.

From a theoretical perspective, the results of this study support the findings of other studies such as Brown and Irby (1993), Grogan (1996), Ortiz and Marshall (1988), Maienza (1986), Merle (1999), Tallerico and Burstyn (1996), Whitaker and Lane (1990), and Wesson and Grady (1994), all of which attempt to describe the perceptions, perspectives, deep concerns, and thoughts of women superintendents through a narrative process. Transformation of leadership theory (Shakeshaft, 1989) occurs by studying the field perspectives of women, their experiences and value orientations regarding leader effectiveness. Grogan (1996) asserts that educational administration is currently undergoing a shift, with directive, top-down administrative styles losing favor to shared leadership. Brunner (2000) posits that this new soft approach, shared leadership, has the potential for being perceived as non-confrontational and supportive to others. Thus instead of being perceived as weak and not direct enough, caring relationships are turned into the strengths of empathy and inspiration.

These collaborative leadership traits dovetail with requirements for value-added growth in achievement in state accountability systems. Empirically, the women in this study demonstrated their ability to lead districts in articulating a vision, establishing a mission, providing an instructional focus, managing budgets, and addressing building and grounds projects. They managed these areas through their collaborative approach to effective leadership. They were seen as trustworthy, caring, and relational people who targeted all students for success. They also were seen as leaders who could make the tough decisions and who could survive when going against the grain of the community to promote and ensure safety for the well being of students.

Thus, against the backdrop of instructional leadership consistent with the effective schools research, the women superintendents of Kentucky demonstrated a leadership style that is aligned with expectations that superintendents improve achievement for all students, as required by KERA. Based on educational, political, and managerial aspects, this type of leadership provides promising perspectives for the reconceptualization of the role. Gossetti and Rusch (1995) concur that these skills close the gaps and blank spaces of the traditional hierarchical form of school administration. Wesson and Grady (1994) indicated that these skills constitute the wholeness of leadership and are aligned with the 21st century model of leadership that represents a framework for instructional improvement in school districts.

Collaborative-based instructional leadership represents a paradigm level shift. The current study, and others in the literature on women's studies, suggests that the feminine model (priorities for children and an instructional focus delivered via an empowering style of leadership that cultivates respect and emphasizes human relations) is consistent with the leadership required to be successful under KERA. But this research does not imply, and should not be construed as, an endorsement that only women behave and lead in this manner. Murphy's (1994) work suggests that more superintendents in Kentucky are changing from the top-down, traditional style of management to collaborative leadership focused on school improvement. Thus the "feminine style" may well not be the sole province of women. Nor should it be presumed, at this early stage of research on what works to achieve value-added results, that there is one best way. Other leadership models may emerge as alternatives to the feminine model described in the current study. After all, this research is based on only 12 cases. And "effective" male superintendents were not examined.

The Serial Superintendency

However, such instructional changes by women superintendents presume that they get hired. As the results from Research Question 4 indicated, covert ol' boy networks seem still to be prevalent, preventing many females from being hired. But this network may have another dimension as well. In addition to the fact that the remaining Kentucky districts are still run by male superintendents, there is the longitudinal career path. The superintendency is a politically sensitive position in which competing interest groups frequently disagree on specific issues or the direction of district policy. Decisions made to resolve these conflicts inevitably please some groups and leave others disgruntled. All such decisions use up a certain amount of social and political capital. Over time, the superintendent's base of approval wanes and the point is reached where the board decides new leadership is needed. This process is accelerated when the superintendent takes an activist role and pushes reform or change. Accordingly, the incumbency of superintendents tends to be relatively brief, with four to seven year terms not uncommon (cf. Tallerico & Burstyn, 1996).

Because of the relatively short tenure for the CEO role, the career path for many individuals becomes a serial superintendency. Individuals who represent this career path are and have been overwhelmingly male (Shakeshaft, 1995). It is obviously too soon to determine whether the pioneering group of female superintendents in this study will be permitted to join this serial-superintendency career path. But it needs to be stated that as long as this longitudinal dimension of hiring remains a male bastion, then strong evidence for the continuing effects of the good ol' boy network would still exist. The particular double standard for this situation would be conceptualized as second (or third or fourth) chances are routine for males, but a female who had her shot need not expect another chance.

FUTURE RESEARCH

As with most research efforts, new questions and concerns are inevitably raised. Several of these are briefly related below. Attention to these issues has the potential to advance significantly the knowledge base on women in school administration as well as increase understanding about school reform, effective district leadership, career superintendents, and gender-based discrimination.

1. Has the Kentucky Education Reform Act (KERA) contributed to the progress of women breaking through the glass ceiling of leadership? Given the emphasis on both student accountability and site-based decision making in KERA, and the concomitant increase in women who are moving into leadership positions, are these increases due to the specific demands of school reform under KERA? This could be examined through comparative trends of females moving into leadership positions across states with different reform packages.

2. What is the current number of female applicants waiting in the ranks for the superintendency and other stepping stone positions en route to that role. Both current and, if available, past statistics, would be valuable in this "pipeline" study.

3. An explicit study of the serial superintendency and the distinguishing characteristics of these individuals compared to one-time superintendents is sorely needed. Data on race and gender would be an important aspect of such a study.

4. What is the nature of the behavior that constitutes the good ol' boy relationships? What are the structural and attitudinal components that comprise these informal networks? This study would require extensive qualitative interviews supplemented by a network analysis approach.

5. The current study on tenured female superintendents could be expanded from qualitative to a large-scale survey of districts across the state, examining opportunities for and attitudes about women and minorities in school leadership positions. This would provide more generalizable insights on the issues raised in this and other qualitative research.

6. It has been noticed throughout this study that the leadership style of these female superintendents appears to correlate strongly with the expectations for superintendents as dictated by KERA. In several of the interviews, the leadership of these women was starkly contrasted with their male predecessors who employed the traditional hierarchical leadership style. What is unknown is whether this finding (focus on instruction and student outcomes coupled with a relational, collaborative, empowering style of leading) is the sole province of female superintendents. What are the priorities and leadership of *effective* superintendents under KERA (cf. Murphy, 1994)? Do males as well as females adopt this style? Is there more than one mode of leadership that is considered effective under KERA? Case studies of successful superintendents could help sort out these questions.

CONCLUSION

In summary, the 12 women who participated in this study within the context of their district are transforming the cultural perception of women in a male dominated profession. The record that is emerging from their leadership, to this point, appears to support a renaissance for the children of Kentucky. To be objective, it is too early to disentangle the broader dictates of KERA from the accomplishments of a feminine approach to leadership per se (emphasis on children; instructional focus; relational, collaborative-based, empowering administrative style). It is not too early, however, to note that the leadership of these women superintendents is clearly aligned with and supports the goals and objectives of Kentucky's reform perspectives. With data pointing to the ability of these female superintendents to lead school districts effectively, one can only imagine the ultimate legacy these women will leave and the impact of their pioneering leadership in the larger national arena: promoting social justice through successful school experiences for all children.

REFERENCES

Aburdene, P., & Naisbitt, J. (1992). *Megatrends for women.* New York: Villard Books.

Adkison, J. A. (1981). Women in school administration: A review of the research. *Review of Educational Research, 51*, 311–343.

Bell, C., & Chase, S. (1993). The under representation of women in school leadership. In C. Marshall (Ed.), *The new politics of race and gender: Yearbook of the Politics of Education Association* (pp. 141–154). Washington, DC: Falmer.

Bell, D. (1989). *And we are not saved: The elusive quest for racial justice.* New York: Basic Books.

Bjork, L. G. (2000). Introduction: Women in the superintendency: Advances in research and theory. *Educational Administration Quarterly, 36*, 5–17.

Bjork, L. G., & Rogers, L. (1999, November). *Opportunity in crisis: Women and people of color in the superintendency. Prelude to a new millennium.* Paper presented at the Yearbook of the Southern Regional Council of School Administrators, Charlotte, NC. Retrieved from www.hehd.clemson.edu/screa/YrBkV1N1/Bjork.htm

Brown, G. H., & Irby, B. J. (1993, August). *Women in educational leadership: A research-based model course design.* Paper presented at the annual meeting of the National Council of Professors of Education Administration, Williamsburg, VA.

Brunner, C. C. (1997). Working through the riddle of the heart: Perspectives of women superintendents. *Journal of School Leadership, 7,* 138–164.

Brunner, C. C. (2000). *Principles of power: Women superintendents and the riddle of the heart.* Ithaca: State University of New York Press.

Chase, S., & Bell, C. (1994). How search consultants talk about female superintendents. *The School Administrator, 51*(2), 36–42.

Chliwniak, L. (1997). *Higher education leadership: Analyzing the gender gap* (ERIC Clearinghouse on Higher Education, D 410 846). Retrieved October 30, 2002, from www.ed.gov/databases/ERIC_digest/ed410846.html

Dorn, S. M., O'Rourke, C. L., & Papalewis, R. (1989). Women in educational administration: Nine case studies. *National FORUM of Educational Administration and Supervision Journal, 17*(4), 23–28. Retrieved from www.nationalforum.com/DORNeas.html

Estler, S. E. (1975). Women as leaders in public education. *Signs: Journal of Women in Culture and Society, 1,* 363–387.

Gallos, J. V. (1992). Educating men and women in the 21st century. *Journal of Continuing Higher Education, 40*(1), 2–8.

Glass, T. (1992). *The 1992 study of the American school superintendency.* Arlington, VA: American Association of School Administrators.

Glass, T. (2000). *The 2000 study of the American school superintendency.* Arlington, VA: American Association of School Administrators.

Gosetti, P. P., & Rusch, E. (1995). Reexamining educational leadership: Challenging Assumptions. In D. M. Dunlop & P. A. Schmuck (Eds.), *Women leading in education* (pp. 11–35). Albany: State University of New York Press.

Grogan, M. (1996). *Voices of women aspiring to the superintendency.* Albany: State University of New York Press.

Gupton, S. L., & Slick, G. A. (1996). *Highly successful women administrators: The inside stories of how they got there.* Thousand Oaks, CA: Corwin.

Hackney, C. (1994). The interaction of epistemological position, performance self-esteem, and the organizational culture: A study of women at entry and staff levels of educational administration. *Dissertation Abstracts International, 55* (09), 2659A.

Hansot, E., & Tyack, D. (1981). *The dream deferred: A golden age for women school administrators* (Policy Paper No. 81-C2). Stanford, CA: Stanford University, Institute for Research on Educational Finance and Governance. (ERIC Document Reproduction Service No. ED 207 161)

Helgesen, S. (1990). *The female advantage: Women's ways of leadership.* New York: Doubleday.

Heller, T. (1992). *Women and men as leaders.* New York: Praeger Publishers.

Hoyle, J. R. (1989). Preparing the 21st century superintendent. *Phi Delta Kappan, 70,* 376–379.

Keller, B. (1999, September 15). Women superintendents: Few and far between. *Education Week,* pp. 23–27.

Konnert, M. W., & Augenstein, J. J. (1995). *The school superintendency: Leading education into the 21st century.* Lancaster, PA: Technomic Publishing Co.

Logan, P. (1998). School leadership of the 90's and beyond: A window of opportunity for women educators. *Advancing Women in Leadership Journal.* Retrieved January, 2000, from www.advancingwomen.com/awl/summer98/LOGAN.html

Lougheed, J. I. (1998). *Fifteen year study, 1984–1998: Assessing attitudes of women and men toward women leaders and a comparison of leadership styles of women and men* (Monograph). Women in Leadership Forum, Oakland University, Oakland, CA.

Maienza, J. G. (1986). The superintendency: Characteristics for men and women. *Educational Administrative Quarterly, 4,* 39–40.

Marshall, C., & Rossman, G. B. (1995). *Designing qualitative research* (2nd ed.). Thousand Oaks, CA: Sage.

Merle, A. M. (1999). *Women's journeys to educational administration positions.* Unpublished master's project, University of Saskatchewan, Saskatoon, SK.

Meyer, J. W., & Rowan, B. (1978). The structure of educational environments. In M. W. Meyer & Associates (Eds.), *Environments and organizations* (pp. 78–107). San Francisco: Jossey-Bass.

Miller, S. K. (1992). Changing conceptions of "good schools": Implications for reforming urban education. *Education and Urban Society, 25,* 71–84.

Morris, T. (2000). A personal account of leadership in an academic setting. *Advancing Women in Leadership Journal, 3*(2), 1–8. Retrieved from www.advancingwomen.com/awl/summer2000/m2_morris.html

Murphy, J. (1994). The changing role of the superintendency in restructuring districts in Kentucky. *School Effectiveness and School Improvement, 5,* 349–375.

Naisbitt, J. (1985). *Re-inventing the corporation.* New York: Warner Books.

Naisbitt, J., & Aburdene, P. (1990). *Megatrends 2000: Ten new directions.* New York: Morrow.

Ortiz, F. I. (1991). An Hispanic female superintendent's leadership and school district culture. In N. Wyner (Ed.), *Current perspectives on the culture of school* (pp. 45–50). Cambridge, MA: Brookeline.

Ortiz, F., & Marshall, C. (1988). Women in educational administration. In N. J. Boyan (Ed.), *Handbook of research on educational administration* (pp. 123–141). New York: Longman.

Owen, W. F. (1986). Rhetorical themes of emergent female leaders. *Small Group Behavior, 17,* 475–487.

Patterson, J. A. (1994, March). *Shattering the glass ceiling: Women in school administration.* Paper presented at the Women's Studies Graduate Symposium, Chapel Hill, NC. (ERIC Document Reproduction Service No. ED 383 098)

Pavan, B. N. (1987, April*). Sex role stereotyping for household chores by aspiring and incumbent female and male public school administrators.* Paper presented at the annual meeting of the American Educational Research Association, Washington, DC. (ERIC Document Reproduction Service No. ED 283 303)

Powell, G. N. (1988). *Women and men in management.* Newbury Park, CA: Sage.

Restine, N. (1993). *Women in administration: Facilities for change.* Newbury Park, CA: Corwin Press.

Rogers, E. M., with Schumacher, F. F. (1971). *Communication of innovations: A cross cultural approach* (2nd ed.). New York: The Free Press.

Rost, J. C. (1994, April). *Moving from individual to relationship: A postindustrial paradigm of leadership.* Paper presented at the annual meeting of the American Educational Research Association, New Orleans.

Sadker, M., & Sadker, D. (1985). The treatment of sex equity in teacher education. In S. Klein (Ed.), *Handbook for achieving sex equity in teacher education* (pp. 145–161). Baltimore, MD: Johns Hopkins University Press.

Schmuck, P. (1980). Changing women's representation in school management: A systems perspective. In S. K. Biklen & M. Brannigan (Eds.), *Women and educational leadership* (pp. 239–359). Lexington, MA: Lexington Books.

Shakeshaft, C. (1987). Theory in a changing reality. *Journal of Educational Equity and Leadership, 7*(6), 4–20.

Shakeshaft, C. (1989). The gender gap in research in educational administration. *Educational Administration Quarterly, 25,* 324–337.

Shakeshaft, C. (1995). Gendered leadership styles in educational organizations. In B. Limerick & B. Lingard (Eds.), *Gender and changing educational management* (pp. 73–81). Rydalmere, NSW, Australia: Hodder Education.

Skrla, L., Reyes, P., & Scheurich, J. J. (2000). Sexism, silence, and solution: Women superintendents speak up and speak out. *Educational Administration Quarterly, 36,* 44–75.

Tallerico, M., & Burstyn, J. (1996). Retaining women in the superintendency: The location matters. *Educational Administration Quarterly, 32*(Suppl.), 642–665. Retrieved from wpnet.com/cgi-bin/epwtop/page

Tilly, C. (1998). *Durable inequality.* Berkeley: University of California Press.

Washington, Y. O. C. (2002). *Women in school leadership: A study of female superintendents in Kentucky.* Unpublished doctoral dissertation, University of Louisville.

Wesson, L. H., & Grady, M. L. (1994). An analysis of women urban superintendents: A national study. *Urban Education, 24,* 412–424.

Whitaker, K., & Lane, K. (1990). Is a woman's place in school administration? *The School Administrator, 47*(2), 8–12.

Wilson, W. J. (1987). *The truly disadvantaged: The inner city, the under-class and public policy.* Chicago: University of Chicago Press.

Worell, J., & Remer, P. (1992). *Feminist perspectives in therapy: An empowerment model for women.* New York: Wiley & Sons.

Preparing Administrators for Gifted, Talented, and Creative Education Programs

Julie Milligan and Joe Nichols

In 1986, Gifted, Talented, and Creative (GTC) Education was mandated in the state of Arkansas. With the mandate, Arkansas State University (ASU) established a program, which provided a master's degree in gifted education. The master's degree certified an educator to serve as a facilitator or coordinator of a program for gifted children in grades kindergarten through 12. Within the last year, licensure programs for the state have changed to allow flexibility for the university to oversee a program of study toward additional licensure. Consequently, the Department of Educational Leadership, Curriculum and Special Education at ASU has added a new program of study, which provides GTC educators the opportunity to become Administrators of GTC Programs. This new program of study involves the prospective administrator in authentic field-based preparation through an internship. During the internship, students explore a problem in the area of emphasis to become eligible for licensure.

The program incorporates competencies from the Council for Exceptional Children (CEC), Interstate School Leadership Licensure Consortium (ISLLC), and Arkansas Department of Education (ADE). Further, professional literature (Mulkeen & Tenenbaum, 1990; Sparks & Hirsh, 1997), reports that holistic field-based preparation is essential in order for administrative candidates to: (a) effectively solve problems, (b) work productively with all stakeholders, (c) make adequate decisions regarding financial matters, and (d) facilitate policy making and curriculum development.

WHY FIELD-BASED PREPARATION?

Within the past two decades, researchers (Pepper, 1988; Mulkeen & Tenenbaum, 1990) have provided ample justification for the use of authentic field-based experiences as an effective and necessary tool in training administrators. Pepper (1988) indicated that practitioners complained about the lack of knowledge and skills in

Julie Milligan, Arkansas State University
Joe Nichols, Arkansas State University

coursework to prepare them to be effective administrators. Muth (1989) went further to say that field-based experiences, diversity issues, and training in skills were all lacking in administrative preparatory programs.

Until the early 90's, programs to prepare administrators were driven by coursework, which engaged students in "lecture learning." Further, assessments were paper-pencil examinations, which were seldom substantive (Mulkeen & Tenenbaum, 1990).

More recently, the benefits of authentic field-based learning to prepare administrators have been reported (Bridges & Hallinger, 1995; Wiggins, 1993). More effective preparatory programs have included: (a) essential, intriguing, field-based problems, (b) employee cooperation and teamwork, (c) understanding people and environments by focusing on cultural diversity, (d) self-analysis regarding beliefs and values about leadership, and (e) student accountability for guiding and directing their own learning (Bridges & Hallinger, 1995; Smith, 1993).

Arkansas State University has incorporated the authentic learning, assessment, and reflection into all the administrative programs. One component of this process is the internship. The Graduate Bulletin defines district-level internship as "an educational leadership experience in a school setting" (2002, p. 156). The internship begins as the student chooses a problem and a plan for action.

THE INTERNSHIP PROCESS

Personnel involved in the internship include the candidate, a clinical supervisor and a university supervisor. A clinical supervisor is assigned at the district level. He or she must be in an administrative possession (i.e., building principal, assistant superintendent, special education administrator or superintendent). When the program is further developed and GTC Administrators exist, such qualified persons may serve as the clinical supervisor. The university supervisor is the director of the GTC Program of ASU. The clinical and university supervisors must approve the field-based project. A contract is completed and signed by all three members of the team—the program candidate, clinical supervisor, and university supervisor. The final product for the internship is a portfolio.

During the internship, candidates and faculty advisors meet on four separate dates in a three-hour session. The first session is dedicated to discussing the syllabus and to answering questions about the requirements of the internship. The second and third sessions involve discussions regarding the progress of the field activities. The final session prepares candidates for finalizing the portfolio.

The administrative candidate is required to e-mail 11 weekly reflections to faculty supervisors during the internship. The primary focus of the reflections is the intern's analysis of the problem solving process. In turn, the university supervisor responds to each candidate's reflection by critiquing it and offering advice about the issues described by the intern.

Candidates, along with the field-based supervisor, are required to identify an area in gifted education of district-wide concern or to construct an innovative gifted education program in the school district of employment. This concern is expected to be one, which is shared or perceived as a need by the district school staff, board of education, the community, and/or the students who have been identified to receive services by the gifted education program. The study and conclusions are all applicable to solving a problem or addressing an issue related to the gifted, talented, and creative students.

The following are requirements for the internship toward fulfillment of the portfolio project. Students must: (a) identify a problem related to the field of gifted education which is pertinent to the school district, classroom teachers, parents, and/or community, (b) determine which Council of Exceptional Children Standards, Interstate School Leadership Licensure Standards, and Arkansas Department of Education. Standards will be addressed in the problem solving process, (c) complete a review of literature related to the problem, (d) identify activities involved in the problem, (e) establish a budget for implementing a plan or solution, (f) articulate a timeline for completing the project, (g) construct a project evaluation instrument that will provide measurable feedback, (h) write 11 reflections, and (i) collect artifacts that demonstrate the procedures used during the project.

With the exception of the weekly reflections, these program components are included in an internship report. The reflections are submitted to the candidate's university supervisor through e-mail at the end of each week for 11 consecutive weeks of the internship.

Effective Problem Solving

In order to become a program candidate and before qualifying for licensure in Gifted Education Administration, the candidate must hold a license or master's degree in Gifted, Talented, and Creative Education. During the preparation for such a degree, students obtain expertise in identification procedures, program options, curriculum planning, creativity, affective issues, and assessment issues for students who are gifted, talented and/or creative. In order to extend the intern's expertise and experiences into the realm of administrative duties, the student is immersed in a course of study, which emphasizes problem solving strategies central to the administrative duties. However, this program requires knowledge more complex than those encountered by the generalist in educational leadership (Christenson, 1990).

Therefore, a unique aspect of this course of study incorporates expertise in gifted education issues, coursework in educational leadership, and problems associated with the two combined. For example, the student might choose to examine the effective directorship of classroom teachers to provide an enriched curriculum. Or the candidate might incorporate leadership strategies to improve the numbers of minority students identified for gifted program services. Such an experience authenticates the exploration and practice of both administration and gifted education issues.

Working Effectively with Stakeholders

The internship provides another opportunity for the prospective Gifted Education Administrator. An opportunity to work with other administrators, classroom teachers, parents, and community members is innate to the process. An administrator within the school district supervises the candidate's project. Typically, the superintendent or a building principal guides, monitors, and evaluates the progress of the candidate.

The student is also required to demonstrate his or her ability to work effectively with classroom teachers in a leadership capacity. For example, the intern might organize and lead staff development training for teachers regarding the identification and education of gifted children. Further, the candidate must demonstrate her or his ability to communicate effectively with parents and community in regard to giftedness.

Adequate Financial Planning
One requirement of the internship is for the prospective administrators to develop a budget for the project. During this process, the intern must seek a source for financial support. This may include funds from a grant or building level administrators. Most schools are willing to invest in the process since the school is benefiting from the implementation of an innovative venture or is receiving a solution to a problem within the system. During the process, the students engage in authentic budget planning regarding cost of materials, program or service implementation, and/or fees for staff development.

Policy Making and Curriculum
Finally, a benefit of the internship is the development of policies or curriculum as a result of leadership and group efforts. As the student engages in a problem, the opportunities for shared decision-making about policies and curriculum are limitless. For example, if a student oversees classroom teachers' use of advanced curriculum for gifted students, a goal might be the development and use of curriculum.

Further, if an internship is guided by a problem such as the lack of standards within a secondary school to provide affective guidance to gifted children, a policy might result from the process. As the intern involves other administrators, teachers, parents, and community members in the process, a logical conclusion is new perspectives and a policy for serving gifted students' affective needs.

CONCLUSION
Professional literature (Bridges & Hallinger, 1995; Sparks & Hirsh, 1997; Wiggins, 1993) maintains that the most effective programs for educational leadership engage prospective administrators in an authentic learning process—an internship. The characteristics suggested by the Danforth Foundation (Ubben, 1991) regarding Educational Leadership preparation programs, articulate the need to utilize both university and school district cooperation in the preparation process. The suggestions include: (a) joint university and school district selection of interns, (b) cohort experiences, (c) mentors acting as site supervisors for interns, (d) collaborative planning by faculty and practitioners, (e) full-time internships of at least 720 hours, and (f) completion of the internship outside the university setting.

The Gifted Education Administrator Program is geared toward the authentic field-based experiences described above. The goals of the internship program are a combination of the theoretical, mechanical, and affective dimensions of educational leadership. The experience is both process and product oriented to provide an authentic opportunity, which is intended to prepare students for real-world interactions in her or his future administrative career.

REFERENCES

Arkansas Department of Education. (1999). *Rules and regulations for gifted, talented, and creative education*. Little Rock, AR: Author.

Arkansas State University. (2002). *Graduate bulletin: 2002–2003*. Jonesboro, AR: Arkansas State University.

Bridges, E. M., & Hallinger, P. (1995). *Implementing problem based learning in leadership development*. Eugene, OR: ERIC Clearinghouse on Educational Management.

Christenson, S. L. (1990). Differences in students' home environments: The need to work with families. *School Psychology Review, 19*, 505–517.

Mulkeen, T., & Tenebaum, T. (1990). Teaching and learning in knowledge organizations: Implications for the preparation of school administrators. *Journal of Educational Administration, 13*(1), 139–147.

Muth, R. (1989). *Reconceptualizing training for educational administrators and leaders: Focus on inquiry*. Charlottesville, VA: National Policy Board for Educational Administration.

Pepper, J. B. (1988). Clinical education for school superintendents and principals: The missing link. In D. E. Griffiths, R. T. Stout, & P. R. Forsyth (Eds.), *Leaders for America's schools* (pp. 360–366). Berkeley, CA: McCutchan.

Smith, S. (1993). *The ATLAS communities design: A comprehensive approach to school reform*. Presentation at the meeting of the Coalition of Essential Schools, Louisville, KY.

Sparks, D., & Hirsh, S. (1997). *A new vision for staff development*. Oxford, OH: National Staff Development Council.

Ubben, G. (1991). Strategies for organizing principal preparation: A survey of the Danforth principal preparation programs. In F. Wendel (Ed.), *Enhancing the knowledge base in educational administration* (pp. 7–26). University Park, PA: University Council for Educational Administration. (ERIC Document Reproduction Service No. ED 3666 091)

Wiggins, G. (1993). Assessment: Authenticity, context, and validity. *Phi Delta Kappan, 75*(3), 200–214.

The Principalship Cohort Leadership Academy: A Partnership that Connects Theory and Practice

Judith A. Zimmerman, Jeffry S. Bowman,
Marcia Salazar-Valentine, and Roger L. Barnes

"The nation's reservoir of experienced principals is about to become seriously depleted, leaving reform to the rookies" (Klempen & Richetti, 2001, p. 34). Other authors have also written about the shortage of principals expected once the "baby boom" generation retires (Ferrandino, 2001; Houston, 2001). A recent survey conducted by the Educational Research Service (ERS) for The National Association of Elementary School Principals (NAESP) and the National Association of Secondary School Principals (NASSP) provides evidence of a shortage of qualified school leaders (1998). This reported shortage occurred among surveyed districts in rural schools (52%), suburban schools (45%), and urban schools (47%) (ERA, 1998). Northwest Ohio, similar to other areas across the state and country, also experiences a shortage of qualified building principals.

This manuscript describes the highlights of the first five years of Bowling Green State University's Principalship Cohort Leadership Academy (PCLA), and reports on the results of its annual program evaluations and a new longitudinal survey. It also addresses the future challenges that the PCLA faces and the challenges that the program presents to the university.

REASONS FOR SHORTAGE

To address the lack of qualified administrative candidates in Ohio, work groups were convened in November 2000 at the request of the Ohio Department of Education (Ohio Department of Education, 2001). The work groups were made up of members of both the Ohio Association of Elementary School Administrators (OAESA) and the Ohio Association of Secondary School Administrators (OASSA). The work

Judith A. Zimmerman, Bowling Green State University
Jeffry S. Bowman, Bowling Green State University
Marcia Salazar-Valentine, Bowling Green State University
Roger L. Barnes, Bowling Green State University

groups identified barriers to recruiting qualified individuals into the principalship that included the following:

- complexities, demands, and time constraints associated with the job
- salary differentials in comparison with teachers, with greater responsibilities
- loss of respect for the position, and less understanding of and appreciation for the role of the principal (Ohio Department of Education, 2001, p. 2).

In DiPaola and Tschannen-Moran's (2003) study of principals in Virginia, participants reported the same types of issues regarding their conditions of employment, the changing role of the principal, and supply and demand. These barriers and new expectations for principals are different from the traditional roles.

EXPECTATIONS OF PRINCIPALS

Today's principals must be more than just school managers; they must be instructional leaders. "Aspiring principals would do well to recognize that superintendents . . . are seeking strong educational leaders to improve their schools academically. The days of hiring building managers appears to have gone by way of the dinosaur" (Lease, 2002, p. 41).

Leadership matters. Principals' actions, attitudes, collaborative behaviors and communication all have an impact on the culture and the performance of the buildings they lead (Fullan & Hargreaves, 1996; Short & Greer, 2002; Sparks, 2002). Principals are change agents. At a time when more demands are placed on principals, they must find innovative ways to create and sustain learning communities in their buildings. One of the most important keys to establishing and leading a learning community in a building is for the principal to model lifelong learning and strive for excellence himself/herself (Copland, 2001; Franklin, 2002; Fullan, 2002; Hessel & Holloway, 2002).

Although the expectations and challenges for principals are greater than ever before, the position still provides rewards not realized in many other positions. Members of the Ohio Department of Education work groups described the principalship as a "calling . . . [with the] power . . . to impact the lives and learning of children [as] one of the intangible and inherent incentives associated with this unique role" (Ohio Department of Education, 2001, p. 1). With all of its frustrations, the principalship continues to be a noble calling. Eighty-eight percent of the principals in Di-Paola and Tschannen-Moran's (2003) study reported that, if given the same opportunity, they would become principals again. The problem then, is how can current educational administrators and higher education professionals recruit the next generation of principals?

History and Background of the Principalship Cohort Leadership Academy (PCLA)

In 1997, in response to the shortage of qualified principals in Northwest Ohio, the Department of Educational Administration and Supervision (EDAS) at Bowling

Green State University developed an off-campus, cohort-based leadership academy for prospective building principals. The choice for the cohort format followed one of the recommendations from the report, *Leaders for America's Schools: The Report and Papers of the National Commission on School Excellence* (Griffiths, Stout, & Forsyth, 1988), which encouraged learning through *collaboration among peers*, one of the main advantages of cohorts. More recent research studies on this design stress the fact that this "adult learning [design] provides support, social learning, security and potential for long-term networking" (Mitchel, 2001, p. 11) and teaches "the collaborative skills needed in today's more complex and connected environment" (Houston, 2001, p. 432).

It was important that this new PCLA program reflect best practices from the literature. In addition to the cohort design, the EDAS Department identified *reflective practice and skills application* as essential components for the preparation program to be successful. Again, recent authors have stressed the importance of educational administrators being reflective practitioners (Gilman & Lanman-Givens, 2001; Houston, 2001). Houston (2001) argued, "preparation programs for the next generation of leaders must involve a constant dance between doing the work and thinking about it" (p. 433).

Current administrators need to take the responsibility for identifying and recruiting teachers with leadership abilities (Gilman & Lanman-Givens, 2001; Ohio Department of Education, 2001; Practical how to's, 1997). According to Houston (2001, p. 433), these are the "oughtabes" and they must be identified, encouraged and then mentored into the jobs. Therefore, during late fall 1996 and winter 1997, the first Principalship Cohort Leadership Academy coordinator presented the concept of the new program to area superintendents at monthly meetings of area Educational Service Centers. At these meetings and at subsequent breakfast and luncheons organized by EDAS, superintendents in Northwest Ohio were given the opportunity to discuss the new program. The area superintendents were asked to help the Bowling Green State University EDAS department recruit teachers who possessed leadership potential to become future principals and thus help reduce the gap between demand and supply for school leaders. It was suggested that recruiting would focus on recommendations not only by the superintendents, but also by other school administrators, who would forward their suggestions to the superintendents.

As a result of this initial collaboration, the program coordinator received a list from the superintendents of over 80 prospective candidates for the PCLA program. Information materials were then personally delivered to these individuals at their school sites. Over thirty-six school buildings were visited during this recruiting phase. Following these personal visits, regional informational meetings for teachers who showed interest in the program were scheduled. As a result, the first three cohorts, with a total of 38 teachers, were established: one 90 miles south, one 36 miles west, and a third 60 miles east of the university.

Other factors that played an important role in the successful recruiting of these first students were:

1. The opportunity to take classes close to the students' school district. As an average, teachers who were referred to the program were within their first five years of teaching, many of whom were also starting families. Many were also responsible for coaching or advising extra-curricular activities in their districts. A convenient location close to their home school was an attractive bonus in pursuing their graduate degree and license. Site-based administrator preparation programs continue to be supported in the literature (Ohio Department of Education, 2001).

2. A three-year course of study, with teachers receiving their master's in education at the end of the second year and finishing all the coursework required for the principal's license in the state of Ohio at the end of year three.

3. A financial incentive provided by BGSU's College of Continuing Education, International and Summer Programs (now Continuing and Extended Education). Students enrolled in the program received a one-hour tuition waiver for every three credit hour class taken.

4. A convenient schedule, with classes always offered on Wednesday evenings in the fall, spring, and first summer sessions, and twice a week on main campus during the second summer session. The summer session classes on main campus met the Ohio Board of Regents' residency rule.

5. Quality instructors, who had administrative experience, taught classes. True to the approach that there should be a focus on practical applications, three practicing administrators with terminal degrees were identified as the first instructors for the program. Hiring faculty with terminal degrees, including adjuncts, has been the preference of universities (Schneider, 2003). Additionally, adjuncts typically have specific knowledge about the operations of school districts in the university's region (Fauske & Larkin, 2003).

6. In the summer, when students came to main campus, tenure-track faculty taught classes.

In order to maintain the original concept of the program, especially its emphasis on personalized attention, the program coordinator's/director's role included:

1. Site visits: a minimum of one visit per cohort every semester to discuss curriculum issues and class schedule; to get feedback from students regarding classes, location, and other logistic issues; to register students on-site; and to sell textbooks. In addition to these visits, phone calls and email were the main means of communication between the program coordinator and cohorts.

2. Responsibility for recruiting new students for future cohorts and retaining existing students by acting as mentor, advisor, and liaison with the main campus.

3. Responsibility for acting as the liaison between the department and adjunct faculty in order to ensure the same academic quality as was found on the main campus courses. For that matter, instructors were asked to use the same textbooks used on main campus and instructed as to the expectations of students' comprehensive examination at the end of the program.

4. Responsibility for maintaining the relationship with area administrators in order to keep the flow of referrals for future participants in the program.

THE PRINCIPALSHIP COHORT LEADERSHIP ACADEMY TODAY

The PCLA program has grown in five years from the 38 students in the first three cohorts to an enrollment of over 150 students. There are currently eight cohorts in seven sites located approximately 40 to 90 miles away from the main campus. The program still retains these characteristics:

1. Site-based
2. A three-year course of study
3. A financial incentive
4. A convenient schedule, and
5. Classes taught by both practitioners with terminal degrees and tenure-track faculty. This practice helps to align academic expectations with the real-world demands that principals face (Beem, 2002; McCay, 2001; Schneider, 2003; Tingley, 2002; Tirozzi, 2001).

The PCLA program coordinator's/director's responsibilities continue to include:

1. Making site visits
2. Recruiting new students
3. Acting as the liaison between the department and adjunct faculty, and
4. Maintaining a relationship with area administrators

Beginning with the first graduates of the PCLA program, from the fall of 1999 through the fall of 2002, 138 students completed the required thirty-three semester-credit hours and have earned their master's degrees in educational administration. Of the 138 graduates, 79 have obtained their administrative licenses. Twelve semester-credit hours beyond the master's degree are required for licensure and thirty of the 138 graduates are currently enrolled in one of the four additional courses.

METHODOLOGY FOR ANNUAL SUMMATIVE EVALUATION

As part of the program's evaluation process each year, PCLA students are asked to complete a confidential survey indicating their satisfaction with the program. The data are studied to determine trends within the areas covered by the questions and to aid in future planning. The results for each of the annual program evaluation areas are consistently high.

Subjects

Students who are currently enrolled in the PCLA program, either as master's degree students or as post-master's students working on licensure, form the subject pool for this annual study. As the program has been in existence for only five years, only those who have already completed their degrees have been able to continue with their licensure coursework. All of the subjects are experienced educators, some of whom have elected to remain in the classroom following graduation (in some cases, following completion of additional administrative licensure requirements), as well as others who have chosen to take administrative positions in districts.

Instrument

As part of the program's annual evaluation process, during the summer session a confidential survey is given to the students asking them to evaluate the program in several areas, including: (a) the convenience of the program schedule, (b) the students' thoughts about having the classes taught by a mix of tenure-track faculty and adjunct faculty, (c) the use of a cohort format, during which the group of students take their classes together throughout the program, (d) the usefulness of having the program director make regular visit to the off-campus classroom sites, and (e) an evaluation of the overall program experience. Because the students were surveyed within their cohort context, demographic or other personally identifiable information was not collected from them for the annual survey.

The survey instrument consists of several general questions about students' level in the program (i.e., first year, second) and location of cohort site. All questions were rated on 5-point Likert-type scales, with "1" standing for "Low Opinion" and "5" standing for "High Opinion." The number of respondents varied from year to year, based on cohort sizes. In addition to the scaled responses, space is provided for written comments concerning each evaluation question.

As stated previously, the students are given the program evaluation surveys during the summer, following each year's classes. The responses are confidential.

Data Analysis

The data from the scaled responses are entered into a database and descriptive statistics are produced for the questions. The numerical data are studied to determine trends within the areas covered by the questions and to aid in future planning (addition or change/removal in aspects of the program). In addition, the subjective responses to the evaluation questions are gathered, transcribed, and studied, for utilization as part of the annual program improvement planning process. The results for the annual evaluation areas for the first five years of the program are presented in Table 1.

RESULTS OF ANNUAL SUMMATIVE EVALUATION

As can be seen from Table 1, the means for all questions regarding student satisfaction were quite high. In reviewing the results of the first question (convenience of the program schedule), the trend of positive responses (mean scores of 4.4 and above) has been consistently increasing over the years. There was, however, a slight drop for 2002. This decrease, it is believed, may be the result of combining two potential cohorts into one in order to maintain a viable enrollment level. This caused the students in the combined cohort to travel farther for their classes than they had originally expected.

Table 1. Descriptive Statistics from Annual PCLA Program Evaluations (1998–2002)

Item	1998	1999	2000	2001	2002
1. Program Schedule	4.46	4.55	4.62	4.61	4.43
	(0.62)	(0.63)	(0.70)	(0.67)	(0.84)
	n = 30	n = 56	n = 50	n = 59	n = 72
2. Teaching by Practitioners	4.40	4.56	4.59	4.66	4.69
	(0.72)	(0.53)	(0.64)	(0.61)	(0.46)
	n = 30	n = 55	n = 49	n = 59	n = 72
3. Cohort Format	4.46	4.84	4.74	4.73	4.76
	(0.68)	(0.59)	(0.53)	(0.52)	(0.49)
	n = 30	n = 57	n = 50	n = 59	n = 72
4. Use of Director Site Visits	4.67	4.35	4.21	4.28	4.19
	(0.47)	(0.76)	(0.85)	(0.81)	(0.85)
	n = 28	n = 52	n = 50	n = 58	n = 72
5. Quality of Overall Experience	4.46	4.56	4.48	4.50	4.44
	(0.57)	(0.50)	(0.61)	(0.60)	(0.85)
	n = 30	n = 55	n = 49	n = 59	n = 72

( )—s.d. Evaluation Scale- 1 (Low Opinion) to 5 (High Opinion)

Question Two involves the students' thoughts about having the classes taught by a mix of tenure-track faculty and adjunct (practitioners) faculty. The trend of positive responses has increased from year to year on this item (mean scores ranging from 4.40 to 4.69). Adjunct faculty members are frequently hired to teach the core courses in educational administration that emphasize practice or skills application (Schneider, 2003). Both adjunct and tenure-track faculty can encourage aspiring administrators to be reflective practitioners. Tenure-track faculty may have more knowledge about theories of adult learning, including the importance of reflection (Egley, Reck, & Rields, 2003; Wegner, Watson, & Macgregor, 2003). However, adjunct faculty members are able to model reflective practice as they share with students the consequences of decisions they have made. Smith (2003) stressed that her work as an adjunct made her a better practitioner, not only because of remaining current in the field, but also because of regaining enthusiasm for her profession. Students see practitioners, as adjuncts, as credible sources of information and experience relative to the scenarios presented to them for their reflection in class (Smith, 2003).

The third survey question addresses the use of a cohort format, during which the group of students take their classes together throughout the program. After the first year (4.46), the scores have been even higher and consistent (ranging from 4.73 to 4.84). The cohort format seems to suit the students. The PCLA students' preference appears to support the literature (Griffiths, Stout, & Forsyth, 1988; Houston, 2001; Mitchel, 2001).

Question Four measures the students' perceptions of the usefulness of having the program director make regular visit to the off-campus classroom sites. Although positive, the responses to this question showed a consistent decline in mean scores over the five years (ranging from a high of 4.67 the first year to a low of 4.19 in the last year). Regarding the lower mean scores, one could assume that more recently, students do not believe the director visits are as important or necessary as in the past. Perhaps the students' on-campus advisors are doing a better job of serving their needs than they had in the past.

Finally, the students are asked to evaluate the overall PCLA program experience in the fifth question. This score has stayed quite consistent over the period, with a mean of approximately 4.50. The results indicate that the students appear to have a very good overall impression of the PCLA program.

METHODOLOGY FOR LONGITUDINAL STUDY (FOLLOW-UP) SURVEY

In addition to the annual program evaluation survey, an additional survey has been developed to serve as a follow-up study of those students who have graduated with their master's degrees, current students in the post-master's licensure courses, and program completers. Ludwig, Salazar-Valentine, and Sanders (1998) recommended such a longitudinal study to evaluate the effectiveness of the PCLA program and the success of its graduates. Recently, Young (2003, p.7) called for professors to "practice what we teach" relative to collecting data for informed decision-making in order to determine the relationship between leadership preparation programs and leadership practice.

Subjects

As the numbers of cohort members and graduates increased, it was decided that additional information was needed from the PCLA members, present and former. The target population for the longitudinal (follow-up) study was all master's degree graduates of the Principalship Cohort Leadership Academy (PCLA) between 1999 and 2002 (N = 139). These graduates included those who were still serving in K–12 teaching capacities and those who have since assumed administrative positions in K–12 systems. Due to the relatively small numbers of program graduates, the entire population was sent a follow-up survey. The subjects were divided into two distinct groups, based on completion of state administrative licensure requirements. Group I (n = 71) consisted of those PCLA graduates who had completed their master's degrees and had also completed the additional coursework required for their state administrative licenses, whether or not they had actually applied for the license. Group II (n = 68) consisted of those graduates who had completed their master's degrees between 1999 and 2002 and might or might not currently be working on administrative licensure coursework. Members of Group II have not currently completed all the coursework required for provisional administrative licensure in Ohio.

Instrument

As stated earlier, the focus of this study was to gather information about the attitudes of the graduates about the program in general and whether the program has had an impact on their performance, either as an educator and/or as an administrator. In order to gather the needed information, a standard program evaluation survey, given to all PCLA students at the end of each academic year, and two recently constructed follow-up surveys were utilized. The follow-up surveys were identical except for one additional question asked of the Group II graduates. Both follow-up surveys began with questions requesting demographic data from the subjects. The remaining questions concerned information pertaining to the PCLA, such as how the graduates first heard about the Academy, the type of position they were currently occupying, whether their PCLA experience had had a significant impact on their careers as educators and/or administrators, whether or not the graduates would recommend the program to colleagues, whether colleagues to whom the graduates had recommended the program were currently enrolled in the PCLA, and whether those who had not yet completed their licensure requirements (Group II) were planning to apply for an administrative position within the next five years. Ultimately, from a total of 138 surveys mailed in Spring 2003, a useable response rate of 51.1% was realized.

Data Analysis

The demographic information was compiled and descriptive statistics were calculated for the items, including: gender, ethnicity, years of teaching experiences, level of licensure (elementary or secondary), and enrollment of respondent's current school. Those survey questions that were answered as *Yes* or *No* were dummy coded and subjected to independent samples t-tests to determine if there were differences in responses between the two groups. In addition, space was provided for written comments as part of the questions concerning the PCLA, and those comments were transcribed. The descriptive statistics related to the follow-up survey are presented in Tables 2 and 3.

RESULTS OF LONGITUDINAL STUDY (FOLLOW-UP) SURVEY

The descriptive statistics related to the follow-up survey demographic requests are presented in Table 2. More (64.8%) members of Group I (master's degree plus state license) responded than did members (35.2%) of Group II (master's degree only—possibly working on state licensure). Relative to gender of respondents, male graduates formed the majority. In terms of ethnicity, there were extremely few non-Caucasian respondents, with African/African Americans making up only 2.9%, Hispanics accounting for 1.4%, and Caucasians making up the remainder (95.7%). This ethnic makeup of the respondents is consistent with that in the total educator population in most schools in Northwest Ohio. In terms of teaching experience, the average years of experience for both groups was 11.4.

Percentages of licensure levels (elementary and secondary) were nearly the same, overall, with nearly one-fifth of respondents holding or working on administrative specialist licenses, as opposed to principal licensure. In terms of building size (enrollment), a majority of respondents were from buildings with between 200 and 499 students, with most of the remainder of respondents being from schools with more than 500 students. Additional information was collected that does not appear in Table 2. Of both groups, 52.2% (n = 24) of Group I respondents now hold administrative positions as do 16.0% (n = 4) of Group II respondents. The lower percentage for Group II makes sense in that these respondents have not yet completed their provisional licensure requirements. However, some pre-licensure students have been employed under temporary licenses, thus underscoring the lack of qualified administrators in this area.

Ninety-five point five percent (n = 20) of the Group I respondents and 100.0% of the Group II respondents currently holding administrative positions felt that the PCLA experience had a significant impact on their performance as administrators. These PCLA results are in accord with DiPaola and Tschannen-Moran's (2003) findings that the majority of principals (88.3%) considered their graduate education to be of value in the performance of their jobs. In addition, 100.0% (n = 23) of the Group I respondents and 89.5% (n = 17) of the Group II respondents who are not currently filling administrative positions, felt that the PCLA experience has had a significant impact on their performance as educators. As stated before, the use of both practitioners/adjuncts and tenure track faculty has paid dividends in the PCLA

Table 2. Demographic Information

Heading/Question	N	Percentage
Group	Group I (master's plus license)-46	64.8%
(n = 71)	Group II (master's only)-25	35.2%
Gender	Male-40	56.3%
(n = 71)	Female-31	43.7%
Ethnicity	Caucasian-67	95.7%
(n = 70)	African/African American-2	2.9%
	Hispanic-1	1.4%
Licensure Level	Elementary-26	37.1%
(n = 70)	Secondary-28	40.0%
	Other-16	22.9%
Building Size	< 200 students-1	1.5%
(n = 67)	200–349 students-24	35.8%
	350–499 students-16	23.9%
	500–649 students-10	14.9%
	650–799 students-3	4.5%
	> 800 students-13	19.4%
How did you first hear about the PCLA? (check all that apply) (Group I, n = 54) (Group II, n = 31)	Group I Program recommended by a school administrator-18	33.3%
	Program recommended by a participant in the program-9	16.7%
	Program recommended by a fellow teacher-7	13.0%
	BGSU advertisement-20	37.0%
	Group II Program recommended by a school administrator-8	25.8%
	Program recommended by a participant in the program-5	16.1%
	Program recommended by a fellow teacher-7	20.6%
	BGSU advertisement-11	35.5%

preparation program involving "a constant dance between doing the work [skills application] and thinking about it [reflective practice]" (Houston, 2001, p. 433).

The question concerning how the respondents first heard about the Principalship Cohort Leadership Academy allowed any number of the four possible responses to be checked. With regards to Group I, the majority of respondents heard about the program through either a school administrator or literature from BGSU (70.3%). This might be due to the fact that school district administrators were very actively involved in the recruiting of the first three cohorts. Considerably smaller percentages of respondents acknowledged that they had heard about the program through either a participant or a fellow teacher. For Group II, the largest percentage response was that literature from BGSU was the first source of information about the PCLA that they encountered (35.5%, n = 11). Nearly equal percentages responded that a school administrator or a fellow teacher was where they first heard about the program, with a recommendation from a program participant being the least reported source of information about the PCLA.

Table 3 presents the results of independent sample t-tests, which were run to determine whether there were differences in responses between Groups I and II on the substantive questions from the follow-up survey. As can be seen, only Question B, "Do you currently hold an administrative position?" showed a significant difference between groups. In addition, there was one question on the survey for Group II that did not appear on the Group I survey. This question asked, "Do you anticipate pursuing course work for an administrative license in the next five years?" As stated previously, Group II graduates from the PCLA had not yet earned their state administrative licensure. For this question, 77.8% (n = 21) stated that they did anticipate pursuing course work for an administrative license in the next five years. *Discussion*

The only demographic result that was skewed was the outcome from the questions concerning ethnicity. However, the results closely match the true ethnic demography of this part of the state. Likewise, the results of the t-tests were those that were expected. The major points to acknowledge are that, as expected, those students in Group II would not be expected to be holding as high a proportion of administrative positions as those in Group I, and the results of the other questions were as to be expected, based

Table 3.   Independent Sample T-Tests

Question	n	df	t	Significance
Do you currently hold an administrative position?	71	69	3.427	$p<.001$*
If yes, has your PCLA experience had a significant impact on your performance as an administrator?	25	23	−0.429	$p<.672$
If no, has your PCLA experience had a significant impact on your performance as an educator?	42	40	1.455	$p<.163$*
Have you recommended PCLA to any of your colleagues?	71	69	0.630	$p<.531$
If yes, did they enroll or are they currently enrolled in the program?	59	57	−1.021	$p<.321$

*Equal variances are not assumed for these analyses.

on spoken comments and written responses to the open ended questions within the surveys. The scaled and written responses only served to reinforce the responses that have been heard by faculty over the five-year life of the PCLA. In the open-ended questions, many respondents stressed the ability of adjunct faculty and regular tenure-track faculty to pull together the importance of theory and practice to show the applicability of the material to "real" life situations. According to one respondent,

> The Principal Cohort was one of the most positive learning experiences I have had with Bowling Green State University. The quality of professors—practicing administrators— is very high. The learning curve is steep since actual experiences are shared and troubleshooting is done together. Many aspects of the principalship are independent and these classes have taught me ways to look for collaborative problem solving.

CHALLENGES FOR THE FUTURE

Although the first five years of the Principalship Cohort Leadership Academy have been successful, by a variety of measures, the program stills faces some challenges for the future.

Connection of Adjuncts to Tenure-Track Faculty

Adjunct professors teach not for financial gain but for their own continuing education and the chance to interact with aspiring administrators (Schneider, 2003). Besides sharing their expertise, an advantage of using adjuncts includes the networking opportunities for students and the help in placement of graduates (Egley, Reck, & Rields, 2003). Another advantage is that these instructors can help to recruit additional students for the program (Egley, Reck, & Rields, 2003). According to McCay (2001, p. 77), "by collaborating, college and university faculty and principals . . . develop new ways to connect theory and practice" (2002, p. 18). Therefore, the challenge for preparation programs is to provide opportunities to better connect our on-campus tenure-track professors with our adjunct professors. Adjunct professors may be less familiar with current research in the field, with standards-based instruction, and with appropriate instructional methods that address adult learners (Egley, Reck, & Rields, 2003; Wegner, Watson, & Macgregor, 2003). Moreover, the administrative coursework taken by the adjuncts, during their preparation programs in the past, may have focused more on the managerial aspects of the position and less on the more recent focus of student outcomes and learning (Waddle & Shepard, 2003). We must continue to provide appropriate support and assessment of PCLA faulty to assure program vigor (Ludwig, Salazar-Valentine, & Sanders, 1998). Shakeshaft (2002), among others, has criticized the inappropriate use of adjuncts in educational administration programs, particularly when the motive of the university is simply to save money.

It is also important for both the EDAS and PCLA programs to ensure that the educational administration curriculum is aligned, so that we can better control the quality of our students' experiences, regardless of who is teaching their courses. Reviewing our curriculum alignment should also pay dividends in our programs meeting the revised Educational Leadership Constituent Council standards (National Policy Board for Educational Administration, 2002).

With their busy time schedules, it is unlikely that practitioners will attend regular on-campus faculty meetings. However, the challenge of connecting on-campus tenure-track professors with adjunct professors may be met in a number of other ways. In addition to being given sample syllabi and possible texts, Egley, Reck, & Rields (2003) suggest an orientation program for adjuncts, a procedural handbook, and personal contact by tenure-track faculty. Waddle and Shepard (2003) encourage tenure-track faculty to develop notebooks for adjuncts that include course syllabi, suggested topics and activities for each class session, and copies of suggested supplemental readings. Finally, Smith (2003) suggested using a newsletter to keep adjuncts informed.

In spring 2003, the College of Continuing and Extended Education hosted a dinner at the university's student union for adjunct faculty members. Following the dinner there were structured small group discussions about adjunct faculty issues and concerns. As an outcome of these discussions, frequent meetings will be held among the department chairs, cohort coordinators, and the associate dean of off-campus programs.

Recruitment of Aspirants by Superintendents

Although enrollment in the PCLA program has increased since its inception, it is still a challenge to get current administrators to take responsibility for recruiting and mentoring prospective administrators. The recent PCLA follow-up survey indicates that there is a slight decrease in the number of students who were recruited by their administrators. "While some aspiring administrators are self-identified, others may not realize their potential . . . and [need encouragement] to think about administration" (Practical how to's, 1997, p. 1). If mentors follow the progress of these potential administrators, including discussing what they are "learning and how it might apply to situations you're both familiar with," it not only provides support to the aspirants but also helps to retain students in the PCLA program (Practical how to's, 1997, pp. 1 & 2). While adjuncts are helpful in recruiting students for the PCLA program, other practicing administrators must also see the need. Therefore BGSU tenure-track faculty members attend local superintendent meetings, especially those at the county or regional educational service centers. This practice not only keeps the faculty current with the problems of administrators, but also provides opportunities to encourage practitioners to recruit aspirants.

Retention

A third challenge is to retain our students in the PCLA program after they obtain their master's degrees. There are a number of possible reasons why students do not finish the licensure requirements. Some reasons are financial or personal. Only five PCLA follow-up survey respondents indicated that they did not plan to seek an administrative position within the next five years. These individuals cited the following reasons: their love for teaching, family commitments, love of coaching, and the lack of monetary incentive between their current pay and the beginning administrative salaries in their area. Family responsibilities have been cited in the literature as deterrents, particularly for women pursuing administrative positions (Dunlap & Schmuck, 1995; Glass, 2000). Additionally, because entry year teachers in Ohio must obtain a master's degree within their first ten years, the PCLA and on-campus master's programs are experiencing an increase in the number of younger teachers in educational administration courses. As a consequence of their youth and lack of experience in the classroom, some of the students have expressed an interest in delaying completion of their coursework for administrative licensure until they have a few more years of teaching "under their belts." In order to realize the major goal of the PCLA program, increasing the pool of qualified administrators in the area, retention of our students through the remainder of their licensure coursework is important. Additional incentives, including a change in the fee waiver structure to reward students who have "stayed the course," are being discussed for the future.

On-Campus Enrollment

A final challenge relates to the impact the PCLA program might have on enrollment in the main campus master's degree program in educational administration. One way to lessen the potential impact has been to enforce the policy that only those students who live and work at least thirty miles or more away from the main campus are eligible for the PCLA program. However, there is still a concern that some students who otherwise would have come to the main campus are now driving just as far to attend one of the off-campus cohort programs. Aside from the convenience of travel, another reason for the gravitation to off-campus sites is most likely the reduced tuition rates for the PCLA program versus the cost of full tuition for the main campus program. This tuition incentive was created in 1997 as a way to attract students who would not otherwise have come to BGSU. Although decreasing tuition rates for on-campus students is not possible, the EDAS faculty determined that it is crucial to be more proactive in recruiting students for the main campus program. A new brochure to recruit on-campus students has been designed and distributed to area superintendents and principals to use in encouraging potential administrators in their districts to consider the PCLA program. BGSU tenure-track faculty members' attendance at local superintendent meetings also provides opportunities to encourage practitioners to recruit students for the on-campus program.

CONCLUSION

The Principalship Leadership Cohort Academy (PCLA) concept was started as a response to the developing shortage of qualified candidates for administrative positions in the northwestern section of Ohio. One of the basic tenets of the program was that it provided practicing teachers with an opportunity to earn a master's degree and administrative licensure without having to drive long distances after school to the regular university campus. This program has made use of facilities in many districts and has utilized a mix of regular tenure-track university faculty and experienced adjunct faculty (holding terminal degrees) to provide a strong practitioner-focused program. The PCLA program has witnessed a 244% increase in enrollment in its first five years. Current students and graduates have given high ratings to the PCLA on annual evaluations and on a recent graduate follow-up survey. The PCLA has increased the pool of qualified administrators in Northwest Ohio. The program has produced 78 licensed administrators since its inception in 1997. Ninety percent of the follow-up survey respondents indicated that they either held an administrative position or planned to seek one within the next five years. A majority of the respondents who have not yet earned a license indicated that they plan to pursue the required additional twelve semester hours. Although the first five years of the Principalship Cohort Leadership Academy have been successful by a variety of measures, the program stills faces some challenges for the future. These challenges include: better connection of adjuncts with tenure-track faculty, recruitment by practitioners, retention after the master's degree, and potential impact on-campus enrollment.

REFERENCES

Beem, K. (2002). The adjunct experience. *The School Administrator, 59*(10), 6–10, 12.

Copland, M. A. (2001). The myth of the superprincipal. *Phi Delta Kappan, 82*(7), 528–532.

DiPaola, M., & Tschannen-Moran, M. (2003). The principalship at a crossroads: A study of the conditions and concerns of principals. *NASSP Bulletin, 87*(634), 43–65. Retrieved May 15, 2003 from www.nassp.org/news/bltn_principalship_crossroads.html

Dunlap, D. M., & Schmuck, P. A. (Eds.). (1995). *Women leading in education.* Albany: State University of New York Press.

Educational Research Service. (1998). *Is there a shortage of qualified candidates for openings in the principalship? An exploratory study.* Alexandria & Reston, VA: National Association of Elementary School Principals and National Association of Secondary School Principals. Retrieved November 25, 2002 from www.naesp.org/misc/shortage.htm

Egley, R. J., Reck, B., & Rields, L. J. (2003). Cheap labor or valuable resource? Adjunct professors. *The AASA Professor, 26*(1), 7–10.

Fauske, J. R., & Larkin, E. Alternative calendar course scheduling and adjunct faculty. *The AASA Professor, 26*(1), 11–17.

Ferrandino, V. L. (2001). Challenges of 21st-century elementary school principals. *Phi Delta Kappan, 82* (6), 440–442.

Franklin, J. (2002, Winter). The necessary principal: The importance of instructional leadership. *Curriculum Update,* 6–7.

Fullan, M. (2002). The change leader. *Educational Leadership, 59*(8), 16–20.

Fullan, M., & Hargreaves, A. (1996). *What's worth fighting for in your school?* New York: Teachers College Press.

Gilman, D. A., & Lanman-Givens, B. (2001). Where have all the principals gone? *Educational Leadership, 58*(8), 72–74.

Glass, T. (2000, June). Where are all the women superintendents? *The School Administrator.* Retrieved July 29, 2003 from www.aasa.org/publications/sa/2000_06/glass.htm

Griffiths, D. E., Stout, R. T., & Forsyth, P. B. (Eds.). (1988). *Leaders for America's schools: The report and papers of the National Commission on School Excellence.* Berkeley, CA: McCutchan.

Hessel, K., & Holloway, J. (2002). *A framework for school leaders: Linking the ISLLC standards to practice.* Princeton, NJ: Educational Testing Service.

Houston, P. (2001). Superintendents for the 21st century: It's not just a job, it's a calling. *Phi Delta Kappan, 82*(6), 429–433.

Klempen, R. A., & Richetti, C. T. (2001). Greening the next generation of principals. *Education Week, 21*(15), 34.

Lease, T. (2002). New administrators need more than good grades. *The School Administrator, 59*(6), 40–41.

Ludwig, R., Salazar-Valentine, M., & Sanders, E. (1998, October). *A collaborative model between university and practicing administrators to create a geographically-based administrative preparation program.* Paper presented at the meeting of the Midwest Educational Research Association, Chicago, IL.

McCay, E. (2001). The learning needs of principals. *Educational Leadership, 58*(8), 75–77.

Mitchel, C. P. (2001). The quest for better preparation programs. *The AASA Professor, 24*(4), 10–14.

National Policy Board for Educational Administration. (2002, January). *Standards for advanced programs in educational leadership.* Arlington, VA: Author.

Ohio Department of Education. (2001, February). *Toward the development of statewide policy to address the Ohio principal shortage: Recommendations of OAESA/OASSA work groups.* Columbus, OH: Author.

Practical how to's: Mentoring future administrators benefits you both now and later. (1997). *Administrative Solutions, 29*(5), 1–2.

Schneider, J. (2003). The invisible faculty within departments of educational administration. *The AASA Professor, 26*(1), 3–6.

Shakeshaft, C. (2002). The shadowy downside of adjuncts. *The School Administrator, 59* (10), 28–30.

Short, P., & Greer, J. (2002). *Leadership in empowered schools: Themes from innovative efforts.* Upper Saddle River, NJ: Merrill-Prentice Hall.

Smith, P. H. (2003). Value added by practitioners/professors: How institutions can maximize their contributions. *The AASA* Professor, 26(1), 22–26.

Sparks, D. (2002). *Designing powerful professional development for teachers and principals.* National Staff Development Council. Available: https://www.nsdc.org

Tingley, S. (2002). Nine reasons why I love my adjunct status. *The School Administrator, 59*(10), 18–20.

Tirozzi, G. N. (2001). The artistry of leadership: The evolving role of the secondary school principal. *Phi Delta Kappan, 82* (6), 434–439.

Waddle, J., & Shepard, S. (2003). The adjunct problem: NCATE, ELCC and performance assessment. *The AASA Professor, 26*(1), 17–21.

Wegner, S. K., Watson, R. W., & Macgregor, C. J. (2003). *The AASA Professor*, 26(1), 27–32.

Young, M. D. (2003). From the director . . . Let's practice what we teach. *UCEA Review, 45*(2), 6–7.

The Educational Leadership Program at Edgewood College Showing the Way—Best Practices in Educational Leadership Programs

Peter J. Burke

Graduate programs in educational leadership for the working professional educator are available from coast to coast. From St. John's University on Long Island (www.new.stjohns.edu) to the University of Southern California (www.usc.edu) faculty in educational leadership departments have designed and implemented graduate degree programs that are school-focused and based on a cohort model with strong ties to the local school or district. This article is an examination of one such program in the Midwest, the Doctorate in Education (Ed.D.) program at Edgewood College in Madison, Wisconsin.

THE COLLEGE—ITS MISSION, TRADITION AND GOALS

Edgewood College was founded in the Catholic tradition of the Sinsinawa Dominican Sisters. It is a tradition guided by a heritage committed to teaching, which is defined by reflection. Reflection and sharing the results of reflection with others is the philosophical foundation of the College. The goals of the College include intellectual competence, personal development, Christian community and a sense of responsibility for service. Edgewood College is a Catholic, liberal arts college that has a mission of professional service with a vision of peace and justice informing that service. The profession of education is one of the representative service groups within the larger community that is a focus of the College mission.

Graduate programs at Edgewood College are rooted in the Sinsinawa Dominican Catholic traditions of peace and justice, intellectual competence, and reflective judgment. Programs are conceptually linked through a core of shared interdisciplinary studies and experiences. Programs provide graduate academic learning experiences centered on integrating theory into practice and on developing leaders in their fields who make responsible decisions from an ethical base. A central purpose of the grad-

Peter J. Burke, Edgewood College

uate programs at Edgewood College is to provide students with an opportunity to pursue personal academic development aimed at enhancing the skills needed to keep pace, maintain, grow and expand professional careers in a rapidly changing and multicultural world. Programs are flexible to accommodate the roles and responsibilities of adults in modern society.

Edgewood College has a mixture of traditional and modern facilities blended into one campus location. The campus is accessible to students and provides ample parking space for commuter students, especially in the off-hours of the graduate classes. Classrooms have up-to-date technology available for faculty and student use. The library facilities are accessible and contain print copy and electronic access to the major publications and journals in the field.

Faculty members have access to a computer course management and instruction system, Blackboard Learning Systems, Inc. This Internet based teaching tool is used to supplement on-campus classes. The campus also has available a two-way interactive classroom that allows both visual and audio interaction to off-campus sites and resources.

THE EDUCATION DEPARTMENT

The Edgewood College Department of Education, as a unit for professional study and preparation is dedicated to the development of reflective practitioners committed to student learning and continuing professional development in a dynamic world. The Educational Administration component strives to prepare prospective administrators in a learning environment consistent with the characteristics of effective schools. The program provides a solid grounding in content for administration and leadership based on a foundation of knowledge drawn from fields of curriculum, organizational systems, law, policy, finance, supervision and the cultural and historical roots of the profession.

The philosophy of the school administration preparation includes an interdisciplinary approach to the knowledge base combined with practice through planned and monitored performance of basic professional components. The mission and tradition of the college support the development and attestation of the professional dispositions necessary for successful practice. A research base of humanism in leadership, school effectiveness and school improvement provides a foundation for the planned integration of theory into practice. National accreditation and state program approval provide objective quality assurance to the program.

The Education Department has a long history of positive interaction with the public and private schools in the local geographic area. Teachers in area schools serve as cooperating teachers for student teachers at the elementary, middle and high school levels. Local school and district offices host graduate practicum students. Professional educators from area schools serve on campus committees and commissions fulfilling various educational functions.

The faculty in educational administration is comprised of highly trained and experienced professionals in the field. All faculty members are current or former practitioners who possess specific expertise and experience in their major areas of concentration. All full- and part-time instructors in the content areas of educational administration hold earned doctorates from regionally accredited and nationally recognized universities.

The College has Wisconsin Department of Public Instruction (DPI) approved programs leading to licenses for the principal, director of instruction, director of special education and pupil services, school business administrator, and instructional technology coordinator at the master's degree level. There is a superintendent license program at the doctorate level. The design and organization of that doctorate program is outlined below following a review of the foundation structure for all administration programs.

PROGRAM ORGANIZATION

The overall educational administration program at Edgewood College has interdisciplinary requirements and prerequisites combined with a core of professional education courses and specialized professional studies. The program is based on state and national standards and is actualized through action research, portfolio preparation and specialized practica for students.

The prerequisite requirements are teacher preparation and licensure and teaching experience. The interdisciplinary components include studies in ethics and change. Through this foundation students gain an increased awareness of change, interrelationships, and ethical issues in the context of personal and professional growth and development. In the process education students interact with other professionals in business, nursing and religious studies.

The professional core includes a survey introductory course to the administration and management of the school enterprise, a focus on curriculum and an introduction to educational research. The specialized professional studies are in the areas of business including accounting and risk management, principalship, law, special education and pupil services, supervision of instruction, politics, program planning and evaluation and staff development.

The program is standards based and assessment driven. Students are assessed upon entry to the program, during the completion of the required coursework, as part of their action research and during their practicum in the specialty area of license. Documentation of student competence as measured against program standards is through completion of course assignments and is compiled by the student in an instructional portfolio. The portfolio is structured according to the program standards and includes student-selected artifacts that document successful performance.

Faculty members who teach in the programs are responsible for continuous, formative assessment during required coursework and practica. This ongoing assessment becomes increasingly more complex as the student moves through each course and across all courses in the planned sequence. It culminates with the faculty support in the design and development of the student portfolio. Summative assessment is the faculty analysis and appraisal of the student portfolio based on Education Department rubrics.

RESEARCH BASE

The educational administration program at Edgewood College has a strong research base. The writing of the National Policy Board for Educational Administration, the Interstate School Leaders Licensure Consortium (ISLLC) of the Council of Chief

State School Officers, the Educational Leadership Constituent Council, the National Council of Professors of Educational Administration (NCPEA), the American Association of School Administrators, the National Association of Secondary School Principals, the National Association of Elementary School Principals and the Wisconsin affiliates of the national groups have all served to influence the program. The work of national assessment groups and the criticism of the current status of school leadership from national sources is also part of the program research base.

Recent research in educational administration has focused on the standards and assessment movement for preparation, licensing and continued development of school administrators. Emerging national standards have influenced state standards, which, in turn, have been incorporated into the program standards that form the basis of administrator preparation at the campus level. The current Edgewood College program in educational administration and leadership reflects continuing study, analysis and integration of various government, policy and professional literature in the field of educational administration and leadership.

The influence of the research and writing in the field of educational administration has resulted in a solid knowledge base voiced through commonly accepted standards of practice—what an administrator needs to know and be able to do to be successful. Students are required to become reflective practitioners who can draw on many resources, recognize opportunities for development, assimilate new knowledge, skills and attitudes, build networks of support and assistance and integrate those resources and acquisitions into successful and effective professional service. Faculty advisors direct program aspects and course selection to maximize the opportunities for demonstration of competence through performance.

PROGRAM STANDARDS

The basic standards for all educational administration license programs at Edgewood College are the Wisconsin state standards for program approval. These standards and the rules for approving licensure programs are in Chapter PI 34.03 of the Wisconsin Administrative Code (see www.dpi.state.wi.us/dpi/dlsis/tel/pi34.html). The Wisconsin standards for administrator preparation are an adaptation of the ISLLC Standards (CCSSO, 1996). Content guidelines made available from the Wisconsin Department of Public Instruction (DPI) for the separate categories of license form a second tier of program standards. Additionally, the 17 knowledge base subfields synthesized by the National Council of Professors of Educational Administration (Wildman, 2003) were used to expand on the basic state standards and to define performance standards including required knowledge, dispositions and performance items essential to student success in the field.

The performance requirements for the program are organized by the DPI state standards. The state standards, adapted from the Interstate School Leaders Licensure Consortium of the Council of Chief State School Officers are as follows:

WISCONSIN DPI STANDARDS FOR ADMINISTRATOR LICENSING

As mentioned above, the Edgewood College program standards are the Wisconsin DPI standards adopted as written in administrative rule. The Wisconsin DPI standards are listed in Table 1.

Table 1.   Wisconsin Standards for Administrator Licensure

Teacher Standards	The administrator has an understanding of and demonstrates competence in the ten teacher standards. [Note: The teacher standards are the Wisconsin adaptation of the Interstate New Teachers Assessment and Support Consortium (INTASC) Standards].
School Culture	The administrator manages by advocating, nurturing and sustaining a school culture and instructional program conducive to pupil learning and staff professional growth.
Organizational Management	The administrator ensures management of the organization, operations, finances, and resources for a safe, efficient, and effective learning environment.
Community Interests and Needs	The administrator models collaborating with families and community members, responding to diverse community interests and needs, and mobilizing community resources.
Integrity	The administrator acts with integrity, fairness, and in an ethical manner.
Political Context	The administrator understands, responds to, and interacts with the larger political, social, economic, legal and cultural context that affects schooling.
Vision of Learning	The administrator leads by facilitating the development, articulation, implementation and stewardship of a vision of learning that is shared by the school community.

Students fulfill the performance requirements through coursework assignments, action research and field work. The NCPEA subfields are integrated under the DPI program standards and DPI content guidelines. The required courses and the DPI standards integrated into those courses form the structure wherein the performance standards requirement is met. The list of knowledge, dispositions and performances for the Edgewood College Educational Administration (ECEA) program, including the Program Coordinator license, follows.

PERFORMANCE STANDARDS
(KNOWLEDGE, DISPOSITIONS, AND PERFORMANCE)

Each of the performance standards may be conceptualized as the knowledge expected of the student, the dispositions that must be demonstrated through the program experiences and the performance of duties that evidence the standards being met. That is, there is documented evidence of what an administrator needs to know, be able to do and value as a program outcome. The Performance Standards items expand upon the NCPEA (Wildman, 2003) knowledge base subfields with action statements added as skill measures. The program standards are listed in Table 2 and referenced as follows (K = knowledge; D = disposition; P = performance).

These 17 performance standards, with their integrated knowledge, disposition and performance items, form the foundation of the Edgewood College Educational Administration (ECEA) theoretical framework. In order to provide evidence of meeting state standards the performance standards need to be aligned with the state standards for licensing. This alignment is provided in Table 3.

Table 2. Knowledge (K), Disposition (D), and Performance (P) Items

#	Program Standard	K	D	P
1	The prospective administrator should know the practical, educational administrative implications of major cultural, historical and philosophical perspectives and should exhibit an appreciation and support for all cultures in school settings.	x	x	x
2	The prospective administrator should know research methods (including design, quantitative, qualitative, historical and ethnographic issues), should have a commitment to ethical research and must complete field-based action research projects as part of class assignments.	x	x	x
3	Prospective administrator should know learning theory (including theories and ideas pertaining to human growth and development, personality and intelligence) and should exhibit an attitude that all students can learn given the appropriate instructional objectives and tasks and appropriate support for learning.	x	x	x
4	The prospective administrator should know curriculum (decision-making, content, instructional methodology, student evaluation, and curriculum change processes) and should value a curriculum that is representative of the multicultural and pluralistic nature of society and of students.	x	x	
5	The prospective administrator should know student services (counseling, psychology, social work, career guidance, student discipline, and dropout prevention strategies) and recognize the importance of a solid student services team to support student social, emotional, psychological and educational well-being.	x	x	
6	The prospective administrator should know the administration of special programs (special education, bilingual education, migrant education, and compensatory education) and must exhibit equity in the support of these programs.	x	x	x
7	The prospective administrator should know personnel and human resources management (certification, recruitment, selection, assignment, academic freedom, compensation, collective bargaining processes, formative and summative teacher evaluation, teacher rights, counselor evaluation, administrator evaluation, classified employee evaluation, staff development), support the design and implementation of professional and support staff development programs and value the existence and continuation of a diverse administrative, teaching, pupil services and support staff.	x	x	x
8	The prospective administrator should know educational management (administrative theories, decision making theories) and use that knowledge in making ethical and educationally appropriate decisions.	x	x	x
9	The prospective administrator should know educational leadership (theories, processes and skills) and value those theories that offer teamwork and inclusion of all stakeholders.	x	x	
10	The prospective administrator should know human relations (conflict resolution, team building, inter-personal and inter-group relations) and should exemplify integrity and fairness in all human relations activities.	x	x	x
11	The prospective administrator should know systems analysis and design (organizational structure, flow charts, strategic planning, computer spreadsheets and databases, quality control) and use those support items in an efficient, effective and ethical manner.	x	x	x

(continued)

Table 2. **Knowledge (K), Disposition (D), and Performance (P) Items (*Continued*)**

#	Program Standard	K	D	P
12	The prospective administrator should know site-based leadership (participatory vs. top-down decision making, empowerment) and exhibit skill in the design and implementation of shared decision-making structures.	x		x
13	The prospective administrator should know school law and policy development (local, state and federal policy, the legal system, church and state, compulsory attendance, student rights, torts) and make informed decisions based on that knowledge.	x		x
14	The prospective administrator should know school finance (local, state, and federal roles, budgeting and accounting, equity and equality issues) and exhibit fair and impartial decisions relating to school budget issues.	x	x	x
15	The prospective administrator should know school public relations (developing and evaluating public support for education) and should be a positive role model for professionalism in the school and community.	x		x
16	The prospective administrator should know school facilities (planning facilities and grounds, educational specifications, energy and conservation, health and safety, maintenance and operation) and give evidence of working to provide safe and healthful facilities for learning to occur.	x		x
17	The prospective administrator should know district and community leadership (board and superintendent roles, relations, and evaluation, district governance models) and be able to follow the appropriate chain of command for decisions.	x		x

In summary, the Edgewood College performance standards (knowledge, dispositions and performance) and the performance requirements for students for the educational leadership and administration program meet the Wisconsin DPI Standards for Administrator Development and Licensure. This integration allows for the assessment done in the program to certify students as competent when

Table 3. **Administrator Program Standards Integrated into State Standards**

State Standards	Program Standards
Teacher Standards	ECEA #1, #3 and #4.
Vision of Learning	ECEA #2, #3, #7, #9 and #11.
School Culture	ECEA #3, #4, #7 and #16
Organizational Management	ECEA #5, #6, #8, #11, #12, #14, #16 and #17
Community Interests and Needs	ECEA #7, #10, #15 and #17
Integrity	ECEA #2, #5, #8, #10, #11 and #15
Political Context	ECEA #13, #14, #15 and #17

measured against state and national standards for performance as required in state rules for all licenses.

ASSESSMENT

Student assessment will take place at four distinct junctures in the program. The formal stages of assessment are as follows:

1. Preliminary Entry Transition
2. Aspiring Professional Transition
3. Emergent Professional Transition
4. Licensure Endorsement Transition

The Preliminary Entry Transition Stage begins with review of formal application materials, a completed criminal background check and preparation of a degree pan and portfolio outline. Following the substantiation of prerequisite items including undergraduate and graduate grade point average, previous coursework and admission to the program there will be an assessment at program entry that will measure communication skill including skill with modern technology, human relations skills including professional dispositions, content knowledge for the license specialty area, pedagogical knowledge including knowledge of and experience with the 10 teacher standards, and professional practice.

Entry assessment takes into account the previous training and coursework the student has completed. An analysis is done to determine through documented evidence what knowledge or performance items required in the program that the student might already exhibit. Special care is taken to assess the content knowledge of prospective students with teaching and learning standards for PK–12 students, the Wisconsin Model Academic Standards in this state, and the Wisconsin Teacher Standards. There are special entry requirements unique to the doctoral program that ore outlined below. The student program plan may be varied by way of this analysis.

The second assessment takes place at the Aspiring Professional Transition stage and is a knowledge assessment based on the specific content standards for the license. A second background check will be done, along with a review of course grade point average (GPA) and an initial human relations (administrator dispositions) endorsement. The content assessment continues over time in the required courses and includes the Edgewood College Educational Administration knowledge, disposition and performance items. In addition, the DI Content Guidelines for the superintendent license are verified at this stage. The content of the superintendent program, as provided by the DPI, are given in Table 4 (see http://www.dpi.state.wi.us/dpi/dlsis/tel/te.html).

The third assessment required in the program at the Emergent Professional Transition Stage includes a third background check, a GPA review, an initial content endorsement, and an advanced endorsement for human relations and a practicum experience advanced endorsement. There is a review of the student's portfolio. The

Table 4. State Content Guidelines for the Superintendent License

A School District Administrator or Superintendent will . . . demonstrate knowledge of and skill in:

1. Diversity as identified in PI 34.15(4)(c).
2. The organization, history and operation of public schools, including program planning and evaluation, theory, research and practice at both the school and district level.
3. The governance of education at the national, state and local levels.
4. Supervision of instruction.
5. Personnel administration.
6. The economics of education including school finance and taxation.
7. School business administration.
8. School law including Chapter 115 to 121, especially those related to pupils, special education, employee contracts and collective bargaining.
9. District, school and community relations.
10. The politics of education, at both the basic and advanced level, including local, state and national politics of educational decision making, and the role of pressure groups in shaping educational policy at these levels.
11. Educational leadership at the district level including participatory management, long-range strategic planning and change agent processes.
12. Oral and written communication.
13. The role and responsibility of the superintendency including the official functions of the school board.
14. The operational tasks and instructional leadership of the principalship.
15. Coordinating special school programs, including organizational structure, program planning, policy formation and curriculum development.
16. Curriculum development at the district level.
17. Different levels of school administration through documented work experience in a school setting.
18. Facilities management.
19. The role, function and responsibility of the superintendent through a supervised practicum or internship in a school district setting.

portfolio framework is proscribed, and structured according to the Edgewood College Educational Administration Standards. Students select and include artifacts that best represent the content of the standard. Students are provided cover sheets to be used for each artifact to maintain consistency of evaluation. The worksheet requires a description of the artifact and a reflection regarding its value in assessing the selected program standard and performance standard.

Formative evaluation focuses on communication skills, content knowledge, professional dispositions and practice. Faculty review and approve artifacts for the portfolio as part of each class in the program. Summative evaluation of the portfolio takes place prior to endorsement for the license and is a partnership endorsement done by campus faculty and school-based educators.

The final assessment of student performance is at program exit, which is the Licensure Endorsement Transition Stage. In addition to the background check, GPA review and portfolio review there are summary assessments of the student's growth in communication skills, dispositions (human relations), content knowledge, knowledge of the teaching standards and evidence of successful practice through practicum experiences and action research completed. The Licensure Endorsement Transition Stage includes a professional practice endorsement and an administrator development statement. The administrator development endorsement is based on the completion of the DPI Professional Development Plan for administrators. The DPI Professional Development Plan for Administrators (see http://www.dpi.state.wi.us/ dpi/dlsis/tel/t2tqeg.html#admin) is the tool new administrators will use for license renewal in Wisconsin in lieu of the previously required six credits every five years. The end result at this final stage of assessment is licensure endorsement.

PORTFOLIO

The accomplishment of program goals is documented in a student portfolio. The portfolio must include artifacts that demonstrate the student's success in meeting each standard, and those artifacts must give evidence of all three categories—knowledge, disposition and performance (K, D and P). The compilation of evidence will be mastered by the students work in graduate classes. Students are provided a cover sheet to be completed for each artifact in their portfolio. The artifact cover sheet will capture the information necessary for faculty to make informed judgments about the artifact and the portfolio fulfilling the purpose of evidence, and to provide the opportunity for an evaluative judgment regarding the student. Table 5 is the portfolio artifact cover sheet.

THE ED.D. PROGRAM AND THE SUPERINTENDENT LICENSE

Edgewood College received program accreditation for the doctoral degree from the Higher Learning Commission of the North Central Association in the fall of 2001. The report noted that the "College's mission, purposes and history clearly encompass the proposed change. The proposed degree program is congruent with the core values of the institution and the delivery methods are in keeping with recognized changing needs of public education." The report pointed out the importance of the ". . . school improvement initiatives within a cohort partnership mentoring arrangement involving full-time faculty, clinical faculty, and doctoral candidates . . . to expand and strengthen ties between institutions of higher learning and K–12 school districts to the benefit of both."

Wisconsin Department of Public Instruction program approval for the superintendent license followed, and the first cohort Group was admitted to study in January of 2002. This first cohort completed coursework in December of 2003 and qualified for the superintendent license. These students are now engaged in the research and dissertation writing that will qualify them for the doctoral degree. Two additional cohorts have been admitted and are pursuing the license by way of completing the modules of study.

The Wisconsin administrative code requires the specialist degree or the equivalent for the superintendent license. The Edgewood College superintendent license program, which includes a Doctorate in Education (Ed.D.), was designed to qualify candidates for the superintendent license. It was further designed with a true partnership between a school district and the college in mind. The two are linked together in the preparation

Table 5.　Portfolio Artifact Cover Sheet

PORTFOLIO ARTIFACT COVER SHEET

1. Title of artifact—describe the piece of evidence in a few words (e.g., "budget items prepared for annual meeting").
2. Date prepared or selected—provide the date you selected or prepared the item for the portfolio.
3. Origin of artifact—list the course or other program experience where the artifact had its inception.
4. Summary description of the artifact—a brief summary of what the artifact is or what it includes should be provided.
5. Standard(s) evidenced—check the administrator standard or standards where the selected artifact provides evidence of professional competence:
Teacher_____
Vision_____
Culture_____
Organizational Management_____
Community_____
Integrity_____
Political Context_____
6. Component of standard documented—identify whether the artifact documents a knowledge (something you read, heard, or now know), a disposition (how you feel or an attitude that the artifact helped you analyze or synthesize) or a performance (something you did that gives evidence of the standard):
Knowledge_____
Disposition _____
Performance_____
7. Reflection—how do you see the evidence documenting the selected standard or standards, and how does that documentation support your educational leadership?

of a highly qualified superintendent candidate, one who could easily take the reins in a local school district. The program was created with the knowledge of the research base in school leadership outlined above, with the foundation of the new administrative rules for licensing created at the Wisconsin Department of Public Instruction, and with the same theoretical framework that was structured for all license programs.

Admission requirements include the master's degree, administrative licensure at the building or staff level, references including a commitment to the partnership component, a letter of intent, curriculum vita and an interview that includes a structured writing component. The interview conducted by doctoral cohort faculty plays a crucial role in determining candidates' administrative disposition and research potential.

The Edgewood College school superintendent license program is a three-year program. The required course work is completed in the first two years, and the student qualifies for the superintendent license after two years. The courses in the program are designed as credit modules with planned pro-seminar experiences woven in at appropriate intervals. The sequence of modules and pro-seminars is provided in the 42 credits in the program's first two years, when combined with the credits taken for the prerequisite master's degree provide the 60 graduate credit minimum that defines

Table 6.   Proseminar and Module Sequence in the Doctor of Education Program

Pro-seminar I	Introduction to Doctoral Study	3 Credits
Module 1	The District Superintendency	6 Credits
Module 2	Leadership Behavior and Policy	6 Credits
Module 3	Curriculum, Instruction and the Learning Environment	6 Credits
Pro-seminar II	Research and Leadership for School Improvement	3 Credits
Module 4	Budget, Finance and Resource Allocation	6 Credits
Module 5	Media and Legal Foundations of District Administration	6 Credits
Module 6	Research Design and Methodology	6 Credits

the equivalent of the specialist degree in Wisconsin administrative code. The third year of the program is devoted to research and writing a dissertation to qualify for the Ed.D. Degree.

The program was designed with the working professional in mind. The courses are in the summer or on Saturdays during the school year so as not to interfere with the duties of the job. The students enroll as a cohort group and take all classes as a group, so that the non-availability of courses that may occur at other colleges and delay an individual's progress through a program never becomes an issue for students in the Edgewood College program.

Course work and research projects are to be centered on the student's work site. Each class is devoted to helping the student translate the theory discussed in the class session to action items at the home site. One aim of the program is to have the students return to their work place on Monday with a new approach to an existing situation or problem. Mentors, cohort members and faculty in the program work together to not only help the student experience success at their current job but also to realize and practice the knowledge and skill necessary to be a good superintendent. Superintendents who already hold the license are cohort members, recognizing the value of the doctorate degree. These sitting administrators add greatly to the preparation of those in the principal or other central office roles as they all "work on the work" of being and becoming highly qualified administrators.

The most important foundation component of the program is the partnership required with the home school district or school. Students must have a mentor from their home district or area who becomes part of the instructional team for the program. The mentor is considered adjunct faculty of the college, and is paid a stipend for that work. In many cases the student is a principal in the district and the district superintendent is the student's mentor. Since the program design is flexible other mentor arrangements have been made that fit the student and district situation.

A key structural element to the partnership component is the faculty visits to the home district. Students, mentors and faculty consultants meet in the district on a regular basis to analyze and synthesize strategies for individual and school success. The value of the faculty visit to the school extends beyond the student and includes the district as a whole.

The ongoing assessments done by each cohort group reinforces the original plan for the cohort as a community of learners in a partnership model. Collaborative learning, district partnership, faculty visits and mentor involvement have substantially reinforced the accomplishments of the modules with content and embedded research. Students, faculty, mentors and dissertation advisors have emerged as a network of scholarship and service—teaching and learning—for administration and leadership at the district level. Inter-cohort sharing and urban and rural district interaction have enhanced the program.

In sum, the Doctor of Education degree program in educational leadership at Edgewood College provides a supportive system of orientation, preparation, advising and assessment. It has a standard of excellence for the preparation of educational leaders at the district level and promotes school improvement efforts through a cohort partnership and mentoring arrangement. It truly epitomizes the best practices in educational leadership programs and is "showing the way" to a better future for schools and those who manage them.

REFERENCES

Council of Chief State School Officers (CCSSO). (1996). Interstate School Leaders Licensure Consortium: Standards for school leaders. Washington, DC: CCSSO. St. John's University website www.new.stjohns.edu.

Edgewood College Graduate Handbook (n.d.).

Education Department Educational Administration Program Handbook (n.d.)

Higher Learning Commission of the North Central Association. (2001). Edgewood College Program Report. University of Southern California website www.usc.edu/education.

Wildman, L. (2003). Pass the Educational Testing Service's Administrative Licensure Examination as an alternative to completing an accredited university educational administration program. National Council of Professors of Educational Administration website www.ncpea.net/.

Wisconsin Department of Public Instruction website www.dpi.state.wi.us.

IV

GOING THE WAY

The Power to Mistreat: Examining Ourselves

Joseph Blase and Jo Blase

Historically, research in the areas of school leadership and university-based and professional development programs have focused on the positive aspects of school leadership; by and large, dark side topics have been ignored. Consequently, prospective and practicing administrators have been given little assistance in dealing with dark side issues. In this chapter, we specifically discuss the critical importance of preparing school leaders to deal with one category of dark side issues that we have studied, namely school principals' misuse of power and, in particular, mistreatment of teachers. Following this, we also draw on several theoretical perspectives to discuss the importance of preparing prospective and practicing school principals to deal with personal and organizational factors that may interact to produce the kinds of leadership that seriously damage teachers, teaching, and student learning.

During the last decade and a half, researchers have produced a strong stream of "bright side" empirical studies in the field of educational administration focusing on the considerable contribution of exemplary school principals to schools in general (e.g., Blase & Blase, 2001; Blase & Kirby, 2000; Good & Brophy, 1986; Hallinger & Heck, 1996; Leithwood, Thomlinson, & Genge, 1996; Murphy & Louis, 1994a, 1994b) and teacher development and student learning in particular (e.g., Blase & Blase, 1999; Heck, Larsen, & Marcoulides, 1990; Heck & Marcoulides, 1993; Joyce & Showers, 1995; Sheppard, 1996). Notably, this knowledge base provides ample theoretical and empirical evidence that effective principal leadership can have important effects on student learning (Wang, Haertel, & Walberg, 1993). Specifically, effective principals develop positive relationships based on mutual trust, respect, openness, support, and understanding (Blase & Blase, 1998, 2001; Glickman, Gordon, & Ross-Gordon, 2001; Lambert et al., 1995; Sergiovanni, 1996; Walton, 1990);

Joseph Blase, University of Georgia
Jo Blase, University of Georgia

develop learning communities of professionals and constituents able to openly communicate, make decisions, solve problems, and resolve conflicts (Schmuck & Runkel, 1994; Wald & Castleberry, 2000); maintain a collaborative focus on teaching and learning (Fullan, 1997; Joyce & Calhoun, 1996); and encourage teacher reflection, peer coaching, and shared critique and inquiry (Blase & Blase, 1998; Calhoun, 1994; Joyce & Showers, 1995; Schön, 1987). The importance of related leadership skills and corresponding attitudes and values to the development of strong, positive relationships between principals and teachers cannot be overemphasized; indeed, respectful, constructive relationships between principals and teachers are essential for school improvement (Boyer, 1995; Cotton, 2001; Hoachlander, 2001; Schlechty, 1997; Senge, 2000).

In stark contrast, only one empirical study has systematically examined the "dark side" of school leadership, in particular principal mistreatment/abuse of teachers, and the extremely harmful consequences such forms of leadership have on life in schools (see *Breaking the Silence: Overcoming the Problem of Principal Mistreatment of Teachers* [Blase & Blase, 2003] and recently published articles in *Educational Administration Quarterly* and the *Journal of Educational Administration*). Undoubtedly, the failure of both academic and professional educators to study principal mistreatment of teachers, applying the same rigorous research protocols we use to investigate other educational problems, has resulted in incomplete, naïve, and even false understandings of how some, perhaps a noteworthy percentage, of school leaders and teachers experience their work (Hodgkinson, 1991). Moreover, this failure allows mistreatment to continue without challenge and without hope of improvement (Ashforth, 1994; Keashly, Trott, & MacLean, 1994; Robinson & Bennett, 1995; Einarsen et al., 2003). As a first step, our study of principal mistreatment of teachers provides an inductively derived knowledge base and initiates an area of inquiry essential to developing a constructive approach for university preparation and development of prospective and practicing school administrators.

TERMS AND CONSTRUCTS

Internationally, systematic research on the problem of workplace abuse, notably nonphysical forms of abuse, has increased significantly during the last two decades in countries such as Sweden, Norway, Germany, Austria, Australia, and Britain. Several of these countries have also enacted legislation against workplace abuse and private organizations have been created to help victims of abuse (Björkvist, Österman, & Hjelt-Bäck, 1994; Davenport, Schwartz, & Elliott, 1999; Keashly, 1998; Namie & Namie, 2000). For most of this same period, organizational scholars in the United States have largely ignored the problem of work abuse. In recent years, however, scholars have begun to address the problem; indeed, the emerging national literature suggests that workplace abuse may lead to serious deleterious consequences for both employees and organizations (Baron & Neuman, 1996; Davenport et al., 1999; Hornstein et al., 1995; Keashly, 1998; Keashly et al., 1994).

Using a variety of research methods, organizational scholars have used a number of terms in the conceptual, theoretical, and empirical literature to describe the workplace mistreatment/abuse phenomenon including *incivility* (Andersson & Pearson, 1999), *mobbing* (Davenport et al., 1999; Leymann, 1990), *bullying* (Einarsen & Skogstad, 1996; Namie & Namie, 2000), *harassment* (Björkvist et al., 1994); *petty tyranny* (Ashforth, 1994), *abusive disrespect* (Hornstein, 1996), *interactional injustice* (Harlos & Pinder, 2000), *emotional abuse* (Keashly, 1998), mistreatment (Folger, 1993; Price Spratlen, 1995), *abuse* (Bassman, 1992), *aggression* (Neuman & Baron, 1998), *deviance* (Robinson & Bennett, 1995), and *victimization* (Swedish National Board of Occupational Safety and Health, 1993).

OUR STUDY

What types of principal conduct do teachers define as abusive? What effect does such conduct have on teachers, teaching and learning? How does a principal's abusive conduct undermine teachers' performance in the classroom and in the school in general? These are some of the basic questions we used in our study to examine how teachers experience abusive conduct by school principals.

Over a one and a half year period, we conducted several in-depth interviews with each of 50 teachers who had experienced long-term (6 months to 9 years) mistreatment by their principals. The sample consisted of male ($n = 5$) and female ($n = 45$) teachers from rural ($n = 14$), suburban ($n = 25$), and urban ($n = 11$) school locations. Elementary ($n = 26$), middle/junior high ($n = 10$), and high school ($n = 14$) teachers participated. The average age of teachers was 42; the average number of years in teaching was 16. The sample included tenured ($n = 44$) and nontenured ($n = 6$), married ($n = 34$) and single ($n = 16$) teachers. Degrees earned by these teachers included B.A./B.S. ($n = 7$), MED/MA ($n = 31$), Ed.S. ($n = 11$), and Ph.D. ($n = 1$). The mean number of years working with the abusive principal was 4. Forty-nine teachers resided in the United States and one resided in Canada. Fifteen of the teachers we studied were with an abusive principal at the time of this study; most others had experienced abuse in recent years. In total, these teachers described 28 male and 22 female abusive principals.

Examination of the personal and official documents submitted to us and reports from those who had worked with and referred us to the veteran teachers we studied suggest that the teachers were highly respected, accomplished, creative, and dedicated individuals. In most cases, they had been consistently and formally recognized by their school and district not simply as effective teachers but also as superior teachers; in many cases, such recognition for their exceptional achievements as public educators extended to state levels.

OUTLINE OF OUR FINDINGS ON
PRINCIPAL MISTREATMENT OF TEACHERS

We found that abusive principals, like abusive bosses, in general, engage in similar behaviors. However, in contrast to the existing literature on boss abuse, we have conceptualized abusive conduct in terms of three levels of aggression: Level 1 principal mistreatment behaviors (indirect and moderate aggression) include discounting teachers' thoughts, needs, and feelings, and isolating and abandoning them; withholding or denying opportunities, resources, or credit; showing favoritism toward other teachers; and offensive personal conduct. Level 2 principal mistreatment behaviors (direct and escalating aggression) include spying, sabotaging, stealing, destroying teacher instructional aids, making unreasonable work demands, and both public and private criticism of teachers. Level 3 principal mistreatment behaviors (direct and severe aggression) include lying, being explosive and nasty, threats, unwarranted reprimands, unfair evaluations, mistreating students, forcing teachers out of their jobs, preventing teachers from leaving/advancing, sexual harassment, and racism. Such behaviors and related patterns of conduct are consistent with studies of abusive bosses conducted throughout the world in both profit and nonprofit organizations (Björkvist et al., 1994; Davenport et al., 1999; Einarsen et al., 2003; Harlos & Pinder, 2000; Hornstein, 1996; Keashly et al., 1994; Leymann, 1990; Lombardo & McCall, 1984; Namie, 2000; Namie & Namie, 2000; Neuman & Baron, 1998; Robinson & Bennett, 1995; Rayner et al., 2002; Ryan & Oestreich, 1991).

We also found that the effects of such mistreatment are extremely harmful to teachers' professional and personal lives. Like many thousands of workers represented in the extant literature—a number that has been extrapolated to be multimillions of workers—abused teachers experienced the same devastating effects. Beyond the teachers' responses of shock and disorientation, humiliation, loneliness, and injured self-esteem, principal mistreatment seriously damaged in-school relationships, damaged classrooms, and frequently impaired all-school decision-making. In addition, principals' abuse of teachers resulted in severe psychological/emotional problems including chronic fear, anxiety, anger, and depression; a range of physical/physiological problems; and adverse personal outcomes also discussed in the general empirical literature on boss abuse (Björkvist et al., 1994; Davenport et al., 1999; Harlos & Pinder, 2000; Hornstein, 1996; Keashly et al., 1994; Leymann, 1990; Lombardo & McCall, 1984; Namie, 2000; Namie & Namie, 2000; NNLI, 1993; Pearson, 2000; Ryan & Oestreich, 1991).

In addition, we learned that teachers victimized by abusive principals seldom had viable opportunities for redress. This is consistent with other research that had demonstrated that victims' complaints about abusive bosses typically result in (a) no action (no response) from upper management, (b) efforts to protect abusive bosses, and (c) reprisals against victims who complain (Bassman, 1992; Davenport et al., 1999; Hornstein, 1996; Keashly, 1998; Keashly et al., 1994; Leymann, 1990; Namie, 2000; Namie & Namie, 2000; Pearson, 2000; Rayner, 1998). In fact, according to our findings, teachers rarely complained to district-level administrators because they expected "no help" and because they "feared" reprisals.

Further, our findings point out that teachers were often unable to leave a school in which they were abused, at least in a timely manner. Several factors of considerable importance frequently result in strong feelings of being "trapped," for example, district policies prohibiting transfers, the high probability of negative letters of reference (and blackballing), weak unions, need for a job and health insurance, and the chronic effects of long-term abuse itself. These chronic effects include chronic fear, depression (self-doubt, feelings of helplessness), and fatigue, all factors that diminish one's ability for proactive action, particularly in difficult circumstances (Izard & Youngstrom, 1996).

ABUSE OF POWER

It is widely acknowledged that power is a fundamental aspect of all human relationships (Muth, 1989; McClelland, 1987; Russell, 1938) and is especially significant for understanding relationships between administrators and subordinates (Blase & Anderson, 1995; Burns, 1978; Gardner, 1990; Gibb, 1954; Kets de Vries, 1989, 1993). It is also acknowledged that power in and of itself is morally neutral; it can be exercised in constructive or destructive ways in pursuit of self-serving or other-oriented purposes (Lee-Chai, Chen, & Chartrand, 2001; Chaleff, 1995; Sampson, 1965).

The destructive use of power may be primarily related to individual factors such as one's stability of identity, capacity for reality testing (i.e., "the ability to distinguish inner from outer reality, fact from fantasy" [Kets de Vries, 1993, p. 179]) and, more concretely, tolerance for anxiety and impulse control. Individuals who lack "balance" in dealing with the vicissitudes of power are more likely to abuse power and engage in pathological behavior (Kets de Vries, 1993). Lack of balance can lead to a mental and moral dualism and "power intoxication" wherein administrators view themselves above precepts of right and wrong, and good and evil (Sorokin & Lunden, 1959, p. 44).

More frequently, however, the use and abuse of power is a function of the interaction between individual and organizational factors (Andersson & Pearson, 1999; Ashforth, 1994; Baron & Neuman, 1996; Folger, 1993; Hornstein, 1996; Kipnis, 1972; Leymann, 1990). To wit, prominent power theorists have demonstrated that the acquisition of power itself may have transforming or "metamorphic" (i.e., corrupting) effects on powerholders and those over whom power is exercised (Adams & Balfour, 1998; Baumeister, 1997; Lee-Chai & Bargh, 2001; Kekes, 1990; Kets de Vries, 1989; Kipnis, 1972, 2001). Lord Acton's (1948) famous aphorism, "power tends to corrupt and absolute power corrupts absolutely," speaks directly to the problematic nature of power. Indeed, some educational scholars have explicitly acknowledged the temptations of power and the "dark side" of school leadership (Hodgkinson, 1991; Kimbrough, 1985; Kimbrough & Nunnery, 1988; Starratt, 1991).

Kipnis's (1972; 1976) research on the "metamorphic" effects of power has shown that individuals can be significantly transformed as a result of gaining power. Kipnis found that after acquiring power, individuals typically increased their attempts to influence those who were less powerful; devalued those who were less powerful; attributed the cause of a less powerful persons' efforts to themselves, rather than to the less powerful persons' motivation to do well; viewed less powerful people as objects of manipulation; and preferred maintaining psychological distance from less powerful people. That is, Kipnis (1972) demonstrated that power affects a powerholder's self-perceptions; the powerholder tends to develop an inflated and vain view of self that inhibits compassion for others. He also noted that many who hold power value it above all else and pursue the acquisition of more power; power often becomes an end in itself, results in abuse, and thus cannot be justified on ethical or moral grounds.

The Inadvertent Misuse of Power

Although much misuse of power is undoubtedly deliberate—"an internal, strategic, and knowing act on the part of the abuser" (Bargh & Alvarez, 2001, p. 45)—"the misuse of power by those who do not realize they are doing so, who at the conscious level believe they are acting in an objective and fair-minded manner and in the best interests of their subordinates" is considered a more insidious and prevalent problem (Bargh & Alvarez, 2001, p. 45). Along these lines, stereotyping of individuals and, in particular, automatic negative evaluations of subordinates have been found to frequently occur unintentionally and in a split-second fashion (Fiske & Neuberg, 1990).

Self-deception theory also provides insight into why individuals (and groups [Janis, 1982]), under certain circumstances, abuse power (Baumeister, 1997). Self-deception is believing that which an individual is motivated to believe; it entails maintaining a given idea in one's consciousness while suppressing a conflicting idea (Silver, 1989); in addition, self-deception processes tend to occur unconsciously (Ford, 1996; Peck, 1983; Silver, 1989). The psychological literature is filled with theoretical and empirical work on various ego mechanisms used by individuals to create or preserve a state of self-deception including denial, projection, distortion, dissociation, displacement, reaction formation, and suppression (Ford, 1996); rationalization, evasion, and jamming (Bach, 1981); and selective perception, biased reasoning, and isolation of incidents (Baumeister, 1996). Self-deception is also considered central to certain personality types (e.g., controlling disposition and self-deceptive narcissism) and a range of destructive forms of leadership (Kets de Vries, 1989).

Finally, the role of emotion should be examined with regard to the inadvertent use of power. Emotion is always present in work in organizations, and, as such, is considered a catalyst to human motivation (Fineman, 1993, 2000); furthermore, much emotion is unconscious and yet it has a profound influence on human behavior (Goleman, 1995). An awareness and understanding of emotions (even as they occur), the ability to manage one's emotions, and the ability to express emotion in appropriate ways, given the context, are regarded as critical to effective school leadership (Beatty, 2000; Goleman, 1995).

IMPLICATIONS FOR ADMINISTRATOR PREPARATION AND PROFESSIONAL DEVELOPMENT

Compelling empirical and theoretical work on the misuse of power in organizational settings and the fact that most prospective administrators have been teachers (and as such have undoubtedly experienced, observed, or heard about abusive conduct with regard to colleagues and its devastating effects on victimized teachers and on schools as a whole) notwithstanding, preservice (e.g., university-based programs in educational leadership) and inservice programs (e.g., those provided per school district policy, by union contracts, and within staff development opportunities) seldom directly address the "dark side" of school leadership. Consequently, such programs fail to equip prospective and practicing administrators and teachers with an understanding of and ability to deal with this incredibly destructive problem (Blase, 1991; Blase & Blase, 2003; Blase & Anderson, 1995; Hodgkinson, 1991; Nyberg, 1981). Relatedly, school leaders typically receive little help from either preparatory or in-service programs in understanding and managing their own emotions or understanding the emotions of others (Beatty, 2000; Ginsberg & Davies, 2001; Ackerman & Maslin-Ostrowski, 2002).

We believe our findings about principal mistreatment of teachers, as troubling as they are, have special significance for prospective and practicing administrators. To test this notion, we created a 2-hour presentation and discussion of our research findings about principal mistreatment for school administrators and teachers taking graduate coursework at a major research university. Following this, participants were given 30 minutes to respond to a survey that included one open-ended question: *What importance, if any, does knowledge about principal mistreatment (abuse) of teachers have for your development as an educational leader?* Over 400 administrators and teachers responded to this survey between 1999 and 2002. One wrote:

> When people are mistreated at work, their focus of attention is diverted from completing their work to trying to understand and manage the mistreatment . . . in other words, to surviving. A fearful and stressed teacher will generally downshift to the lowest mode of functioning. Creativity and innovation suffer. Paths of communication change in the school as teachers either talk among themselves or shut down entirely. Mistreatment of teachers is especially damaging because such mistreatment is often clearly visible to students. Even when mistreatment is more subtle, the subliminal perception of it by students is certain to undermine teachers; in fact, in some cases a mistreated teacher may become angry and the anger may be directed back toward students. Students then resort to further aggressive behavior as they internalize the hostility that has been directed toward them. . . . Thus, not only do teachers suffer, but the bullying is passed down the line. The implication for my development as an educational leader is that . . . I must be very mindful of how I treat other people. What goes around comes around in many destructive ways.

Without exception, respondents affirmed the merits of studying the mistreatment problem and suggested a number of immediately practical uses for our findings. Respondents typically used phrases such as "very important," "extremely useful," "incredibly significant," and "shocking but extremely significant" to characterize the importance of the topic for their professional development. They reported that *knowledge of the "negatives," that is, "what not to do as an educational leader, is as important as just studying the positive, effective things."* Specifically, respondents reported that such knowledge provoked in them a long-term commitment to a "truly reflective" orientation to school leadership, based on an understanding of how *personal factors* (e.g., one's weaknesses, values, assumptions, attitudes, and behavior) alone or in conjunction with *organizational conditions* (e.g., stress, accountability expectations, unreasonable expectations by superiors) can contribute to destructive forms of leadership and abuse of teachers.

Our presentation had special significance for teachers and principals who had been victimized by principals (and others) at some point in their careers:

> During the presentation, I began to feel the exact same feelings I felt during a 3 year period of emotional abuse by a principal. I compiled a journal during our discussion to relieve my physical reactions. All of us must work to understand this problem and take responsibility for it.

Lombardo and McCall (1984) studied successful executives who had been victimized by abusive bosses earlier in their careers. These researchers found that executives derived some of their *most profound lessons about effective leadership from reflection on abusive experiences.* Blase and Blase (1998) reported similar findings for teachers and administrators preparing for careers in educational leadership, as did Ginsberg and Davies (2001) for school administrators and administrators generally. Clearly, these studies strongly confirm the significance of knowledge of and reflection on the dark dimensions of school leadership for professional growth (Butler, 1996). Without such reflection, administrators routinely fail to recognize and confront personal values, attitudes, and behaviors that contradict their own espoused theories of effective leadership and this failure can produce substantial adverse outcomes for individuals and organizations (Argyris, 1990, 1994; Bass, 1981). This latter point is especially important in light of countless studies that demonstrate that some school principals typically employ leadership approaches that adversely affect teachers as well as classroom instruction (e.g., Blase, 1990; Blase & Blase, 1998; Diehl, 1993; Farber, 1991; Malen & Ogawa, 1988; McNeil, 1988); such studies have revealed that, in many cases, principals may not be aware of the consequences of their actions (Adams, 1988, Gunn & Holdaway, 1986; High & Achilles, 1986; Reitzug & Cross, 1994).

Thus, university-based programs and field-based professional development programs can examine the phenomenon of principal mistreatment of teachers and consider questions such as (a) What conduct by school principals do teachers and administrators perceive as abusive? (b) What is it about a school's context, the principal's role (e.g., negative role modeling by superiors, conflicting role expectations, unreasonable district policies), and those who occupy this role that can result in abusive conduct? (c) What effect does such conduct have on teachers? (e.g., What are the emotional and physical consequences for teachers, and how does such conduct affect teachers' classroom instruction and student learning?) (d) What are the consequences of abusive conduct by principals on school climate and school culture? (e) What coping strategies are efficacious for mistreated teachers? (f) What actions can mistreated teachers take to deal with the problem? (g) What actions can school-based administrators, school district office personnel, and school boards take to help principals deal with this problem (e.g., providing opportunities for principals to consider ways they encourage or discourage a respectful and supportive climate in the school, ways to become more aware of the impact of their behavior on teachers, and ways to deal with teachers' concerns about being mistreated)? (h) What policies and procedures can school personnel develop to protect teachers and provide relief from mistreatment? and (i) At what point should district office personnel move beyond counseling, guiding, and providing performance reviews of principals who mistreat others, and move to disciplinary action or discharge?

CONCLUSION

As professors of educational leadership, we have spent decades researching and teaching about school leadership. We are aware that school principals are confronted with what seem to be insurmountable challenges and pressures: Their work is characterized by long hours and inadequate compensation (Olson, 1999); and they now face an explosion of demands and pressures related to school safety and violence, drugs, diversity, inclusion, site budgeting, aging teaching staffs, and unresponsive bureaucracies (Rusch, 1999) as well as new responsibilities linked to school reform including new power arrangements, collaborative planning, evaluation, and accountability (Murphy & Louis, 1994a). We are also aware that principals are confronted with unique challenges associated with the retention of quality teachers, inadequate facilities and instructional materials, and discouraged, disillusioned faculties (Steinberg, 1999). Moreover, we recognize that such challenges can result in dramatic emotional experiences for principals (Ginsberg & Davies, 2001); feelings of anxiety, loss of control, disempowerment, insecurity, anger, and frustration are not uncommon (Beatty, 2000; Evans, 1996). Indeed, we cannot adequately express our appreciation and respect for the women and men who meet such challenges with professional integrity, courage, and ingenuity.

However, more than ever before, school reform efforts require that principals and teachers at the school level work together collaboratively to solve educational problems. Such collaboration is successful when school principals build trust in their schools; trust, in turn, serves as a foundation for open, honest, and reflective professional dialogue; problem solving; innovative initiatives; and, more directly, the development of the school as a powerful community of learners willing to take responsibility for and capable of success. All principals need to work toward these ends, and all individuals and organizations associated with public education should willingly confront the kinds of administrative mistreatment that, most assuredly, undermine such possibilities. In his forward to *Breaking the Silence: Overcoming the Problem of Principal Mistreatment of Teachers* (Blase & Blase, 2003), Don Saul, American Association of School Administrators (AASA) Superintendent of the Year 2000, described the link between mistreatment and mistrust and urged educators to seriously address the mistreatment problem:

Leaders who attempt to work with teachers and principals to promote systemic change within this environment realize district efforts to create a positive atmosphere and common purpose leading to improved student achievement and well-being are hindered by behaviors which create a loss of trust among school professionals. Funding difficulties, curricular narrowing, high stakes testing of debatable utility, special interest advocacy and other factors already conspire to evoke a feeling of powerlessness and frustration among staff. When these elements are combined with a teacher's perception that "I will probably never truly trust an administrator again," it's hard to imagine how the organizational *gestalt* essential for reform and improvement can be generated and sustained in a district or school. In this vein, [Blase and Blase] aptly quote Bok, whose statement that "trust and integrity are precious resources, easily squandered, hard to regain" illustrates what we all know about administrative-staff relations.

For all these reasons, this [study] should come with a warning. The challenges implicit in these findings reflect issues affecting the gamut of school performance and the success of related initiatives to guide and improve teaching and learning: abuse and denigration of staff members is seldom dealt with easily or without creative, dedicated effort and courage. The . . . findings . . . must not be brushed aside as a natural outcome of human interaction in the form of so-called personality conflicts or as grousing from poorly performing staff members. On the contrary, the complexity and depth of change required to assure consistent progress in education demands that the problem of mistreatment of teachers be taken very seriously and that appropriate preventative and corrective action serve as one of the keystones of growth and productivity in district and school cultures. (Blase & Blase, 2003, p. ix)

REFERENCES

Ackerman, R. H., & Maslin-Ostrowski, P. (2002). *The wounded leader: How real leadership emerges in times of crisis.* San Francisco: Jossey-Bass.

Acton, J. E. E. Dahlberg (Lord). (1948). *Essays on freedom and power.* Boston: Beacon Press.

Adams, B. P. (1988). *Leader behavior of principals and its effect on teacher burnout.* Unpublished dissertation, University of Wisconsin-Madison, Madison.

Adams, G. B., & Balfour, D. L. (1998). *Unmasking administrative evil.* Thousand Oaks, CA: Sage.

Andersson, L. M., & Pearson, C. M. (1999). Tit for tat?: The spiraling effect of incivility in the workforce. *Academy of Management Review, 24*(3), 452–471.

Argyris, C. (1994). *On organizational learning.* Malden, MA: Blackwell.

Argyris, C. (1990). *Overcoming organizational defenses: Facilitating organizational learning.* Boston: Allyn & Bacon.

Ashforth, B. (1994). Petty tyranny in organizations. *Human Relations, 47*(7), 755–778.

Bach, K. (1981). An analysis of self-deception. *Philosophy and phenomenological research, 41*(3), 351–370.

Bargh, J. A., & Alvarez, J. (2001). The road to hell: Good intentions in the face of nonconscious tendencies to misuse power. In A.Y. Lee-Chai & J. A. Bargh (Eds.), *The use and abuse of power: Multiple perspectives on the causes of corruption* (pp. 41–56). Philadelphia, PA: Psychology Press.

Baron, R. A., & Neuman, J. H. (1996). Workplace violence and workplace aggression: Evidence on their relative frequency and potential causes. *Aggressive Behavior, 22,* 161–173.

Bass, B. M. (1981). *Stogdill's handbook of leadership: A survey of theory and research.* New York: Free Press.

Bassman, E. S. (1992). *Abuse in the workplace: Management remedies and bottom line impact.* New York: Quorum.

Baumeister, R. F. (1996). *Evil: Inside human cruelty and violence.* New York: W. H. Freeman.

Beatty, B. R. (2000). The emotions of educational leadership: Breaking the silence. *International Journal of Educational Leadership, 3*(4), 331–357.

Björkvist, K., Österman, K., & Hjelt-Bäck, M. (1994). Aggression among university employees. *Aggressive Behavior, 20,* 173–184.

Blase, J. (1990). Some negative effects of principals' control-oriented and protective political behavior. *American Educational Research Journal, 27*(4), 725–753.

Blase, J. (1991). *The politics of life in schools: Power, conflict, and cooperation.* Newbury Park, CA: Sage.

Blase, J., & Anderson, G. L. (1995). *The micropolitics of educational leadership: From control to empowerment.* London: Cassell.

Blase, J., & Blase, J. (1998). *Handbook of instructional leadership: How really good principals promote teaching and learning.* Thousand Oaks, CA: Corwin Press.

Blase, J., & Blase, J. (1999). Principals' instructional leadership and teacher development: Teachers' perspectives. *Educational Administration Quarterly, 35*(3), 349–378.

Blase, J., & Blase, J. (2001). *Empowering teachers* (2nd ed.). Thousand Oaks, CA: Corwin Press.

Blase, J., & Blase, J. (2003). *Breaking the silence: Overcoming the problem of principal mistreatment of teachers.* Thousand Oaks, CA: Corwin.

Blase, J., & Kirby, P. C. (2000). *Bringing out the best in teachers: What effective principals do* (2nd ed.). Thousand Oaks, CA: Corwin Press.

Boyer, E. (1995). *The basic school: A community of learning.* Princeton, NJ: The Carnegie Foundation for the Advancement of Teaching.

Burns, J. M. (1978). *Leadership.* New York: Harper & Row.

Butler, J. (1996). Professional development: Practice as text, reflection as process, and self as locus. *Australian Journal of Education, 40*(3), 265–283.

Calhoun, E. (1994). *How to use action research in the self-renewing school.* Alexandria, VA: Association for Supervision and Curriculum Development.

Chaleff, I. (1995). *The courageous follower: Standing up to and for our leaders.* San Francisco: Berrett-Koehler.

Cotton, K. (2001). *Principals of high-achieving schools: What the research says.* Portland, OR: Northwest Regional Educational Laboratory.

Davenport, N., Schwartz, R. D., & Elliott, G. P. (1999). *Mobbing: Emotional abuse in the American workplace.* Ames, IA: Civil Society Publishing.

Diehl, D. B. (1993). *The relationship between teachers' coping resources, feelings of stress, and perceptions of the power tactics employed by the administrators.* Unpublished dissertation, Georgia State University, Atlanta.

Einarsen, S., Hoel, H., Zapf, D., & Cooper, C. (2003). *Bullying and emotional abuse in the workplace: International perspectives in research and practice.* London: Taylor & Francis.

Einarsen, S., & Skogstad, A. (1996). Bullying at work: Epidemiological findings in public and private organizations. *European Journal of Work and Organizational Psychology, 5*(2), 185–201.

Evans, R. (1996). *The human side of school change.* San Francisco: Jossey-Bass.

Farber, B. A. (1991). *Crisis in education: Stress and burnout in the American teacher.* San Francisco: Jossey-Bass.

Fineman, S. (Ed.). (1993). *Emotion in organizations.* Newbury Park, CA: Sage.

Fineman, S. (Ed.). (2000). *Emotion in organizations* (2nd ed.). Thousand Oaks, CA: Sage.

Fiske, S. T., & Neuberg, S. L. (1990). A continuum of impression formation, from category-based to individuating processing: Influences of information and motivation of attention and interpretation. In M. P. Zanna (Ed.), *Advances in experimental social psychology, Vol. 23* (pp. 1–74). New York: Academic Press.

Folger, R. (1993). Reactions to mistreatment at work. In J. K. Murningham (Ed.), *Social psychology in organizations: Advances in theory and research* (pp. 161–183). Englewood Cliffs, NJ: Prentice Hall.

Ford, C. V. (1996). *Lies! Lies!! Lies!!!: The psychology of deceit.* Washington, DC: American Psychiatric Press.

Fullan, M. (1997). *What's worth fighting for in the principalship?* New York: Teachers College Press.

Gardner, J. W. (1990). *On leadership.* New York: Free Press.

Gibb, C. (1954). Leadership. In G. Lindzey (Ed.), *Handbook of social psychology* (Vol. 1, pp. 877–920). Cambridge, MA: Adison-Wesley.

Ginsberg, R., & Davies, T. (2001, April). *The emotional side of leadership.* Paper presented at the annual meeting of the American Educational Research Association, Seattle, WA.

Glickman, C. D., Gordon, S.P., & Ross-Gordon, J. M. (2001). *Supervision and instructional leadership: A developmental approach* (6th ed.). Needham Heights, MA: Allyn & Bacon.

Goleman, D. (1995). *Emotional intelligence.* New York: Bantam Books.

Good, T. L. & Brophy, J. E. (1986). School effects. In M. C. Wittrock (Ed.), *Handbook of research on teaching* (3rd ed., pp. 570–602). New York: Macmillan.

Gunn, J. A., & Holdaway, E. A. (1986). Perceptions of effectiveness, influence, and satisfaction of senior high school principals. *Education Administration Quarterly, 22*(2), 43–62.

Hallinger, P., & Heck, R. H. (1996). Reassessing the principal's role in school effectiveness: A review of empirical research, 1980–1985. *Educational Administration Quarterly, 32*(1), 5–44.

Harlos, K. P., & Pinder, C. C. (2000). Emotion and injustice in the workplace. In S. Fineman (Ed.), *Emotion in organizations* (2nd ed., pp. 255–276). Thousand Oaks, CA: Sage.

Heck, R. H., Larsen, T. J., & Marcoulides, G. A. (1990). Instructional leadership and school achievement: Validation of a causal model. *Educational Administration Quarterly, 26*(2), 94–125.

Heck, R. H., & Marcoulides, G. A. (1993). Principal leadership behaviors and school achievement. *NASSP Bulletin, 77*(553), 20–28.

High, R., & Achilles, C. (1986). An analysis of influence-gaining behaviors of principals in schools of varying levels of instructional effectiveness. *Education Administration Quarterly, 22*(1), 111–119.

Hoachlander, G. (2001). Leading *school improvement: What research says.* Atlanta, GA: Southern Regional Education Board.

Hodgkinson, C. (1991). *Educational leadership: The moral art.* Albany: State University of New York Press.

Hornstein, H. A. (1996). *Brutal bosses and their prey.* New York: Riverhead Books.

Hornstein, H. A., Michela, J. L., Van Eron, A. M., Cohen, L. W., Heckelman, W. L., Sachse-Skidd, M., & Spencer, J. L. (1995). *Disrespectful supervisory behavior: Effects on some aspects of subordinates' mental health.* Unpublished manuscript, Teachers College, Columbia University.

Izard, C. E., & Youngstrom, E. A. (1996). The activation and regulation of fear and anxiety. In R. A. Dienstbier & D. A. Hope (Eds.), *Perspectives on anxiety, panic, and fear* (pp. 1–59). Lincoln: University of Nebraska Press.

Janis, I. L. (1982). *Groupthink: Psychological studies of policy decisions and fiascoes.* Boston: Houghton-Mifflin.

Joyce, B., & Calhoun, E. (1996). *Creating learning experiences: The role of instructional theory and research.* Alexandria, VA: Association for Supervision and Curriculum Development.

Joyce, B., & Showers, B. (1995). *Student achievement through staff development,* 2nd ed. New York: Longman.

Keashly, L. (1998). Emotional abuse in the workplace: Conceptual and empirical issues. *Journal of Emotional Abuse, 1*(1), 85–117.

Keashly, L., Trott, V., & MacLean, L. M. (1994). Abusive behavior in the workplace: A preliminary investigation. *Violence and Victims, 9*(4), 341–357.

Kekes, J. (1990). *Facing evil.* Princeton, NJ: Princeton University Press.

Kets de Vries, M. (1993). *Leaders, fools, and imposters: Essays on the psychology of leadership.* San Francisco: Jossey-Bass.

Kets de Vries, M. F. R. (1989). *Prisoners of leadership.* New York: Wiley.

Kimbrough, R. B. (1985). *Ethics: A course of study for educational leaders.* Arlington, VA: American Association of School Administrators.

Kimbrough, R. B., & Nunnery, M. Y. (1988). *Educational administration* (3rd ed.). New York: Macmillan.

Kipnis, D. (1972). Does power corrupt? *Journal of Personality and Social Psychology, 24*(1), 33–41.

Kipnis, D. (1976). *The powerholders.* Chicago: University of Chicago Press.

Kipnis, D. (2001). Using power: Newton's second law. In A.Y. Lee-Chai & J. A. Bargh (Eds.), *The use and abuse of power: Multiple perspectives on the causes of corruption* (pp. 3–18). Philadelphia, PA: Psychology Press.

Lambert, L., Walker, D., Zimmerman, D. P., Cooper, J. E., Lambert, M. D., Gardner, M. E., & Slack, P. J. F. (1995). *The constructivist leader.* New York: Teachers College Press.

Lee-Chai, A.Y., & Bargh, J. A. (2001). *The use and abuse of power: Multiple perspectives on the causes of corruption.* Philadelphia, PA: Psychology Press.

Lee-Chai, A.Y., Chen, S., & Chartrand, T. L. (2001). From Moses to Marcos: Individual differences in the use and abuse of power. In A.Y. Lee-Chai & J. A. Bargh (Eds.), *The use and abuse of power: Multiple perspectives on the causes of corruption* (pp. 57–74). Philadelphia, PA: Psychology Press.

Leithwood, K., Thomlinson, D., & Genge, M. (1996). Transformational school leadership. In K. Leithwood, J. Chapman, D. Corson, P. Hallinger, & A. Hart (Eds.), *International handbook of educational leadership and administration* (pp. 785–840). Dordrecht, The Netherlands: Kluwer Academic.

Leymann, H. (1990). *Mobbing and psychological terror at workplaces. Violence and victims,* 5(2), 119–126.

Lombardo, M. M., & McCall, Jr., M. W. (January, 1984). The intolerable boss. *Psychology Today,* 44–48.

Malen, B., & Ogawa, R. (1988). Professional-patron influence on site-based governance councils: A confounding case study. *Educational Evaluation and Policy Analysis, 10*(4), 251–270.

McClelland, D. C. (1987). *Human motivation.* New York: Cambridge.

McNeil, L. M. (1988). *Contradictions of control: School structure and school knowledge.* London: Routledge.

Murphy, J., & Louis, K. S. (Eds.). (1994a). *Reshaping the principalship: Insights from transformational reform efforts.* Thousand Oaks, CA: Corwin Press.

Murphy, J., & Louis, K.S. (1994b). Transformational change and the evolving role of the principal: Early empirical evidence. In J. Murphy & L. G. Beck (Eds.), *Reshaping the princi-*

palship: Insights from transformational reform efforts (pp. 20–53). Thousand Oaks, CA: Corwin Press.

Muth, R. (1989). Toward an integrative theory of power and educational organizations. *Educational Administration Quarterly, 20*(2), 25–42.

Namie, G. (2000). *U.S. hostile workplace survey 2000.* Benicia, CA: Campaign Against Workplace Bullying.

Namie, G., & Namie, R. (2000). *The bully at work: What you can do to stop the hurt and reclaim your dignity on the job.* Naperville, IL: Sourcebooks.

Neuman, J. H., & Baron, R. A. (1998). Workplace violence and workplace aggression: Evidence concerning specific forms, potential causes, and preferred targets. *Journal of Management 24*(3), 391–419.

NNLI (Northwestern National Life Insurance Company) (1993). *Fear and violence in the workplace.* Minneapolis, MN: Author.

Nyberg, D. (1981). *Power over power: What power means in ordinary life, how it is related to acting freely, and what it can do to contribute to a renovated ethics of education.* Ithaca, NY: Cornell University Press.

Olson, L. (1999, March). Demands for principals growing but candidates aren't applying. *Education Week, 18*(20), 20.

Pearson, C. (2000). *Workplace "incivility" study.* Chapel Hill: University of North Carolina.

Peck, M. S. (1983). *People of the lie: The hope for healing human evil.* New York: Simon & Shuster.

Price Spratlen, L. (1995). Interpersonal conflict which includes mistreatment in a university workplace. *Violence and Victims, 10*(4), 285–297.

Rayner, C. (1998). *Bullying at work.* Stoke-on-Kent, UK: Staffordshire University Business School.

Rayner, C., Hoel, H., & Cooper, C. (2002). *Workplace bullying: What we know, who is to blame, and what can we do?* New York: Taylor & Francis.

Reitzug, U. C., & Cross, B. E. (1994, April). *A multi-site study of site-based management in urban schools.* Paper presented at the Annual Meeting of the American Educational Research Association, New Orleans, LA.

Robinson, S. L., & Bennett, R. J. (1995). A typology of deviant workplace behaviors: A multidimensional scaling study. *Academy of Management Journal, 38*(2), 555–572.

Rusch, E. A. (1999). The experience of the piñata: Vexing problems. In F. K. Kochan, B. L. Jackson, & D. L. Duke (Eds.), *A thousand voices from the firing line: A study of educational leaders, their jobs, their preparation, and the problems they face* (pp. 29–43). (UCEA Monograph Series). Columbia, MO: University Council for Educational Administration.

Russell, B. (1938). *Power: A new social analysis.* New York: Norton.

Ryan, K. D., & Oestreich, D. K. (1991). *Driving fear out of the workplace: How to overcome the invisible barriers to quality, productivity, and innovation.* San Francisco: Jossey-Bass.

Sampson, R.V. (1965). *The psychology of power.* New York: Pantheon.

Schlechty, P. (1997). *Inventing better schools: An action plan for educational reform.* San Francisco: Jossey-Bass.

Schmuck, R., & Runkel, P. (1994). *Handbook of organization development in schools* (4th ed.). Prospect Heights, IL: Waveland Press.

Schön, D. A. (1987). *Educating the reflective practitioner: Toward a new design for teaching and learning in the professions.* San Francisco: Jossey-Bass.

Senge, P. (2000). *Schools that learn: A fifth discipline fieldbook for educators, parents, and everyone who cares about education.* New York: Doubleday.

Sergiovanni, T. J. (1996). *Moral leadership*. San Francisco: Jossey-Bass.

Sheppard, B. (1996). Exploring the transformational nature of instructional leadership. *The Alberta Journal of Educational Research, 42* (4), 325–344.

Silver, M. (1989). On knowing and self-deception. *Journal for the Theory of Social Behavior, 19*(2), 213–237.

Sorokin, P., & Lunden, W. (1959). *Power and morality: Who shall guard the guardians?* Boston: Porter Sargent.

Starratt, R. J. (1991). Building an ethical school: A theory for practice in educational leadership. *Educational Administration Quarterly, 27*(2), 185–202.

Steinberg, J. (1999, November 14). Federal funds for teachers reveal surprising hurdles. *New York Times*, p. 18.

Swedish National Board of Occupational Safety and Health (1993). *Statute Book*, Ordinance (AFS 1993: 17), Section 1 & 6.

Wald, P., & Castleberry, M. (2000). *Educators as learners: Creating a professional learning community in your school*. Alexandria, VA: Association for Supervision and Curriculum Development.

Walton, M. (1990). *Deming management at work*. New York: Perigee.

Wang, M. C., Haertel, G. D., & Walberg, H. J. (1993). Toward a knowledge base for school learning. *Review of Educational Research, 63*(3), 249–294.

Architect and Steward: Shaping a Vision of Learning: Examining the Role of the Principal in the Immersion of New Teachers into Existing Urban School Climates

Clint Taylor, Albert Jones, John Shindler, and Herminia Cadenas

One of the problems that continue to confound principals and other school leaders is why so few beginners remain in teaching. The problem is most acute among the urban teacher population. In Los Angeles, more than fifty percent of first-year non-credentialed teachers leave the Los Angeles Unified School District after their first year. More troubling is that those who leave, in many cases, are those judged to have the greatest potential to be excellent teachers. As a result, Los Angeles and other urban areas face deficits of both quantity and quality in their teacher forces.

While teacher education programs have responded to the high demand for teachers by increasing the number of graduates, the problem at the root of high attrition rates has not been well addressed (Bondy, 2002; Fox & Singletary, 1986). Improving the quality of teacher preparation has been a step in the right direction (Zeichener & Gore, 1990), yet what happens when these new teachers enter the field appears more influential in the shaping of their practice than their formal preparation (Cuddapah, 2002; Jordell, 1987; Zeichener & Gore, 1990).

However, too often the pedagogical paradigm the new candidate takes away from the university conflicts with the paradigms of the schools they enter (Angelle, 2002). This disjuncture can create stress and cognitive dissonance in new teachers and lead to their disillusionment (Bondy, 2002). This study examines the role the principal plays in shaping the experiences, perceptions, and adjustment of novice teachers as they are faced with beginning their career in schools with established climates. The principals' role is also examined in relation to the existing forces in the school, the university training received by these new teachers, and their incoming values and expectations concerning children and schooling.

Clint Taylor, California State University, Los Angeles
Albert Jones, California State University, Los Angeles
John Shindler, California State University, Los Angeles
Herminia Cadenas, California State University, Los Angeles

METHODOLOGY

An emergent qualitative design was used to examine the experience of new teacher immersion from both the perspective of novice teachers and principals. The principal participants were chosen from four urban and three suburban schools within the California State University, Los Angeles, service area, all of which enrolled a majority of English language learners. The principals ranged in experience from two to twenty-seven years. The principal participants represented diverse ethnic and cultural backgrounds. The principal participants showed a real willingness to discuss their ideas and beliefs about novice teachers, and their strategies for supporting the needs of their new hires. Each of the principal participants was interviewed separately using a structured interview protocol.

The seven teacher participants all received their training from California State University, Los Angeles. Each of the participants was trained in pedagogical methods including progressive classroom management strategies. Each of the teacher participants had taken a position in a local urban school. These participants were purposefully selected to reflect a range of ideologies and backgrounds. Four taught elementary school, two taught high school and one taught at a middle school. The participants reflected a range of ethnic and cultural backgrounds; three were male and four female. The teacher participants took part in four focus group interview sessions of two hours each.

Data from each set of interviews were transcribed and analyzed after each session. Emergent themes were developed using a grounded theory approach for data analysis. Analytic themes were triangulated by verification within the research team, previous research and ultimately the participants themselves. The result of the analysis produced a three-factor research framework used for interpreting and displaying data.

ANALYTIC FRAMEWORK

An organizing theme for the study arose from the implications of a statement repeatedly expressed by many of the participants, "That won't work in my school." This belief provided a multi-layered context for a holistic data analysis. In essence, the statement implied that what was taught at the university was neither effective nor acceptable in the schools where the beginning teachers worked.

When the beginning teacher participants in the study suggested that "That won't work in my school," this raises the question; what does *that* mean? What practices constitute what were perceived as the strategies and approaches that would not work in these schools?

In the area of classroom management, a common classifying system known as the Teacher Behavior Continuum is employed to categorize classroom management models from those most teacher-centered to those most student-centered (Edwards, 2000). The investigators, applying the rationale for this continuum and extending upon the work of Coloroso (1994) and Canter and Canter (1976), devised a four-cell matrix of teaching practice classification by inserting a y-axis across the continuum that ranges from productive and highly functional to dysfunctional and unproductive (see Figure 1). These quadrants can be assigned numbers from one to four and pro-

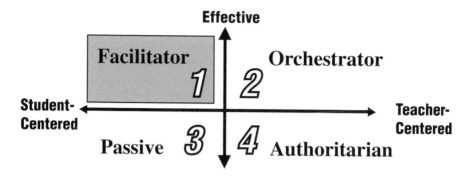

Figure 1. Four-Quadrant Matrix of Teaching-Style Orientation and Practice

vide four distinct quadrants for classifying teacher behavior. According to this model, One schools are characterized by student-centered communities that feature self-directed learning and cast the teacher as a facilitator. Their climate could be inferred to be highly productive and functional. Two schools would also be classified as highly productive and functional climates, but these schools are teacher-centered places where teaching is well orchestrated and the teacher is conductor. Three and Four schools exhibit dysfunctional and unproductive climates in as much as they do not promote student motivation and/or emotional health. Three schools may be student-centered, but passive leadership and instruction prevail while students' efforts are self-centered. Four schools are teacher-centered where leadership aims to forge conformity by repression, which often gives rise to rebellion among the students.

RESULTS

New teacher participants had previously developed a classroom management plan as part of their credential program. In many cases, these management plans described the practices of a One School teacher. Yet, when asked how they would classify the management style/culture in the schools they had entered, the participants suggested that their schools could be most accurately classified as at best, Two Schools, at worst, Four Schools. They said they did not see One or Three Schools in common use. They added:

> Our schools are very strict, very Canter-centered (2 orientation). Everything is very external, very extrinsic.

> Our school follows deanism—kids that act out are sent to the dean.

Also, participants suggested that the discipline climate of the schools was driven primarily by the beliefs of the veteran teachers.

> The younger teachers are more Two and the experienced teachers more Four. There is kind of a split between the new thinking and the old-school thinking.

Some experienced teachers just don't care. Kids are going to write standards even if they go to training and learn that is a bad idea. [Writing standards is a common method of punishment in which the students write many times the rule that has been violated—well-known as "write-offs."]

When I ask my colleagues for advice, what I get are [Four school] suggestions like "just write names on the board and have them write standards."

In addition, participants reported the belief that the One school approaches would require their students to make a significant adjustment inasmuch as it would be so unfamiliar.

If the students came to a One classroom, they would not know what to do after 4 years of Four teaching.

I try to be more student-centered and the students get really uncomfortable. They look at me and say basically "just tell us what to do."

I want to see someone teach with a One style in an inner-city school and be successful.

THE PRINCIPALS' PERCEPTION

When the principals were asked how many of their new teachers possess classroom management plans that reflect a philosophy of learning, all seven reported that few if any of their new teachers presented such plans. Furthermore, the principals observed that the teachers saw no connection between managing a classroom and promoting higher achievement among their students. One remarked, "My new teachers have tunnel vision about their work. They are hung up on trying the latest idea promoted in the teachers' lounge." When asked why they believed this occurred, two of the principals reported that beginners are capricious and have not thought about how they view children and how their views influence their day-to-day work with students.

When asked what assistance they give their new teachers, most principals suggested offering help in the form of sending them to workshops such as the popular "assertive discipline" series. However, the principals believe most training to be ineffectual because it did not lead their new teachers to the development of a philosophical rationale for their actions. One principal quipped, "New teachers don't know *why* they do what they do."

To support this contention, it appeared from the data that participants who lacked philosophical anchors more readily default to the school's existing climate or the culture as expressed by the veteran teachers. In this urban district these existing climates seem to be heavily influenced by the approaches of Canter's Assertive Discipline Program (Canter, 1976). The Canter program could be said to produce what might be classified as Two-style practices. This was especially prevalent with elementary level participants.

The principal participants expressed dissatisfaction with the quality of the novice teachers due to the principals' perceptions that novice teachers lack an understanding of the mission and vision of the schools and the districts they enter. Moreover, the principals stated that the novice teachers lack the skills to create classrooms that are consistent with that mission and vision. However, the principals themselves had difficulty in articulating the mission and vision of the school beyond the state and national directives of improving student achievement; i.e., test scores through standards-based instruction. Though the principals accepted this directive is beneficial to the academic development of children, they showed an inability to articulate their philosophical beliefs to create school climates that achieve. The principal participants also expressed a lack of control in the development of distinct school climates that promote learning. First, they stated that external forces in the form of district and state mandates defined the existing school mission and vision and in turn the learning climate of the school. In addition, the principals related the significance of veteran teachers in determining the school climate. The principals related an acceptance of the power of veteran teachers at school climate construction. They reported that veteran teachers had developed their own distinct vision of a school climate that promotes achievement based on their experiences and acculturation into the school. Principals said that they found difficulty in transformation of school climate due to the teachers' prior acculturation to the school environment and faculty. As a result, the values and beliefs expressed by veteran teachers became the accepted manner of dealing with students and in turn the accepted school climate.

THE MISPERCEPTION OF A LOGICAL/LINEAR PATH TO NEW TEACHER INDUCTION

It might be inferred from the logic applied in teacher training that there is a linear relationship among the incoming values of the teacher, the university and the schools where they work. This logic implies that all learning leads in a developmental progression toward improved practice. However, the data in this study suggested that the values that drive new teachers and the values of the schools they enter are often at odds. Furthermore, the values of the school are at odds with those of the university where the teacher was trained. These conflicts became evident when the new teacher participants reported that very often they jettisoned their management plans when they attempted to achieve a functional set of strategies with their students.

The data suggest that it is common for new teachers to enter a school with certain values and beliefs but during their first year of teaching they are faced with the challenge of negotiating and reevaluating these values and beliefs to be consistent with the existing culture of the school (see Figure 2). While the new teachers' values may vary due to many factors including their university training, the participants in this study reported a willingness to adopt One school approaches and strategies. Yet because these new teachers have not seen One school in operation, their ability to replicate One school environments is not well-grounded.

The new teacher participants entered schools that exhibited a wide range and combination of practices, from One to Four, but most were Two and/or Four. For many of the beginners, this created a problem. Their values clashed with those of their school. This conflict took the form of cognitive dissonance, job uncertainty, and disagreements with their mentors, administrators, or other veteran teachers. The conflicts with

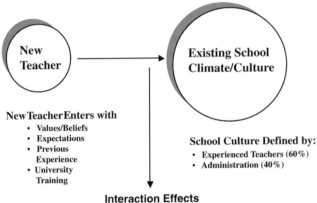

Figure 2.   New Teacher Interaction with Existing School Climate

their principals became the most unsettling. The teacher participants reported that this conflict forced them to ask themselves whether they were willing to pay the price of disapproval to retain their emerging beliefs that they felt were best for their students.

Many of the teacher participants reported that they faced the choice of fitting in or being marginalized; to do what they thought made sense or to do what worked in their school; to ultimately align themselves with the culture of the university or the culture of the school in which they found themselves. These participants explained that the expectations that they had entering the school were not reinforced by the actions of the administration or the veteran teachers. First, these new teachers found behaviors among the veterans that placed their needs above the needs of the students.

> The advice I got from many teachers is "don't smile 'til Christmas."

> They asked the teachers to be there early and someone said, "that is not in our contract."

Secondly, these participants noticed an unwillingness of the veterans to create an environment in which all the stakeholders were respected.

> Unless the students are empowered, I don't think it will work and I don't know how the culture will change.

> There are not only physical practical barriers; there are emotional barriers that create separations in the school.

Thirdly, the new teacher participants found the administration ineffectual in changing the culture of the school defined heavily by the actions of the veteran teachers and the expectations of external forces.

I think everyone has to buy in. I noticed that the administration has an expectation but everybody has to buy in.

I don't blame the administration [for not doing enough to change the situation]. They have other things to worry about—all these standards and tests and . . . standards to meet. All those assessments. They are not in a position to support us being [One school teachers].

HOW PRINCIPALS' VIEW THE NEEDS OF THEIR NEW TEACHERS

When asked to cite key reasons for beginning teachers' failure to demonstrate a coherent and effective approach to their classroom management, the principal participants suggested that it was a result of poor lesson planning, a lack of instructional savvy, and a lack of time to properly prepare plans, with most identifying the absence of a personal philosophy about the best way to promote learning as the most notable cause of drift and disillusionment. The principals also stated that few if any beginners ask the principal for help. In fact, many observed a conspicuous avoidance of the principal during the first years of a teacher's work. They suggested that beginners often want to know about routine procedures, how to obtain supplies, how to deal with serious examples of misconduct and other "survival issues" as one principal characterized them. Another principal felt that his beginning teachers didn't know what to ask, which compounds their isolation from him.

Overall, the principal participants suggested that few, if any, of the beginning teachers actively sought help from them. However, three of the seven principals responded to this tendency by requiring new teachers to meet with them. They reported holding regular (at least monthly) meetings with their new teachers to discuss their problems and concerns. These principals embrace the opportunity to shape the views of their beginners, thereby building a common culture for productive learning. Cultivating this shared vision seemed to help promote a more intentional climate in the schools where it was practiced.

While the principal participants typically viewed the climate at their schools as well-defined and conducive to professional growth, the experience of the teacher participants was not often consistent with this characterization. New teacher participants suggested that in most cases the climates in which they found themselves were more accidental than intentional (see Figure 3).

Moreover, the degree of intentionality seemed to contribute to the teacher participants' confidence in their ability to navigate successfully the demands and challenges of a new position in a new career. Teacher participants recognized that in the absence of what would be considered an intentional climate, the resulting disintegration led to more apathetic and uncritical practice school-wide. These participants expressed a deep awareness of the effects of climate of their schools.

There is no collective/intentional culture or set of expectation. We do not create the culture, it just happens, and when we just let it happen then (the culture) is just this accident. What is produced is something that we are not very proud of . . . I think that

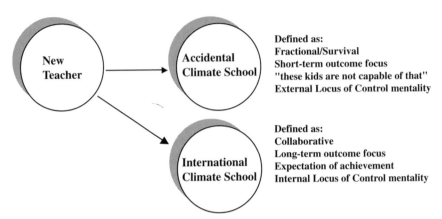

Defined as:
Fractional/Survival
Short-term outcome focus
"these kids are not capable of that"
External Locus of Control mentality

Defined as:
Collaborative
Long-term outcome focus
Expectation of achievement
Internal Locus of Control mentality

Figure 3.   Comparison of Intentional and Accidental School Climates

mission statements and vision statement are great, but without the school having a collective sense of what they are about. . . . The staff needs to have buy in.

At my school [right now] there is virtually no time to work with anyone else. The meetings are always business-oriented. There is not really any governance for the teachers
right now. We are working on a way for teachers to have input. I just think it would be
so much more powerful if I/we could work collaboratively during the day.

The development of an intentional school climate was shown to be essential in the
success of these novice teachers, supporting earlier research (Bondy, 2002: Clement,
1998; Hope, 1999). Shown in both the principal participant interviews and the focus
group findings, the creation of an intentional climate had a significant impact on the
development and retention of beginning teachers. One new teacher participant put it
this way:

So new teachers who see things getting better will stay in a school as they see progress
and the bad teachers will leave as they see their style becoming inconsistent with the
emerging culture. Likewise, the new teacher will get burned out because they see that
nothing is changing and they feel like the culture is unfriendly to their values, and so
they quit.

Yet, the principals, unlike the teachers, did not express a lack of intentionality in
the operation of their schools. They explained that the improvement of student
achievement is a well-accepted goal among the faculty and that a great deal of professional development reinforces their schools dedication to this goal. Nevertheless,
the principals did express that veteran teachers played a great role in the creation of
school climate. To counter this phenomenon, the principals related the need to take
an active role in the acculturation of beginning teachers. From the data, the need for
a deliberate effort by principals in the acculturation of new teachers appeared critical in promoting both a positive experience for the teachers and simultaneously an
intentional school climate.

DISCUSSION

It appears from the data that school climate may be a significant variable in the new teachers' thoughts and feelings related to their first year. While training and support were useful, a school with a sense of purpose that was defined by a critical reflection of practice was more welcoming to the new teacher than a school with no such sense of purpose. As the new teacher participants suggested when there was no sense of purpose, they experienced a climate defined by accidental and haphazard practices. These practices were often the result of less critical reflection and a less student-centered mindset. Principal participants who promoted a more intentional climate seemed to reap a more thoughtful brand of practice, practices that were more consistent with what is considered "best practice" at most universities. It appeared that the ability and effort of the principal to create and promote an intentional climate was essential in encouraging and supporting superior quality teaching from these novices. It could be inferred from these data that these efforts may in turn lead to an increased willingness on the part of these beginning teachers to remain in the profession. Moreover, the process of acculturation and inner conflict resolution nurtured between the beginning teacher and the administrator may produce greater linear relationship between university teacher education training and induction to the teaching profession.

IMPLICATIONS FOR PRINCIPALS

1. The principal appears to be the stakeholder who is in the best position to create the intentional climate that will promote a sound and coherent induction climate. In the absence of administrative leadership the most powerful teacher constituency will dictate the climate.
2. Principals should assert their role as the chief determiner of the school's climate and culture.
3. Principals should reflect on their relations with veteran teachers and challenge their "folk wisdom" which may inhibit new teachers as they attempt to apply what they have learned during their university preparation programs.
4. With regard to the immersion of new teachers, the principal's most important roles are *architect* of the school's shared vision of learning and *steward* of this vision with new teachers and veterans alike.

IMPLICATIONS FOR TEACHER PREPARATION/INDUCTION

1. New teacher acculturation does not appear to be within the exclusive control of any single stakeholder within the chain of the teacher preparation/induction system. Thus issues affecting retention can be positively or negatively affected by any link in the chain, and coordination among members appears necessary for successful teacher preparation/induction.
2. School climate cannot be viewed as homogenous. Nor can teacher immersion be viewed as a common experience. The interaction of the teacher's beliefs and

training with those of the school climate that they enter can produce multiple results.
3. Institutions of higher education might consider preparing their candidates with skills for cultural immersion as well as for best practice.
4. K–12 schools that make an effort toward cultivating an intentional school climate will likely be better equipped to help new teachers face the substantial demands related to the social, psychological, and pedagogical transitions into teaching.

CONCLUSION

It is often the case that new teacher candidates graduate from institutions of higher education with idealistic views related to classroom management and the job of teaching. Constructivist and progressive, learner-centered approaches are frequently advocated by university faculty. While this trend is encouraging in many respects, it often puts the new teacher in a difficult position when they find that those same values are not shared by those in their school. New teachers are often torn between conforming to existing environments and doing what they see as most noble; survival versus long-term gains; doing what seems to work versus what they feel makes the most sense. Principals are often unaware that this conflict is taking place. Moreover those administrators that are unable to take an intentional approach to constructing a school climate/culture may find that new teacher acculturation is more accidental and therefore more uncertain. While this research sheds new light on the dynamics between institutions of higher education and K–12, it is clear from the alarming rate of teacher dropout in our urban schools that more emphasis must be placed on effective teacher induction and the crucial role of the principal in supporting the induction and acculturation of new teachers into intentional school climates. In our view, the principal could stem this unfortunate acculturation by taking charge of new teachers; supporting their attempts to practice what they learn at the university, and by challenging the status quo environments promoted by entrenched teachers.

REFERENCES

Angelle, P. (2002, April). *Socialization experiences of beginning teachers in differentially effective schools.* Paper presented at the Annual Meeting of the American Educational Research Association, New Orleans, LA.
Bondy, E. (2002, April). *Who learns what and how? An emerging theory of learning in teacher education.* Paper presented at the Annual Meeting of the American Educational Research Association, New Orleans, LA
Canter, L., & Canter, M. (1976). *Assertive discipline: A take charge approach for today's education.* Seal Beach, CA: Canter and Associates.
Clement, M. (1998). *Beginning teachers' perceptions of their stress, problems, and planned retention in teaching.* Paper presented to the meeting of the Midwest Association of Teacher Education, Urbana, IL.
Coloroso, B. (1994). *Kids are worth it: Giving your child the gift of inner discipline.* New York: William Morrow.

Cuddapah, J. (2002, April). *Supporting new teachers through mentoring relationships.* Paper presented at the Annual Meeting of the American Educational Research Association, New Orleans, LA.

Edwards, C. (2000). *Effective classroom management.* New York: Allyn Bacon.

Fox, S., & Singletary, T. (1986). Deductions about supportive induction. *Journal of Teacher Education, 37*(2), 12–15.

Hope, W. (1999). Principals' orientation and induction activities as factors in teacher retention. *Clearing House, 73*(1), 54–56.

Jordell, K. (1987). Structural and personal influences in the socialization of beginning teachers. *Teaching and Teacher Education, 3*(3), 165–177.

Zeichener, K., & Gore, J. (1990). Teacher socialization. In *Handbook of Research on Teacher Education* (pp. 329–348). Madison: University of Wisconsin.

Democratic Leadership:
Meeting the Needs of Our Children[1]

Patrick M. Jenlink and Karen E. Jenlink

Being an educational leader today isn't easy. Being an educational leader who is able to foster democratic practice and nurture advanced citizenship is even harder. Educational leadership is about advanced citizenship: about justice, equity, caring, freedom, and about ensuring the rights, hopes, and success of all children. Currently, leading the educational enterprise, on all levels, has become an increasingly problematic and unavoidably political activity, complicated further by the growing complexity of cultural and linguistic diversity that is redefining the very essence of our society and educational systems. We are challenged with meeting the needs of our children in uncertain times. Uncertainty for children fostered by educational inequities (failure to close the achievement gap in schools for non-White and poor White children) and uncertainty for all by social inequities (failure to close the income and resource gap in society). Amidst this uncertainty, Giroux (2002) draws our attention to the necessity of "rethinking the role of educators and the politics of schooling" (p. 1138), as America is redefined by the "cataclysmic political, economic, and legal changes inaugurated by the monstrous events of September 11" (p. 1138). The implications for education of such uncertainties and changes draw attention to the very meaning of democracy, freedom, and social justice. A pressing question guides current discourses, "What type of leadership do we need to meet the challenges confronting schools in America today?"

Dewey (1916, 1927) understood the importance of education in a democracy and the nature of the problems often confronted by the public. The influence of recent domestic policy events, such as the No Child Left Behind Act[2], the impact of state standards and accountability, a redefining of political democracy, and the need for a strong democratic citizenry have directed attention to reconsidering leadership for

Patrick M. Jenlink, Stephen F. Austin State University
Karen E. Jenlink, Stephen F. Austin State University

schools—leadership that is concerned with democracy, freedom, and social justice (Freire, 1998; Giroux, 1994; Starratt, 2001).

Arguably, leadership preparation in current times has not focused "on how to educate prospective administrators and teachers to address the problems facing public schools in the United States as a crisis of citizenship, authority, and ethics" (Giroux, 1994, p. 33). Recent domestic policy events and the political fallout of September 11 have cast a heightened sense of need for strong leadership—concerned with democracy, freedom, and social justice. Unfortunately, as Kincheloe (1999) notes,

> the last quarter of the twentieth century has been marked by a crisis of democracy—a crisis seldom referenced in the public conversation or in educational institutions. The crisis has been initiated by a growing imbalance of power and a perverted concept of neutrality that undermines analysis of the crisis. (p. 74)

Giroux (1992) argues that the crisis lies, in part, "in a refusal to address how particular forms of authority are secured and legitimized at the expense of cultural democracy, critical citizenship, and basic human rights" (p. 7). Problematically, schools exist in a democracy that is marked "by an undemocratic economy, by undemocratic communications and media industries, by undemocratic cultural institutions, and by a form of representative government many see as serving special interests and itself more than the broad needs of the people" (Starratt, 2001, p. 341). Respectively, public schools and colleges of education are equally affected by the undemocratic nature of society.

In this paper, the authors argue the need for reconsidering democratic leadership beyond modernist definitions. Legislation, policy, and educational trends in Texas schools will serve as a backdrop for contextualizing the need for democratic leadership. The authors will examine specific considerations with respect to preparing democratic leaders, particularly the need to prepare preservice teachers and administrators conjointly (Heckman, 1996), *in situ*—communities of practice (Lave & Wenger, 1991).

EDUCATION AND THE RETREAT FROM DEMOCRACY

Nearly two decades ago, Barbara Finkelstein (1984), in *Education and the Retreat from Democracy in the United States, 1979–198?*, noted that contemporary reformers

> seem to be recalling public education from its traditional utopian mission—to nurture a critical and committed citizenry that would stimulate the processes of political and cultural transformation and refine and extend the workings of political democracy. . . . Reformers seem to imagine public schools as economic rather than political instrumentalities. They forge no new visions of political and social possibilities. Instead, they call public schools to industrial and cultural service exclusively. . . . Reformers have disjoined their calls for educational reform from calls for a redistribution of power and authority, and the cultivation of cultural forms celebrating pluralism and diversity. (p. 280)

We are three years deep into the new millennium, and Finkelstein's words seem to describe current political reform agendas. Standards and accountability, No Child

Left Behind, and the deprofessionalization agendas of the conservative right continue to recall public education from its democratic imperatives.

Meier (2000) notes that "because of the disconnection between the pubic and its schools, the power to protect or support them now lies increasingly in the hands of public or private bodies that have no immediate stake in the daily life of the students" (p. 15). Reflecting on the past two decades, current federal and domestic policy, high-stakes testing proponents, and advocates of deregulating teaching are engaged in "ideological surgery" on public schools, "cutting them away from the fate of social justice and political democracy completely and grafting them onto elite corporate, industrial, military, and cultural interests" (Finkelstein, 1984, p. 281).

As Kincheloe (1999) notes, "the last quarter of the twentieth century [was] marked by a crisis of democracy—a crisis seldom referenced in the public conversation or in educational institutions. The crisis has been initiated by a growing imbalance of power and a perverted concept of neutrality that undermines analysis of the crisis" (p. 74). Evidence of this imbalance of power is found in current and recent past efforts of the standing conservative political agenda that has resulted in harmful policy effects on the quality of life and education of African American and other racial minorities (Feagin, 2000; Lugg, 1996).

More specifically, current debates concerning standards and high-stakes testing acknowledge both the inequities and the effects of accountability systems on poor and minority youth. This is in large part because schools for such students are teaching to the test and, thus, weakening the curriculum and widening the gap between the White middle- and upper-class students and the low-income children from minority schools (Anderson, 2001; Carnoy, Loeb, & Smith, 2000; Fuller & Johnson, 2001; Haney, 2000, 2001; Klein, 2001; Klein, Hamilton, McCaffrey, & Stecher, 2000; McNeil, 2000; McNeil & Valenzuela, 2000; Valenzuela, 1999).

DEMOCRACY AND EDUCATION

In *Democracy and Education*, Dewey (1916) identified the "widening of the area of shared concerns, and the liberation of greater diversity of personal capacities" (p. 87) as hallmarks of democracy. He noted that only after "greater individualization on one hand, and a broader community of interest on the other have come into existence" (p. 87), could these characteristics be sustained by voluntary disposition and interest, which must be made possible by means of education. While Dewey's ideas of democracy and education were never realized during his life time, and were often the focus of criticism during the progressive era, nonetheless, the role of education in a democratic society has been a constant and central element of education discourse. However, as Dewey stated, "the conception of education as a social process and function has no definite meaning until we define the kind of society we have in mind" (1916, p. 97).

Democracy

Democracy is not an all-or-nothing affair, but a definition of degree; societies and institutions can vary in both the extent and the intensity of their commitment to democratic practice. Therefore, there are many degrees and definitions of democracy, each marked by its idiosyncratic nature within particular cultural-political contexts. Dewey (1916) explains that democracy is

> more than a form of government; it is primarily a mode of associated living, a conjoint communicated experience. The extension in space of the number of individuals who participate in an interest so that each has to refer his own action to that of others, and to consider the action of others to give point and direction to his own, is equivalent to the breaking down of those barriers of class, race, and national territory which kept men from perceiving the full import of their activity. (p. 87)

Democracy is not merely a belief in a form of government. The "foundation of democracy is faith in the capacities of human nature; a faith in human intelligence" (Dewey, 1937, p. 458). Democracy is belief in freedom, "the basic freedom of mind and of whatever degree of freedom of action and experience is necessary to produce freedom of intelligence" (p. 459). A democracy ensures freedom of "expression, general diffusion of knowledge, the marketplace of ideas, and open pursuit of truth so that citizens continuously educate themselves to participate, learn, and govern beyond the limited ideas of individuals" (Glickman, 2003, p. 274). As Dewey (1916) states, a democratic society "makes provision for participation for the good of all its members on equal terms and which secures flexible readjustment of its institutions through the interaction of the different forms of associated life" (p. 105).

Important to defining democracy is the caution posited by Scheurich (2003). Proposing a definition of democracy, however historical or radical the definition, and

> then proceeding to build a view of educational reform (or societal reform) on that definition without taking serious and careful account of dominant social assumptions and practices, is dangerously naïve (and by "dangerously naïve" I mean the naïveté itself is a social practice with dangerous effects). (p. 288)

Relatedly, American democracy, over the past decade, has been devalued and dismissed in reform proposals that "pit a romanticized view of the laws and logic of the market against the discourse of ethics, political agency, and social responsibility" (Giroux, 1992, p. 5). A new American naïveté that calls for "schools to be dispensers of an unproblematic cultural tradition in which the emergence of cultural difference is seen as a sign of fragmentation and a departure from rather than an advance toward democracy" (Giroux, 1992, p. 5). The responsibility of determining the type of democratic society befalls the citizenry, both the adult citizenry and the future generations of citizenry. Therein lies the critical connection between education and society—the educating of a critical democratic citizenry.

Education

Amy Gutmann (1987) explains that "the primary aim of a democratic theory of education is not to offer solutions to all the problems plaguing our educational institutions, but to consider ways of resolving those problems that are compatible with a commitment to democratic values" (p. 11). With this aim in mind, is important to note that just as there are many degrees and definitions of democracy, there are "multiple, legitimate definitions of 'a good education' and 'well-educated,' and it is desirable to acknowledge that plurality" (Meier, 2000, p. 16). A healthy democratic, pluralistic society is characterized by openly differing viewpoints. Juxtaposed to mainstream (consensus) views, "alternative views that challenge the consensus are critical to the society's health. Young people need to be exposed to competing views, and to adults debating choices about what's most important" (Meier, 2000, p. 16). Amidst the tensions of standards and accountability, growing diversity, and political mandates, education for democracy is a central concern. Torres (1998) focuses the concern of education for democracy:

> how to build better schools, intellectually richer schools, particularly for those who are the bottom of the society; how to build a democratic multicultural curriculum where everybody learns from the rich diversity of the society and where the trends toward balkanization and growing separatism in modern societies can be prevented and even reversed. School should play a central role in the constitution of democratic discourse and citizenship. (p. 259)

Toward effecting solutions that address the concern of education for democracy, "a democratic theory of education [must provide] principles that, in the face of our social disagreements, help us judge (a) who should have authority to make decisions about education, and (b) what the moral boundaries of that authority are" (Gutmann, 1987, p. 11). Education for democracy concerns the conjoining of individuals through communicative action, the sharing of personal voice in the "between" space that forms a public sphere, wherein individuals participate in identifying social issues and share in social action to address the issues, thereby breaking down the barriers of class, race, ethnicity, language, and culture.

Making education for democracy problematic, high-stakes testing has, as Giroux (1994) explains,

> become the new ideological weapon in developing standardized curricula that ignore cultural diversity, in defining knowledge narrowly in terms of discrete skills and decontextualized bodies of information, and in ruthlessly expunging the language of ethics from the broader purpose of teaching and schooling. (pp. 32–33)

As state and federal policy exact stronger controls on curriculum and testing, "standardized testing can become a more sophisticated technology of control—a form of official surveillance that controls populations through normalization" (Anderson, 2001, p. 323). Such normalization leads to a normativity, a standing ideology of socially reinforced or iterated norms (Scheurich, 2003). When education is considered in terms of being a form of cultural capital, then there is a need to examine the relationship between cultural capital and social capital. This is needed in large part because in the past two decades, "we have seen an inequitable redistribution of economic and social capital that has made social equity more elusive than at any time in our history since the 1920s" (Anderson, 2001, pp. 324–325).

Relatedly, when we reflect on the ideological control of high-stakes testing and its widening of the achievement gap, we recognize the marginalizing of non-White and poor White students. Problematically, the majority has established what could be called a normativity, a standing ideology of socially reinforced or iterated norms (Scheurich, 2003). Thus, what democracy and democratic education means to the majority and what it means to a minority is often vastly different. This, then, is political because minority "realities" are dominated, suppressed, ignored by the majority "reality'"(Scheurich, 2003, p. 291).

There remains an American naïveté in matters of education and democracy, evident in the differing realities for White majority and non-White minorities, differing realities of democracy and democratic education that continue to advantage some while disadvantaging others. Such naïveté will not be addressed unless we create "in-between" spaces in our communities, and more importantly in our schools. Creating such spaces—democratic spaces—will require a rethinking of educational leadership and by extension education that is animated by democratic imperatives and a concern for social justice and equity.

MEETING OUR CHILDREN'S NEEDS

What do our children need? Our children need a sense of hope and social responsibility, a realization of the possibilities before them and an expectation that they can achieve these possibilities. Our children need a promise that inequities and injustices won't become their inheritance as it was for their parents. Our children—all children—need to believe that the teachers and schools they visit each day are concerned with helping them learn, and not places where their identities are less important than their scores on tests. However, if we look at schools today, within the larger cultural-political context of the American educational system, this is not the story being written.

Ayers (2000), writes that the purpose of education in a democracy is to break down barriers, to overcome obstacles, to open doors, minds, and possibilities . . . to assist people in seeing the world through their own eyes, interpreting and analyzing through their own experiences and thinking, feeling themselves capable of representing, manifesting, or even, if they choose, transforming all that is before them. Education, then, is linked to freedom, to the ability to see and also to alter, to understand and also to reinvent, to know and also to change to a world as we find it. (pp. 67–68)

This is what our children need. "Can we imagine this at the core of all schools, even poor city schools?" (Ayers, 2000, p. 68).

Children need schools hallmarked by the "possibilities and opportunities for students to share their experiences, work in relations that emphasize care and concern for others, and be introduced to forms of knowledge that provide them with the opportunity to take risks and fight for a quality of life in which all human beings benefit" (Giroux, 1994, p. 44). This means that educators must replace pedagogical practices which emphasize accountability and disciplinary control with practices that are based on a democratic authority, ones which enable students to develop critical voices and engage in critical analysis and to make choices regarding what is most desirable and morally appropriate for living in a just and democratic society. Equally important is the need for students to engage in civic-minded action in order to resist the normativity of standing ideologies and remove the social and political constraints that victimize members of this society, preventing them from the promise of a democracy for all. We must understand as Dewey (1939) argued, that the "task of democracy is forever that of creation of a freer and more humane experience in which all share and to which all contribute" (p. 245).

THE NEED FOR DEMOCRATIC LEADERSHIP

Hannah Arendt (1958), in *The Human Condition*, wrote about the importance of diverse persons speaking to one another as "who" and not "what" they are and, in so doing, creating an "in-between" among themselves. The human condition that children face in our schools today suggests that we have reached a point in education where we are charged with bringing into being a space "in which things are saved from destruction of time" (p. 57), a space where all children are prepared for their future. Arendt went on to say that the reality of such a space will rely

On the simultaneous presence of innumerable perspectives and aspects in which the common world presents itself and for which no common measurement or denominator can ever be devised. For though the common world is the common meeting ground of all, those who are present have different locations in it. . . . Being seen and heard by others derive their significance from the fact that everybody sees and hears from a different position. . . . Only where things can be seen by many in a variety of aspects without changing their identity, so that those who are gathered around them know they see sameness in utter diversity, can worldly reality truly and reliably appear. (1958, p. 57)

Creating such a reality will require mediating the normativity that conditions our schools and our society—the standing ideology that widens the gaps in cultural and social capital. It will require that we critically examine the redefining of political democracy and equally important that we critically examine the distancing of education from democracy.

Crisis in Democracy

Democracy, by its nature, is an unfinished project, continually open to reform and reinterpretation. As a way of life, it produces a "set of principles on which institutions, schools in particular, are constructed" (Kincheloe, 1999, p. 73). In order to sustain democracy within society, the balance between the values of individuality and community must be maintained. In this context "democracy is a value system, a method of associating with one another, a way of confronting problems together within the boundaries of solidarity, and a means of validating human dignity" (p. 73).

However, there is currently a crisis in democracy and a crisis in American education. More specifically, there is a crisis in leadership as "exemplified in the debates that have been waged around the issues of choice, testing, and diversity that have recently informed the educational reform movement" (Giroux, 1994, p. 31). Ayers (2000), delineating the crisis to American schools, notes that it is "neither natural nor uniform, but particular and selective; it is a crisis of the poor, of the cities, of Latino and African-American communities. All the structures of privilege and oppression apparent in the larger society are mirrored in our schools" (p. 66).

The crisis of leadership and schooling has to be seen as part of the wider crisis of democracy itself. Past and present efforts, on the part of neoconservatives, to define leadership through technical-rational and structural-functional lenses work to "develop a notion of educational leadership that undermines the responsibility of public service, ruptures the relationship between schools and the community, and diverts educators from improving access to and equality of public education for all children" (Giroux, 1994, p. 33).

Leadership for Democratic Schools

In order for educational leadership to address the issues and problems of education and in particular public schools, we must make the social responsibility of school leaders and teachers and the role of public schools and higher education in society a high priority in the current discourses concerned with the crisis in democracy. We must revisit, critically, their "wider political and social function" (Giroux, 1994, p. 31) in relation to standing ideologies and political agendas that work against social justice and democratic principles.

Democracy and democratic education, from an ethical and critical perspective, will require that "who" is considered as educational leaders in educational institutions be expanded to engender the imperative of an inclusive democracy—that is, we can no longer simply define leadership by role or office such as principal. Rather, we must recognize the complex and dynamic nature of leading in the public schools and that democracy is a function of community that recognizes the potential of all members and the necessity of all voices being valued.

Therein, those who work toward effecting democracy must constantly "reflect and become consciously aware of the power struggles that further alienate the voices of the disadvantaged and oppressed . . . leaders in education must emulate those democratic principles of emancipation and empowerment if democracy is to be truly embraced" (Lees, 1995, p. 223). Such a view of leadership is rooted "in the necessity of enhancing and ennobling the meaning and purpose of public education by giving it a truly central place in the social life of a nation" (Giroux, 1994, p. 38). A central challenge then for democratic leaders is to come to terms with society's contradicting ideas of democracy, and more specifically, the ideologically imposed normativity that works against the very premise of democracy. "On one hand, society claims an ideology for emancipation; on the other hand, society's flawed structure builds dependencies on a dominating power that further binds any human potential or growth" (Lees, 1995, p. 223). Democratic leaders must necessarily work to create schools as democratic cultures, as "a public forum for addressing preferentially the needs of the poor, the dispossessed, and the disenfranchised as part of a broader concern for improving the quality of civic life" (Giroux, 1994, p. 38).

Considerations for Leadership Preparation

Leadership or teacher preparation programs have been, and continue to be, largely removed from a perspective and a set of practices dedicated to the fostering of critical democracy and social justice. Practitioner education often fails to address either the moral implications of societal inequalities or the ways in which schools function to reproduce and legitimate these inequalities.

Democratic Pedagogy

Pedagogically, the type of leadership preparation we are proposing is fundamentally concerned with leadership experience insofar as it takes the problems and needs of the leadership students themselves—that is, experiences these practitioners bring with them from their respective places of practice—as its starting point (Clark, 1997; Jenlink, 2001). If we are to cultivate democratic leadership, we must necessarily situate learning to lead within the practical and pragmatic problems of public schools. On the one hand, pedagogical considerations of practitioner experience encourage a critique of dominant forms of knowledge and cultural mediation that collectively shape practitioner experiences; on the other hand, they attempt to provide practitioners with the critical means to examine their own particular lived experiences and subordinate knowledge forms. This means working within a framework of democratic imperatives as a critical lens while assisting practitioners in analyzing their own experiences so as to illuminate the processes by which they were produced, legitimated, or disconfirmed, enabling the practitioner to understand what is and isn't democratic about their experiences (Giroux, 1994).

Practitioner experience is the stuff of culture, agency, and identity formation and must be given preeminence in a democratic curriculum. Importantly, conjoining practitioners in preparation brings the differing experiences to the foreground and situates leadership preparation within a more authentic context made problematic by the dynamic and complex interactions of experience—reflecting more nearly what the school setting is like for leaders (Jenlink, 2001). It is therefore imperative that practitioners preparing to be democratic leaders learn how to understand, affirm, and analyze such experience. This means not only understanding the cultural and social forms through which practitioners learn how to define themselves and their identity, but also learning how to engage practitioner experience in a way that neither unqualifiedly endorses nor delegitimates such experience (Giroux, 1994).

Reconceptualizing schools/colleges of education as democratic cultures, and practitioner preparation programs by extension, will require that administrator and teacher educators—all preparation program faculty as well as partner school practitioners—embrace imperatives of democracy. Schools/colleges of education, and educators of democratic leaders will need the democratic language and conceptual apparatus necessary for them not only to critically analyze the democratic and political imperatives and issues of reconceptualizing preparation, but also to develop the knowledge and skills that will advance the possibilities for generating curricula, classroom social practices, and organizational arrangements based on and cultivating a deep respect for a democratic and ethically based community.

In effect, this means that the relationship of practitioner preparation programs to public schooling would be self-consciously guided by political and moral considerations. Such considerations connect the work of schools/colleges of education with the work of public schools in a democratic society. Dewey (1916; 1927) expressed well the need for educators to make political and moral considerations a central aspect of their education and work when he distinguished between "education as a function of society" and "society as a function of education." Simply, education can function either to create passive, noncritical citizens as agents of society controlled by dominant ideologies or to create a critical citizenry to question existing conditions and fight for various forms of public life informed by a concern for equity, justice, democracy, and equality. At issue here is whether schools/colleges of education, and equally public schools, are to serve reification of existing cultural patterns and social structures and reproduce the existing society or to adopt the more critical role of challenging the existing patterns and structures so as to develop and advance America's democratic imperatives.

Communities of Democratic Practice

Democracy, democratic education, democratic schools, and democratic learning involve a transformation of human consciousness, and a transcendence of existing social structures and cultural patterns. Shaping individual identity is social, yet affected by cultural-political conditions in society, in schools, and in classrooms. Democratic leadership must be responsive, culturally and epistemologically, to transforming human consciousness and identity formation. Toward this attainment, democratic leadership must be inclusive, that is many individuals must share the responsibilities within the school/classrooms and between the school/community. Shared responsibility will work to create an "in-between" that affords students the ideological and institutional space to engage, through dialogue and practice, in shared experiences.

Specific considerations must be given with respect to preparing democratic leaders, particularly the need to prepare preservice teachers and administrators conjointly (Heckman, 1996), *in situ*—communities of practice (Lave & Wenger, 1991). Such communities of practice, within and across preparation programs, and within and across public schools and classrooms reflect small democratic cultures that are the foundation of a larger democratic society. We need democratic spaces in which, as Giroux (1994) argues, participants conjoin to critically examine the state, and "engage in struggles to eliminate structural social inequalities, and work for the creation of a number of active critical public cultures engaging in multiple literacies and democratic practices" (p. 37).

Considerations for Democratic Leadership Preparation and Practice

Some thoughts for reconceptualizing leadership preparation and practice within the philosophical and theoretical context of democratic leadership include:

- Practitioners will learn and practice together, conjointly, in communities of practice authentically situated in schools, blurring historical-traditional boundaries between teacher, principal, counselor, etc., instructed by democratic imperatives necessary to fostering democratic practices—pedagogical, cultural, social, ethical, and critical;

- Practitioners will necessarily deal with the diversity of ideas represented in educational settings, and how to identify and assimilate interdisciplinary ideas, methods, knowledges, and theories as well as utilize the techniques offered by each idea when relevant to school or college and student needs, thus facilitating commonality instead of divisiveness;
- Practitioners will learn the importance of creating, sustaining, and participating in a democratic community, and how to develop authentic collegial community of inquiry and practice for intellectually purposeful practice/behavior contextualized by ethical and moral responsibility to the self, others, community, and society;
- Practitioners will learn, through authentic experience and democratizing inquiry, to ground theory in current practice by having the opportunity, through critical reflection, to synthesize theory—both formal and practical—with the authentic practice and problems encountered in the practical setting, recognizing the transformative value of theory in practice as well as the value of practice in transforming existing theory;
- Practitioners will learn the importance of engaging in personal and professional democratic praxis—critically examining their experience and the theory and practice relations that they create individually and collectively to ensure democratic imperatives;
- Practitioners understand the relevance and importance of critical and democratic theory to educational and social change in relation to leading the educational enterprise, on all levels;
- Practitioners, as cultural workers and scholars of practice, constantly engage in practice to explore, create, and transform knowledge through the integration of criticality in relation to leadership efforts, especially in the form of race, gender, ethnicity, linguistics, sexual orientation and class; and
- Practitioners value collegiality and community, recognizing the importance of diversity to fostering cultures of democracy and communities of inquiry.

Three questions frame the work ahead for the preparation and practice of democratic educational leaders. Importantly, these questions are catalyzed by a concern for realizing the imperatives of a socially just and democratic society, realizing these imperatives as the foundation of reconsidering education for its role in a democratic society. The questions:

1. What are the democratic imperatives that should be considered in fostering a more democratic culture in public school, colleges of education, and society?
2. What are the challenges (theoretical, practical/pragmatic, political, cultural, etc.) to implementing these imperatives in our schools, colleges of education, and society?

3. What are the political issues related to democratic schools/democratic leadership for a democratic society—i.e., such as the disconnects between standards and accountability and fostering a democratic culture in schools and educational settings?

The challenges confronting American education and America's democratic way of life, bring to the foreground of discourse an awareness of the critical work ahead for educational leadership. In particular as politics and policy on the domestic front continue to redefine the federal government's role in education, compounded by the threat of war and terrorism, which redefine what it means to be an American in disquieting times.

NOTES

1. The chapter was originally presented at the 57th Annual Conference of the National Council of Professors of Educational Administration (NCPEA), August 5–8, 2003, Tucson, AZ.

2. Introduced as H.R. 1, in the 107th Congress. Retrieved June 1, 2003 from http://www .ed.gov/legislation/ESEA02/107–110.pdf

REFERENCES

Anderson, G. L. (1996). The cultural politics of schools: Implications for leadership. In K. Leithwood, J. Chapman, D. Corson, P. Hallinger, & A. Hart (Eds.), *International handbook of educational leadership and administration* (Vol. 1, Part 2, pp. 917–966). Boston, MA: Kluwer Academic Publishers.

Anderson, G. L. (2001). Promoting educational equity in a period growing social inequity: The silent contradictions of Texas reform discourse. *Education and Urban Society, 33*(3), 320–332.

Arendt, H. (1958). *The human condition*. Chicago: University of Chicago Press.

Ayers, W. (2000). The standards fraud. In D. Meier (Ed.), *Will standards save public education?* (pp. 64–69). Boston, MA: Beacon Press.

Carnoy, M., Loeb, S., & Smith, T. L. (2000, April). *Do higher state test scores in Texas make for better high school outcomes?* Paper presented at the annual meeting of the American Educational Research Association, New Orleans, LA.

Clark, D. (1997, March). *The search for authentic educational leadership: In the universities and in the schools*. Division A invited address presented at the annual meeting of the American Educational Research Association, Chicago.

Dewey, J. (1916). *Democracy in education: An introduction to the philosophy of education*. New York: Macmillan.

Dewey, J. (1927). *The public and its problems*. New York: H. Holt.

Dewey, J. (1937). Democracy and educational administration. *School and Society, 45*(1162), 457–462.

Dewey, J. (1939/1993). Creative democracy: The task before us. In D. Morris & I. Shapiro (Eds.), *John Dewey: The political writings* (pp. 240–245). Indianapolis/Cambridge: Hackett Publishing Company. (Originally published in 1939)

Feagin, J. R. (2000). *Racist America: Roots, current realities, and future reparations*. New York: Routledge.

Finkelstein, B. (1984). Education and the retreat from democracy in the United States, 1979–198? *Teachers College Record, 86*(2), 275–282.

Freire, P. (1998). *Pedagogy of freedom: Ethics, democracy and civic courage*. (P. Clarke, Trans.). Lanham, MD: Rowman & Littlefield.

Fuller, E. J., & Johnson Jr., J. F. (2001). Can state accountability systems drive improvements in school performance for children of color and children from low-income homes? *Education and Urban Society, 33*(3), 260–283.

Giroux, H. (1992). Educational leadership and the crisis of democratic government. *Educational Researcher, 2*(4), 4–11.

Giroux, H. A. (1994). Educational leadership and school administration: Rethinking the meaning of democratic public cultures. In T. A. Mulkeen, N. H. Cambron-McCabe, & B. J. Anderson (Eds.), *Democratic leadership: The changing context of administrative preparation* (pp. 31–47). Norwood, NJ: Ablex Publishing Corporation.

Giroux, H. A. (2002). Democracy, freedom, and justice after September 11th: Rethinking the role of educators and the politics of schooling. *Teachers College Record, 104*(6), 1138–1162.

Glickman, C. D. (2003). *Holding sacred ground: Essays on leadership, courage, and endurance in our schools*. San Francisco, CA: Jossey-Bass.

Gutmann, A. (1987). *Democratic education*. Princeton, NJ: Princeton University Press.

Haney, W. (2000). The myth of the Texas miracle in education. *Education Policy Analysis Archives, 8*(41). A printed version of this monograph is distributed by the Harvard Education Publishing Group. [Online]. Available: http://epaa.asu.edu/epaa/v8n41/

Haney, W. (2001). Commentary response to Skrla et al.: The illusion of educational equity in Texas: A commentary on "accountability for equity." *International Journal of Leadership in Education, 4*(3), 267–275.

Heckman, P. E. (1996). Democratic leadership and places to practice. *Journal of School Leadership, 6*(2), 142–154.

Jenlink, P. M. (2001, April). *Scholar-practitioner leadership: A critical analysis of preparation and practice*. Paper presented at the annual meeting of the American Educational Research Association, Seattle, WA.

Kincheloe, J. L. (1999). Critical democracy and education. In J. G. Henderson & K. R. Kesson (Eds.), *Understanding democratic curriculum leadership* (pp. 70–83). New York: Teachers College Press.

Klein, S. P. (2001). Commentary Response to Skrla et al.: Is there a connection between educational equity and accountability? *International Journal of Leadership in Education, 4*(3), 261–266.

Klein, S. P., Hamilton, L. S., McCaffrey, D. F., & Stecher, B. M. (2000). *What do test scores in Texas tell us?* (RAND Education Issue Paper) [Online]. Available: www.rand.org/publications/IP/IP202

Lave, J., & Wenger, E. (1991). *Situate learning: Legitimate peripheral participation*. Cambridge, UK: Cambridge University Press.

Lees, K. A. (1995). Advancing democratic leadership through critical theory. *Journal of School Leadership, 5*(3), 220–230.

Lugg, C. A. (1996). *For God and country: Conservatism and American school policy*. New York: Peter Lang.

McNeil, L. M. (2000). Contradictions of reform: The educational costs of standardized testing. New York: Routledge.

McNeil, L. M., & Valenzuela, A. (2000). The harmful impact of the TAAS system of testing in Texas: Beneath the accountability rhetoric. In G. Orfield & M. Kornhaber (Eds.), *Rais-*

ing standards or raising barriers? Inequality and high stakes testing in public education. Harvard Civil Rights Project 2000. New York: Century Foundation.

Meier, D. (2000). Educating in democracy. In D. Meier (Ed.), *Will standards save public education?* (pp. 3–34). Boston, MA: Beacon Press.

Scheurich, J. J. (2003). Commentary: The grave dangers in the discourse on democracy. In C. D. Glickman, *Holding sacred ground: Essays on leadership, courage, and endurance in our schools* (pp. 286–293). San Francisco, CA: Jossey-Bass.

Starratt, R. J. (2001). Democratic leadership theory in late modernity: An oxymoron or ironic possibility? *International Journal of Leadership in Education, 4*(4), 333–352.

Torres, C. A. (1998). *Democracy, education, and multiculturalism: Dilemmas of citizenship in a global world.* Boulder, CO: Rowman & Littlefield.

Valenzuela, V. (1999). *Subtractive schooling: U.S.-Mexican youth and the politics of caring.* Albany, NY: State University of New York Press.

Why Don't Our Graduates Take Administrative Positions, and What's the Cost?

Rodney Muth and Tricia Browne-Ferrigno

Many educators who complete administrator preparation programs either have no intention of becoming or may never become administrators (Browne-Ferrigno & Muth, 2001). Although greater knowledge and skill of those trained but not practicing still benefit schools, such advantages neither offset the current shortage of trained administrators nor the costs of preparing large numbers of people who do not fully use their knowledge and skills. An informal survey conducted by the Kansas Board of Regents in the late 1980s, for example, suggested then that as many as 4,000 to 5,000 administrative certificate or degree holders *per state* were not using their credential or degree for its intended purpose. Today, significant resources are still being used toward ends that remain unrealized.

What keeps these graduates from entering the profession, and what are the costs to university programs, the state, and especially districts that now desperately need high-quality administrators? These questions are critical in a time of shortage of quality applicants, particularly for the most challenging assignment in education (Roza, Cello, Harvey, & Wishon, 2003).

BACKGROUND

Typical administrator-preparation programs nationwide offer three-credit courses with total credits ranging from 36 hours to 45 hours. Typical class are comprised of 12 to 30 students, depending on recruiting success, types of classes, program structure, professorial preference, university requirements for class size, and the like. For this chapter, case studies of several cohorts in Colorado supplied data about the intent of program participants when they complete their preparation (Browne-Ferrigno & Muth, 2001). These data are used to project the costs—programmatic, institutional, state—of

Rodney Muth, University of Colorado at Denver
Tricia Browne-Ferrigno, University of Kentucky

Table 1.   Composition of Cohorts

Cohort	Total Number Students	Age Range (years)	Age Groups ≤40	Age Groups ≥40	Gender Female	Gender Male	Number Minority Students*
A	18	25–61	12	6	11	7	2
B	18	28–53	11	7	11	7	2
C	24	29–54	6	18	16	8	4
Totals	60	25–61	29	31	38	22	8

Note: *African American, Hispanic, or Pacific Rim.

Table 2.   Educational Experiences and Goals

Cohort	P–12 Work Experience (years)	Level of Current Position* ES	MS	HS	DO	Degree Level at Program Entry** B	M	D	Exit Goal Earn Degree	Exit Goal License Only
A	3–28	3	9	3	3	12	6	0	18	0
B	3–30	8	3	3	4	10	8	0	14	4
C	4–33	8	5	8	3	5	18	1	8	16
Totals	3–33	19	17	14	10	27	32	1	40	20

Note: *ES = elementary school, MS = middle school, HS = high school, DO = district office or work experience in district office; **B = Baccalaureate, M = Master's, D = Doctorate.

Table 3.   Goals and Leadership Readiness

Cohort	Total Number Students	Position Anticipated within Two Years P	AP	D	T	NS	Ready for Principalship Yes	Ready for Principalship No	Ready to Assume Leadership Position P	AP	Total
A	18	7	2	2	0	7	8	10	44%	22%	66%
B	18	6	5	2	1	4	7	11	39%	17%	56%
C	24	10	7	1	0	6	8	16	33%	29%	62%
All	60	23	14	5	1	17	23	37	38%	23%	62%

Note: *P = principal, AP = assistant principal, D = district administrator, T = teacher, NS = not sure.

Table 4.   Factors Contributing to Unreadiness for Principalship

Participant Responses Separated According to Categories and Gender							
Need More Experience* 20		Be Assistant Principal First* 14		Conflicting Personal Issues 5		Other Career Interests 3	
Female	Male	Female	Male	Female	Male	Female	Male
7	13	10	4	2	3	3	0

Note: *Nine respondents said that they both "need experience" and desire to be "assistant principal" first.

the attrition of large numbers of potential administrators who choose not to enter school administration. Analysis of reasons for the attrition, ways of identifying and preventing it, and the probable savings and benefits to the profession are explored.

Each cohort in the study averaged about 20 students, with an age range of 25 to 61 and a gender distribution of 38 women and 22 men. See Table 1 for additional information about the students in these cohorts. Table 2 shows the background of the students, and indicates that one-third wanted only the license while two-thirds also wanted a graduate degree. For degree-seeking students, the program involved 31 hours of licensure work and 9 hours of additional course work to complete an MA or EdS. The program leads to a provisional license, and an MA or other graduate degree is required along with a district-sponsored induction to earn a professional license.

ATTRITION

A typical administrator preparation program may see at least 50% of its graduates delay entering school administration, and most of these may never become school administrators (Educational Research Service, National Association of Elementary School Principals, & National Association of Secondary School Principals, 2000; Grogan & Andrews, 2002; McAdams, 1998; Young, Petersen, & Short, 2002). Table 3, Goals and Leadership Readiness, shows information from a study that combined data from three typical principal-preparation cohorts in Colorado (Browne-Ferrigno & Muth, 2001). These data are a bit more optimistic, indicating that, even though 37 of 60 (62%) said that they were not ready to assume a principalship on completing their program, 62% did say that, when adding the assistant principalship to possible leadership positions, they felt ready to assume a leadership role in schools. Even so, for candidates who were generally handpicked for the program, 30% still planned to be teachers within two years of graduation.

Table 4 provides additional information about the aspirations of these students at the time that they were completing their programs. Of the 42 who had indicated that they were not ready to assume a principalship, 14 did say that they felt prepared to become an assistant principal. This left 28 (47%) who indicated that they either needed more experience, had personal issues that prevented them from considering school administration at the time, or had other career interests. Interestingly, most of the students (39 or 65%) felt that they lacked sufficient technical skills at the end of the program, which may explain the reticence of many of them to consider immediately seeking a position as principal or assistant principal (see Table 5).

ISSUES FACING STATES, UNIVERSITIES, PREPARERS, AND DISTRICTS

The data show that the investments made—by students in terms of time, tuition, and other personal and financial sacrifices; by states in terms of support for graduate programs; and university programs in terms of the commitment of resources—are not realizing the ends possible: close to 100% of graduates seeking and attaining leadership positions in schools. As indicated earlier, about 30% of the students in the cohorts described here did not intend to enter school administration. Could any business survive if 30% of its products were rejected on inspection or by consumers?

Table 5. Learner Perceptions: School Leadership Skills

Cohort	Perceived Most Important Skill			Identified Least Understood Skill		
	Technical	Social	Awareness	Technical	Social	Awareness
A	5	4	8	11	3	3
B	1	5	12	12	4	1
C	6	10	7	16	4	4
All*	12	19	27	39	11	8

Note: *Totals do not equal 60 responses as two respondents added "all" for most important skills, and two wrote "none" for least understood skill.

Estimated Costs

What are the costs, then, to produce a licensed graduate who is prepared with an administrative license to lead in a school with a provisional license? As Table 6 shows, at a tuition rate for a public institution of $240 per credit, a 31-hour program for 20 students raises about $231,000 in tuition and state support for the university. University-faculty costs are estimated, based on an academic-year salary of $75,000 for five three-hour courses, at $5,000 per credit hour. For clinical faculty, the rate per three-hour course is $3,600 or $1,200 per credit hour. Benefits for both are 8.6%. Thus, instructional support for a cohort of 20 for 31 hours with university faculty teaching 15 and clinical faculty teaching 16 of the 31 credits runs about $102,000. Net revenues for the university are estimated at $129,000.

In addition to the costs presented in Table 6, transportation and parking, books, room rental, fees, and similar indirect costs vary considerably by cohort, year, location (field vs. campus), and so forth. Other costs not included here range from meetings of as many as 10 university and clinical faculty to plan a cohort's curriculum and sharing progress with successive instructional teams, site supervisors who work with students during clinical practica, or mentors who remain in contact with students throughout the program. Another cost that is unknown but significant is the tuition reimbursed by some districts when a student completes a course or a program. Even with this incentive, some students may not become school administrators, yet they often must stay in the district for two or more years or repay the support.

Lost Opportunity Costs

With estimates of about 50% of students nationwide not going into school administration on completing their certificates or licenses, the "lost-opportunity cost" to the preparation system is considerable. That is, the investments made by all parties, purportedly directed toward the formal professional development of future school administrators, are not realized when program graduates do not seek or accept administrative positions in schools. In this case, though, 30% is used as a local estimate, which means that about $55,000 per cohort is "lost." Student tuition is not included because students do get what they sought: a license, degree, or a bump on the salary scale. The net cost to the "state," then, in unrealized investments is about $55,000, and these lost-opportunity costs—investments made versus return—are significant, even though the university and

Table 6.   Estimated Costs to Prepare a Cohort of 20

Revenues/Costs	Cost per Credit	Per Cohort: 20 Students	Totals for 31 Licensing Hours	Benefits at 8.6%	Net Revenue/ Costs (NR/C)	Lost Opportunity (NR/C × 30%)	Net Cost to State, Programs, and Districts
Revenues/Costs							
—tuition	$240	$4,800	$148,800	NA	$148,800	NA	
—state support	$133	$2,667	$82,667	NA	$82,667	$24,800	$24,800
Subtotals	$373	$7,467	$231,467	NA	$231,467	$24,800	$24,800
Costs							
—university faculty	$5,000	$5,000	$75,000	$6,450	$81,450	$24,435	$24,435
—clinical faculty	$1,200	$1,200	$19,200	$1,651	$20,851	$6,255	$6,255
Subtotals	$6,200	$6,200	$94,200	$8,101	$102,301	$30,690	$30,690
Net Revenue/(Cost)		$1,267	$137,267	$8,101	$129,166	($55,490)	($55,490)

the program "profit" from tuition and state support regardless of the numbers who actually use their preparation to enter administrative life. (In the case presented here, the profit margin appears to be about 56%, but it actually could be considerably less, given all of the necessary university support structures.)

Scarce Resources

In an age when higher education is under concerted attack and state support for higher education is decreasing alarmingly, it seems unwise to squander resources. Universities often respond to declining state support with increased tuition or new admissions to generate additional revenues. However, an alternative for colleges and departments responsible for the preparation of educational leaders may be to rethink the needs of the field and the multiple investments of the parties involve. The problem, then, is to lower the lost-opportunity costs to the entire "profession" by ensuring that more of those entering principal-preparation programs complete them and then assume administrative positions as soon as they finish or very shortly thereafter. Otherwise, university-based programs may risk being viewed as inefficient, as misusing scarce resources, or as irrelevant.

Cash Cow

The scenario outlined in Table 6 also perpetuates the "cash-cow" role that administrator-preparation programs have played, in which universities expect high enrollments while providing low levels of resources (Murphy, 1993; Twombly & Ebmeier, 1989). Unfortunately, keeping enrollments high generally necessitates a "batch-processing" approach to preparation that only can work against quality programming and quality graduates.

Inadequate Preparation Experiences

It is more costly for districts and universities to provide in-depth, long-term, authentic experiences during preparation than to provide the batch-processing programs so prevalent today. Yet in these tight times, districts are simply not able to support apprentice-like experiences for large numbers of potential administrators, particularly if many of them may not then seek administrative roles after their professional training. And as long as most students in preparation programs are full-time school-district employees, it is less likely that they can engage in the high-quality clinical experiences that would prepare them well for the challenges of administrative positions and give them much needed reality tests of their resolve to be leaders. In the study data reported above, students also indicated concern about the quality of their clinical experiences and the quality of the mentoring that they received during their clinical practice (Browne-Ferrigno & Muth, 2001). Costs of district-based mentoring are high, and the batch-processing model does not lend itself to the intensive commitment required.

Easy MA for Salary Advancement

As is well known, many students, probably most particularly those who do not intend to become administrators, attend administrator licensing or degree programs to get a bump on the salary scale. A perspective "out there" is that administration programs are "easy" and therefore a low-effort way to increase one's salary. For those who take this approach, the probability of entry into or success in administration is quite low.

District Pay for Student Tuition

Some districts in Colorado and other states reimburse students for the credits that they take, assuming that the investment in university-based professional development improves district capacity to improve learning outcomes. Some suggest that this form of investment by a district can be returned by teachers who now understand what leadership means to school success and can contribute to the school and district whether or not they become administrators. From this perspective, the net cost to the state, shown in the last column of Table 6, can be viewed as an asset for the district proportionate to the district's investment.

SOME BARRIERS TO CHANGING THE WAY THINGS ARE DONE

Why do administrator-preparation programs continue such inefficiencies? They do so primarily because institutional demands structure how an administrative preparation program responds to its environment. Among the constraints that affect program are the status quo, the need for bodies, the full-time jobs of students in preparation programs, and university-based programming.

Status Quo

For most of us, it is simply easier to continue doing what we do. Change is always difficult: uncertain, threatening, even scary. Yet, to improve their success rates, programs will have to consider making serious changes that will upset the status quo, perhaps decreasing the number of university-based faculty while increasing the number of clinical faculty, tightening the criteria for program admissions, modifying the places of learning, and altering the ways in which students come to the program and are supported by it. Changing the status quo will also decrease the profit margin for universities.

Need for Bodies

One way to overcome the status quo is decrease the number of students going through principal-preparation programs. To do this, however, will require reconceptualization of programs, admission standards, settings in which learning takes place, people and methods that facilitate learning, and the role of university-based faculty. For example, Table 6 shows that the most costly part of the program described here is university faculty, as should be expected. Even though university faculty have an essential role in ensuring academic quality, by decreasing the proportion of university faculty time (credits) in a program, the numbers prepared can be reduced while quality is maintained.

Full-Time Employees

As long as students in preparation programs are part-time, their exposure to administrative life, responsibilities, and learning options will be severely constrained, with faculty necessarily expecting less than is preferable. Ways need to be found for future administrators to spend focused time working on problems of practice with experienced administrators who can guide and mentor them. As students in the Browne-Ferrigno and Muth (2001) study indicated, clinical experiences were insufficient to overcome student anxieties about their technical expertise (see Table 5).

University-Based Programming

If all a prospective administrator had to learn came from books, lectures, or simulations, programs would have no need to change what they do. On the other hand, because learning may best occur by doing (Dewey, 1938; Schön, 1983, 1987), the more that students can apply what they are learning to practice, the more likely their learning will be usable and transferable (Getzels, 1979; Lindblom & Cohen, 1979). Thus, closer relations with districts, more extensive clinical engagements, and intensive mentorships could be developed more effectively as programs move from campus to the field.

POSSIBLE SOLUTIONS

Can these problems be overcome? Can the costs be lowered while the numbers completing a program who take administrative positions increase? The possibilities are positive, but the changes to the status quo—how students come to a program, the places where learning occurs, and how they are assessed and counseled—imply that programs need to be reconfigured in important ways.

Data from the study cited here suggest that students want more exposure to field learning and stronger mentoring but find it difficult to pursue these preferences because of the nature of their work lives (Browne-Ferrigno & Muth, 2001). If more attention needs to be paid to authentic learning opportunities in administrator training (Cordeiro & Smith-Sloan, 1995; Crow & Glascock, 1995; Lumsden, 1992; Milstein & Krueger, 1997), then ways need to be found to get potential leaders out of the classroom and into positions where they can readily apply their knowledge in real settings to real problems. Increasing opportunities for hands-on practice is paramount as is providing students with mentors who can coach them as they address problems of practice.

Admission Standards

One way to affect the outcomes positively is to tighten admission standards in several ways. Many programs, including the one cited here, have minimal standards that focus mostly on academic measures such as GPA and test scores based on the assumption that an academic program requires a certain level of intellectual ability. While no one would argue that intellectual ability should not be a criterion for leadership, it is not enough.

Commitment.   First, establishing commitment to leadership through an administrative position needs to become part of the admissions process. It is not enough simply to ask. Rather, performance indicators—success in past and current leadership roles, for example—and recommendations from school leaders that include statements about ability and commitment to leadership responsibilities are needed to establish higher probabilities that graduates will seek administrative positions on program completion.

Experience. The greater the experience, the greater the likelihood that program applicants will understand the prospects and difficulties of administrative work. Thus, a floor of 5 to 7 years working as a licensed professional in a school or district should be the minimum for program entry. The data show that students with less experience in schools, with only few exceptions, are less likely to seek an administrative position following exit from the program (Browne-Ferrigno & Muth, 2001). Added to this expectation might be time working directly with adults in various quasi-administrative roles (see Commitment to Leadership Development below).

With time, opportunities comes for leadership experience on leadership teams, work as a literacy or math coach or curriculum developer, and other ways to experience the problems and meaning of leading adults. This transformation from a focus on children to a focus on adults is significant, and without some adult-level experience the likelihood of making the transfer from teacher or counselor to leader of adults may be difficult. The differences in power relations alone can be intimidating, particularly for less mature professionals.

Preparation. Just as research shows that competence in subject matter is important to success as a teacher, it may be that principals and other administrators need to be subject-area experts to lead others in instructional activities. Thus, an advanced degree in curriculum or another area may provide potential leaders with substantive confidence and credibility in their work with teachers. This type of expectation would also remove the "easy MA" as an attractant to those with no intention of entering administration.

Partnering

Preparing educational leaders is necessarily a collaborative process, involving the university and the field in some combination to identify the best candidates and provide them the best possible preparation. Taken seriously, such partnerships can produce excellent outcomes but involve considerable investment from both parties.

District needs. Districts and universities can work together to develop clear criteria for the kinds and numbers of leaders needed by a district over time. Doing so requires paying attention to the nature of the district's student population, the kinds of skills that successful principals in the district demonstrate, and the district's outcome expectations. Developing criteria with an eye to admitting only the top candidates nominated by district leaders who meet or exceed such criteria will likely limit the numbers entering a program.

Mentoring. The importance of continuous mentoring cannot be over emphasized, and identifying and supporting mentors to work with students requires a huge commitment by a district to developing leadership capacity. Effective mentors add significantly to a student's learning, competence, and confidence. Students in the three cohorts consistently raised concerns about their need for mentoring and the generally low quality of the mentoring that they did receive.

University commitment. Partnering requires considerable faculty effort and different forms of faculty work: off-campus planning meetings, configuring curricula to meet district needs, team teaching, group assessments, and the like. All of these engagements demand more faculty time and energy.

Periodic Self- and Program Assessments
Members of current cohorts in the program discussed here engage in self-assessments on the state's preparation standards. The students use these assessments throughout the program to chart their progress toward meeting the standards as well as to guide their development of clinical-practice goals and professional development plans. What is not practiced as well are program assessments that "test" whether expected progress occurs sufficiently over time to suggest that the program's and state's standards will be met sufficiently for university endorsement. Data from both sources could be used in counseling students about their career aspirations.

Career Counseling
A seldom-used but oft-raised process is career counseling. It is fairly clear early in a principal preparation program who the weak students are. Given various performance indicators, including quality of academic work and participation in class-based activities, level of achievement in clinical-practice settings, and dispositions such as belief that all children can learn, students who are doing less well on the indicators can be counseled out of the program. In fact, all students in preparation programs probably should receive periodic input on their performance, the likelihood of their success in administration, and any other feedback from clinical and university faculty as well as mentors and site supervisors that can help them become effective leaders. To do such counseling well would require consensus on success indicators and agreement on who provides counseling, how, and when.

Continuous Reflection
Another source of data, particularly for students, is a continuing process of reflection that focuses on what is being learned, a common practice in many preparation programs. Reflections can also be used continuously to test whether a career in administration is the right course.

Commitment to Leadership Development
To improve the quality of leadership in schools requires that districts commit to leadership development as a regular part of their professional-development expectations. This means that districts would invest early in potential leaders, providing them with multilevel experiences that can help the district and the individual determine whether increasing responsibilities in administrative leadership is the right choice. Models that can be used include "teacher on special assignment" (TOSA) and job sharing. These models engage former teachers in applied settings while focusing on the development of knowledge, skill, and dispositions (Hallinger, Leithwood, & Murphy, 1993; Martin, Ford, Murphy, Rehm, & Muth, 1997). They also support transitional plans to ease the shortage of quality school administrators, ensuring that new leaders are fully prepared for administrative responsibilities (Barth, 2001; Cline & Necochea, 1997). Further,

according to national accrediting bodies, programs are now required to be standards and performance based, immersing learners in the critically important day-to-day leadership responsibilities (National Council for the Accreditation of Teacher Education, 1995; National Policy Board for Educational Administration, 1998).

TOSAs. Districts, for example, could seek out and develop teacher leaders through focused TOSA programs that permit teachers to have out-of-classroom experiences in instructional leadership, working with other teachers to increase their classroom effectiveness, developing new curriculum and assessments, and engaging in other practice-improvement activities. In such roles, identified teacher leaders could test whether they like being out of the classroom, enjoy working with adults on skill and practice improvement, and appreciate the "administrative" activities and responsibilities that go with such positions. Then, when preparation-program opportunities come along, these prospective administrators would be able to make realistic decisions about their readiness for increased responsibilities, their ability to work with adults, and their commitment to leaving teaching.

The TOSA model can also be used during principal preparation to allow students to become thoroughly engaged in authentic practice to gain the knowledge and skills needed to lead a school as a principal. Program participants, freed from classroom teaching responsibilities, can serve in quasi-administrative positions (e.g., assistant principal, dean of students, project coordinator) that allow them to work with carefully selected mentor principals. The transfer of classroom learning to authentic practice then becomes almost seamless.

Job sharing. Another model that can be invoked before or during formal preparation is job sharing. In this model, a soon-to-retire principal decreases her or his administrative hours, shares them and classroom duties with an aspiring administrator, helps with crises, or performs tasks not permitted for unlicensed personnel. This model also allows budding administrators to test themselves in administrative practice while allowing district and school personnel to assess whether the candidate has the capabilities to be an effective school administrator.

DISCUSSION

"Making of a principal" (Lane, 1984) begins long before a leadership aspirant starts formal training; it continues beyond formal preparation and placement with focused support during the novice years (Browne-Ferrigno, in press; Browne-Ferrigno & Shoho, 2003; Doyle, 1984; Milstein, Bobroff, & Restine, 1991). The purpose of formal preparation is "to produce leaders" who can assume responsibility for guiding schools (Milstein, 1992, p. 10).

In the Colorado study, more than 62% (37 of 60) of the students—after four semesters in the program—declared that they were not ready for a principalship because they needed to increase their experience or skills, preferred to serve first as an assistant principal, felt conflicts with family or personal responsibilities, or had other career plans or no interest in becoming a principal. "I feel I must prove myself [as an assistant principal] to gain credibility," said one. Others clearly indicated that they did not feel that the principalship was the place for them at this time—perhaps never.

Given that some people in preparation programs have no intention of assuming formal administrative responsibilities, should preparation programs spend precious resources on these learners? Can such students instead be identified and redirected to other programs to reserve space for those who do aspire to administrative positions? On the other hand, can preparation programs remain viable without them?

Models proposed here can decrease costs and increase benefits, connect the university more closely with the field, and turn out a higher percentage of position-ready graduates. Such changes require better assessments of program applicants, greater involvement of districts in identifying potential leaders and in pre-preparation leadership development, more effective recruitment and selection, instruction and ongoing assessment intimately lodged in the day-to-day work of schools, and systematic connection of outcome assessments to standards of practice and district-leadership needs. Without such redirection of resources, preparers will continue costly investments in human capital that probably will not provide the needed return.

REFERENCES

Barth, R. S. (2001). *Learning by heart.* San Francisco: Jossey-Bass.

Browne-Ferrigno, T. (in press). Becoming a principal: Role conception, initial socialization, role-identity transformation, purposeful engagement. *Educational Administration Quarterly.*

Browne-Ferrigno, T., & Muth, R. (2001, November). *Becoming a principal: Role transformation through clinical practice.* Paper presented at the annual meeting of the University Council for Educational Administration, Cincinnati, OH.

Browne-Ferrigno, T., & Shoho, A. (2003, April). *Do admission processes in administrator preparation programs assure students with potential to become effective principals?* Paper presented at the annual meeting of the American Educational Research Association, Chicago, IL.

Cline, Z., & Necochea, J. (1997). Mentoring for school reform. *Journal for a Just & Caring Education, 3*(2), 141–159.

Cordeiro, P. A., & Smith-Sloan, E. (1995, April). *Apprenticeships for administrative interns: Learning to talk like a principal.* Paper presented at the annual meeting of the American Educational Research Association, San Francisco, CA.

Crow, G. M., & Glascock, C. (1995). Socialization to a new conception of the principalship. *Journal of Educational Administration, 33*(1), 22–43.

Dewey, J. (1938). *Experience and education.* New York: Touchstone.

Doyle, C. P. (1984). Obtaining an administrative position. In J. J. Lane (Ed.), *The making of a principal* (pp. 129–152). Springfield, IL: Charles C. Thomas.

Educational Research Service, National Association of Elementary School Principals, & National Association of Secondary School Principals. (2000). *The principal, keystone of a high-achieving school: Attracting and keeping the leadership we need.* Arlington, VA: Educational Research Service.

Getzels, J. W. (1979). Problem-finding and research in educational administration. In G. L. Immegart & W. L. Boyd (Eds.), *Problem-finding in educational administration* (pp. 5–22). Lexington, MA: D. C. Heath.

Grogan, M., & Andrews, R. (2002). Defining preparation and professional development for the future. *Educational Administration Quarterly, 38*(2), 233–256.

Hallinger, P., Leithwood, K., & Murphy, J. (Eds.). (1993). *Cognitive perspectives in educational leadership.* New York: Teachers College Press.

Lane, J. J. (Ed.). (1984). *The making of a principal*. Springfield, IL: Charles C. Thomas.

Lindblom, C. E., & Cohen, D. K. (1979). *Usable knowledge: Social science and social problem solving*. New Haven, CT: Yale University Press.

Lumsden, L. S. (1992). *Prospects in principal preparation*. Eugene, OR: ERIC Clearinghouse on Educational Management. (ERIC Digest No. 77).

Martin, W. M., Ford, S. F., Murphy, M. J., Rehm, R. G., & Muth, R. (1997). Linking instructional delivery with diverse learning setting. *Journal of School Leadership, 7*, 386–408.

McAdams, R. P. (1998). Who'll run the schools? The coming administrator shortage. *American School Board Journal, 29*(8), 37–39.

Milstein, M. M. (1992, October–November). *The Danforth Program for the Preparation of School Principals (DPPSP) six years later: What we have learned*. Paper presented at the annual meeting of the University Council for Educational Administration, Minneapolis, MN.

Milstein, M. M., Bobroff, B. M., & Restine, L. N. (1991). *Internship programs in educational administration: A guide to preparing educational leaders*. New York: Teachers College Press.

Milstein, M. M., & Krueger, J. A. (1997). Improving educational administration preparation programs: What we have learned over the past decade. *Peabody Journal of Education, 72*(2), 100–106.

Murphy, J. (1993). Alternative designs: New directions. In J. Murphy (Ed.), *Preparing tomorrow's school leaders: Alternative designs* (pp. 225–253). University Park, PA: University Council for Educational Administration.

National Council for the Accreditation of Teacher Education. (1995). *NCATE program standards: Advanced programs in educational leadership for principals, superintendents, curriculum directors, and supervisors*. Retrieved October 19, 2000, from http://www.ncate .org/standard/ellcmatrix.doc

National Policy Board for Educational Administration. (1998). NCATE curriculum guidelines: Advanced programs in educational leadership for principals, superintendents, curriculum directors, and supervisors. In National Council for Accreditation of Teacher Education (Ed.), *NCATE curriculum guidelines* (pp. 183–204). Washington, DC: National Council for Accreditation of Teacher Education.

Roza, M., with Cello, M. B., Harvey, J., & Wishon, S. (2003). *A matter of definition: Is there truly a shortage of school principals?* Seattle: Center for Reinventing Public Education, Daniel J. Evans School of Public Affairs, University of Washington.

Schön, D. A. (1987). *Educating the reflective practitioner*. San Francisco: Jossey-Bass.

Schön, D. A. (1983). *The reflective practitioner: How professionals think in action*. New York: Basic Books.

Twombly, S., & Ebmeier, H. (1989, December). Educational administration programs: The cash cow of the university? *Notes on reform*. Charlottesville, VA: National Policy Board for Educational Administration.

Young, M. D., Petersen, G. T., & Short, P. M. (2002). The complexity of substantive reform: A call for interdependence among key stakeholders. *Educational Administration Quarterly, 38*(2), 137–175.

Principals: Motivating and Inhibiting Factors in Texas, Missouri, and Oregon

*Sandra Harris, Michael Arnold, Carolyn S. Carr,
and Sarah E. Worsham*

It was a cold, gray Friday in February with a light snow beginning to fall. The fifty year old high school principal looked up at the clock in the hallway. "Amazing," he thought to himself, "Four o'clock and it's already dark outside." He walked past classrooms empty of most students and teachers as he headed toward the gym. The girls junior varsity basketball game would be starting soon, followed by the girls varsity game. Tomorrow night he had to attend the boys games. In between basketball games, he must begin working on his "to-do" list. The first draft of the budget was due, he had three evaluations to complete, two parents to call, and a board member who had asked to meet with him before Monday. Only an hour ago, the chemistry teacher had handed in his resignation. Just thinking about trying to fill that vacancy, exacerbated the headache that had been forming all day until now it was raging.

As the principal walked into the gymnasium, his mind slowly returned to those earlier days before he became the principal, when he and his wife never missed one of their son's basketball games, days when the telephone ringing at home was probably one of his son's buddies calling, rather than an irate parent, and days when Friday evening was eagerly looked forward to as the beginning of family time and some rest. He smiled at those long-ago pleasant thoughts. Just then, a parent touched his arm and said, "Oh, Mr. Smith, I'm so glad you're here, I really need to talk with you about something that happened today in my daughter's Math class." Even before he could respond, the thought ran through his mind, "Maybe changing jobs or retiring isn't such a bad idea."

Sandra Harris, Stephen F. Austin State University
Michael Arnold, Southwest Baptist University
Carolyn S. Carr, Portland State University
Sarah E. Worsham, Southwest Baptist University

THE PROBLEM

Attracting and keeping qualified principals is an issue with more and more school districts across the country in rural, urban, and suburban schools of all grade levels (Educational Research Service, 2000; Harris, Arnold, Lowery, & Crocker, 2000; Potter, 2001). In fact, Southern Regional Education Board Senior Vice President, Gene Bottoms, emphasized that the problem is not in the availability of *certified* principals, but in the availability of *qualified* principals (Norton, 2002). Still, New York State experienced a principal shortage when the 2000 school year began with 163 substitute principals according to the *New York Times* (Goodnough, 2000). Kentucky and Texas have reported alarming situations of dwindling numbers of applicants; and in Vermont one out of five principals left at the end of the 1999–2000 school year through either retirement or resignation (Steinberg, 2000). Additionally, large numbers of principals are reaching retirement age, more principals are moving into central office positions, and some are just leaving because of the enormous responsibilities (ERS, 1998). In fact, it has been estimated that over the next ten years, over 42% of today's principals will resign or retire (Doud & Keller, 1998). Therefore, the purpose of this study was to explore reasons why current principals in three different states stayed in the principalship and why they considered leaving.

HISTORY OF THE PRINCIPAL ROLE

The role of the principal is a challenging, ever-changing role with even more change occurring due to the changes in our 21st century society (Goodwin, Cunningham, & Childress, 2003). In fact, principals today reported that the job "involved more work, more pressure and frustration, greater demands, and more responsibilities than when they assumed the position" (Mertz, 1999, p. 17). There is no doubt that the job of the principal has changed. For example, early schools were small and ungraded, and teachers performed administrative, clerical, and janitorial tasks that came with running the school (Pierce, 1935; Sheets, 1986). The headmaster was the person who kept attendance, reported to the lay school committee, and made sure the building was maintained (Knezevich, 1969, p. 279). By the 1900s, the headmaster/principal had become a "directing manager" with increasing responsibilities in the day-to-day management of the school (Pierce, 1935). In fact, according to Tyack and Hansot (1982), leadership in American public schools by the turn of the century . . . "had gravitated from the part-time educational evangelist of the mid-nineteenth century to a new breed of professional managers, who made education a life-long career and who reshaped the schools according to the canons of business efficiency and scientific expertise" (p. 120).

In the 1920s, the principal was the person who accepted and promoted certain values and worked to connect spiritual issues with those of scientific management (Beck & Murphy, 1993). The 1930s saw the principal as a financial manager, and the '40s viewed the role as that of a democratic leader (Barnard, 1938; Beck & Murphy, 1983). With the '50s came the role of applying laws such as *Brown vs. Board of Education of Topeka* in combination with implementing school activities (Beck & Murphy, 1993). The '60s brought on additional turmoil and the principal's role became more bureaucratic. According to Haynen (1973), humanistic facilitator best described the role of the principal in the '70s.

The '80s cast the principal into the role of instructional leader, the '90s as a leader vs. a manager, and now in the new 21st century the principal must be all things to all people as she is considered the strategic leader of the school who is both "visionary and a change agent" (Goodwin et al., 2003). There was a time when the principal could be successful if she was a good manager; but today demands are placed on the principal from increasingly vocal and demanding private and public sectors. As schools involve a variety of external and internal stakeholders ascribing to school-based management, the role of the principal has continued to become more time consuming and stressful. It is no wonder that many qualified principals are considering leaving the position for another career or retiring even though their services are still needed in today's schools.

Despite the increasing complexity of the principalship, it is generally agreed by scholars and practitioners alike that this role is vital to the success of the school (ERS, 2000; NPBEA, 2001; Sergiovanni, 2001). Effective principals must be skilled instructional leaders, change initiators, managers, personnel directors, problem solvers, and visionaries (Blase & Kirby, 2000; Goodwin et al., 2003; Sergiovanni, 2001). In fact, how the principal prioritizes leadership skills needed to be an effective administrator is critical to the effectiveness of the school (Gordon, Stockard, & Williford, 1992). Certainly, the challenge to keep top leaders is vital to any organization. In fact, replacing a leader can cost up to 1.5 times the individual's salary, when taking into account the cost for replacement, advertising, loss of productivity and training (Ream, 2001). Additionally, changing leadership at an inopportune time in the life of a school can halt the momentum for change. Strong leaders must be able to understand the whole picture and analyze "current progress in order to chart future direction" (Wasley, 1992, p.5).

MOTIVATORS OF THE PRINCIPALSHIP

What attracts men and women to the position of principal? Why would anyone willingly assume this role with the complex demands of the principalship? Beginning with the seminal work of Herzberg, Mausner, and Snyderman (1959), Motivation Hygiene Theory identified achievement, recognition, interpersonal relations, advancement, responsibility, the work itself and policy as contributors to job satisfaction. Building on this foundation, Pounder and Merrill (2001) suggested that there are two theories that contribute to a willingness to accept such a complex job: the objective theory and the subjective theory. In the objective theory, candidates are viewed as "economic beings who seek to maximize their economic status by joining the organization that is perceived as being the most economically competitive" (pp. 29–30). This suggests that those who are motivated by the economic stability of the district or by means of improving their own economic standing, make their decision by looking at factors that are more objective, such as salary and benefits.

The subjective theory recognizes the individual's need to have their psychological or emotional needs met (Pounder & Merrill, 2001). The desires to achieve and impact education are subjective motivational factors that must be addressed. Research conducted among students enrolled in a university principalship program indicated the number one factor that motivated individuals to enter the principalship was a desire to make a positive impact (Harris, Arnold, Lowery, & Crocker, 2000). The same study also indicated that wanting to make a difference ranked very high as a motivator to enter the principalship. Additionally, Pounder and Merrill (2001) surveyed assistant principals and middle school principals and found that the desire to achieve and influence education had the highest positive influence. These data were supported by other research conducted by Moore (2000) and the National Education Association (1997). Thus, a key motivating factor for individuals seeking this job and keeping it is the intrinsic reward of helping children and their teachers. Clearly, principals recognize the tremendous difference they can make in the lives of others (Pellicer, 1999; Sergiovanni, 2001). Additionally, Moore (2000) and Harris et al. (2000) identified other service reasons, such as the personal and professional challenge and the opportunity to initiate change as critical motivating factors for principals.

INHIBITORS TO THE PRINCIPALSHIP

Today's principal spends too much time in areas that have nothing to do with students, such as paperwork, and endless meetings and activities (Green, 2001). Yerkes and Guaglianone (1998) cited a number of reasons associated with the difficulty of the principalship all related to the increasingly complex society of today that included: workload, supervision of night activities, the 60 to 80 hour work week, paperwork associated with state and district mandates, and high expectations from various publics and insufficient compensation. Added to these issues, Educational Research Services (ERS) in 1998 reported that "lack of sufficient compensation" was the strongest barrier for filling the high school principalship (p. 30). Other studies have echoed many of these same factors, as well as too much stress, difficulty of satisfying stakeholders, societal problems that make it difficult to focus on instruction, increased litigation, and discipline issues (ERS, 2000; Harris et al., 2000; Moore, 2000; Pounder & Merrill, 2001).

STUDY DESIGN

Sample

We surveyed a representative sample of school districts in Texas, Missouri, and Oregon, using systematic sampling (Gay & Airasian, 1996). Having selected the district, one school from each district was chosen by its composition (elementary, middle school, or high school). For example, in Texas, which has 1036 school districts, 150 districts were selected to sample which included principals in 98 elementary schools, 30 middle schools and 22 high schools. Three hundred fifty principals from the three states were mailed questionnaires and invited to participate in the study. Two hundred fifty one principals in Oregon, Missouri, and Texas responded—102 in Texas, 83 in Missouri, and 66 in Oregon, which was a 71% response rate.

Data Collection

A three-part questionnaire was constructed. Part I of the survey asked for general biographical and school demographic information. Part II asked participants to identify motivating factors for becoming a principal and for remaining in the principal-ship. Part III asked participants to identify inhibiting factors for these same issues. Participants responded to these items on a Likert scale of 1—no importance, to 4—great importance. Questions on the survey for parts II and III were drawn from the literature (ERS, 2000; Harris et al., 2000; Moore, 2000; Pounder & Merrill, 2001) and pilot tested among 150 principalship students. After pilot testing, the survey was revised for increased reliability and validity.

Data Analysis
All responses were compiled, tallied, and frequencies generated. Using SPSS 10.1, means were generated, crosstabs disaggregated data, and ANOVA's analyzed for sig-nificance at the $p > .05$ level. Multiple comparisons were conducted with a Post Hoc Scheffe test to locate differences among the states (George & Mallery, 2001).

FINDINGS AND DISCUSSION
General Biographical Demographics
Over 60% of principal participants were 46 years or age or older. An additional 20% were between the ages of 41 and 45. Sixty-seven percent were male and 33% were female. Seventy-five percent had a master's degree, 19% had completed work on a specialist degree or certificate. Only 6 percent reported having a Ph.D. or Ed.D. Consistent with the number of minority principals nationwide, only 2.9% were His-panic, 2.4% were African American, and 2.4% marked the Other category. An over-whelming 91.6% of principals responding were Anglo.

While only 8% of these principals were in their first year, 35% had served as principal for two to five years, 23% had served from six to ten years, and the re-maining 34% had served from eleven years to over twenty years. When asked about their employment prior to becoming a principal for the first time, 52% re-ported moving directly from the classroom to becoming a principal and 41% had been assistant principals before assuming the principal position. Only 5% came from central office and only one individual had transitioned directly from the business world into the principalship.

Building Level Information
The schools represented many different configurations. Forty-one percent were principals of elementary schools, 20% led middle schools, 29% were principals of high schools and 10% led schools of grades K–12. Nearly half of the schools had less than 300 students (45.5%), 35% had populations of 301–600, and 5 percent were between the size of 601 and 800 students. Thirteen percent of these princi-pals led schools with over 800 students. The majority of the principals reported that their schools were in rural areas (80%), 15% were located in suburban areas and 4% (l0 schools) were located in urban areas.

All three states rate their school districts based on a state test. In Texas, the rating is exemplary, recognized, acceptable, or not acceptable; while in Oregon the rating is exceptional, strong, satisfactory, or not acceptable. Missouri rates its schools as accredited, provisionally accredited and unaccredited. For consistency of reporting, Missouri schools that were accredited were tallied as exceptional, provisionally accredited schools were reported as acceptable and unaccredited schools were tallied as not acceptable. Therefore, when state ratings of schools were reported collectively, 47.4% indicated their school had an exemplary or exceptional rating, 27% were recognized or strong, 22% were acceptable or satisfactory, and only 1.6% (four schools) were rated as not acceptable.

Identified Motivating Factors

Responding on a Likert-type scale of 1–4 from "no importance" to "very important," seven of the ten factors had means of 3.01 or higher as reported in Table 1. Four categories, the desire to make a positive impact ($M = 3.75$), the desire to make a difference ($M = 3.69$), the personal challenge ($M = 3.46$) and the professional challenge ($M = 3.44$) were the strongest motivators in all three states. The ability to initiate change ranked fifth in each state with an overall mean of 3.36. Only support and encouragement from others ($M = 2.98$), increased prestige or status ($M = 2.08$), and the opportunity to relocate to a desirable location ($M = 1.67$) had means lower than 3.0. All three states considered these the least motivating of the factors. All of the means ranged from a low of 1.67 to a high of 3.75.

The mean for the category of salary and fringe benefits was 3.01. This was the only motivator that was significant at the .05 level when the three states were compared with an ANOVA. Upon further analysis using a Scheffe for multiple comparisons, Oregon principals were significantly less motivated by salary and fringe benefits ($p = .017$) than either Missouri or Texas counterparts (see Table 1). While the survey did not address causal factors, this suggested that perhaps reviewing the salary and fringe benefits and information about economies in these three states might contribute to a better understanding of the role of these economic factors when individuals consider whether to enter or remain in the principalship.

Table 1. Motivating Factors for Principals by States

Motivators	Oregon Mean	SD	Missouri Mean	SD	Texas Mean	SD	Total Mean	SD
Desire make positive impact**	3.77	.42	3.78	.44	3.7	.52	3.75	.47
Desire to make a difference	3.74	.51	3.70	.60	3.66	.54	3.69	.55
Personal challenge**	3.53	.56	3.48	.70	3.40	.66	3.46	.65
Professional challenge**	3.47	.68	3.47	.72	3.40	.66	3.44	.69
Ability to initiate change	3.44	.64	3.30	.69	3.35	.74	3.36	.70
Teacher of teachers**	3.24	.77	3.11	.80	3.04	.78	3.12	.78
Salary and fringe benefits* **	2.79	.79	3.11	.66	3.08	.77	3.01	.75
Support/encourage by others**	3.06	.82	3.04	.80	2.89	.84	2.98	.82
Increased prestige/status	2.98	.79	2.12	.80	2.06	.76	2.08	.78
Relocate to a desirable location	1.62	.94	1.72	.80	1.66	.85	1.67	.88

*Significant $p<.05$ between states
** Significant $p<.05$ by gender when all responses combined
Key: 1 = no importance, 2 = little importance, 3 = important, 4 = great importance
(Texas n = 102; Missouri n = 83; Oregon n = 66; Total n = 251)

When all responses from the three states were combined and analyzed with independent samples *t*-tests by gender, six categories were significant at $p<.05$. These were: salary and fringe benefits ($p = .023$), desire to make a positive impact ($p = .033$), personal challenge ($p = .002$), professional challenge ($p = .001$), support/encouragement from others ($p = .033$), and opportunity to be a teacher of teachers ($p = .001$). Salary and fringe benefits were more powerful motivators for males, but the other factors were more motivating for females.

Identified Inhibiting Factors

On a Likert-type scale of 1 to 4 with "1" being "no importance" and "4" being "very important," inhibitors' means ranged from a low of 2.17 to a high of only 3.10 as can be seen in Table 2. Only the category that addressed amount of paperwork and bureaucracy ($M = 3.10$) had a collective mean above 3.0. This was followed by increased time commitment/longer day ($M = 2.90$), and the increased emphasis on standardized tests ($M = 2.88$). Also, increased litigation had a collective mean of 2.7 among the three states. Items that appeared to have the least inhibiting influence on the decision to become a principal or stay in the principalship were the isolation from students and staff ($M = 2.29$), the longer school year ($M = 2.17$) and the opportunity to take jobs outside of education ($M = 2.17$).

Upon further analysis, we found that the strength of the inhibitors did not appear to be as influential as the strength of the motivators. For example, the top three motivators had means of 3.75, 3.69, and 3.46, while the top three inhibitors had means of 3.10, 2.9, and 2.88. Also, when items were analyzed by gender with independent samples *t*-tests, there were no statistically significant differences.

When one-way ANOVAs were computed for inhibiting factors among the three states, two factors were significant at $p<.05$: salary too small ($p = .000$), and opportunities for jobs outside education ($p = .002$). The "salary too small" was a more inhibiting issue in Texas than in either Missouri or Oregon. Also, "job opportunities outside education" was a greater issue in Texas than in Oregon. These findings further emphasized the importance of the job possibilities and economic conditions within states as likely contributors to the decision of whether to become a principal or remain a principal.

Because this was an exploratory study, the researchers also looked at the data between states for issues that were significant at $p < .10$ level (Gay & Airasian, 1996). The data suggested that discipline issues ($p = .053$) were a significantly greater inhibitor in Texas than in Oregon. The issue of no tenure ($p = .059$) was also a significantly greater inhibitor in Texas than in Oregon. Thus, the ANOVAs calculated for each of these inhibiting issues suggested that there were indeed some differences among states in the areas of salary, other job opportunities, job security (tenure), and discipline issues.

RECOMMENDATIONS

Increasing salaries, improving retirement income that recognizes the additional contracted months, streamlining special education paperwork, lowering the number of

314 *Sandra Harris et al.*

Table 2. Inhibiting Factors for Principals by States

	Oregon		Missouri		Texas		Total	
Inhibitors	Mean	SD	Mean	SD	Mean	SD	Mean	SD
Inc. paperwork/bureaucracy	2.95	.90	3.22	.75	3.10	.81	3.10	.82
Inc. commitment/mtgs/day	2.86	1.02	2.95	.88	2.88	1.02	2.90	.97
Increased emphasis std. tests	2.74	.98	2.90	.81	2.94	.89	2.88	.89
Increased litigation	2.61	.96	2.80	.88	2.68	.97	2.70	.94
Student discipline problems**	2.38	.89	2.63	.88	2.74	.77	2.61	.85
Salary too small*	2.20	.98	2.53	.99	2.89	.99	2.59	1.03
No tenure**	2.06	.93	2.29	1.07	2.47	1.01	2.30	1.02
Isolation from staff/students	2.44	.96	2.25	1.00	2.23	.88	2.29	.94
Longer year	2.18	.82	2.16	1.01	2.17	.99	2.17	.97
Job opportunity outside edu.*	1.77	.87	2.20	1.04	2.39	1.04	2.17	1.03

* Significant p<.05 between states
** Significant p<.10 between states
Key: 1 = no importance, 2 = little importance, 3 = important, 4 = great importance
(Texas n = 102; Missouri n = 83; Oregon n = 66; Total n = 251)

students/administrators and having staff take care of some of the routine activities such as bus duty and supervision of extracurricular activities are some ways state and local officials could help in the retention of principals (Hertling, 2001). Other suggestions for recruiting, and, thus, retaining quality administrators included restructuring job responsibilities; reducing the work week and the work year; adding support services; and increasing the principal's authority and nurturing; and developing future administrators to recruit and, thus, retain, quality administrators (McAdams, 1998).

Some districts have considered job sharing to ease the burden of the principalship. Muffs and Schmitz (1999) reported one school where a veteran principal worked the morning hours and an intern principal worked in the afternoon hours. This was organized so that at least one hour a day the shifts overlapped to allow for communication. Another school in Tennessee had a team of six people—one for each grade level—which acted collectively as the principal (Ashford, 2000). Additionally, mentor programs provide ongoing support for principals. These programs can be formal and informal, but provide networking and training opportunities that strengthen resolve for those involved in the challenging job of the principal (ERS, 2000; Whitaker, 2001). University preparation programs can better support principals in training by emphasizing training in time management, delegation of duties, legal issues, discipline management strategies, and standards accountability.

CONCLUSION

Clearly, individuals who choose to remain in the principalship are motivated by an intrinsic desire to make a positive impact on the world and make a difference in the lives of others. They are motivated by being challenged personally and professionally, by the opportunity to initiate change, and the opportunity to be a teacher of teachers. This is especially so for females. In our study, of the ten motivating issues, the category salary and fringe benefits was listed seventh. While, not high on the survey list, its overall mean of 3.01 indicated that it was still an important item to be considered. Thus, the data from this study regarding motivators are consistent with previous literature (ERS, 2000; Harris, et al., 2000; Moore, 2000; Pounder & Merrill, 2001).

Inhibitors, while not identified as strongly as the motivators, were still generally consistent with findings from previous studies identifying paperwork, endless meetings and increased time commitment, low salaries, discipline issues and the complexity of today's society as primary inhibitors (ERS, 2000; Green, 2001; Harris et al., 2000; Yerkes & Guaglianone, 1998). Our findings also suggested that other inhibiting factors in the job of the principalship included bureaucracy, emphasis on standardized tests, litigation surrounding education today, and discipline problems.

When we looked at differences among states, our findings suggested that there were many similarities. However, there were some differences among states when educators considered motivators and inhibitors to becoming principals and remaining principals. These differences included salaries, job opportunities outside education, and, to a smaller degree, discipline problems, and the lack of tenure. This is critical information for districts and school boards when considering reform strategies to restructure the job of the principalship. Additionally, this implies that exploring area economic conditions could contribute much needed information toward understanding how best to recruit and retain principals in different states.

Men and women who become principals are committed to a vision that is almost spiritual; they are motivated by an inner desire to do something good for someone. Yet, sometimes, the difficulties of the job overshadow and so inhibit the positive aspects that even these dedicated individuals consider leaving the job. Educators must begin to understand that the task of building and maintaining an effective school culture and climate can not rest solely on the shoulders of the principal. It is the responsibility of the internal and external publics to help provide leadership and this cannot be done without considering the wider school community. In doing so, some of the burden will be lifted from the principal and the outlook for retaining quality administrators should be brighter.

REFERENCES

Ashford, E. (2000, December 19). Creative solutions ease burdens on principals. *School Board News,* 1–5. Retrieved: December 12, 2000. Available On-Line. Http://www.nsba.org/sbn/00-dec/121900-1.htm

Barnard, C. I. (1938). *The functions of the executive.* Cambridge, MA: Harvard University Press.

Beck, L. G., & Murphy, J. (1993). *Understanding the principalship: Metaphorical themes 1920s-1990s.* New York: Columbia University Teachers College Press.

Blase, J., & Kirby, P. (2000). *Bringing out the best in teachers: What effective principals do* (2nd ed.). Thousand Oaks, CA: Corwin Press.

Doud, J., & Keller, E. P. (1998). The K–8 principal in 1998. *Principal, 78*(1), 5, 6, 8, 10–12.

Educational Research Service. (1998). *Is there a shortage of qualified candidates for openings in the principalship? An exploratory study.* Alexandria, VA.: National Association of Elementary School Principals, and Reston, VA: National Association of Secondary School Principals.

Educational Research Service. (2000). *The principal, keystone of a high-achieving school: Attracting and keeping the leaders we need.* Arlington, VA: Author.

Gay, L. R., & Airasian, P. (1996). *Educational research: Competencies for analysis and application.* Upper Saddle River, NJ: Merrill.

George, D., & Mallery, P. (2001). *SPSS for windows: Step by step.* Boston: Allyn & Bacon.

Goodnough, A. (2000, September 8). Mrs. Clinton proposes grants for principals. *New York Times,* 25.

Goodwin, R., Cunningham, M., & Childress, R. (2003). The changing role of the secondary principal. *NASSP Bulletin, 87*(634), 26–42.

Gordon, B., Stockard, J., & Williford, H. (1992). The principal's role as school leader. *Educational Research Quarterly, 14*(4), 29–38.

Green, L. (2001). Incentives aim to aid principal retention. *The Capitol,* Annapolis, MD. Retrieved: April 2, 2002. Available On-Line: http://www.hometownannapolis.com/egi-bin/read/2001/04_01-02/TOP

Harris, S., Arnold, M., Lowery, S., & Crocker, C. (2000). Deciding to become a principal: What factors motivate or inhibit that decision? *ERS Spectrum, 18*(2), 40–45.

Haynen, R. V. (1973). Special leaders need for special problems. *NASSP Bulletin, 57*(374), 89–92.

Hertling, E. (2001). Retaining principals. *ERIC Digest 147.* Retrieved: March 20, 2002. Available http://eric.uoregon.edu/publications/digests/digest147.html

Herzberg, F., Mausner, B., & Snyderman, B. (1959). *The motivation to work* (2nd ed.). New York: John Wiley.

Knezevich, S. J. (1969). *Administration of public education* (2nd ed.). New York: Harper & Row.

McAdams, R. (1998). Who'll run the schools? *American School Board Journal, 35*(4), 37–38.

Mertz, N. (1999). Through their own eyes: Principals look at their jobs. In F. Kochan, B. Jackson, & D. Duke (Eds.), *A thousand voices from the firing line* (pp. 15–28). Columbia, MO: University Council of Educational Administration.

Moore, D. (2000). The vanishing principals: Perceptions of graduate students in two university leadership programs. *Journal of the Intermountain Center for Educational Effectiveness, 1*(1), ll–14.

Muffs, M., & Schmitz, L. (1999). Job sharing for administrators: A consideration for public schools. *NASSP Bulletin, 83*(605), 70–73.

National Education Association (1997). *Status of the American Public School Teacher 1995–96.* Washington DC: Author.

National Policy Board for Educational Administration for the Educational Leadership Council (2001). *Recognizing and encouraging exemplary leadership in America's schools: A proposal to establish a system of advanced certification for administrators.* Arlington, VA: Author. Retrieved March 4, 2002 from http://www.npbea.org/projects/able_project.htm

Norton, J. (2002, Fall). *Preparing school leaders: It's time to face the facts.* Atlanta, GA: Southern Regional Education Board.

Pellicer, L. (1999). *Caring enough to lead: Schools and the sacred trust.* Thousand Oaks, CA: Corwin Press.

Pierce, P. R. (1935). *The origin and development of the public school principalship.* Chicago: University of Chicago Press.

Potter, L. (2001). Solving the principal shortage. *Principal, 80*(4), 34–37.

Pounder, D., & Merrill, R. (2001). Job desirability of the high school principalship: A job choice theory perspective. *Educational Administration Quarterly, 37*(1), 27–57.

Ream, R. (2001, April). Holding on to the best and brightest. *Information Today.* Retrieved: March, 2002. Available On-Line: http://www.infotoday.com

Sergiovanni, T. (2001). *The principalship: A reflective practice perspective* (4th ed.) Boston: Allyn & Bacon.

Sheets, W. W. (1986). *The perceptions and expectations of principals, teachers, and parents from selected elementary schools regarding the role of the elementary school principal.* Unpublished doctoral dissertation, George Peabody College, Nashville, TN.

Steinberg, J. (2000, September 3). Nation's schools struggling to find enough principals. *New York Times,* A1, A4.

Tyack, D. B., & Hansot, E. (1982). *Managers of virtue: Public school leadership in America 1920–1980.* New York: Basic Books.

Wasley, P. (1992). When leaders leave. *Educational Leadership, 50*(3), 1–6. Available On-Line: http://www.ascd.org/readingroom/edlead/9211/wasley.html

Whitaker, K. (November 1–4, 2001). *Candidates for the principalship in the current era: Superintendent perceptions.* Paper presented at the University Council of Educational Administration, Cincinnati, OH.

Yerkes, D. M., & Guaglianone, C. L. (1998). Where have all the high school administrators gone? *Thrust for Educational Leadership, 28*(2), 10–15.

Creating an Environment for Learner Centered Leadership: An Emerging Model of Professional Development for School Administrators

Arnold Danzig, Gary Kiltz, Elsie Szescy, Terrence Wiley,
Azadeh Osanloo, Josué González, Kay Hunnicutt,
Donna Macey, and Charlotte Boyle

Since October 2002, the College of Education at Arizona State University has been implementing an emerging professional development program for school leaders in collaboration with the Southwest Center for Educational Equity and Language Diversity and four diverse, urban school districts in the Phoenix area. The receipt of a three-year grant from the United States Department of Education's School Leadership Program has provided the opportunity to create the Learner Centered Leadership program (LCL) for language and culturally diverse schools in high needs, urban districts. The intention of the federal grant program is to assist high need local educational agencies in developing, enhancing, or expanding their innovative programs to recruit, train, and mentor principals and assistant principals (U.S. Department of Education, 2002). The grant draws from both university knowledge and theory and the applied expertise of practicing administrators from the four participating school districts by: (a) recruiting and training new candidates for school leadership positions, (b) building the knowledge and competencies of beginning principals and assistant principals based on current research and understandings of the commitments required of educational leaders, and (c) encouraging the retention of expert school principals through participation in mentoring activities (Danzig, 2002).

Arnold Danzig, Arizona State University
Gary Kiltz, Arizona State University
Elsie Szescy, Arizona State University
Terrence Wiley, Arizona State University
Azadeh Osanloo, Arizona State University
Josué González, Arizona State University
Kay Hunnicutt, Arizona State University
Donna Macey, Arizona State University
Charlotte Boyle, Creighton Elementary School District, Phoenix, Arizona

WHAT IS LEARNER CENTERED LEADERSHIP?

As the title of the grant indicates, attention is given to the primary role of teaching and learning in the development of school leadership expertise. This view, by definition, involves changing the major source of inspiration for educational leadership away from management and toward education and learning. Murphy (2002b) proposes a role for leadership which entails developing a learning community, one in which greater attention is needed to promote an atmosphere of inquiry with greater focus on collaboration and shared decision making. In this new role, leaders will need to develop the capacity for reflection and promote self-inquiry among the entire school community.

Focus on Learning

Learner centered leadership involves a balance between the professional norms and personal dispositions of educators, with the larger good as defined by a learning community (Danzig & Wright, 2002). Without this focus on learning, there is considerable risk that the daily press of management tasks and a crisis mentality will override the school leader's attention. This enlarged role of leadership implies a movement away from bureaucratic models of schooling which monitor and track children based on efficiency to a model of schooling with the goal of educating all youngsters well. Two challenges that exist will be to reorient the principalship from management to leadership and to refocus the principalship from administration and policy toward teaching and learning.

This alternative framing, one in which leaders are learners, is central to this grant and to the experiences that we are developing as part of this program. Many leadership actions are implicit in a learner centered approach:

- The leader translates guiding ideas into educational practices that engage all members of the community.
- The leader designs effective learning processes so that individuals and organizations learn.
- The leader provides relevant school data that can be used as a tool for developing a learning community that strives to improve.
- The leader surfaces mental models that people bring to the world and helps faculty and staff identify strengths and weaknesses of these models.
- Leadership embraces a deeper understanding and learning about one's own work and practice.

This view of learner centered leadership implies that leaders individually commit to their own learning. Leaders committed to their own learning must therefore have the necessary time to reflect and answer these questions and the additional opportunities to apply what they have learned to their performances as school leaders. This application of a learner centered approach to educational leadership is complicated given the current political demands on leadership along with demands for greater accountability and press for increased individual and school academic performance. These demands must be balanced by recognitions that learning cannot always be reduced to a product and that learners have multiple reasons for engaging in learning. Therefore, the learning embedded in learner centered leadership must also take into account dilemmas and contradictions for practicing school leaders who adopt a learner centered focus.

Focus on the Central Role of Community in Learner Centered Leadership

Leadership that connects with community implies leadership at three distinct levels. On the first level, it implies embracing an external community of parents, families, and neighborhoods and using the resources available outside the school structure. Within this first level is the idea that the external community is an asset rather than deficit to learning. On the second level, it implies creating a community of learning within the school among teachers and staff in which learning is embraced and valued. At the third level, community leadership implies a focus on the creation of personalized learning communities among students. At all three levels, it implies leadership that is less bureaucratic in which others are empowered through dialogue, reflection, and democratic participation. Under the principles of learner centered leadership, the metaphor of principal as "captain of the ship" or as CEO no longer sustains critical scrutiny in the 21st century.

Focusing on community also presses school leaders to ask questions about community values, particularly values around educational equity and social justice. If the earlier discussion of re-culturing the profession is to be taken seriously, then the leaders of tomorrow's schools will be more heavily involved in defining purpose and establishing vision than in maintaining the status quo. This commitment involves greater attention to the culture of schools and to the values of parents, families, and communities. Learner centered leadership is built around the ability to understand, articulate, and communicate community culture and values and the ability to make sense of conflicting values and cultures. Learner centered leadership models democratic participation, considers new ideas, and embraces differences. One of the central aspects of the leader's work each day is to help clarify the day-to-day activities of participants as they contribute to a larger vision of educational purposes. In this view, the leader is a "moral steward" heavily invested in defining purposes which combine action and reflection. Leadership is more than simply managing existing arrangements and keeping fires from burning out of control. Putting out fires is not enough to nourish the minds and hearts of today's principals and school leaders. For that matter, even fire fighters define their work more broadly than just putting out fires and see a broader mission as serving people, whatever it takes.

The theme of community that is part of learner centered leadership asks leaders to translate guiding ideas into educational practices that engage all members of the community. Learner centered leaders serve the community and its ideals, and at the same time, recognize that the community is a work in progress. Schools simultaneously contribute to and reflect the development of local culture and democratic participation. This image of principal as community builder encourages others to be leaders in their own right and see to it that leadership is deeply distributed in the organization (Murphy, 2002a; Sergiovanni, 1994).

Focus on a Systems Approach to Change for Leadership in Urban Settings

The third strand or pillar of our grant, relates to understanding the combination of embedded constituents, multiple stakeholders, and complex relationships in urban school systems that require a systems approach to change. Learner centered leadership provides this alternative framing for school leadership, one in which leaders translate guiding ideas into educational practices that engage all members of the community. Lieberman, Falk, and Alexander (1995) define learner centered leadership as requiring school leaders to simultaneously be educators, problem solvers, crisis managers, change agents, enablers, consensus builders, and networkers. Learner centered leadership is built around these new conceptions for principals of our schools. Without this learner focus to leadership, traditional management tasks override the leader's time.

A systems approach recognizes various levels at which leadership must operate in order to change the status quo, solve problems, and meet human needs (Senge, Kleiner, Roberts, Ross, Roth, & Smith, 1999). A system approach to school reform and change necessarily involves collaboration among educators and others within and outside the traditional boundaries of the school. This approach requires understanding of one's own organizational culture, values, and priorities, and those of other organizations and providers. Systems thinking implies a collaboration and sharing which professionals do not routinely value. School principals expect to be held accountable for school-site stability and control. Teachers expect to be in control of their classrooms. When things go wrong, individuals are identified, not organizations. This leads to territorialism as a problem in organizations. One result is that the norm of reciprocity prevails: a quid pro quo of arrangements is typical of schools, between teachers and students, between principals and teachers, between administrators and school board, etc. Without powerful incentives, stakeholders will resist collaboration to preserve their individual control over their respective domains.

School leaders and stakeholders must learn different terminologies, find common interests, and resolve ideological conflicts in order to maintain day-to-day operations. Institutional disincentives to collaboration must also be understood and recognized: autonomy, time, non-accountability, control over one's own clientele, a sense of personal accomplishment, discretionary decision making, and the control of space are all rewards for non-collaboration. A model of school leader as community builder and the development of strong incentives are required for systems approaches to take hold, and for conditions to improve. In the grant, achieving this level of collaboration is a daily effort, both within the University team and among the University partners. The effort to collaborate, in itself, requires crossing of organizational boundaries in both university and school settings.

PRELIMINARY OUTCOMES AND FINDINGS FROM YEAR ONE

In order to carry out this mission of developing leaders who are learners, the grant project team is working with 93 participants who are in three distinct categories.

Table 1. Participant Information (Gender and Ethnicity)

	Gender	Ethnicity
Prospective Leaders (N = 32)	Female = 18 (56%) Male = 14 (44%)	African American = 7 (22%) Caucasian = 14 (44%) Hispanic = 11 (34%)
Rising Leaders (N = 31)	Female = 23 (74%) Male = 8 (26%)	African American = 6 (19%) Asian American = 1 (3%) Caucasian = 13 (42%) Hispanic = 10 (32%) Native American = 1 (3%)
Accomplished Leaders (N = 30)	Female = 17 (57%) Male = 13 (43%)	African American = 9 (30%) Caucasian = 16 (53%) Hispanic = 5 (17%)

The first group is a collection of prospective administrators who are currently enrolled in courses and working toward administrative certification. The second is a group of rising administrators who are in entry level administrative positions and hope to continue working in educational leadership. The final is a group of experienced and accomplished administrators who are serving as mentors for groups one and two. One of the goals of the grant is to encourage the promotion and retention of a diverse set of leaders within the four participating districts. This includes both gender and ethnic diversity. The outcomes reported are drawn from *The Annual Performance Report-Year One* (Kiltz & Danzig, 2003). Table 1 provides the numbers and percentages of participants related to gender and ethnicity for each of the three groups.

Educational Positions
Table 2 provides the professional positions that are held by participants in each group.

Table 2. Participant Information (Educational Positions)

	Professional Position	Number/Percent
Prospective Leaders (N = 32)	Elementary Teacher Secondary Teacher	24/75% 8/25%
Rising Leaders (N = 31)	Assistant Principal Dean of Students District Personnel Intervention Specialist Principal	15/49% 4/13% 2/6% 4/13% 6/19%
Accomplished Leaders (N = 30)	Assistant Superintendent Directors Principal	2/7% 3/9% 25/84%

Table 3.   Participant Retention-First Year (*)

Group	# of Participants-Start of Yr. One	# of Participants-End of Yr. 1
Prospective	32	29
Rising	31	31
Accomplished	30	30

(*) These figures represent the actual loss of seven participants out of 93 during the first year. The grant team has been able to add four new participants since the beginning of the program in January 2003 to replace those who have left.

Retention and Movement

Overall, the grant project team has been able to retain the participants in the program during the first year. With the prospective administrators, 32 participants began taking classes in the spring 2003 semester. Twenty-seven signed up to continue with coursework during the summer 2003 semester. Three of the individuals who are no longer enrolled expressed concern with balancing job and family responsibilities with coursework. Another participant decided that staying in the classroom as a teacher is the direction to go. The fifth person gave no reason for withdrawing from the program. Two new students were added to the program in summer 2003. Finally, one student has accepted a half-time administrative position with another high poverty, urban district that is not affiliated with the grant program. This student is being allowed to stay with the cohort through the completion of the program and hopes to return to her current district as a future administrator.

The group of rising administrators lost one from the program. This person decided to move back into the classroom to teach. One rising administrator will be moving to Group 3 for the beginning of the 2003–2004 school year. Two new administrators will join Group 2 participants at the beginning of the 2003–2004 school year.

The group of accomplished administrators has lost one participant over the course of the first year. This person has decided to make a career change and become a chef. Table 3 summarizes this information.

RISING ADMINISTRATORS—SOME INITIAL AREAS OF INTEREST AND CONCERN

In some of the early sessions, we did some needs assessments to get an idea of the issues or problems that rising administrators faced as new administrators. They identified three critical issues/challenges that they face: student achievement for all, effecting change/dealing with resistance, and the challenge of leadership versus management. A second question probed the types of support or training that was desired: dealing with parents effectively, changing faculty attitudes, legal issues/discipline, special ed/legal issues, getting buy-in school community (establishing shared vision), grant writing, cross grade opportunity for articulation, planning, running, facilitating meetings so that they are effective and meaningful, getting resources for parents, students, school from the community (i.e. counseling).

Along with this discussion, we asked all of the rising administrators to complete the Training and Educational Leadership Self Assessment (TELSA). The purpose of the assessment is to provide educational leaders with a tool for assessing their development needs. The assessment is divided into ten general functions: lead analysis, design, and development of instruction; lead implementation of instruction; lead evaluation of instruction; lead staff development; perform learner-related duties; perform staff-related duties; perform budgetary and other administrative duties; communicate and use communication technology; self development; and crisis management. All 32 rising administrators completed the TELSA. Table 4 provides the general results from the TELSA.

During the month of February, rising administrators were also asked to have five individuals complete the Leadership Development Needs Assessment (LEADNA). This is a 360 degree assessment in which the participants selected five individuals (two who are people whom they supervise, two who are colleagues, and one who supervises them) to complete the survey. The survey provided information in the following categories: strategy, communication, knowledge, learning, influence, relationships, delegation, priorities, integrity, and confidence. Twenty-six out of the 32 participants received scores. The scores are provided in Table 5.

Accomplished Administrators

During the first meeting, accomplished administrators also had an opportunity to meet each other and talk about areas of need within the principalship. In their dis-

Table 4. TELSA Average Results (Rising Administrators, February 1, 2003)

Category	Difficulty	Importance	Frequency	Sum
Lead Analysis Design and Development	2.84	3.46	4.1	10.4
Lead Implementation of Instruction	2.24	4.2	2.93	9.37
Lead Evaluation of Instruction	2.39	3.69	3.66	9.74
Lead Staff Development	2.48	4.01	3.46	9.95
Learner-Related Duties	1.86	4.49	2.2	8.55
Staff-Related Duties	2.42	4.43	3.32	10.17
Budget and Other Admin. Duties	2.83	4.2	3.9	10.93
Communication Skills	1.83	4.0	2.58	8.41
Self-Development	2.34	4.55	1.6	8.49
Crisis Management	2.09	4.58	3.87	10.54

Use the following scale to interpret scores.
Score of 3–7—No formal training or development necessary—address your specific needs through reading and/or coaching from a mentor.
Score of 8–11—Initial formal training and development necessary (train one time). Take a college or commercial training course. Attend a seminar.
Score of 12–15—Initial and ongoing formal training and development necessary. Take a college or commercial training course, attend a seminar. Follow up with refresher courses and seminars.

Table 5. LEADNA Average Results (Rising Administrators, February 2003)

Number of Completed Surveys: 102		LEADNA Class Score: 4.22
Area	*Class Average*	*Norming Group Score*
Strategy	3.82	3.33
Communication	4.29	3.50
Knowledge	4.20	4.50
Learning	4.35	4.00
Influence	4.12	4.00
Relationships	4.49	4.00
Delegation	3.33	3.70
Priorities	4.42	4.00
Integrity	4.59	3.11
Confidence	4.11	3.78

cussion, they identified four important strands: management, communication, human relations, and learner centered leadership. They also completed a self-assessment that used the same categories as the TELSA, but was scored using a Likert scale. All 32 accomplished administrators completed the survey. Table 6 provides the average results of this assessment.

Using this information from the assessments and the discussion, topics for future Learner Centered Leadership workshops were discussed and planned. Based upon the assessments and session information, the project team decided to develop curriculum and experiences for the next series of workshops that focused primarily on developing relationships and secondarily on five topics that repeatedly came to the front in discussions and assessments with participants: (a) leadership versus management, (b) using data to improve student achievement, (c) ensuring achievement for diverse learners, (d) leading schools through a reform process, and (e) facilitative leadership.

Table 6. Average Results of Self-Assessment (Accomplished Administrators, February 1, 2003)

Participants were asked to rate their expertise using a Likert scale (1 = weak, 5 = strong) on processes related to ten administrative categories.

Category	*Mean*
Lead Analysis Design and Development	3.83
Lead Implementation of Instruction	3.92
Lead Evaluation of Instruction	3.79
Lead Staff Development	4.38
Learner-Related Duties	4.27
Staff-Related Duties	4.49
Budget and Other Admin. Duties	4.0
Communication Skills	3.81
Self-Development	3.64
Crisis Management	4.03

BUILDING RELATIONSHIPS: THE KEY TO CREATING THE CAPACITY FOR AN INTER-DISTRICT MENTORING PROGRAM FOR SCHOOL ADMINISTRATORS

The Learner Centered Leadership program provides professional development opportunities for school administrators, focusing on meeting the needs of beginning administrators through an emerging mentoring model. In order to develop the capacity at an inter-district level for a successful mentoring experience, the first eight months have focused on building relationships between district participants. To do this, the project team has focused its energy on sponsoring district-led workshops, informal socials and activities that provide opportunities for reflection, and participation in a Team Challenge activity that is modeled after ropes and challenge courses. All of these activities have been valuable, and have led to better relationships between participants from the four districts. This is reflected in the feedback forms and personal comments that have been gathered by the project team. As the project moves into the implementation of a mentoring experience, the relationships that have been established in this first phase will continue to flourish and to help the mentoring activities in the future.

Description of Participating Districts

Before looking at the mentoring model and the development of relationships, a description of each of the participating districts is necessary. All four districts are high needs, urban districts with language and culturally diverse student populations. One of the districts is an urban high school district. The other three districts are urban elementary school districts that feed into this high school district. The community in which these districts are located can be described as lower income with a high percentage of ethnic minorities and immigrant populations. The percentage of children living in poverty among these four districts ranges from 50.4% to 89%. In the high school district, 50.4% of the students are identified at the poverty level. The student population is comprised of 69.2% Hispanic, 10.4% African American, 15.5% Anglo, 1.7% Asian, and 3.1% Native American students. Over 60% of the student population speaks English as a second language. In one of the three elementary districts, the schools serve approximately 8,300 students, with a minority enrollment of 88%. Eighty-two percent of the students live at the low income/poverty level, and 74% are English language learners. Since the 1985–86 school year, there has been a 446% increase in students who have immigrant status within this district. The second elementary school district has about 11,500 students in twenty schools and is facing rapid growth. Four additional schools will be built. The student population has the following breakdown: 75% Hispanic, 19% African American, 5% Anglo, 0.9% Native American, and 0.15% Asian. Eighty percent of the school population is at or below the poverty level with over 65% of the students enrolled as English language learners. The final elementary school district is comprised of fifteen school sites serving over 14,000 students. The student population is comprised of 61.05% Hispanic, 21.127% Anglo, 9.4% African American, 5.17% Native American, and 3.1% Asian. This elementary school district has an 85%

poverty level, and has over 60% of its student population speaking English as a second language.

Looking at student achievement on the Stanford 9, a norm-referenced test, and on the Arizona Instrument to Measure Standards (AIMS), the state's standards-based assessment, the participating schools do worse than other schools in these four districts and within the state. The Learner Centered Leadership program includes 33 schools out of 57 from the four participating districts. On the AIMS, students are assessed in reading, writing, and math. On average, students from participating schools score 2.5 points lower than the average score of all schools from the four districts and 26.75 points lower than the average student score at the state level (see Figure 1).

When looking at the percentage of students demonstrating proficiency or better on the AIMS, the same pattern is revealed. The average percentage of students from participating schools showing proficiency or better is 2.3 percentage points below the average for all schools from the four districts and 24.4 percentage points below the state average (see Figure 2).

Finally, on the norm-referenced Stanford 9 assessment, students from participating schools again lagged behind other schools from participating districts and within the state. Looking at average percentile ranks, students from participating schools are 2.3 percentile points below the percentile rank average of all schools from the four districts and 19.5 percentile points below the state average percentile rankings (see Figure 3).

As these statistics show, students from the participating schools struggle academically to do well on both the AIMS and Stanford 9 assessments. This disparity may be the result of any number of factors including student demographics, mobility rates of both students and teachers, and access to educational resources within the schools. With the high percentage of students who are non-English speakers, who

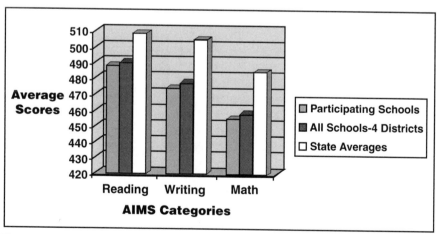

Figure 1. Average Student Scores on AIMS for Reading, Writing, and Math for Participation Schools, Districts, and State Averages.

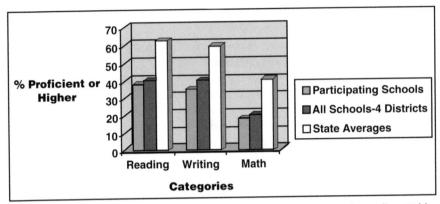

Figure 2.   Average Percentage of Students at or above Proficiency on AIMS in Reading, Writing, and Math by Schools, Districts, and State Average.

live in poverty, and who do poorly academically, the issues that these districts face are complex. In order to work through these issues associated with being an urban school district with a diverse student population, a collaborative model of professional development for school leaders is important. The Learner Centered Leadership Program provides a means for the four districts to share model programs, to provide research on best practices, and to support each other through the chaotic process of school leadership and administration in these urban, diverse districts.

FINAL THOUGHTS

In order to create a leadership professional development program, a mentoring model has emerged as the way to develop university-district and inter-district col-

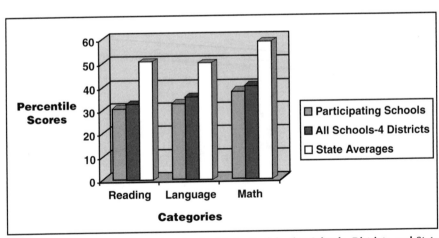

Figure 3.   Average Percentile Ranks—Stanford 9 for Participating Schools, Districts, and State Averages.

laboration. Research has shown the importance of mentoring for prospective administrators who are in the process of doing an internship (Daresh & Playko, 1992; Crow & Matthews, 1998) as well as rising administrators who may be in their first couple of years in administration (Daresh & Playko, 1997; Daresh, 2001). Mentoring serves as a great opportunity for professional growth and development.

Effective mentoring relationships require a level of trust, respect, ethics, and communication (Shea, 1994; Hay, 1995; Johnson, 1997). In order to engage in intense dialogue about tough and complicated issues in meaningful ways, participants must establish a level of trust including the insurance that confidences will not be betrayed. Along with this, the participants must respect opinions and experiences that each brings to the mentoring relationship. Without this mutual respect, individual growth may not occur as a result of the dialogue and mentoring. Finally, mentoring is about effective communication that embraces listening and providing constructive feedback. This does not mean that ideas and opinions should not be challenged. On the contrary, a mentoring relationships should encourage shifting of thoughts, roles, and ideas. At times, this requires confrontation, but if the relationship is built on trust, respect, and ethics, then the result of this confrontation will be personal and professional growth. To ensure that the appropriate foundation is set to engage in these difficult conversations, relationships need to be formed that reflect trust, respect, and communication.

During the past eight months, the LCL program has been focusing on the building of relationships so that participants have the capacity to embed the mentoring model into their daily practices. Although the four districts are in close proximity with each other, they historically have done little inter-district planning or sharing of resources and expertise. One of the goals of the grant project has been to ensure that inter-district collaboration occurred. For this reason, it was important for the project team to begin breaking down barriers that may have existed at the very beginning of the grant project. The hope was to accomplish this through a three-fold process: formal activities and workshops that introduced each district and its administrators including needs and expectations; informal activities that broke down personal barriers and developed a pattern of networking; and participation in a Team Challenge activity that focused on team-building. The three elements provided a comprehensive plan for building inter-district relationships that create the capacity for effective mentoring.

NOTE

This paper is based on a symposium presentation at the annual meeting of the National Council of Professors of Educational Administration, August 5–8, 2003, Sedona, AZ. Research in this article is supported by a grant from the United States Department of Education, Office of Innovation and School Improvement under NCLB, Title II, Subpart 5, Section 2151, School Leadership.

REFERENCES

Crow, G., & Matthews, L. J. (1998). *Finding one's way: How mentoring can lead to dynamic leadership.* Thousand Oaks, CA: Corwin Press.

Danzig, A. (2002). *Learner-centered leadership for language and culturally diverse schools in high need urban settings*: Grant Application to USDOE, Office of Innovation and School Improvement un NCLB, Title II, Subpart 5, Section 2151, School Leadership. Arizona State University, Tempe, AZ.

Danzig, A., & Wright, W. (2002). *Science versus service: Narrative and story-based professional development with school administrators at a county regional school district*. Paper presented in Division A—Symposium, New Models of Professional Development for Learner-Centered Leadership at the annual meeting of the American Educational Research Association, April 1–5, 2002, New Orleans, LA.

Daresh, J. (2001). *Leaders helping leaders: A practical guide to administrative mentoring*. Thousand Oaks, CA: Corwin Press.

Daresh, J., & Playko, M. (1992). *The professional development of school administrators: Pre-service, induction, and inservice applications*. Boston: Allyn & Bacon.

Daresh, J., & Playko, M. (1997). *Beginning the principalship: A practical guide for new school leaders*. Thousand Oaks, CA: Corwin Press.

Hay, J. (1995). *Transformational mentoring: Creating developmental alliances for changing organizational cultures*. New York: McGraw-Hill.

Johnson, H. (1997). *Mentoring for exceptional performance*. Glendale, CA: Griffin Publishing.

Kiltz, G., & Danzig, A. (2003). *Learner-centered leadership for language and culturally diverse schools in high need urban settings: Annual performance report-year one*. Tempe, AZ: Arizona State University.

Lieberman, A., Falk, B., & Alexander, A. (1995). A culture in the making: Leadership in learner-centered schools. In J. Oakes & K. H. Quartz (Eds.), *Creating new educational communities* (Ninety-fourth yearbook of the National Society for the Study of Education, Part I, (pp. 108–129). Chicago: University of Chicago Press.

Murphy, J. (2002a, April). *A design paper for the Ohio Principals Leadership Academy: A discussion draft*. Paper presented at the annual meeting of the American Educational Research Association, New Orleans, LA.

Murphy, J. (2002b). Reculturing the profession of educational leadership: New blueprints. *Educational Administration Quarterly, 38*(2), 176–191.

Senge, P., Kleiner, A., Roberts, C., Ross, R., Roth, G., & Smith, B. (1999). *The dance of change: The challenges to sustaining momentum in learning organizations*. New York: Currency/Doubleday.

Sergiovanni, T. (1994). *Building community in schools*. San Francisco: Jossey-Bass.

Shea, G. (1994). *Mentoring: Helping employees reach their full potential*. New York: American Management Association.

United States Department of Education. (2002). *Application for grants under the school leadership program*. Washington, DC: United States Department of Education.

United States Department of Energy. (1998). *TELSA — Training and Educational Leader Self Assessment*. U.S. Department of Energy, Carlsbad Area Office: Westinghouse Electric Company.

United States Department of Energy. (1998). *LEADNA — Leadership Development Needs Assessment*. U.S. Department of Energy, Carlsbad Area Office: Westinghouse Electric Company.

Profiles of Outstanding Female and Male Superintendents: A Comparative Study of Leadership Dimensions

Carole Funk, Barbara Polnick, Anita Pankake, and Gwen Schroth

> Extraordinary leaders are those who inspire people during their lives and make lasting contributions . . . many of these leaders have been school superintendents, dedicated public servants charged to work with boards of education and communities to provide the best possible education for all children and youth.
>
> (Hoyle, 2002, p. 1)

When Hoyle, English, and Steffy (1985) worked with the American Association of School Administrators (AASA) regarding skills needed by school superintendents, they determined that eight major skill areas were needed for success in the public schools at the time. However, statistical analyses indicated that these works reflected mostly the responses of males who dominated the work force in the 1980s. Candoli, Cullen, and Stufflebeam (1997) highlighted the work of the Texas LEAD Center by identifying over 50 basic required skills needed by superintendents, the nearly 14,000 men and women who provide day-to-day executive leadership for nearly 90,000 schools (Glass, 2001), but did not make any distinctions between skill areas for male and female superintendents. As more female school administrators continue to enter positions as superintendents, the significance of their leadership roles and behaviors become more important to the profession of education (Funk, Pankake, & Schroth, 2003; Pankake, Schroth, & Funk, 2000; Glass, Bjork, & Brunner, 2000; Slick & Gupton, 1993). However, limited research has been conducted regarding these women, especially those who are highly successful in their positions as superintendents.

Beckley (1999) found that female and male superintendents differed from one another particularly regarding ethnicity, marital status, career paths, and political

Carole Funk, Sam Houston State University
Barbara Polnick, Sam Houston State University
Anita Pankake, University of Texas-Pan American
Gwen Schroth, Texas A&M University–Commerce

persuasions from their male counterparts, revealing quite different patterns between males and females who occupy positions as school superintendents. No attempts in this study, however, to provide information regarding differences between leadership characteristics of male and female leadership were made. Funk, Polnick, Pankake, and Schroth (2004), however, did find differences between successful male and female superintendents, but their findings were limited to qualities of leadership, impact of developmental experiences, and responses to failure that led to later success in their lives and careers. Critical information regarding the differences between successful male and female leadership characteristics, essential superintendent roles, ethical behaviors, communication styles, motivational efforts, relationships with school board members, and other critical areas has been limited. To date, few studies have been concerned with differences and similarities between male and female superintendents and the ways in which they lead.

"In earlier studies and leadership theories related to the study of leadership, gender differences were completely ignored" (Lougheed, 2001, p. 185), resulting in beliefs that women did not have the ability to meet the norms of behavior and possess individual characteristics considered to be critical for success in the field of school administration. The findings in her study revealed few significant differences in leadership styles of men and women, noting that Lougheed's research results are congruent with findings of social science researchers. She also revealed that "women just didn't fit, and if they wanted to fit they would have to act more like men and learn to play games their mothers never taught them. The consensus was that women were not socialized to compete with men" (p. 185). Another interesting finding in this research revealed that both women and men were equally concerned with task and people, and the higher the educational level of these administrators, the more they related to relationships with others. From her research results, this author determined that leadership characteristics of males and female differed by age, education, occupation, marital status, and upward mobility. In addition, they kept their distinctive leadership styles over time. Other data indicated that an increasing number of women were seen by their female and male counterparts as "being better communicators, sharing power, and being more people-oriented" (p. 186).

Brown, Irby, and Iselt (2002) studied the gender perspectives of superintendent preparation programs, noting that "female superintendents found the programs less relevant than did male superintendents" (p. 163). In the analyses of these data, the researchers found that men and women viewed the relevance of eight of the 30 topics included in the program differently in terms of how the topics related to their job performance. The topics that were shown to be more important to the males than the females included: legal issues, organizational culture/climate, ethics, working within the cultural/political system, collaboration, networking, use of mentors, and interviewing practices. According to these authors, insufficient attention was given to these areas in their superintendent's certification program.

Results from another comparison study of male and female school leadership (Bradshaw & Phillips, 2002) indicated that male and female responses to questions regarding key events that changed their approach to leadership, described their challenges, mistakes, and disappointments as well as organizational events not related to their actions. Overall, responses of these women and men indicated that female and male participants were more similar than different. Both males and females reported that they were concerned about building positive relationships with others, involving others in planning and decision-making processes, ensuring that members of the faculty are given the information that they needed, and receiving appropriate staff development. The results of this research also supported the fact that male and female school leaders are concerned with the concept of both task and people. In a related study, Gupton and Slick (1996) found that the leadership style of female respondents revealed that women leaders were more "verbally oriented, more concerned bout personal relationships, and more cooperative than males in similarly oriented" (p. xxxi). These women also believed themselves to share the following characteristics with their male counterparts, seeing themselves as: aggressive, competitive, spatially oriented, career oriented, family oriented, and androgynous. These female respondents also noted that they were different from their male counterparts because they used transformational leadership, motivating others by transforming their self-interest into the goals of the organization, while men used transactional leadership.

Overall, superintendents in the United States make visionary leadership the driving force for school change (Hoyle et al., 1985), strive to achieve organizations in which all children can be successful through the use of strong policy and governance, oversee the design of curriculum and development of a plan to enhance teaching and learning in multiple contexts, and create and manage a personnel system successfully. Other leadership characteristics for school superintendents include focusing their attention to clearly identified major priorities, interests, and commitments; using goal-directed activities to put in place an orderly and systematic monitoring and assessment of progress for identified focus areas; modeling positive behavior, interacting frequently with teachers and administrators; being directly involved in the instructional process; providing an emphasis on human resources; emphasizing staff empowerment and sophisticated staff development process; and giving close attention to hiring practices in the district. According to Hutchinson (2002), noteworthy differences existed between men and women who served in positions of educational administration which also included differences in "personal characteristics, professional preparation, and career paths. Differences were also noted in the effect of mentors, networking, gender-related myths, and career aspirations" (p. 364). Other differences between male and female superintendents were revealed by Glass et al. (2000), who indicated in his national study that female superintendents were found to be younger than male superintendents, a change from previous years, when women superintendents were much older than the men superintendents. In addition, distinctly different characteristics between female superintendents and the males revealed that fewer of the women had been married, women had spent more time as teachers before going into administration, and more women than men had taught in elementary schools.

Brunner (1997) described differences between female and male superintendents, noting that there is proportionally more diversity among female superintendents than among the 93% of the males who occupy the superintendency. In her research, Brunner indicated that male superintendents are primarily Caucasian, Protestant, married with children, and Republicans. In contrast, female superintendents are more often people of color; Catholic or Jewish either never married or divorced or widowed and Democrats. In 2001, Brunner noted that it was still difficult for a woman to be appointed as a school superintendent, especially in large urban districts—rebutting the idea that the playing field for male and female candidates for these positions was now even. Furthermore, she stated that only 14 percent of women are school superintendents and indicated that women who are school superintendents have to be outstanding. Differences between male and female superintendents revealed in Brunner's work indicate that women have to be well-liked in order to be respected by others and considered successful. However, she stressed, men are not required to have these characteristics. Other differences noted by this author regarding differences between male and female superintendents show the following: men more often define power in terms of dominance, authority, influence, and control, while female superintendents tend to work together with their colleagues to get things done through the use of transactional leadership. According to Brunner, female superintendents will be successful when using a traditional feminine process but will not succeed if they use the masculine construct of leadership. She found in her research that women as superintendents use power in collaboration with others, building circles of consensus (2001). From her research findings, she also suggested that women use a type of collaborative power that meshes with a shift toward administrative styles of superintendents that matched well with the current shift to shared leadership, providing a nonconfrontational approach that supports the participation of others in the decision-making process.

As a result of the literature review regarding male and female superintendents, there are some distinctions made between the leadership characteristics, practices and styles of male and female school district leaders but no substantive research comparing outstanding male and female superintendents. In contrast, the results of this research study regarding highly successful male and female superintendents provide an inside look at the differences and similarities between these groups of educational leaders.

PURPOSE OF THE STUDY

The purpose of this study was to determine the profiles of outstanding male and female superintendents that would reveal comparisons between these two groups regarding leadership themes, unique characteristics, qualities, essential roles, and critical skills that made them highly successful school district leaders. The twelve subjects selected for this study included six female superintendents and six male superintendents who had either been named or nominated for the Superintendent of the Year Award by the Texas Association of School Administrators (TASA), thereby defining the term "outstanding superintendent." The female subjects in this study represented six of the seven women who met the criteria for outstanding superin-tendents, and each of the males who was selected represented the same years in the study in which the female superintendents were nominated for or won this out-standing superintendent award.

The original study from which the data for this research were utilized was based on the work of Bennis (1989) who noted that leaders learn from their experiences; asserting that making mistakes in their roles as leaders produces "potent lessons" that lead to future successes. Hoy and Miskel (1996) agreed with Bennis' premise, noting that overcoming failure leads to success and also contributes to the devel-opment of self-efficacy of leaders. The initial research using the idea of "failure leading to subsequent success" was first conducted with highly successful, out-standing female superintendents in Texas (Pankake, Schroth, & Funk, 2000). The results of this initial study revealed a striking similarity between and among these women with regard to their beliefs about the importance of their responses to fail-ure as a learning experience and how that played out in their lives but also the qualities of leadership, vital developmental experiences, turning points in their lives, what they learned from failure, people they admired, and the positive and negative organizational effects on leaders. The next stage of this research involved selecting outstanding male superintendents who also responded to the Bennis questions, allowing the researchers to collect comparative data for these two groups of successful leaders. The questions utilized in both studies were utilized by the researchers with the permission of Bennis (1989). These questions used by this author are noted here.

1. What do you believe are the qualities of leadership?
2. What experiences were vital to your development?
3. What were the turning points in your life?
4. What role has failure played in your life?
5. How did you learn from this (failure)?
6. Are there people in your life, or in general, whom you particularly admire?
7. What can organization do to encourage or stifle leaders?

METHODOLOGY

The methodology of this research was conducted using structured, face-to-face in-terviews with each of the male and female superintendents in the study. All inter-views were conducted in person, audio-taped, and transcribed in order to provide rich database for the analysis of the resulting verbatim transcripts. A content analy-sis technique was utilized by the researchers to identify significant descriptors for the characteristics of subjects that were identified and collected during these inter-view sessions. Overall, the average length of the interviews was one hour to one and one-half hours in length. These data were collected over a three-year period with these interviews involving the same twelve outstanding male and female superin-tendents. The database resulting from the responses to the questions for both out-standing female and male leaders led to a separate analysis of each data set in order to determine differences between the themes, qualities, roles, and skills — one for the female superintendents and one for the male superintendents.

Following this analysis of the survey data from the outstanding female and male superintendents, the researchers determined the leadership themes, unique qualities and characteristics, essential roles, and critical skills that emerged from the initial content analysis regarding comparisons between these two groups of outstanding superintendents. Using an inductive process, the researchers made generalizations regarding specific leadership data that were identified in the thought units during the initial analysis. These data were analyzed separately to allow the leadership categories to reveal leadership differences by gender. After the completion of this step, the researchers developed profiles of these two groups of outstanding male school district leaders. Comparisons were then made between the profiles of the two groups, revealing the commonalities and differences between the overall profiles of these successful male and female superintendents.

FINDINGS FROM THE DATA ANALYSIS
Review of the Findings from Interviews with the Female Superintendents

The six superintendents included in this initial phase were all female and had been nominated for the Texas Association of School Administrators' Outstanding Superintendent of the Year Award. A personal interview with each of these women was conducted by the research team, using Bennis' (1989) seven questions listed in *On Becoming a Leader*. All interviews ranged from one to one and one-half hour in length. All interviews were audio-taped and scripted. Audiotapes were transcribed to facilitate analysis. Content analysis techniques were used in examining the data to discover common theses/threads between and among the interviews.

Five questions were used here to organize the information gleaned from analysis of the interviews with the six female superintendents.

1. What Actions and Beliefs Did Each of the Six Superintendents Identify as Qualities of Leadership?

Vision, passion, and commitment, and promoting leadership in others were the qualities of leadership most often identified by these six female superintendents. Additionally, three other qualities were identified by more than one but not by a majority of these superintendents. Integrity and honesty, knowledge and energy or stamina were repeated themes.

2. What Experiences Did They Report as Being Especially Important in Their Own Leadership Development?

The six female superintendents identified five major categories of vital experiences. These categories were support from family, variety of work experiences, mentors, formal education, and learning about the organizational context. Experiences described in each of these categories ranged from special attention received during childhood from a parent or grandparent to incidents in their administrative careers that brought about major perspective changes regarding issues such as politics in the public schools and the strength of support one can expect from colleagues and community during difficult situations.

3. Did These Superintendents Perceive Any Mistakes or Failure Incidents as Contributing to Their Development as Successful Leaders? The Follow-up Question Asked "What Role Has Failure Played in Your Life?"

The female superintendents tended to reject the term "failure." They renamed the experiences with terminology having a less negative connotation, e.g., "setbacks," "conflicts," and "hot stoves." After renaming the incidents, each of the women went on to describe at least one event, either personal or professional, in response to the follow-up question.

4. Did the Superintendents Make Specific Efforts to Learn from These Experiences? The Follow-up Question Was "How Did You Learn?"

Responses from each of these leaders indicated that their mistakes/failures had taught them some valuable lessons. Most intriguing, however, was that the words and phrases used by these women in describing the lessons learned from failure/ mistakes were in many cases echoes of the assertions regarding learning from failure made by the experts in their writings and research on motivation and leadership. Some examples of what we found are included in the following quotes.

> When I have encountered a failure situation, I really make myself go through the discipline of sitting down and trying to analyze what went wrong . . . what could I have done differently, and then, what can I do about it?
>
> I think failure strengthens a person. I think it helps you understand who you are and allows you to focus or look at those areas that need to be developed.

5. Were Any "Lessons in Common" Identified Regarding What These Superintendents Learned about Themselves and Their Organizations through These Mistakes/Failure Experiences?

The common themes in the lessons learned from failure for the female superintendents focused on support, loyalty, and commitment to the big issues of education. These women told stories about learning the extent to which they could count on others' support or when they would truly be "on their own." They had used these experiences to help them understand that this limited loyalty in difficult situations was not planned but was rather a consequence of the situation in which people need to survive.

Reviews of the Findings from Interviews with the Male Superintendents

This phase of the research study involved interviews with six more superintendents, this time all males. This second group of successful superintendents was also selected from nominees for the TASA's Outstanding Superintendent of the Year Awards. One individual was randomly selected from among all the male nominees for each of the years in which there was also a female nominee but the individual selected might or might not be the award recipient for that year. The same interview procedures, interview questions, and data analysis techniques from the initial phase were used in this phase of the research. Data from this phase of the study have been organized to address the five questions guiding the research.

1. What Actions and Beliefs Did Each of the Six Superintendents Identify as Qualities of Leadership?

The leadership qualities most often identified by the six male superintendents were vision, integrity and credibility, honesty, working hard/work ethic. Additionally, three of these superintendents identified being a good listener as a leadership quality, and two of them noted that knowledge was an important leadership quality.

2. What Experiences Did They Report as Being Especially Important in Their Own Leadership Development?

Two areas common to the six superintendents' responses to the question regarding what experiences were vital to their development were "support from family" and "formal education." All six of these individuals specifically mentioned their parents and the home environment in which they grew up as being a vital part of their development. The home environments for five of these superintendents had been in small/rural communities with some involvement in farming and other agriculture-related activities. A supportive spouse was identified by four of the six superintendents as important to their leadership development.

Regarding formal education, five of the six male superintendents interviewed mentioned completing the doctoral degree as an important experience in their leadership development. Even further back in their formal schooling, all of them told of going to college and deciding to go into teaching as important life experiences for them as leaders. Three individuals told stories of their work experiences in their own businesses as being vital to their development. Being entrepreneurs and having to compete to succeed (though not all of the stories were about success) were included in the descriptions of why these experiences were viewed as important. One individual mentioned his involvement with the governance and operation of a professional association as vital to his leadership development; another mentioned the various experiences gleaned through a variety of administrative positions as being important for his development as a leader.

3. Did These Superintendents Perceive Any Mistakes or Failure Incidents as Contributing to Their Development as Successful Leaders? The Follow-up Question Asked "What Role Has Failure Played in Your Life?"

Responses to the original question varied from reporting that no failures (at least not big ones) had occurred to not getting a job that the individuals desperately wanted. All described failures were either school ones (if early years) or professional ones (if mature years) as well as ones involving personal interactions or responsibilities. Still everyone responded to the question in some way. As the researchers found with the female superintendents, responses to the follow-up question reflected that they learned from failure. This type of response occurred even from those who noted no big failure experiences occurring in their lives.

4. Did the Superintendents Make Specific Efforts to Learn from These Experiences?

Each of the male superintendents interviewed had something to offer regarding lessons learned from mistakes/failure experiences. Much of what the male superintendents had to say regarding their efforts to learn from their mistakes/failures reflected what was found in the literature on this topic. Following are quotes from the male superintendents regarding failure.

> Well, we learn from failures and we all fail . . . . You got to learn from the failure and you got to try to analyze why you did what you did, what you need to do or not to do and learn from those . . .
>
> I learned a lot. I learned about myself, I learned a lot about people in general, and there again was exposed to some situations that I think put me in a good position for a lot of years.

5. Were Any "Lessons in Common" Identified Regarding What These Superintendents Learned about Themselves and Their Organizations through These Mistakes/Failure Experiences?

Comments regarding what these individuals had learned from their failure experiences seemed to have a common theme of introspection and behavior analysis. The lessons learned included learning to be a little more reflective, analyzing why something was done and what needed to be done or not done in the future, and looking at situations differently in the future. Generally, the individuals' judgments of the events they reported were positive even though they were responding to a set of questions regarding their mistakes and/or failures.

Learning to be persistent was another lesson these superintendents learned through their mistakes and/or failure experiences.

RESULTS OF THE ANALYSIS OF FEMALE SUPERINTENDENTS

The results of this study began with the separate analysis of the responses made by the six female superintendents and the six male superintendents. The results of the analysis of the data for the themes, qualities, roles, and skills for female superintendents are presented below.

1. Vision, commitment, and promoting leadership for others were those most often identified by all these women, followed by integrity, honesty, knowledge, energy, and stamina that were repeated themes but were not noted by a majority of these superintendents.
2. Vital experiences toward their developmental themes included support from family, having a variety of work experiences, mentors, formal education, and learning about the organizational context. Experiences described included

special attention given by a parent or grandparent, incidents in their careers that brought about major changes regarding political issues, and the strength of support one can expect from colleagues and community during difficult situations.

3. Perceptions regarding mistakes or failures and their effects revealed that female superintendents tended to reject the term "failure" and renamed their experiences with terms that had a less negative connotation such as having setbacks, conflicts, and hot stoves.

4. Learning from failure led to responses that indicated that these women taught them valuable lessons about learning from failure and mistakes. Analyzing what went wrong, strengthens you, allows you to focus on developing the areas regarding the failure, learning that you don't have to get credit for what you do, and not to quit.

5. Lessons in common regarding mistakes learned about their organizations through their failures include the importance of loyalty, support and commitment to the big issues of education, and being aware of the danger of limited loyalty from those you work because of their survival needs.

RESULTS OF THE ANALYSIS OF MALE SUPERINTENDENTS

The results of this phase of the study began with the separate analysis of the themes, qualities, roles and critical skills that were reported by the six male superintendents. The results of the analysis of the data for the themes, characteristics and qualities, roles, and critical skills for male superintendents are presented below.

1. Leadership qualities and beliefs most often identified by male superintendents were vision, integrity, credibility, honesty, working hard, and having a strong work ethic. Those qualities that were noted by half of these male leaders were being a good listener, and two others indicated that knowledge was also an important trait.

2. Vital experiences common to the six male superintendents include support from family and formal education. All members of this group specially mentioned their parents and home environment where they grew up (five were from small/rural communities). A supportive spouse was identified by four of the six male superintendents as being very important to their leadership development.

   In addition, five of the six superintendents mentioned the completion of their doctoral degree was an important experience, but all agreed that going to college and deciding to teach was also a factor leading to their development. Three noted that their strong experiences also involved succeeding in work outside of education, being an entrepreneur, having to compete, leading a professional association, and being given a wide variety of administrative experiences.

3. The role of failure in the lives of these men indicated that some reported no failures (at least not big ones), not getting a job one wanted desperately, and all

these failures were involved with school, professional failures, and those involving personal interactions or responsibilities. As noted with their female counterparts, male superintendents stated that they learned from failure even though they did not note a "big" failure experience in their lives.

4. Each of the male superintendents shared something regarding lessons learned from their mistakes or failure experiences that included forcing me to be introspective, regroup, create a new vision, and do whatever necessary to achieve a goal. Others indicated that their behavior was changed, were more careful with relationships, took advantage of the moment/day, learned a lot about myself and to have faith, made the best of things, and didn't look back on decisions made. Others noted that they had to learn that they had to want it bad enough to be successful, not to get out of balance because of failure or rejection, not to wallow in self-pity, and do what you need to do differently next time for you to succeed.

   Common lessons learned regarding failure experiences for male superintendents included learning to be more reflective, analyzing why you did what you did and what you should do to change, looking at things differently the next time, and knowing if I want this bad enough, I'll do what I need to do to be successful.

5. Responses regarding organizational themes included a need to build trust, set boundaries, be extremely professional, be more reflective, take decisions seriously, have a little faith, and don't look back on the decisions you make.

COMPARISON OF OUTSTANDING
FEMALE AND MALE SUPERINTENDENTS

A comparison of male and female superintendents as revealed in the data analysis allowed the following comparisons regarding actions and beliefs as they related to qualities of leadership of these successful school leaders. These can be found in Table 1.

Both male and female superintendents identified vision, integrity, and honesty, knowledge, and working hard (energy and stamina) as important qualities of leadership. The women included passion and commitment and promoting leadership in others in their list of qualities. Neither of these appears in the list of qualities offered by the men. Being a good listener and having credibility were two qualities identified by men but not women. Overall the lists are more alike than different. Additionally, both lists are quite similar to the one offered by Bennis (1989), i.e., guiding vision, passion, integrity, trust, curiosity, and daring.

Table 1. Comparison of Leadership Actions and Beliefs

Female Superintendents	*Male Superintendents*
Vision	Vision
Passion and Commitment	Credibility
Integrity and Honesty	Integrity and Honesty
Promoting Leadership in Others	Being a Good Listener
Knowledge	Knowledge
Energy and Stamina	Working Hard/Work Ethic

Table 2. Comparison of Important Experiences

Female Superintendents	Male Superintendents
Support from Family	Support from Family
Variety of Work Experiences	Formal Education
Mentors	Supportive Spouse
Formal Education	Business Experiences
Learning the Organizational Context	Leadership in Professional Associations; Variety of Administrative Positions

A comparison of male and female superintendents as revealed in the data analysis also allowed the following comparisons regarding experiences that were especially important in their development as successful school leaders. These can be found in Table 2.

Once again, comparing lists from the male and female interviews offers some important similarities and differences. For both males and females, "education" and "support of family" are common themes in what these successful leaders see as being important to their development as leaders. Stories about events during their childhoods, strong and continuing relationships with parents and grandparents, especially as they relate expectations for performance, and the critical role their spouses have played in education, especially earning a doctorate, were identified by both males and females. Learning about the organizational context as well as business experiences were related to "people lessons" they learned. Understanding competition, realizing that not everyone can be trusted, finding out that sometimes good people are held back because they are too good to lose from the boss's perspective, and discovering that not everyone has good intentions—were lessons embedded in these experiences.

Some male superintendents and some female superintendents denied having experienced any failures at all; however, each of the subjects in the study ended up telling one or more incidents involving mistakes or failures in response to the questions posed to them. The females' incidents, however, were more often personal than those shared by the males. The women shared failures in family relationships as well as in professional settings. Incidents shared by the men were related to formal schooling experiences of females and two of the males as either a turning point or a mistake failure incident influencing their development as leaders.

Relationships and trust were often at the heart of both the personal and professional incidents. The relationship incidents ranged from difficulties with a spouse or parent to sabotage attempts from board members of community groups. Stories about trust issues with employees, between themselves, and their board members were frequent.

Both the females and the males were able to identify lessons learned from mistakes and/or failure incidents in their lives. The lessons shared by both groups mirrored the information in the literature about mistakes and failures. In addition, each of these groups indicated that they became more reflective and analytical about themselves and their behavior as lessons learned and renewed resolve to act differently in order to succeed in subsequent attempts at a particular relationship or achievement goal.

Learning to "read the organization" was a common theme among the lessons learned from mistakes and failures from these superintendents. Issues of trust, the volatility of seemingly simple issues that escalate to major controversies, commitment and loyalty of individuals during controversial episodes in the organization's development, and decisions regarding when to "lay down the gauntlet," when to "back off," were themes told during these interviews. The themes of reflection and reevaluation of their goals was also common between these two groups of superintendents as they voiced commitments to make changes in themselves and to persevere in their efforts regarding their mistakes or failures. These superintendents reinterpreted their stories, seeing them as times when they became much wiser about themselves and their work.

SUMMARY AND CONCLUSIONS

Perhaps the most interesting finding from this study of highly successful female and male superintendents was that there were more similarities than differences between these two groups. Overall these superintendents agreed on the importance of vision, integrity, honesty, knowledge, and credibility to success in the superintendency. Common themes between these male and female superintendents regarding education and family support in their leadership development included: positive childhood experiences, supportive parents and grandparents, and helpful spouses who also assisted both male and female superintendents in performing well in their roles. Lessons learned from private sector experiences as well as in organizational perspectives were seen as important commonalities for both groups as well. One factor that resonated most often for superintendents of both genders was getting the doctoral degree.

Renaming failure events or denying having failed at all was common to both female and male superintendents; however, in spite of their efforts to prove that they had not been unsuccessful or failed, every male and female subject in this study shared information regarding at least one "failure" that had occurred in their lives. Other interesting differences between these groups with relation to mistakes made revealed that female superintendents were more likely to describe personal mistakes, while their male counterparts more often described mistakes in terms of their experiences in school settings. Failure also influenced their leadership development.

The following conclusions have been generalized from the data regarding outstanding female and male superintendents who had been nominated for or won the Superintendent of the Year award. The conclusions presented here highlight the most salient findings of the data from the interviews with the male and female superintendents in this study.

- Relationships, both personal and professional, are important factors in the development and success of outstanding superintendents.
- Scanning the environment and ensuring that communication channels are open allows for early-warning systems for superintendents that reveal emerging misunderstandings, conflicts, and power plays.

- Powerful school district leaders utilize failure events in their professional and personal lives to reflect on their behaviors and actions and make necessary changes to grow and be more successful in the future.
- Strong school executives do not admit to failures but reframe such experiences in a positive manner when reflecting on trying times in their positions.
- Mentors and family members (especially supportive spouses for male superintendents) are important to the development of outstanding male and female superintendents.
- Commonalities between successful female and male superintendents regarding leadership qualities include vision, integrity, honesty, knowledge, and hard work (energy and stamina).
- Outstanding male and female superintendents agree that the doctoral degree is essential to their leadership development.
- Highly successful superintendents, both male and female, exhibit leadership qualities that are quite similar to the qualities of successful managers in the private sector.

REFERENCES

Beekley, C. (1999). Dancing in red shoes: Why women leave the superintendency. In C. C. Brunner (Ed.), *Sacred dreams: Women and the superintendency* (pp. 161–175). Albany, NY: State University of New York Press.

Bennis, W. (1989). *On becoming a leader.* Reading, MA: Addison-Wesley.

Bradshaw, L. K., & Phillips, J. C. (2002). Women school leaders: Lessons of experience. In S. Korcheck & M. Reese (Eds.), *Women as school executives: Research and reflections on educational leadership* (pp. 196–203). Austin, TX: Texas Council of Women School Executives.

Brown, G., Irby, B. J., & Iselt, C. (2002). Gendered perspectives of superintendent preparation programs. In S. Korcheck & M. Reese (Eds.), *Women as school executives: Research and reflections on educational leadership* (pp. 163–167). Austin, TX: Texas Council of Women School Executives.

Brunner, C. C. (1997). Women's way of succeeding in educational administration. *ERS Spectrum, 15*(4), 25–31.

Brunner, C. C. (2001). New faculty member examines power and female school superintendents. *The link.* Retrieved on March 18, 2004 from http://education.umn.edu/alum/link/2001fall/female.html.

Candoli, C., Cullen, C., & Stufflebeam, D. L. (1997). *Superintendent performance evaluation: Current practice and directions for improvement.* New York: Kluwer Academic Publishers.

Funk, C., Pankake, A., & Schroth, G. (2003, February 20–23). *Outstanding female superintendents in Texas: Profiles in leadership.* Paper presentation at the 2003 American Association of School Administrators' Annual Conference-within-a-Conference, New Orleans, LA.

Funk, C., Polnick, B., Pankake, A. M., & Schroth, G. (2004). *Profiles of outstanding female and male superintendents.* Paper presentation at the 2004 American Association of School Administrators' Annual Conference-within-a-Conference, San Francisco, CA.

Glass, T. E. (July, 2001). *Superintendent leaders look at the superintendency, school boards and reform.* Denver, CO: Education Commission of the States.

Glass, T., Bjork, L., & Brunner, C. C. (2000). *The 2000 study of the American school superintendency,* Arlington, VA: American Association of School Administrators.

Gupton, S. L., & Slick, G. A. (1996). *Highly successful women administrators: The inside stories of how they got there.* Thousand Oaks, CA: Corwin Press.

Hoy, W. K., & Miskel, C. G. (1996). *Educational administration: Theory, research, and practice, 5th ed.* New York: McGraw-Hill.

Hoyle, J. R. (2002). Superintendents for Texas school districts: Solving the crisis in executive leadership. *Texas future superintendent advisory team.* Sid Richardson Foundation Forum.

Hoyle, J. R., English, F., & Steffy, B. (1985). *Skills for successful 21st century school leaders.* Thousand Oaks, CA: Corwin Press.

Hutchinson, S. (2002). Women in school leadership: Taking steps to help them make the list. In G. Perreault & F. C. Lunenburg (Eds.), *The changing world of school administration* (pp. 363–375). Lanham, MD: Scarecrow Press.

Lougheed, J. (2001). Understanding leadership styles of women and men. In T. J. Kowalski (Ed.), *21st century challenges for school administrators* (pp. 178–188). Lanham, MD: Scarecrow Press.

Pankake, A., Schroth, G., & Funk, C. (2000). Successful women superintendents: Developing as leaders, learning from failure. *ERS Spectrum, 18*(3), 3–13.

Schroth, G., Pankake, A., & Funk, C. (1999). *Failure incidents in career success of female superintendents in Texas.* Paper presented at the 1999 AERA annual meeting, Montreal, Canada.

Slick, G. A., & Gupton, S. L. (1993). Voices of experience: Best advice to prospective and practicing women administrators from education's top female executives. In G. Brown & B. J. Irby (Eds.), *Women as school executives: A powerful paradigm* (pp. 74–85). Huntsville, TX: Texas Council of Women School Executives.

Author Index

About the Editors

Carolyn S. Carr is an associate professor in the Graduate School of Education at Portland State University in Portland, Oregon. She is currently the coordinator of the Executive Leadership Program. She received her Ph.D. from The University of Texas at Austin after a twenty-year career as a public school teacher, counselor, and administrator. Her research has focused on principal preparation, gender and language issues related to school leadership, and school policy. Dr. Carr recently served as guest editor of a special series in the *Journal of School Leadership* entitled *Professing Educational Leadership: Experiences for the University Classroom.* Her co-authored book, *Bridge to Ourselves: Nine Stories of Award-Winning Women Educators,* is in press.

Connie L. Fulmer earned her Ph.D. in Educational Administration at The Pennsylvania State University. Currently, she serves as coordinator of the Administrative Leadership and Policy Studies Division in the School of Education at the University of Colorado at Denver. Dr. Fulmer coordinates the work of the ALPS faculty and their principal partners in delivering six metro-area leadership academies and one state-wide distance-learning program. Her most recently published article is referenced as Bellamy, G. T., Fulmer, C. L., Murphy, M., & Muth, R., (2003), *A framework for school leadership accomplishments: Perspectives on knowledge, practice, and preparation for principals.* Connie's research has focused on innovations in the preparation of school-district administrators.